THE TRANSLATOR

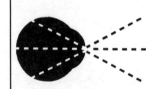

This Large Print Book carries the
Seal of Approval of N.A.V.H.

THE TRANSLATOR

A TRIBESMAN'S MEMOIR OF DARFUR

DAOUD HARI

*AS TOLD TO DENNIS MICHAEL BURKE
AND MEGAN M. McKENNA*

THORNDIKE PRESS
A part of Gale, Cengage Learning

GALE
CENGAGE Learning

Detroit • New York • San Francisco • New Haven, Conn • Waterville, Maine • London

LIBRARY OF CONGRESS CATALOGING-IN-PUBLICATION DATA

Hari, Daoud.
   The translator : a tribesman's memoir of Darfur / by Daoud
Hari ; as told to Dennis Michael Burke and Megan M.
McKenna. — Large print ed.
    p. cm.
   ISBN-13: 978-1-4104-0743-6 (hardcover : alk. paper)
   ISBN-10: 1-4104-0743-8 (hardcover : alk. paper)
   1. Hari, Daoud. 2. Translators — Sudan—Darfur — Biography.
3. Sudan — History — Darfur Conflict, 2003 — Personal
narratives, Sudanese. I. Title.
DT159.6.D27H38 2008a
962.404'3092—dc22   2008011606
[B]

Published in 2008 by arrangement with Random House, Inc.

*To my mother and all
the women of Darfur*

CONTENTS

INTRODUCTION

"If God must break your leg He will at least teach you to limp" — so it is said in Africa. This book is my poor limping, a modest account that cannot tell every story that deserves telling. I have seen and heard many things in Darfur that have broken my heart. I bring the stories to you because I know most people want others to have good lives, and, when they understand the situation, they will do what they can to steer the world back toward kindness. This is when human beings, I believe, are most admirable.

If you know where Egypt is on the map, you can go down from there and find Sudan. The western side of Sudan is called Darfur, which is about the size of France or Texas. Darfur is mostly flat; it has a few mountains but many endless plains of little trees, scratchy bushes, and sandy streambeds.

Darfur is where I lived with my family

until the attack on our village. Our people are called the Zaghawa. We are traditional tribal herdsmen who live in permanent villages; our grass huts are very big around and have pointed roofs that smell very good in the rain. My childhood was as full of happy adventures as yours. While you probably had a bicycle and then a first car, I had a camel, Kelgi, that I loved dearly and could make go very fast. On cold nights he might come into the hut, which was okay with everyone.

While we Zaghawa are not Arabs, many nomadic Arabs lived near us and were a part of my childhood as friends. My father took me to feasts in their tents, and they feasted with us.

Dar means land. The *Fur* are tribespeople farther south who are mostly farmers. One of the Fur leaders was king of the whole region in the 1500s. The region took its name from that time.

Hundreds of thousands of my people have been killed recently, as you may know. Two and a half million others are now living difficult lives in refugee camps or in solitary hiding places in desert valleys. I will explain why this is happening. If you are hungry for more details, I have included a deeper explanation in the back of this book.

As for the future, the only way that the world can say no to genocide is to make sure that the people of Darfur are returned to their homes and given protection. If the world allows the people of Darfur to be removed forever from their land and their way of life, then genocide will happen elsewhere because it will be seen as something that works. It must not be allowed to work. The people of Darfur need to go home now.

I write this for them, and for that day, and for a particular woman and her three children in heaven, and for a particular man and his daughter in heaven, and for my own father and my brothers in heaven, and for those still living who might yet have beautiful lives on the earth.

I write this also for the women and girls of Darfur. You have seen their faces wrapped in beautiful colors, and you know something of their suffering, but they are not who you think. Though they have been victimized, they are heroes more than victims. My aunt Joyar, for example, was a famous warrior who dressed like a man, fought camel thieves and Arab armies, wrestled men for sport — and always won. She refused to marry until she was in her forties. I dedicate this to her and to the girls of my village who

11

were faster and stronger than the boys at our rough childhood games. I dedicate this to my mother, who, as a young woman, kept a circle of attacking lions away from our cattle and sheep in the bush for a long day, a long night, and all the next morning, using only the power of her voice and the banging of two sticks. The power of her voice is something I know very well.

Near my village is a beautiful mountain we have always called the Village of God. Though the Muslim religion is practiced throughout our area both by indigenous Africans like me and by Arab nomads, it is also true that our people, especially our young people, have always gone up on this mountain to put offerings into the small holes of the rocks. Meat, millet, or wildflowers may be placed in these holes, along with letters to God, thanking Him or asking Him please for some favor. These gifts and notes have been left here long before the newer religions came to us. For a young man or woman, a letter may ask that some other young person be chosen for his or her mate. It might be a letter asking that a grandfather's illness be cured, or that the rainy season be a good one, or that a wedding be beautiful and the marriage successful. Or it might simply ask that the year ahead be good for everyone in the village below. So here it is, God: I am up there now in my heart, and I put this book in Your mountain as an offering to You. And I praise You by all Your Names, and I praise our ancient Mother of the Earth, and all the Prophets and wise men and women and Spirits of heaven and earth who might help us now in our time of need.

And for you, my friend, my reader, I thank you so much for taking this journey. It is a hard story, of course, but there are many parts that I think will surprise you and make you very happy that you came with me.

The story I am telling here is based on my memories of a time of great difficulty and confusion. I have done my best to capture the details of my experiences, and to set them down here accurately and to the utmost of my recollection, and I am grateful to those who have helped me focus and occasionally correct my account. Of course, no two people can view the same event in the same way, and I know that others will have their own tales to tell. Surely these collective tales will add up to the truth of the tragedy in Darfur.

1.
A CALL FROM THE ROAD

I am sure you know how important it can be to get a good phone signal. We were speeding through the hot African desert in a scratched and muddy Land Cruiser that had been much whiter a week earlier. Our driver, a Darfur tribesman like me, was swerving through thorny acacia bushes, working the gears expertly in the deep sands of another and always another ravine, which we call a wadi, and sailing over the bumps in the land — there are no roads to speak of. In the backseat, a young news filmmaker from Britain, Philip Cox, was holding on as we bounced and as our supplies thumped and clanked and sloshed around. A veteran of these deserts, he was in good humor — even after a long week of dusty travel and so many emotionally difficult interviews. Survivors told us of villages surrounded at night by men with torches and machine guns, the killing of men, women, and chil-

15

dren, the burning of people alive in the grass huts of Darfur. They told us of the rape and mutilation of young girls, of execution by machete of young men — sometimes eighty at a time in long lines.

You cannot be a human being and remain unmoved, yet if it is your job to get these stories out to the world, you keep going. So we did that.

I was Philip's translator and guide, and it was my job to keep us alive. Several times each hour I was calling military commanders from rebel groups or from the Chad National Army to ask if we should go this way or that way to avoid battles or other trouble. My great collection of phone numbers was the reason many reporters trusted me to take them into Darfur. I don't know how Philip got my cell number in the first place — maybe from the U.S. Embassy, or the U.S. State Department, or the British Embassy, or from the U.N. High Commissioner for Refugees, or from one of the aid organizations or a resistance group. It seemed that everyone had my cell phone number now. He certainly did not get my number from the government of Sudan, whose soldiers would kill me if they caught me bringing in a reporter.

These satellite phone calls — and often

just cell phone calls — frequently were to commanders who said, *No, you will die if you come here, because we are fighting so-and-so today.* We would then find another way.

If one rebel group hears that you have been calling another group, they might think you are a spy, even though you are only doing this for the journalist and for the story — you give the rebels nothing in return. I had to be careful about such things if I wanted to get my reporters out of Darfur alive, and so more stories could go out to the world. Since the attack on my own village, that had become my reason, and really my only reason, for living. I was feeling mostly dead inside and wanted only to make my remaining days count for something. You have perhaps felt this way at some time. Most of the young men I had grown up with were now dead or fighting in the resistance; I, too, had chosen to risk myself, but was using my English instead of a gun.

We needed to arrive at our destination before sundown or risk attack by the Sudanese Army, or by Darfur rebels aligned with government, or by other rebels who didn't know who we were and who might kill us just to be safe. So we didn't like what happened next.

Our Land Cruiser was suddenly blocked

by six trucks that emerged from a maze of desert bushes. These were Land Cruisers, too, but with their roofs cut off completely so men could pile in and out instantly, as when they have to escape a losing battle or get out before a rocket-propelled grenade (RPG) reaches them. Dusty men with Kalashnikov rifles piled out. On the order of their commander, they pointed their guns at us. When so many guns are pulled ready at the same time, the crunching sound is memorable. We moved slowly out of our vehicle with our hands raised.

These men were clearly rebel troops: their uniforms were but dirty jeans; ammunition belts hung across their chests; their loosely wrapped turbans, or *shals* — head scarves, really — were caked with the dust of many days' fighting. No doctors travel with these troops, who fight almost every day and leave their friends in shallow graves. Emotionally, they are walking dead men who count their future in hours. This makes them often ruthless, as if they think everyone might as well go to the next life with them. Many of them have seen their families murdered and their villages burned. You can imagine how you would feel if your hometown were wiped away and all your family killed by an enemy whom you now roam the land to find and kill so you can die in peace.

Among the rebels are the Sudan Liberation Movement, the Sudan Liberation Army, the Justice and Equality Movement, and several others. There are other groups in Chad, and they travel across the borders as they please. Where they get their guns and money is often a mystery, but Darfur has been filled with automatic weapons from the time when Libya attacked Chad and used Darfur as a staging area. Also, it must be understood that Sudan is aligned with radical Islamic groups and is, as a separate matter, letting China get most of its oil. So some Western interests and some surrounding countries are thought to be involved in supporting the rebel groups. It is sad how ordinary people suffer when these chess games are played.

Nearly half of Africa is covered by the pastoral lands of herding villages, and much of this land has great wealth below and poor people above. They are among the three hundred million Africans who earn less than a dollar a day, and who are often pushed out of the way or killed for such things as oil, water, metal ore, and diamonds. This makes the rise of rebel groups very easy. The men who stopped us probably needed no persuasion to join this group.

The men's weary-looking young commander walked to me and said in the Zaghawa language, "Daoud Ibarahaem Hari, we know all about you. You are a spy. I know you are Zaghawa like us, not Arab, but unfortunately we have some orders, and we have to kill you now."

It was easy for him to know I was a Zaghawa from the small scars that look like quotation marks and were cut into my temples by my grandmother when I was an infant. I told him yes, I am Zaghawa, but I am no spy.

The commander breathed in a sad way and then put the muzzle of his M-14 rifle to one of these scars on my head. He asked me to hold still and told Philip to stand away. He paused to tell Philip in broken English not to worry, that they would send him back to Chad after they killed me.

"Yes, fine, but just a sec," Philip replied, holding his hand up to stop the necessary business for a moment while he consulted me.

"What is going on?"

"They think I am a spy, and they are going to shoot the gun and it will make my head explode, so you should stand away."

"Who are they?" he asked.

I told him the name of the group, nodding carefully in the direction of a vehicle that had their initials hand-painted on the side.

He looked at the vehicle and lowered his hands to his hips. He looked the way the British look when they are upset by some unnecessary inconvenience. Philip wore a well-wrapped turban; his skin was tanned and a little cracked from his many adventures in these deserts. He was not going to stand by and lose a perfectly good translator.

"Wait just a moment!" he said to the rebel commander. "*Do . . . not . . . shoot . . . this . . . man.* This man is not a spy. This man is my translator and his name is Suleyman Abakar Moussa of Chad. He has his papers." Philip thought that was my name. I had been using that name to avoid being deported from Chad to a certain death in Sudan, where I was wanted, and to avoid being otherwise forced to stay in a Chad refugee camp, where I could be of little service.

"I hired this man to come here; he is not a spy. We are doing a film for British television. Do you understand this? It's absolutely essential that you understand this." He asked me to translate, just to be sure, which, under my circumstance, I was happy to do.

More than his words, Philip's manner made the commander hesitate. I watched the commander's finger pet the trigger. The gun muzzle was hot against my temple. Had he fired it recently, or was it just hot from the sun? I decided that if these were about to be my last thoughts, I should try some better ones instead. So I thought about my family and how I loved them and how I might see my brothers soon.

"I am going to make a telephone call," Philip explained, slowly withdrawing his satellite phone from his khaki pants pocket. "You will not shoot this man, because your commander will talk to you on this telephone momentarily — you understand?" He looked up a number from his pocket notebook. It was the personal number of the rebel group's top commander. He had interviewed him the previous year.

"Your top man," he said to all the gunmen standing like a firing squad around us as he waited for the call to go through. "Top man. Calling his personal number now. It's ringing. Ringing and ringing."

God is good. The satellite phone had a strong signal. The number still worked. The distant commander answered his own phone. He remembered Philip warmly. Miracle after miracle.

Philip talked on the phone in a rapid English that I quietly translated for the man holding the gun.

Philip held one finger up as he spoke, begging with that finger and with his eyes for one more moment, one more moment. He laughed to show that he and the man on the phone were old friends.

"They are old friends," I translated.

Philip then held out the satellite phone to the commander, who pressed the muzzle even harder against my head.

"Please talk to him now. Please. He says it's an order for you to talk to him."

The commander hesitated as if it were some trick, but finally reached over and took the phone. The two commanders talked at length. I watched his trigger finger rise and fall like a cobra and then finally slither away. We were told to leave the country immediately.

To not get killed is a very good thing. It makes you smile again and again, foolishly, helplessly, for several hours. Amazing. I was not shot — *humdallah. My brothers, you will have to wait for me a little longer.*

Our driver had been wide-eyed through all this, since drivers often do not fare well in this kind of situation. There was joy and some laughter in the Land Cruiser as we sped back toward the village of Tine — which you say "Tina" — on the Chad-Sudan border.

"That was amazing what you did," I said to Philip. We drove a few trees farther before he replied.

"Amazing, yes. Actually, I've been trying to get through to him for weeks," he said. "Lucky thing, really."

The driver, who spoke almost no English, asked me what Philip had said. I told him that he had said *God is good,* which, indeed, is what I believe he was saying.

2.
WE ARE HERE

Philip asked me if my name was Daoud or Suleyman. I told him that I was Daoud when in the Darfur regions of Sudan, but I was Suleyman in Chad. I explained my situation.

"Everyone has lots of names around here," was his reply. He asked what I preferred to be called. Daoud, please, though many of my close friends also call me David, which is where Daoud comes from in the Bible. I asked him for the commander's phone number, which he read to me.

We crossed back into Chad and moved up along the border, then came back into Darfur farther north. It would be worth our trouble not to run into that same rebel group again. But, one way or another, we would get the story for Philip, and Philip would get it out to the world. You have to be stronger than your fears if you want to get anything done in this life.

The problem in dealing with rebel groups is that it is often difficult to know who is on which side on any given day. The Arab government in Khartoum — the government of Sudan — makes false promises to make temporary peace with one rebel group and then another to keep the non-Arab people fighting one another. The government makes deals with ambitious commanders who are crazy enough to think the government will promote them after the war, when in fact they will be discarded if not killed then. These breakaway commanders are sometimes told to attack other rebel groups, or even to kill humanitarian workers and the troops sent from other countries to monitor compliance with cease-fire treaties. This is done so the genocide can carry on and the land can be cleared of the indigenous people. History may prove me wrong in some of these perceptions, but this is how it seems to most people who are there.

It is also believed that the government pays some of the traditional Arab people, many tribes of whom are otherwise our friends, to form deadly horseback militias called the Janjaweed to brutally kill the non-Arab Africans and burn our villages. The word *Janjaweed* may be from an ancient word meaning "faith warriors," or it may be a combination of words meaning "evil spirits on horses," or, some believe, it just means "gunmen on horseback."

This is my prediction: When the government has removed or killed all the traditional non-Arabs, then it will get the traditional Arabs to fight one another so they too will disappear from valuable lands. This is already happening in areas where the removal of non-Arab Africans is nearly complete.

"So why did you come back home to Darfur just in time for this war?" Philip asked me over the roar of the Land Cruiser as we again bounced through wadis and over sand banks.

"A very good question!" I shouted back to him with a laugh.

On a day when you come so close to death, you should think about what you are doing here. Yes, you have a job to do in this place, but maybe you are also a little crazy to be here when you could be far away. But death had been chasing me for a long time now, from when I was thirteen and the world lit up around me, and I first saw men flying in pieces above me.

Here is that story. I was finishing my afternoon chores and thinking about the coming night of playing our village games, *Anashel* and *Whee,* rough-and-tumble sports played on the moonlit sand. Twenty government troop trucks suddenly surrounded our village. The commander gathered everyone from the village and organized the beating of some of the village men — quite old men — and demanded to know the precise whereabouts of the younger men who were presumed to be hiding in the hills with the resistance groups. That in fact was where they were, but the old men did not know exactly where they were, so the commander soon realized that the beatings were useless. He burned six huts to make his point.

Changes in the weather had forced the Arab nomads to graze their animals farther south into Zaghawa lands. In the past they would have asked permission, and a few camels might have changed hands. If no bargain could be reached, and if they used the water and the grass anyway, a challenge would be made for a battle of honor on a traditional battlefield, far from any village. After that fight, the matter would be considered settled and the Arabs and the Zaghawa would immediately be friends again, dining in one another's homes.

What was different now was that the Arab

government of Sudan, because it wanted the more settled people off the land, was taking sides with the Arab nomads and providing some with guns, helicopters, bombers, and tanks to decide the arguments. This had driven many of the young Zaghawa men to join resistance groups. The Sudanese Army commanders were now going from village to village, looking for these fighters, telling the women to make their men turn in their weapons or else see their homes burned. Pressure was also being put on the people to move into the towns and cities "where they would be safe." If they did this, however, they would live in the most severe kind of poverty.

The commander had grabbed me and two of my cousins to be his translators, since he knew that we were of school age and that all students were forced to learn some Arabic, which is what he spoke. If they caught you speaking Zaghawa in the schools, or not knowing your Arab words, they would use camel whips on you. The commander stood us up on the running board of his truck and made us say all his orders about giving up weapons. The women were crying and begging the soldiers to stop the beatings and let the children run away.

Often such commanders would shoot a few people to emphasize the seriousness of the matter. In many instances, whole villages were burned. But this commander was not that strict. He told the three of us children that we must show them the way to a village he needed to visit next. We did not want to go with him, because, unlike the women and the old men who were being beaten, we knew the village defenders were in the steep wadi beyond the village waiting to attack these trucks. But we were pushed into the front seat of the first truck and were soon speeding out of the village.

Suddenly, there were painfully loud explosions all around us and machine-gun fire everywhere as the trucks came to a halt and the soldiers streamed out to find positions. We screamed from the window, "We are here! We are here! It's us!" The commander pulled us out and used us as shields as he ran into the bushes. We put our faces close to the sand and the RPG rounds exploded into some of the trucks, sending any stragglers into the sky with trails of smoke and red mists of blood. The furious gunfight seemed to go on forever, but it was actually just a few minutes: guerrilla fighters always withdraw quickly to fight another day. When the shooting stopped, the commander stood and looked down at us.

"I think you helped make a trap for me," he said, waving his pistol in our faces. We waited to die. He looked at us and, shaking his head, mumbled something we could not make out because our hearing had been hurt badly by the explosions. He then simply walked over to his men. They collected their dead and wounded and drove away in their working trucks. We ran back to the village, yelling, "We are here!" in case the defenders were still in the bushes. Our mothers and sisters greeted us, crying, dancing around us and saying so many times, *Humdallah! Thank you, God!*

The three of us couldn't hear much of anything for a few days. Eleven people died, mostly government soldiers.

Soon after that my father sent me to school in the largest city in North Darfur, El Fasher. I was his youngest son. Living with cousins, I could finish primary school and continue on to intermediate and secondary school. I was very sad to leave home.

Life in El Fasher was overwhelming — too many people, too many cars, too many new things. I got very sick the second week, mostly homesick. El Fasher is a city of mud buildings and sandy streets: so many streets that I got lost all the time. There are some government buildings and a large prison where, everyone knew, terrible things happened.

My brother Ahmed knew from our cousins that I was having a hard time, so he came to see me. He stayed for a week until I got better, walking me to school with his long arm over my shoulder and making me feel like home. He said that fate had given me a blessing, and that I should work hard at school. He came to visit whenever he could, which was quite often. He showed me good things about the town. Eventually I grew to like El Fasher.

I got a job cleaning tables at a restaurant after classes. I watched television for the first time. A cousin would put his TV outside his home so all the cousins and neighbors could watch. I didn't like it much because it was mostly about the government of Sudan's military. I did like the movies, but the first one I saw was a Clint Eastwood movie, and I went running down the street when I thought the bullets would come out of it from all the shooting. My cousins came laughing down the street to get me.

A movie house played American films once a week and films from India the rest of the time. It was very cheap; I went to see every new film with a few coins of my restaurant money.

At the restaurant, and from the older students, I began to learn about politics. There were many military operations against the Zaghawa at that time, and many Zaghawa were leaving El Fasher to join resistance groups. Dictator Omar Hassan Ahmal al-Bashir had just taken over Sudan, which made us all angry. A Chad commander named Idriss Déby was fighting the Chad government for control of that country. He is a Zaghawa and we thought he was a great hero. Some wanted to go join him. He would later become president of Chad.

This fighting sounded like a good idea to me. I dropped out of high school and hid for two weeks, planning with friends to go to Chad and join up with Déby.

Ahmed came and found me. He sat me down under a tree and told me that I should use my brain, not a gun, to make life better. He said it would be wrong to turn away from the gifts given to me by God and my family.

"Shooting people doesn't make you a man, Daoud," he said. "Doing the right thing for who you are makes you a man." So we walked back to town and I returned to school. I became interested in English because of a wonderful teacher, and I became lost in the classic books of England and America. I particularly loved Charlotte Brontë's *Jane Eyre,* Robert Louis Stevenson's *Treasure Island* and *Kidnapped,* Charles Dickens's *Oliver Twist,* George Orwell's *Animal Farm,* and Alan Paton's *Cry, the Beloved Country.* These changed me; they opened and freed my mind. I still paid attention to politics, however.

Around this time my father wanted me to accept an arranged marriage and come home to be a camel herder, just as the men of our family had always done. I thought I might do that, as I loved camels so, but I wanted to see something of the world first, and I wanted to choose my wife and let her choose me, too. A camel, by the way, can be away from its human family or camel family for twenty years and still know them very well when somehow it comes back. Camels are completely loyal and full of love and courage.

My urge to see something of the larger world was perhaps from all the television and movies and mostly the books. I finished my studies and, giving my apologies to my father, who took me for a walk and said I must learn to take care of my family one way or another if I was to be a man, I headed to Libya to find a good job.

I got there by camel and by truck. Déby, the new president of Chad, was traveling overland to Libya at the same time. He and his motorcade got hopelessly lost in the dunes. Helicopters from Libya found most of them and led them onward. The truck caravan I was in found the rest of his vehicles and gave the men much-needed water. At an oasis, I saw Déby standing and went to greet him and shake his hand.

When you travel across the Sahara by camel, or even by vehicle, it is easy to get lost in the dunes — there are no roads. You just go.

A special red salt, dug from North Darfur, is put in camels' water to help them make the long trip. Horses are of no use here, since it would take three or four camels to carry the water and food needed by one horse. It is better just to take the camels.

If you travel in the summer months, the sun and heat will be very hard on the camels; if you travel in the winter months, the freezing sandstorms will cut your face if you do not hide from them deep in your robes. These are not small trips: you might take your camels a thousand miles, which would be like traveling from Athens to Berlin through all of Serbia, Austria, and the Czech Republic, or from Miami Beach to Philadelphia — a very long way without roads or shelter.

There are many human bones in the desert, particularly where North Darfur blends into the great dunes of the Sahara. Some of these bones are still wearing their clothes and leathery skin, while others have been bleached by hundreds of years of the searing sun. Mirages make birds sitting on distant dunes — birds no bigger than your fist — look like camels. Mirages make dry flatlands look like distant lakes. Mirages make the bones of a single human skeleton look like the buildings of a city far ahead. This sounds impossible, but the Sahara is an impossible place. All trails are erased with each wind. You can note the stars at night, if it is clear, or see where the sun rises or sets, also if it is clear, but it is not always clear, and the tilted horizon provided by the great dunes disorients you even under a cloudless sky. From ten in the morning until about four in the afternoon you cannot guess the direction.

You are modern and think your compass and your GPS will keep you from trouble. But the batteries will give out in your GPS, or the sand will ruin it. Your compass may break or become lost as you try to put away your bedding one morning in a hard sandstorm. So you will want to know the ways that have worked for thousands of years.

If you are good, like my father and brothers, you will put a line of sticks in the sand at night, using the stars to mark your next morning's direction of travel; you can extend this line as needed. Be careful: some people die because they look to a distant mountain as their guide, but the wind moves these mountains around; you might travel in circles until your eyes close and your heart withers.

It says everything about this land to know that even the mountains are not to be trusted, and that the crunching sound under your camel's hooves is usually human bones, hidden and revealed as the wind pleases.

3.
THE DEAD NILE

My years away from Darfur were mostly good years. It takes nothing away from them to say that I ended this sojourn as a prisoner in Egypt.

In a prison in Aswan, southern Egypt, a very old jailer — perhaps the age of my own father — was kind enough to let me talk to him through the bars late at night. My Arabic served me well with him, and he asked about my adventures. His company was very welcome.

"Why did you go to Libya? How is it there for a young man like yourself?" he asked as he made a cigarette for himself and one for me.

I told him that I had found a warm community of Zaghawa friends and cousins working along the seacoast there. They made a place for my mattress and found me a restaurant job at a military academy. The Arab students there were also kind to me and lent me their books to study, constantly encouraging me. And always I was asking for more books.

"Ah, you were like the ancient Library of Alexandria once on that shore, demanding the loan of every book from every traveler so it might be copied for the library," he said.

I told him that the library in my head was not quite so good as that, but that I did read about philosophy and history and some politics — and the great novels, of course, which I love and which are read everywhere.

"But you had no passport?"

I told him I did have a visa at first, but I did not have permission to move from Libya to Egypt, where some of my friends had gone and were telling me of much higher wages. Because such workers suffer lonely lives away from home in order to send money to their families, the lure of better pay is very powerful. It is the only thing. So I went to Egypt and worked in restaurants along the Red Sea. I made many friends in Egypt, from every race and background. Then I heard that the wages were even better in Israel. If I could get on the other side of the Red Sea to the Israeli resort town of Eilat, I could go from a hundred dollars a month to about a thousand. This would provide me with enough money to go to college and still send money home. Or perhaps I could find a job in Beersheba, where Ben-Gurion University would be just right for me. I had been working in a restaurant on the Red Sea owned by a Bedouin. I then met a Bedouin man who helped people get across the border to Israel. He showed me where to cross. For me, it was not a good place.

I was immediately captured when I came out of the Gaza Strip into Israel proper. Exhausted, I had fallen asleep by the gushing irrigation pumps of a beautiful farm. I woke to see Israeli soldiers standing around me with their guns pointed at my head.

So I did get to Beersheba, but only to the prison there. It was actually very nice, with television and free international calls. I would recommend it even over many hotels I have known.

I was soon sent back to Egypt, where I was harshly imprisoned. You might have some idea of how bad a prison can be, with the filth and darkness and violence of it, but you would have some ways to go.

"Many die in those Cairo prisons," the old man in Aswan said, but he did not need to tell me that. I had taken my own turn kneeling in the sun all day begging for water and being beaten by the bare fists of a huge guard. I had spent months in a cell so crowded that we had to take turns sitting down. Some of the ninety people in this small room had been there for thirteen years. It was very hot and filled with stench.

A ten-year-old boy was beaten so brutally that he was dying as I tried to comfort him.

How completely sad that he would die so far from his family! In Africa, our families are everything. We do all we can to help them, without question. But I had long known that I could not help my family quite like my brothers did. I could not herd camels and cattle as well as Ahmed, or solve village problems like him; I could not be as hardworking in the bush as Juma, or as patient and good at keeping the family together. For to do such things well requires that they be done happily and forever, and my particular education had inclined me toward a hungry curiosity for the world. But I was not doing so well without my family. *If, if,* if *I am ever released from this place,* I told myself, *I must return home* — not forever, for that was not my life, but for long enough to heal all the wounds of my long separation.

However, nothing is all bad, and there were many good people to meet in prison from all over Africa with interesting stories for us to listen to as we stood through the nights and days, stepping on roaches and scratching lice but at least getting to learn something interesting about other countries and other people.

After too much of this, the Egyptians were going to send me to Sudan, where, as the old jailer in Aswan advised me, I would probably find my doom. From Aswan, I was going to be put on a Nile boat and taken south to Khartoum.

"It's too bad you could not have stayed in the jail in Israel," the old man said.

Indeed, I agreed, it was a shame to leave.

"If you have some friends, you should get them to try to stop you from being deported to Sudan," he advised.

Some Sudanese men had tried to sneak into Israel from Jordan a few years earlier. After the Israelis sent them back to Jordan, the Jordanians in turn sent them back home to Sudan, where they were executed in Khartoum. This harshness was, I believe, the Arab government of Sudan's way of trying not to be embarrassed in front of other Arab nations regarding its poor economy. When this atrocity was made public by Amnesty International and Human Rights Watch, Israel and other countries agreed not to extradite people to Sudan or to other countries that might do so. When Israel sent me to Egypt, they had Egypt sign an agreement promising not to send me to Sudan. It was happening anyway, unless I could get my situation known to the human rights groups.

Besides this problem, the Egyptian prison had taken a heavy toll on my health, and the old man could see I was very weak. He seemed to have a father's concern. I said that I had no way to contact anyone, and I asked if he could perhaps make a call to my Zaghawa friends in Cairo, who might contact the groups.

"That would be very expensive from here, and I have no money, my son," he said sadly. "Maybe you have some money and I will do it for you."

What happened next was not the first miracle in my life, but it was one of the best. It doesn't matter how many times you put your hands in your empty pockets; when someone asks if you have any money, you will put your hands in there again. This time, after so long in prison, after wearing these old jeans for many months in the vilest of prison cells with nothing to do but stand in the heat and put my hands in my pockets, I somehow let my thumb slip into the tiny watch pocket above the right pocket of my jeans — a forgotten pocket. I felt the edges of something. Folded into a small square was an Egyptian hundred-pound note, worth maybe twenty U.S. dollars, that I had no memory of ever putting in there. It was tightly folded and frayed after so long, but I unfolded it carefully. It was more than enough for an expensive phone call, certainly.

I gave this to the old man and asked if he would make the phone call for me at a café and perhaps use the rest for a little food for me and for him. Though it was late at night, he returned with a fine chicken dinner for us. He told me details enough of his phone conversation so that I knew he had made the call. Our dinner together reminded me of sharing meals with my father. I had been away from my family a long time, and perhaps that is what I needed to think about in this dark time. My disconnection from them was causing my life great harm. Most of the money was still left, which I gave to the old man for his kindness and because I didn't think there was more than a one percent chance anything could be done for me in time.

My friends in Cairo soon contacted Zaghawa tribal leaders, one as far away as

Scandinavia. They in turn contacted Human Rights Watch and the United Nations. Somehow, somehow, somehow, all of that worked. On the day when I had already been sent in chains to a boat on the Nile, and just before the boat began its journey to Khartoum, I was taken off and sent back to Cairo. I would stay in the horrible prison there for a few more months. But then, great miracle, I was allowed to fly away.

It is hard to know where grace comes from. Perhaps the money was always there, waiting for the curiosity that comes with right thinking. For a time, I thought the old jailer had perhaps slipped it in there as I slept. But it was so folded and faded that I think it was waiting for me a long time in that pocket, in the way that many things are waiting for us to be ready to receive them.

4.
A Bad Time to Go Home

It was the summer of 2003; an Ethiopian Airlines jet lifted me over the Red Sea in late afternoon. My cousins in Britain had purchased my ticket home. The plane banked over the Nile and then floated south above the river with a view west into the Sahara. Almost as if I had died in the Egyptian prison and was now going home on the wind, there was a magic-carpet feeling to it. I could see, for the first time in my life, the immensity of the Sahara: a forever sea of sand below with scattered dots of green, with the curled and weathered backbones of dead mountains, with the chalk threads of camel trails and dry streams tracing delicate currents around the dunes.

As we continued to rise, the trails disappeared and the dunes became the rough weave of a canvas extending to the distant horizon. This desert of sand is about the size of the entire United States. From above, it is easy to understand why men must build great pyramids to achieve any notice here. *Amazing to be alive and see such things,* I thought as I rested my head beside the window and sipped a tea. I watched a red sunset spill over the land. *Amazing to be alive. Humdallah, humdallah, amazing. God bless my cousins in London. God bless my friends in Cairo and the human rights groups. God bless the old jailer in Aswan. God bless the hundred-pound note in my jeans. God please even bless the person who invented those little pockets in jeans where such a note might become long lost and someday found. God bless Ahmed and all my brothers and sisters and my mother and father.*

After so many years away, I would see them all soon, though they were now, as my cousins informed me, in the middle of a war. My brother Ahmed would be happiest to see me, and would want to know everything of my adventures. *God bless Ahmed.* I could see him already in front of me, delighted to hear each turn of my story.

In the distance somewhere just beyond my view to the west was Khartoum, its lights probably just now blinking on, the blue dusk probably shining in the strands of the Nile River where it is born from the White and Blue Niles. The Blue comes from

Ethiopia and contributes the most water, while the White comes a far greater distance through Lake Victoria, losing much of its water in the vast swamps of southern Sudan. In ancient times there was another great river in Sudan, running through Darfur west to Lake Chad. The great valley where it once ran is the Wadi Howar, also called the Dead Nile by the people. Except for the summer rain time, its waters now flow under the sand.

After a stop in Addis Ababa, I flew in a southern loop through Kenya, Uganda, and the Central African Republic, then cut back up across South Darfur in Sudan. Mostly it was dark below, as most of this land has little or no electricity and goes to bed early. The stars and a new moon were all I could see for most of this time, until suddenly there were some flickering lights below.

"Where are we?" I asked the young flight attendant whom I had come to know a little; she was perhaps my age, about thirty. She leaned over to look out my window, letting her hand rest gracefully on my shoulder for balance.

"Nowhere, I think!" she smiled as she looked patiently into the dark.

By asking the time until landing, I calculated that we were probably crossing over southern Sudan and very probably South Darfur. The lights below were likely the lights of war — the last flaring of huts and villages attacked earlier that day, of great, centuries-old village trees that had become like bonfires. Darfur was burning.

I rubbed the Zaghawa scars on my temple as I looked down at this dark scene. Somewhere down there — though north of there, really — were my friends, my mother and my father, my sisters and my brothers, uncountable cousins, aunts, uncles, our camels, donkeys, our songbirds, our thousand years of stories. You can imagine this for yourself, friend, flying home and seeing your homeland below in points of fire. Whatever warrior blood comes to you from your ancestors would be working inside you.

Yet, perhaps because I had already seen something of the larger world, it was not so simple as that; I was indeed observing from this altitude. I counted among my friends the people of many tribes and many races, and this makes a difference in our hearts. I counted also among my acquaintances Jane Eyre, Long John Silver, and Oliver Twist.

Altitude itself is a powerful thing. When travelers are in space, looking at our small planet from a distance where borders and flags cannot be seen or imagined, this also,

I am told, bends one toward a peaceful view. That is what I wanted, really, just peace. I was sad and anxious for my people but not angry. I didn't want to kill any human person. I didn't even hate the man who was organizing all these crimes, the president of Sudan, though I wished deeply to take him for a long walk through the villages of my childhood and perhaps change his way of thinking about how best to serve the people, which is surely his job.

We floated in the predawn over the deserts of Chad, descending finally into the oasis of N'Djamena (you just say it "Jameena"). Here I had friends and cousins who would give me a place to sleep. With a few dollars from my cousins, I could cross Chad and slip into Darfur in a remote place unnoticed by the Sudan government.

The stairway rolled up to the plane a little after 5 a.m. in N'Djamena. Last off, I paused for a moment atop the stairs; the moist smell of the river, the great starry sky of my freedom greeted me — *Humdallah, humdallah, the Africa of my friends and my family!*

From this small porch I could see, even at this early hour, Chadian military vehicles and aircraft moving around the base beside the small airport. The city, too, was already awake with its normal business and the added seasoning of war's excitement.

The body responds to this. The smells and sounds, the movements of soldiers and vehicles, are all taken in quickly with the keener perceptions that awaken in dangerous times.

Some cousins were at the airport and I was soon eating a wonderful breakfast: kebab meats in rich, very spicy sauces. The news of the war in neighboring Sudan surrounded me: news from cousins here and there in North Darfur; news learned from cell phones and passing travelers; news about villages attacked here, of deaths in the family there, of cousins taking arms to defend their villages, of sisters missing and mothers killed or raped. There was a great sadness and also a great excitement everywhere: our great nest of bees had been swatted hard.

After several days to recover my health, I told my eldest cousin that it was time for me to go to Darfur. He shook my hand and held my shoulder as if he would not see me again. I was given the money I would need for fares in the Land Cruisers that string together the villages of Africa. The women of the family wrapped some food for me to take. I went to a marketplace and found a ride in what looked like a good Land Cruiser with a good driver.

Packed shoulder to shoulder with other travelers, I was soon heading across the rain-flooded wadis.

The Darfur regions of Sudan are on Chad's eastern border, about six hundred miles and two days away from N'Djamena on bad roads. We stopped in village market-places where some riders would leave and others would pile in. The newer riders bore the ceremonial scars of the Zaghawa, my own people. From these people I learned of the troubles ahead: the burned villages, the rush of people across the border into Chad from Darfur. My stomach hurt with fear for my family.

Everyone knows the family of everyone else among the Zaghawa. If you live in a small town, you know a great deal about the families who live there. If your town had no television or other things to take you away from visiting all the time, your town could be very large and you would still know something about everyone. So it is like that. And of course when people travel close together like this on long journeys, you get to know a great deal about many people. Everyone is well-known eventually.

We finally arrived in the sprawling mud-brick, tin-roof city of Abéché, the last big community in Chad before the Sudan border. It is home to sixty or seventy thousand people in peaceful times, but now was thick with refugees and Chadian soldiers arriving to control the long border and prevent trouble. The soldiers let the refugees come across from Darfur since it was the only humane thing that could be done, and because there is a tradition of hospitality that prevents you from turning away your visitors.

In Abéché I found a ride for the last, but very rough, ten miles to the Sudan border, to the town of Tine. I had been able to get very little sleep so far. Tine would be a good place to rest.

As we approached the town, the smell found us before we could see any huts. It was the smell of tea brewing and food cooking. Tine is Zaghawa, so the cooking smells were very nice after such a long time away.

I went to the sultan's home, a fenced enclosure of several large huts. All visitors there are always welcomed with a mattress to sleep outdoors in the enclosure and with good food, for the sultan is there to care for the people.

The war was bringing people by the thousands to the sultan, who was asking his omdas, who look out for the several regions of his kingdom, and his sheikhs, who look out for one village each, to arrange hospitality for the refugees. In North Darfur, for example, there are five such sultans. Several more are in West Darfur, several more in South Darfur, and several more, like this one, in Chad. These compose the ancient nation of Darfur, and Darfur is still organized as it was in the 1500s. The sultanships are hereditary, while the omdas and the sheikhs are appointed by the sultan because they have earned the respect of the people they live among. It is a very different kind of democracy, with the people voting for their local leaders not with ballots, but rather with their attitudes of respect for those who stand out in their service to their communities. The tally is kept in the mind of the sultan. At the national level, of course, there are regular elections, though they are now so corrupted by Bashir that they have no power to reflect the will and wisdom of the people.

The sultan shook my hand and held my shoulder when we first met.

"How is your father and your brother Ahmed?" he asked me. When he said this with such respect, I knew Ahmed would someday be the sheikh of our village.

He told me that I had some cousins who, having fled Darfur, were now living in Tine, and he told me exactly where they could be found. He welcomed me to stay as long as I pleased, then went back to the thousand emergencies pressing down on him.

Some of the arriving people were gravely wounded by bombs and bullets in the attacks on their villages across the border. Some of the children who had come a long way were thin and ill. Some of the women and girls had been raped and were seriously injured by that. Family members were searching from village to village to find one another, and the sultan, omdas, and sheikhs were helping to find these people and take care of everyone.

Amid all this rush of people and trouble, I lay down on the ground to rest. Because it had rained, plastic tarps were put down under the mattresses provided to guests. Despite the constant coming and going of people and the crying of children, I fell deeply asleep.

In the morning, after drinking green tea with many others, I went looking for a Land Cruiser that would be heading north to Bahai, which is forty-five miles up the border and a good place to cross into Darfur without notice.

In the Tine marketplace, men were cleaning their guns — mostly old rifles and Kalashnikovs — and talking about where they might be most useful. They were buying and trading ammunition and supplies. Others, without guns, were also organizing to go back into Darfur to find relatives and friends. That, of course, was my situation, and I was soon on the road.

As we traveled, we could look to our right across the great valley separating Chad from Sudan and see the white bombers and helicopters in the distance. These aircraft were bombing villages. We saw funnels of smoke against the horizon. We saw Janjaweed militia units moving down in the wadi, not far from us.

Bahai, my last stop in Chad, was finally in view. It is a small town of scattered huts and mud-brick stores on the flats near a river crossing. Because it is a different Zaghawa kingdom than Tine, there is a different sultan in the area. I paid my respects to him. Like the sultan in Tine, this one was also surrounded by many people who had crowded over the river. And as in Tine, the town was filled with families seeking their lost members, with wounded men, women, and children seeking care. Vacant-eyed people, shocked by the sudden loss of their homes and families, were walking every-where. Groups of armed defenders were organizing everywhere.

I paid a driver and pulled myself up into the back of the next truck heading deep into Darfur.

We crossed the river against a current of people escaping. All along the muddy roads and along the flats where every vehicle makes its own road, we passed refugees walking toward Chad. We encouraged them as we passed, telling them that safety was only a mile farther, then only two miles farther, only a half day farther, and soon we would only say that they were walking the right way. We gave much of our water to mothers and children.

The white Antonov bombers were visible from time to time, and smoke was often seen rising behind the hills. Village defend-ers and other resistance fighters sometimes stopped us on the road. Our trucks were white, as are any civilian Land Cruisers or other trucks that might otherwise be mis-taken for military vehicles. Even so, the resistance fighters reminded us that the helicopters and bombers would not care about such things. So every turn of our journey was carefully traveled, our eyes watching the sky and the distant hills and wadis. We would lean out and look at the tire tracks beside the road to know who had come this way and that. Fresh tracks from big tires would mean government trucks and death. Fresh horse tracks in great numbers would mean Janjaweed and death. This constant observation was a good travel activity to help pass the hours, as our situation was truly in God's hands, not our own.

When, in the trance and bounce of the long journey, I would think of the whole situation, it did seem like a bad dream. This part of the world, our world, was changing so quickly every day, falling deeper into the fires of cruelty. I wanted to wake up from it. Imagine if all the systems and rules that held your country together fell apart suddenly and your family members were all — every one of them — in a dangerous situation. It was like that. You cannot be thinking of yourself at such a time; you are making calculations of where your friends and family members might be, and where they might go. You are recalculating this constantly, deciding what you might do to help them.

5.
MY SISTER'S VILLAGE

I had decided even before leaving Egypt that I would go first to my older sister's village, so I would then have some news about her to give my mother and father in our own village.

After some rough mountains, the approach into her village was along a dry river. Wells and small pools — the water points of the village — were pocked with bomb craters. The normal rush of village children toward a visiting vehicle was absent. The outlying clusters of huts were burned, though some had mud rooms and enclosures that were still standing.

I had been to this village many times, including for several weddings, which are a big part of life for us. A wedding goes on for four evenings, with wonderful dancing and singing. I saw an area of large trees and remembered all the dancing that used to happen under them. The women form a long line and sing traditional songs about village life, and then dance in this long line — so beautiful in their brightly colored gowns floating about them in the firelight. The men watch and jump in a ceremonial way. In ancient days they would have their spears with them, since this was the symbol of the male. At the last wedding I went to, some men had guns and they fired them in the air, to show their appreciation for the great dancing and singing by the women.

That now seemed so long ago, and forever lost. As we arrived, we could see that many huts were still standing. My sister's hut was among them.

After my sister Halima recovered from seeing the man her baby brother had grown to be, she made a small joke that I was always doing things backward, that a Hari should not come home to roost in the middle of a war. She was joking that our family name, *Hari,* means "eagle." Birds are famous for leaving a village before a battle, not for arriving during one.

Her husband was away somewhere with a group of men. They were perhaps moving the animals to safety or preparing to defend the village. Women are often not told about the troubles of war, though they suffer them greatly.

But whether they are told or not, the women know everything. The children see it all and, as they do their chores, the women ask them to tell what they have seen. I did not ask Halima where my brother-in-law might be. He was somewhere doing what needed doing, just as the women were busy hiding caches of food out in the wadis to the west of the village, should a hasty escape be necessary.

Halima told me of the prior bombings in the village, which killed seven people. I knew these families, though some of the victims had come into the world in the years I was away. Thus I had missed their whole lives, which was very sad to me.

In the evening, when the children of the village finished their chores with the animals and gardens, I talked to them under a tree in a slight rain.

"Tell me what happened," I asked the eldest boy, who was perhaps fourteen and would surely be among the resistance troops in a few days or weeks. He was wearing torn jeans and a shredded UCLA sweatshirt that probably had come through marketplaces from Algeria to El Fasher, having first been donated years ago in the United States.

"All the birds flew up and away. This is the first thing we noticed," he said.

Then he mimicked the noise of the Antonov bomber as it cruised high over the village.

"We could not see it," he said. The others nodded.

"But our mothers knew it was the Antonov as soon as they saw the birds leave, and they yelled at us to go hide in the wadi, and take some animals quickly. So we took the donkeys and some chickens and goats as fast as we could. As we ran, we could hear people in the village yelling to get this person or that person out of a hut and help them get away. We could not hear the Antonov at this time. We thought it had gone away and we were safe, and that our mothers were crazy. Our fathers were far away with the animals.

"Then we heard the Antonov coming back," the boy continued under the tree. "It was coming lower, and we could see it coming up the wadi. It dropped a big bomb on each of the water points along the wadi to destroy the wells and maybe to poison them with this . . ."

The boy then pulled up his sleeve to show me red blisters on his arm. Other boys did the same, revealing backs, necks, legs, and stomachs burned by some chemical.

"The bombs sent balls of fire and sharp

metal everywhere, even to where we were hiding, where the metal came down like rain — *ting, ting, ting, ting* — for a long time. Some trees and huts were on fire when we came running back to find our mothers and grandparents."

I noticed how loud the boys were talking, and then I realized they were not hearing well. I remembered how the RPGs had damaged my own hearing for a long time when I was a little boy caught in an attack.

Seven people were dead, but the toll could have been much worse if not for the vigilance of the women. It could have been much worse if helicopter gunships had chased down the children and women, as happened so many other places. It could have been worse if the attack had been followed by the armed horsemen of the Janjaweed and the government's own troops, who would have raped every girl and woman and then shot everyone they could find. This had not happened yet to this village, but they understood it was yet to come.

Many dead animals still needed to be buried or taken away. I tended to some of this, helping wherever I could.

The smell of the chemical was still heavy on the village. It made everyone, especially the children, suffer diarrhea and vomiting for several days. Many had difficulty breathing, particularly the very young and old. The birds who drank from the water points began to die. Fifty or more camels and other animals who had trusted the water too soon lay dead at the wells.

Junked appliances and other scrap metal had been packed around the huge bombs dropped by the Sudanese government, creating a million flying daggers with each explosion. I had heard that this was happening, but did not believe it until I saw the pieces of junk stuck in the trunks of trees. Most of those killed by the bombs were buried in several pieces.

The women, normally dressed in bright colors or in the white robes of mourning, were now all in dark browns to make themselves less visible in the desert. They had poured sand in their hair, which is a custom of grieving for the dead, and they began to look like the earth itself. The children were in the darkest colors their mothers could find for them. All the bright color of the village, except a sad sprinkling of dead songbirds, was now gone.

After the second day I told Halima that it was time for me to go find our parents and the others of our family in the home village.

We said goodbye very warmly, because we well knew the trouble coming.

6.
THE END OF THE WORLD

There is a small town within a few hours' walk of my home village. Like most towns in the middle of an area of villages, it has a marketplace and a boys' school and a girls' school, all with mud-brick buildings.

As we approached the town in the Land Cruiser, we moved from the flat desert into a wadi between small mountains. We drove along the sand of the dry riverbed. Up ahead would be, in normal times, green trees, the sound of birds, and the smell of cooking. Boys and girls would be tending animals at the water points along the sandy bottom. All that was different now. Many of the trees were now burned and the water points were blackened and cratered. There were very few birds.

The children of the village looked at us seriously instead of running along beside us. Their animals were nowhere to be seen. Some burned huts were still smoking.

Each family compound has a kitchen hut that usually includes three or four red clay vessels inside, called *nunu*s, full of millet. These are sometimes much bigger than you can reach around, and can be fairly squat or as tall as a man. These silos can keep millet for ten or fifteen years and provide some insurance for hard times. From the burned huts, the smoke from these vessels layered the village with a smell of burned cooking, plus the burnt-hair smell of smoldering blankets and mattresses. There was also the smell of the dead, since not every animal had been buried yet.

I went first to the sheikh's huts: I knew him well and so could get the best information there. His huts were partially burned; no doubt everyone had rushed to help put out the fire here, since the sheikh's house is everyone's house. There was a busy coming and going of people now. Burials were being arranged and some of the wounded were being tended to. I was told who was dying over in that family and who over in this family, so that I could visit them before they died. There are no doctors or medicines in these villages, so you will die if you are seriously wounded. You bear your pain as bravely as possible and pray for death to come. Your people come to be with you. I knew everyone except the children in this village, so I visited the seventeen badly wounded people who were dying. Some had lost arms or legs in the explosions or had great wounds loosely held together with stitches of wool thread or animal hair. The only medicine or pain relief was a cup of tea.

These were people I had grown up with and played games with under the moon — we played games at night because we were busy with chores in the day, and the daytime heat was too much.

I visited a young woman whom I had always admired when we played together. She had been so strong and joyful. It was not proper for me to hold her hand, though I longed to do so now. Maybe you can think of who this would be if this happened in your hometown, and you may know how I was feeling.

Two days before my arrival the seven water points of the village had been hit with large bombs, and this had set some of the huts afire. It had not been the first attack. Each day now, the children were sent away from the village. The animals were brought to the few usable water points late at night for watering. In the daytime, anything moving in the village would invite bombs or helicopter attacks. Still, no ground attack had come.

Every cousin I met told me of ten or more deaths in his part of the family. All the villages to the east were under attack, and the men in this village were preparing for what might come next. The women were tending the wounded and were preparing food and supplies to hide in the wadis and pack on the donkeys.

While some men were organized to wait in place and defend the villages, others joined resistance groups that roamed in vehicles to be wherever they could be of most use. The government was attacking so many villages at once that these men were stretched thin and exhausted. The five kingdoms of North Darfur — Dar Kobe, Dar Gala, Dar Artaj, Dar Sueni, and our own Dar Tuar — were all under attack at the same time. Kingdoms in West and South Darfur were also being hit. The resistance fighters — some barely fourteen years old — would come into the villages in pieced-together Land Rovers for water and food, then would speed away to the next emergency, leaving their wounded with the women of the village. While the kingdom's system of sultans, omdas, and sheikhs was until recently a superbly efficient form of military organization, no one was giving orders now; the facts of each new day overwhelmed all plans.

I was told by the sheikh that my own smaller village had been bombed once but was not badly damaged, and that my immediate family was not harmed. Knowing this, I stayed in the larger village a few days to help where I could. There was a great movement of refugees through this town and people needed every kind of assistance.

Many men were joining resistance groups; you would see very young teenage boys jumping into the backs of trucks with a family weapon and that was it for them. No one in the boys' families would try to stop them. It was as if everybody had accepted that we were all going to die, and it was for each to decide how they wanted to go. It was like that. The end of the world was upon us.

"We are leaving now to try to get to Chad," was the anthem of many families as they moved through the sheikh's compound to say their goodbyes. They received advice as to the best ways through the mountains and wide deserts. Chad was far away. Even if they were not attacked by troops or Janjaweed or helicopters, many would not survive the hundred-mile trip through the scorching desert. The rain time would be over in a few days, after which the desert would dry very quickly. But there were not many other choices. Some said they would hide in local wadis and wait for peace. And there are caves in the mountains, as I well knew. But most people were intent on finding safety in Chad, where Zaghawa relatives would take care of them until they could return. Below all these adult conversations gazed the worried eyes of silent children. And in every adult eye was the dullness of a fatal understanding: whatever we do, our world is now ending and we commend ourselves into God's rough or gentle Hands.

"Your home village will soon be attacked," the sheikh told me as we stood together after tea, watching his people go. He kept track of where the refugees were coming from; he knew where the lines of attack were spreading. So I bid him goodbye and thanked him for his lifetime of courtesies to my family and to me. He said that he had always been honored to serve us; he bid me give his greetings to my father and my mother and to Ahmed and my sister, all of whom he respected greatly.

I climbed aboard a Land Cruiser loaded with guns and men headed in the direction of my own small village. There was not much conversation as we bounced quickly through the wadis. There ahead, in a lovely nest of green, was my home village. I stepped off within sight of my family's huts and said goodbye for the last time to these fellows in the vehicle.

"See you soon, Daoud," said an old school friend with a serious smile, meaning *not in this lifetime.*

7.
Homecoming

It was not the homecoming I had longed for after these years away. I was not returning with gifts and money for everyone.

"Daoud is returned," I heard some men say as I walked by groups that were gathered here and there. I nodded to them but it did not seem to be a time for smiles and joyful greetings.

I walked into the family enclosure where a donkey, several goats, and some chickens watched my arrival. My father was on the far side of the village with some other men, as were my brothers. I saw my mother under the shade roof attached to the cooking hut; she was with my sister Aysha and with several other women of the village; they were all in mourning. Mother looked very old now. Her hair was matted with the earth of grieving. She wore dark clothing, a dark shawl over her old head. She saw me and wept into her hands, as if it were even sadder for her to think that my homecoming had to be at such a time.

"*Fatah,*" she managed to say, which is what you say when you greet someone in a time of grieving.

"Fatah," I replied. I stood a distance away from her. We did not touch or embrace, following the custom. She would try to say something, but then begin to cry again into her hands and her shawl. We had lost perhaps twenty cousins in the previous days, and each was like a son or daughter to her. In tribal life, cousins are as close as brothers and sisters and, in such times of loss, it physically hurts. In this tiny village, three children and their mother were killed when the white Antonov bomber came. Six of the fifty houses were burned. This news, which I already knew, was told to me again by the women as I stood with my head bowed a little to my mother.

They recounted the deaths of each person: how it happened, what was happening to that family, and good things to remember about each person. It is good to remember the dead at such times, for soon, after the period of mourning, any photo and reminder of that person will be removed. The person's clothes will be given away to a distant village. The past is past. There is too

I went to look for Ahmed, who had escaped the old men to continue his preparations. I found him in front of his family enclosure, talking to more than twenty men, mostly thirty-five to forty-five years old. They were planning to move the old people and young children in the next two days. Because they also talked about preparing their guns, I later asked Ahmed what this group was going to do.

"We are the village defenders," he said. "We will stay behind to slow the attack if it comes before everyone has left. It is what we are trained to do, and you are not."

He told me that most of the younger men had already gone to the rebel groups. There were other defenders in the mountains from other villages who would come when they were called.

In the old days, the sultan of an area had a great war drum. Actually, some of these drums still exist. They are so big that ten men can beat them with great clubs. The sound of this drum — I heard it more than once as a child — will carry over the desert the distance of a two- or three-day walk. In the rain time, when there are low clouds, it will carry even farther. In this way, all the villages in the sultan's reach would know that there is a sad problem that must be solved with fighting. The sultan would send representatives to the omdas, and the village sheiks would go to the omdas to get the news and learn the strategy. Perhaps, for example, Arabs had stolen some cattle and would not pay. There was no higher court to take the problem to, so there would be a battle at some agreed-upon field of honor. As I have said, it would be far away from the women and children.

We boys would have to go find the strongest of the male camels so that our fathers and older brothers would have good mounts for the battle. Guns and swords would swing from their saddles as they left the village without a word of information or consolation to the children or women. The camels would know what all this meant, and they would grind their teeth in a way that could be heard all over the village. The sound of worried camels was the sound before battle, while the ululation of wailing women was the sound after the battle. The names of the fallen would arrive long before the weary camels and men plodded back into the village. The surviving men would split up and spend up to two weeks in the family enclosures of the widows, so that the women would have company and could overhear their stories. This was how their lost husbands were honored. In time, the widow might be taken as an extra wife by one of her late husband's brothers or another man.

I tell you all this because I was hearing again the grinding sound of worried camels, and the birds flew up and down as if they were unsure of which place might be safe.

Over dinner, Ahmed reminded me of all the paths through the wadi, of all the water points in remote places, and of our childhood caves.

"It will not be easy for all these people to get quickly away," he said. "Men like you, who tended animals so far into the desert when they were boys, could, if they chose, help them find their way." He was not inviting me to go, but he was clearly not inviting me to stay and die — and I had no gun. Ahmed was thinking clearly. He had sent another of our brothers to El Fasher, the safest town in North Darfur, as a kind of family insurance: no matter what happened, there would be one alive to help the surviving women and children of the family. There was no way for all the family to go with him, as there were too many animals to tend.

We ate chicken that evening and the next several evenings — wonderful chicken, usually saved for special occasions. Everyone in the village ate chicken those nights.

I borrowed *jallabiya* robes to wear from Ahmed. I had not been in the flowing clothes for many years, but it was pleasant to wear them now — they were cooler in the sun than my Western khakis. They bring you shade wherever you go. I borrowed one of Ahmed's camels and checked on the animals at the water points. I used the camel whip very lightly to get some speed along the sand. I saw a shadow in the sand of who I might have been had I stayed.

I was happy to find my place again in my big and loving family. Maybe Heaven is like this, a warm reunion of those you love after dark times and a long separation, but with a little excitement to keep things interesting.

Ahmed told me that some of the old people were refusing to leave. They were intent on dying where they had always lived. They would not be humiliated and made to run away from their homes.

I asked about our parents. Ahmed was planning to get them out soon. They were willing to go.

Some families had already left. A few of these had arranged vehicle rides to other villages, but most had children and animals and belongings, and would have to walk.

Our family's animals, like those of most

families, were in faraway places known only to us.

I spent the days helping people get ready. I would ride to the outlying clusters of huts and encourage people to prepare to move. Some did not want to, and would point and say, "We have our great-grandfathers buried over here, and our children buried over there, and so why would this not be a good place for us to die also?" You could not argue with that. This meant we had to think about the women and children and the younger men and help them instead.

Women were getting their children ready for the long journey, and you may know what this is like, though it was probably more serious in this kind of situation. What to take, what to leave — all those difficult choices.

I woke up late one night with a vivid dream. Ahmed was standing in the middle of the village. Two of his fellow village defenders were near him, screaming for him to run. I was shouting down to them from the hillside, telling them to shoot at the attackers. *Don't yell at Ahmed,* I shouted, *shoot the attackers over there, over there,* and I pointed because I could see them taking aim at Ahmed. But it was too late, and Ahmed fell from a bullet. *Why didn't you shoot the attackers?* I shouted when I got down to the men. *Why didn't you shoot them?* But Ahmed was dead, and then maybe I was dead.

This dream kept me awake. I walked out of the village to the hill beside it. I was still up there in the bushes at dawn.

I had tea for breakfast at my father's hut. (Husbands and wives have separate huts, which makes for long marriages.) Ahmed was there and I looked at him like he was a dead man. I could not tell him the dream. Ahmed was telling my father to leave the village right after tea, and to take the rest of the animals out of the village. My father, who said he had heard guns in the night, agreed and left.

At about 9 a.m. I was walking through the village to see how everyone was doing. It was a morning of good weather at the end of the rain time. The birds were singing, which I took to mean we were safe at least another hour. But then there was a strange sound and I stopped walking in order to listen carefully. It was a thumping like a great drum, then more and very rapid thumps of this drum. Then very clearly it was the sound of helicopters turning steeply. I saw two large, green helicopters now through the trees, turning sharply into our narrow wadi. The thumping was their engines as they turned — then the thumping of their guns shook the air. I did not know which way to run so I stood there crazy for a moment and watched the dirt of the village spraying up from the bullets.

I saw Ahmed run from his enclosure with his gun. My other brother, Juma, was with him. Juma is a quiet, very hardworking man. I was not used to seeing him excited and with a gun. Juma and Ahmed seemed now to be running to the sound of this drumming. They were headed to the mouth of the little valley where the ground attackers would have to enter. Their running also drew the helicopters away from the huts. Other defenders were now running up to the hills on both sides of the village, but mostly to the east to intercept the attackers as far down the valley as they could manage.

"Let's go! Let's go!" they shouted to one another over the steady *kata-tata* of the machine guns.

The women started screaming to their children *Let's go let's go* and everything in the village began to move in a swirl of dust and noise. The animals were wild-eyed with fear, and the donkeys screamed and brayed. I did not see where the bullets were going, but little songbirds flew down from the trees, confused and worried. They perched on my shoulders and then hid in the folds of my robes and shawl. But then I saw they were falling dead from me, their hearts broken by this noise. I ran to my mother's hut. She and my sister and her children were already leaving, quickly moving between the huts to the safety of the trees and the rocky wadi west of the village. *Let's go let's go,* she called to her grandbabies as they ran toward the safety of the trees and the steep rocks to the west of the village. I quickly found myself with other men carrying a child here, boosting some children onto donkeys, urging donkeys along *let's go let's go,* finding children and sometimes their mothers standing and crying hysterically and pleading with them to move along.

"You can cry, but you must move also, *let's go.* You must get your children behind those trees and keep going — go, go, go!"

One hundred people had wisely left the village in the days before the attack; we were now struggling with the one hundred and fifty remaining. The older people willing to go needed the most help; we were constantly coming back to help this person and again for the next person, with the bullets cracking in the trees and RPG rounds exploding in the center of the village and setting huts on fire. We were checking flaming huts and carrying the people who could not run. There was a sort of slow dreaminess to all this.

I am dead, I am dead, this is how I died, it is not so bad, I was thinking, afraid to look down at my body because too many bullets were flying around for me still to be okay. I kept moving, moving, carrying the people to the trees and up into the rocky ravine, looking back and hoping to see no one else needing help, but seeing them and going back.

The small, camouflage-painted Land Cruisers of the attackers were now visible at the lower part of the village. The defenders had moved quickly enough to pin them in place and buy us this time. Defenders from other villages nearby had heard the helicopters and were coming over the hills to help. The Sudanese Army troops and the Janjaweed are cruel but they are not stupid, and they did not rush into this little valley so quickly and become trapped; the defenders had thought this out very well.

Large-caliber machine guns were firing into the village from far enough away that attackers could only spray the area and hope to kill people without seeing them. The helicopters were mostly shooting at the defenders at the east end and not at the people escaping to the west. They would all surely come after us when the defenders were dead, so we knew we had to keep moving.

This pushing of the people into the mountains went on for perhaps fifteen or twenty minutes, though it seemed like many hours. You have to keep going, keep going, up steep places and onward to places where Janjaweed horsemen would not be able to follow.

I could see, as we moved the last of the people out of the village, the Janjaweed now charging in on their horses, shooting into the huts as they came. We had everyone but the defenders out by this time. We slipped into the rocks and watched from above for a moment before we continued on, pushing at the rear of this exodus to keep it going.

Being ready to go had worked a great miracle, as all but the defenders were now safely out of the village. I looked behind me, far down to the sand, and could see no children's bodies, no women's bodies, on the sand or between the huts or trees. A very good view, under my circumstances.

Behind us, the defenders held down the attackers and we heard their firing dwindle over the hour. Finally it was silent. We kept moving through all that day and all that night. The fast march was hardest on the children and on the old who had chosen to come, but the great fear now was that the helicopters would come looking for us, as they often did after an attack.

People cried as they walked, thinking of what they had left behind, and they cried for the defenders and some of the old people who had stayed.

We could settle down some of the boys by saying, *Someday you will have this great story to tell your children.* There was nothing, however, that could be said to the young girls and the women, who could not see the future anymore. Our village was gone. Some of the best of our men were dead. There was no reason not to cry as they walked in several dark lines through the mountain.

The surviving village defenders caught up with us toward dark. My brother Juma was among them, but I did not see Ahmed with him. Juma looked at me sadly when he came closer. This was enough.

"Fatah," he said. "Our brother Ahmed is killed. Maybe we will see him soon."

We held each other. He told me that the badly wounded were staying about three hours back on the trail so the women and children would not see them. It is considered impolite for a man, whose job is to be strong, to present himself to women or children when he is badly hurt.

I had thought in my heart that Ahmed and Juma were probably dead. Seeing Juma alive was very good, but Ahmed's death hit me very hard now. We would have to tell Mother and our sister. It might be too much for them.

They stood and listened as Juma and I told them. They appealed to their God for strength that starry night.

In the morning, and the next morning, we could hear bombing and helicopters in the distance; other villages were dying.

On the third day of our flight we came to a water point where some of our people were waiting for us, including Father. He had some of our camels and other animals in his care. He already knew about Ahmed and looked much older on account of this news.

Fifteen of us, the younger men, decided to ride camels back to the village to bury the dead and retrieve the hidden supplies of food and clothing. The attackers would have taken all they wanted by now, burned the village, and gone away. We needed to bury the bodies before the wild dogs and jackals destroyed them. We gathered some tools for burial and rode back.

The village was mostly gone — sixty or so scorched black spots where a whole world once celebrated life. The nunus of millet, many mattresses and blankets, mounds of trees, and parts of huts were still smoking, which we smelled long before we entered the wadi.

Thirteen bodies were on the ground, mostly near the eastern side of the village, where the defense was made. The Sudanese troops and Janjaweed had of course removed their own dead, so these thirteen were the defenders of the village and some who had come to help.

I found Ahmed. The effects of large-caliber weapons and perhaps an RPG round were such that I barely recognized his body, but it was Ahmed. I dug a grave as we do, so that he would rest on his right side with his face to the east. I put the pieces of this great fellow in the deep sand forever.

"Goodbye, Ahmed," I said to him. And I knelt down there for a long time instead of helping the others. It was raining a little.

Finally, I did stand and go help the others.

After we retrieved some hidden supplies and packed them on our camels, we prepared to leave. Mixed deep in the ashes of the smoldering huts were of course the bones of the old people who had refused to go, but we could do nothing for these now until the rains would reveal them. The wild animals would have no use for these fired bones.

A few birds were singing in the trees. Not many, but a few. *Well,* I thought to myself, *they will come back in time, like the people.*

But for now it was ashes and graves. This had been a good village.

8.
THE SEVEN OF US

When we caught up with our people we men stayed mostly together with the wounded defenders, going back and forth to the women for the food and for the traditional medicine and teas they would prepare. In this way our village, though now a moving line in the desert, was still the same people helping one another.

The people of other villages joined us here and there, until we were a great mass of people moving across the land. Every morning we would have to bury several of the wounded who died in the night. It was good for some of them to die, since there was no morphine or other medicine. You can usually see in a man's eyes if he will be blessed to die before morning.

On the fifth day we came to a remote and grassy valley, and some of those with animals to sustain them decided they would hide there and make a temporary life. Those with no animals had no choice but to continue on to Chad. My mother and sister were among these who stayed — she would go no farther. My father would keep moving with some of the animals and the other people while they needed him. The camels provided wonderful milk and rides for the children, who were suffering. He would come back to Mother with our animals when he could. In this way, my mother and sister became what the world calls IDPs, which means internally displaced persons — refugees who are still within their home country.

And in this way, too, the other people continued on for seven more days, walking to Chad, marking their way with graves.

Six of my old friends and I began to scout ahead on our camels. We would take water to the people from the water points we knew. This was becoming critical, because the rain time was over and the little wet spots in the desert quickly dried. We began to find other groups in the desert who needed water, and you must of course help everyone you can. We helped many people to move along, to find one another, to find the safe routes. We brought food from Chad to people who had run out of everything.

We became lost in this work for three

months, sleeping in the bush and watching for the white airplanes, the government troops, and the Janjaweed. We buried men, women, and children who could not finish the trip.

Many other groups of men were doing this as well. And in Chad, camps were forming all along the border. Everyone was helping one another, since the world had not come to help yet.

I met two women, around maybe twenty-five and forty-five in age, who had escaped a village attack, but did so as new widows. They looked behind them to see the men of the village machine-gunned down from helicopters. These two women escaped with two metal boxes, now badly dented. They contained the tools needed by traditional nurses to help deliver babies. They set up a clinic in one of the impromptu camps and were now helping many people every day, long before the first of the white trucks arrived from the aid groups. It was like this everywhere; the best way to bury your pain is to help others and to lose yourself in that.

The sight of the seven of us coming on our camels through the mirages of the desert was strange to people who had been a long time without water and were perhaps a little delirious. They were of course praying for exactly this miracle. It was good to be the miracle, and how can you stop doing that? But we were not always the miracle in time.

"You need to get that baby away from her," some women told me as they swallowed their first sips of water and pointed to a young mother standing alone.

"Her baby is dead and she was carrying it all day yesterday and today. She will not let us have it to bury it," one of them told me.

The little mother sipped water from the cup I held out, and she looked at me very sadly.

"I need to have your little baby now. She has already flown away," I said to her. After a time she let me take the dead child.

Losing a child is so hard, as you may know. It doesn't matter where you live in the world for that. Babies are usually not named in Darfur until several days or even weeks after they are born, because so many babies die here without doctors or medicine. Those who do not live are considered birds of passage who did not want to stay. Naming the child is therefore saved until it is clear the spirit in this child wants to stay.

We continued to move through this odd landscape of pain, saving as many as we could, and burying others.

We came upon a lone tree not far from the Chad border where a woman and two of her three children were dead. The third child died in our arms. The skin of these little children was like delicate brown paper, so wrinkled. You have seen pictures of children who are dying of hunger and thirst, their little bones showing and their heads so big against their withered bodies. You will think this takes a long time to happen to a child, but it takes only a few days. It breaks your heart to see, just as it breaks a mother's heart to see. This woman hanged herself from her shawl, tied in the tree. We gently took her down and buried her beside her children. This moment stays with me every day.

I felt a need to know something about her from others I would later meet. She was about thirty years old. When her village was attacked by the Janjaweed, she and her two daughters and son — the eldest was six years old — were held for a week. The mother was raped repeatedly. They released the mother and her children in the desert far from any villages. That was probably cheaper than using bullets on them, or else they wanted their seeds to grow inside her. She walked for five days in the desert carrying her children without food or water.

When she couldn't carry them anymore, she sat under a tree that she found. There was nothing she could do except watch her children die. She took her shawl and tied it to a high branch in order to end her life. We found her that same day, a few hours too late.

After these months, we began to see white trucks over on the Chad side of the wadi; the aid groups that respond to crises were beginning to arrive. We could see them in the distance over the hot desert — sometimes great lines of them. It was time to go talk to them. Things would be different with these people arriving. I felt good about this, but my friends didn't know about these groups and had no sense of what they could do. These groups had saved my life in Egypt, so I felt warmly toward them.

My six friends and I had tea over a dinner fire. I told them we should go into Chad and see what these groups could do now. We could help them.

"You go ahead, Daoud, and help your friends in the groups; you speak English and so that is what you were meant to do," the eldest of my friends said. In his kind authority I could hear Ahmed. Because of my schooling, my fate would always be a little different from my friends'.

Perhaps because we knew we were about to part, we tossed a little animal bone around in the moonlight, just as we had done as children but a little slower. In the game called Anashel, you have two teams of eight people each. We had three against four that night, but no one cared. Someone throws the bone far away into the sand. Everyone runs for it. If you are the one to find it, you try to run it back to the goal area without being caught and wrestled down, although you can throw it to your teammates. Children play this game at night, when there is at least a half-moon for light and some cool air and no chores left to do. The girls and boys play it together.

There is another game, called Whee, but we were getting too old to play it, so we stayed with Anashel. But so you will know: In Whee you have eight on a team, and try to get your team members across a goal line, as the other team tries to get across theirs. You do battle in the middle, of course. The challenge is that everyone must hold on to one of their feet, so they will be hopping on one leg. This is a very, very hard but very funny game, and it goes on for several hours; you have to be young and strong. The girls would often win because of the work they do carrying water and wood.

On this night, someone finally got the Anashel bone to the goal and that was it for us forever.

I have not described these men carefully because, if I do, they might be killed for what I am about to say, although some are probably dead now anyway. They decided to sell their camels for guns and defend their villages. It was not for me to argue with them.

On that last morning together, we shook hands warmly and embraced one another. While the sun had yet to rise in a very red sky, they rode east toward El Fasher on their camels, and I rode west.

9.

THE TRANSLATOR

I sold my camel in Tine for what would be about four hundred U.S. dollars and began to move around the refugee camps to help where I could. The fact that I spoke Zaghawa, Arabic, and English made me useful to the aid people who were streaming into Chad. Aid groups are usually called NGOs, which stands for nongovernmental organizations.

I soon had a good network of contacts in these groups and, as a translator, I helped to get refugees to the small amount of help that was at first available.

As far as the Chad government was concerned, the refugees were welcome to come across the border, but they were to remain in the refugee camps, and they were not to work at jobs — even for free as I was doing — since this might take work opportunities away from Chad citizens. This was fair, but it meant I could not be of much help unless

I said I was from Chad. So I did this, because it was morally necessary.

As more NGOs came in, and as the camps rapidly expanded, the officials in charge became less willing to look the other way regarding my citizenship. A few reporters began to arrive, mostly from other African nations, and I wanted to take them into Darfur and show them what was happening. I thought I would need some kind of Chad papers to cross the border with the journalists, so I took some of my remaining camel money and went to see my cousins and friends in N'Djamena, who might help me get papers. That is how I became Suleyman Abakar Moussa of Chad. The little scars on my temples were not important; Zaghawa live in Chad as well as Sudan. It was a little strange that I did not speak French, as Chad people do, but many also speak Arabic, so I could manage.

It was a risk, and, yes, I remembered the beatings in the Egyptian jails when I was captured after trying to get into Israel. But you should always do what you need to do to be helpful.

When I was ready to go back to the border area, I went first to one of the big hotels in N'Djamena where the NGOs and reporters often stay when they first come into the area. I had heard that there were journalists there who needed translators to go to the refugee camps and perhaps into Darfur. I was told by a friend who worked in a Chad government ministry to look for a "Dr. John" at the Novotel Hotel. After three days and several trips there and to the other large hotel, I saw some Massalit men I had met in Abéché and who, I knew, spoke some English. The Massalit are a tribe mostly from West Darfur, while my Zaghawa people are mostly in North Darfur, and the Fur are mostly in South Darfur. The two men were in the Novotel's coffee shop, talking to a white man at their table. I went up to them and, in Arabic, asked, *Who is this white man of yours? Who is this hawalya?* That is a not-unkind word for a white person. They explained that this man was looking for translators to go to the camps, and they were going with him. Also, he needed a Zaghawa translator. It seems we had been looking for each other.

"Dr. John, I presume?" is how I introduced myself to him, which I thought was pretty good.

He was not exactly a journalist. He had arrived with people from the United Nations and the U.S. State Department to interview refugees and make a legal determination if a genocide was occurring. If it was not technically a genocide and was instead a more ordinary civil war, that would call for a different international response. For killings to be considered a genocide, the victims have to be targeted because of their ethnic identity.

Dr. John, a young American who looked to be in his late twenties, with blond hair and a bushy beard, said that he was not a doctor, but that this was his nickname. He was glad to meet this Suleyman Abakar Moussa from Chad who spoke Zaghawa, Arabic, and English. After his many questions, he asked if I would be one of their translators for this investigation into possible crimes of genocide. Yes, I would do that. I had found my fate.

10.

STICKS FOR SHADE

Our caravan of white vehicles, the genocide investigation team, was waved through an army checkpoint at the Breidjing refugee camp on Chad's eastern border with Sudan. It was one of about ten such camps along the border at the time.

The horizon ahead was fluttering with plastic tarps and little rags tied to sticks for shade. There were shredded green tents and torn white plastic sheeting wrapped around more sticks to serve as tattered roofs and walls. Where the road lifted a bit, this thin line of twirling rags was revealed as a vast city of desperation, as if all the poverty and sadness of the world came from one endless storage yard somewhere, and here it was. This camp had tripled in new souls during the few weeks I had been away. The thinnest shelters flapped everywhere in the wind now. Some were the torn canvas remnants from Rwanda and Sierra Leone and other previous tragedies, rewoven now into a miserable twig and rag nest for thirty thousand birds of passage.

The sight of so many people suffering pushed my own troubles from my head. Because I had been to this camp before, I had been worrying that the people who knew me here would certainly call me Daoud, when the genocide investigators had hired me as Suleyman, citizen of Chad. I was still wanted by the government of Sudan ever since they tried to extradite me from Egypt for immigration violations. If Chad arrested me for false papers or for working illegally instead of staying in a refugee camp, they might send me to Sudan, which would surely be the end of me. This had been hanging over my thoughts as we traveled.

Familiar smells and the low rumble of a great crowd greeted us as we rolled down the windows: babies crying but also children laughing and running after us, stretching out their fingers to touch ours; mothers calling for their children to be careful, the crunch of bundles of firewood being unloaded from the backs of donkeys, the braying of those donkeys, the smoke and smell of a thousand little fires, of spiced and mint teas brewing, of hot cooking oils and overheated, dirty children. A gauze of this sound, smoke, and dust extended over the tangled nest as far as one cared to look, except where the women wore their beautiful colors, which stood out through the sticks: clean and bright reds, oranges, yellows, brilliant blues and greens. The women of Africa, as the world knows, have a genius for color, and they decorated this place with themselves, as they always do. The bold colors they had put away before the attacks were now waving from their lean bodies with defiance — the flags of resilient life.

Perhaps a thousand women and children were standing in daylong lines for their monthly rations of wheat, cooking oil, and salt from the U.N. World Food Programme. Others, with plastic jerry cans, waited in separate lines for their turns at the water pump.

Every day these same girls and women collected wood for their cooking fires by scavenging sticks from the surrounding wild areas. These areas were quickly stripped, angering the local tribes and forcing foraging trips ever deeper into dangerous territory. As a consequence, rape was now the going price of camp firewood. If the women sent their men to gather wood, or if they came along as protection, the men would be killed. So the women and girls went alone and in small groups, often to be raped by the local men. It is the same in Darfur, but there it is the Janjaweed who rape. Many pregnancies of unwanted children were the next tragedy facing these women. The girls and women who looked at us and blinked away our dust as we drove past had the look of people who had seen all this.

Except for the food and the tattered canvas, and for some drawing paper and pencils so the children could make pictures of huts and cows and helicopters shooting people and airplanes dropping bombs and men with bayonets stabbing the people identified in these drawings as the children's uncles, brothers, sisters — except for these, the world's charity seemed almost invisible here. Perhaps the wealthy nations had finally blown themselves away and were no longer available to send their usual token remedies for the problems that their thirst for resources has always brought to such people as these. It should be said that much was being done that we could not see at first glance: groups such as Médecins Sans Frontières (Doctors Without Borders), Oxfam, and Italy's Intersos were hard at work here, but the smoky misery of homeless human beings stretching to the very horizon cannot but upset your heart.

Canvas and plastic make very hot shelters in a desert, and these were what the world had sent — exactly the wrong thing and not nearly enough of it. Perhaps there was no right thing to send; the grass huts of Darfur, so cool in summer and warm in winter, were impossible here because of an insufficiency of grass and wood poles, of space to put them up, and of young men alive to build them. What, indeed, could be built quickly enough for so many? Even so, with all the bright people in the world and so much wealth, could there not be humane shelters for such times if we are a family? Let a peace prize be reserved for those who can someday do this moral favor for humanity.

I had a pretty good idea where my mother and father were hiding at this time, and also my sister Aysha and her children. My surviving brothers were here and there, according to reports from cousins. My second sister, Halima, who had lived near our home village, was with her children in an area that I cannot mention. I was in regular contact with all of them thanks to cousins on the move.

My third sister, Hawa, who lived in her husband's village in South Darfur, had been missing along with her husband and children since the attack on their village. I thought my new work in the camps might help me find her and her family if they were still alive. I was looking for and asking about them always. More than four thousand villages were being attacked and destroyed, so this would be difficult.

There were perhaps twenty of us in the team: half translators and half genocide investigators from the United States, Canada, Australia, and Europe. We translators had been trained for several days to ask questions without causing further harm to people. I was moved by the sensitivity of these investigators. Some were very young, coming straight from universities, while the elders had worked in Bosnia and Rwanda and other hard places.

The manager of the camp, who worked for one of the big relief agencies, greeted our team. I stood a little back, not wanting to be recognized or introduced by my new name. Our leaders went into the administrator's office and I felt safe momentarily. But then the woman in charge of our group got a cell phone call from one of my cousins, who had tracked me down and wanted to tell me that some of our other cousins had been attacked the previous day. She came out and said she had a call for a *Daoud.* Did anyone know a Daoud?

Some of the other translators knew my secret story and looked at me. I breathed deeply and smiled, walking forward.

"Some of my friends call me that. Sometimes my cousins call me that nickname. Daoud is the same name as David from the Bible. They call me that because I don't mind fighting with bigger men." She still looked a little curious.

"We all have many nicknames," one of my translator friends said quickly to the laughter of others. The woman raised her eyebrows, handed me the phone, and said, "Okay. I get it," and walked back inside. She was going to be cool about these things.

11.
TWO AND A HALF MILLION STORIES

We soon split into groups to begin our work. With one of the investigators, I went to find a sheikh I knew. Each camp is like many villages pushed together, complete with their sheikhs. We asked this sheikh to help us find refugees willing to talk about what had happened to them. As he took us for a walk, I told him where my sister's village had been and asked if he knew about her family. He did not.

"There are many other camps," he said in a gentle way. "Perhaps they are alive and you will find them." I could not imagine how many times he must have had to say this to worried people. There are registries of names in each camp, of course, and I always would check these, but there is too much confused movement, too much fear and illiteracy, and too many displaced people — two and a half million now — for these lists to be complete. The sheikhs, however, always know better than the NGO lists.

We walked with him through this mass of people. Very young boys followed us wearing dirty and torn shirts and shorts. They ran around us, bouncing, trying to shake the white people's hands, practicing the few English words they had learned in their now burned schools, or in the roasting canvas classrooms of the camp, or under trees when the school tents had blown away: *Hello, Good morning, Thank you, How are you? What is your name?*

I looked for a boy I met when I visited the camp some weeks earlier. He was about eight years old and wore huge sunglasses that made him look like a small movie star. I didn't see him — not surprising; he was a pebble in this wide desert, as was my sister if she was alive.

Some brave girls joined the boys in their prancing around us, but most walked shyly along the margins of our moving crowd, holding the ends of their bright shawls tightly and sometimes hiding all but their large brown eyes. Older girls and women were coming and going with water and wood, slowing a little to glance at us. A lucky few had donkeys to help them. Donkeys are the best friends of the refugees, and were the only animals many of these families now had — if they had anything. Compared to a camel, which is like a very good truck for the family, a donkey is like a little brown cart, but well loved and well used, and often hugged and kissed every day by the children.

When I was a young boy I loved our family donkey, but in a different way than I loved my fast camel, Kelgi, who was as intelligent as any person I knew. Once when Kelgi was stolen, he walked the thief around in circles through the night so we could easily catch him the next morning. My father scolded the man and asked his family to pay a debt of some animals, which they did. Father sold these animals to buy us some new clothes and my first shoes. A camel's hooves, by the way, have cracks and other marks as individual as fingerprints, so a camel can be tracked a very long way, and you can see which of your friends has come through this way or that. I cannot say enough about camels. Their milk is a wonderful desert drink — so plentiful and watery that it is often used to pour over your head and arms like a shower after a sandstorm. Camel meat, sadly, is quite delicious and needs no salt.

Like camels, donkeys are loyal unto death.

Donkeys suffered terribly as they carried children out of Darfur into Chad. They kept going without enough food or water — three days without water will kill a donkey. A camel, by comparison, will deflate after many days without water. He will get smaller and older looking, with a drooping head. But when he is refreshed with water and grass, he is beautiful again, strong, big, and young-looking again. Donkeys cannot do that. Some donkeys went longer than three days without water, because if there was any water at all, it was given to the children riding on them. When these animals reached the camps and finally felt the children slide down, many of the donkeys straightaway fell dead, having done their loving work. The NGOs in some camps made piles of hundreds of these dead donkeys and burned them in great fires that were terribly sad for the people to see, especially the children. These animals were like family, so full of modesty and devotion.

The donkeys who survived the trip were happy now to be moving wood and water around the camps.

My investigator and I sat on straw mats in the precious shade of a small tree. Seven people, collected by the sheikh as we walked, sat with us to tell their stories. A few wanted the world to know the terrible things they had suffered and demanded that we tell their stories personally to the U.N. secretary-general, whose name they knew. Some thought we must know him as well as they knew their own sheikh. Others were quieter in their pain and spoke to us only out of respect for their sheikh and his request.

Often, then, the stories came pouring out, and often they were set before us slowly and quietly like tea. These slow stories were told with understatement that made my eyes and voice fill as I translated; for when people seem to have no emotion remaining for such stories, your own heart must supply it.

It helps many people just to have someone listen and write their story down; if their suffering is noted somewhere, by someone, anyone, then they can more easily let loose of it because they know where it is. Only little comfort can be given, however, to a woman or girl who has been ravaged. The pain is written deep into her flat eyes and flat voice. There is, she believes, nothing for her now. We would listen with heads bowed, careful to tread only where she would accept another question and perhaps one or two more.

The first day was very hard on everyone

who told a story and everyone who listened. The dust of the camp was streaked down the faces of even the most experienced investigators. The coming days would be no easier.

The attack stories were often like my own, though I realized how lucky our village had been to have Ahmed's leadership. So many villages were caught completely by surprise: surrounded, burned alive, massacred from helicopters above and Janjaweed below, with only a few escaping, or a few coming from other villages to find everyone dead and the bodies burned in heartbreaking positions; mothers died trying to protect their children and husbands died trying to protect their wives. Hundreds of thousands were dead. Millions were homeless.

While I was waiting that first evening for the return of some teams who had ventured farther toward the horizon of this great camp, an administrator stepped out of the office and saw me. "Daoud!" he said. "What are you doing here?"

He knew the work I was doing was against the law for a refugee in Chad, so I walked slowly toward him, giving myself time to think. Halfway there, a man in his late thirties, wearing a dirty and ragged robe and head shawl, suddenly appeared from the bush at the edge of the camp and walked toward me. He seemed very intense and maybe a little crazy. Pain came from his face like heat from a little stove. He shook my hand and would not let it loose, patting my hand quietly.

"You are Zaghawa," he said, "and I need to tell you something alone."

He led me a short way into the bush and motioned for me to sit down with him in the sand, which, under my circumstances, I was very pleased to do. The man's wife approached quickly and pleaded, "He's not right in his head. Please don't ask him your questions." But I could tell the man had something he needed to get out, so I asked his wife if I could just listen to him, like two Zaghawa men who should be friends anyway. She agreed and stood a few bushes away, pacing a little and watching us.

They were from North Darfur. Their village had been attacked and destroyed a few months before my own.

"Everybody ran away as fast as they could. My wife over there held our two-year-old son tightly in her arms, and she ran one way through the bushes. Thank God she found a good way to go. I took my four-year-old daughter, Amma, and we ran as fast as we could another way around the bushes. They

116

caught me, the Janjaweed, and I let go of her hand and told her to run. But she didn't keep running; she watched from some bushes as they beat me and tied me to a tree with my arms back around it like this" — he made his arms into a hoop behind his back.

"One of the Janjaweed men started to kill me in a painful way. My daughter could not bear to see this, so she ran toward me and called out, *Abba, Abba.*" These words, which mean "Daddy, Daddy," filled his throat with emotion, and he paused a long time.

"The Janjaweed man who had tied me to the tree saw my daughter running to me. He lowered his rifle and he let her run into his bayonet. He gave it a big push. The blade went all the way through her stomach. She still cried out to me, 'Abba! Abba!'

"Then he lifted up his gun, with my daughter on it, with blood from her body pouring down all over him. He danced around with her in the air and shouted to his friends, 'Look, see how fierce I am,' and they chanted back to him, 'Yes, yes, you are fierce, fierce, fierce!' as they were killing other people. My daughter looked at me for help and stretched her arms in great pain toward me. She tried to say *Abba* but nothing came out.

"It took a long time for her to die, her blood coming down so fresh and red on this — what was he? a man? a devil? He was painted red with my little girl's blood and he was dancing. What was he?"

This man had seen evil and didn't know what to do with the sight of it. He was looking for an answer to what it was, and why his little daughter deserved this. Then, after taking some time to cry without talking, he told me he no longer knew who he was.

"Am I a woman who should stay in this camp, or a man who should go fight, and leave my wife and son without protection?" He looked at me as if I should know the answer to his life now. He waited for an answer that I could not give.

"You are still alive," I said. "They didn't kill you."

"What is a better torture than this?" he snapped. "What was better torture than to have to tell my wife and son this?"

His wife came over again and sat near her husband. She picked some small leaves from the shawl that wrapped his head. She told me that his mind was not the same after the attack. "Thank God we have our son, and he is good," she said. "I told my husband that Amma is gone and we must think about the future. But he cannot let go of what he saw."

The woman told me she found a man in the camp who writes and has ink and a quill for that. She had him write down helpful passages from the Koran on small wooden tablets, which were then washed so the inky water could be given to her husband to drink. It is an old cure that often works very well — but had only worked a little for him. They would try again, she told me. Her husband nodded.

When I came back to the same camp a long time later, and I asked the sheikh to help me find this family, the man had gone away, and his wife did not remember me. She seemed more dazed than before. She still had her son, she said, who was at the camp's school that hour. I had come back because the story that would not leave the man's mind was now in my mind, and was in my dreams among other stories, waking me almost every night. I thought that talking to him again might help us both, but now he was gone, perhaps to fight and be done with his life, as I was doing in my own way.

It is interesting how many ways there are for people to be hurt and killed, and for villages to be terrorized and burned, and for children to die in deserts, and for young mothers to suffer. I would say that these ways to die and suffer are unspeakable, and yet they were spoken: we interviewed 1,134 human beings over the next weeks; their stories swirled through my near-sleepless nights. I found that if I made little drawings of the scenes described to me, it would sometimes get the stories out of my head long enough for me to get some sleep. I would wake and make these drawings, and then I could sleep a little. These stories from the camps, mixed with things I had seen with my own eyes, such as the young mother hanging in a tree and her children with skin like brown paper and mothers carrying their dead babies and not letting them go . . . I was thankful that I could not draw them very well — stick figures, really. Even so, it helped.

12.

CONNECTIONS

When the genocide investigation came to its end, I returned to N'Djamena, Chad, and had a last meal with Dr. John and the others. Genocide is not always easy to prove, so the many interviews were necessary. The United States and others used this investigation to determine that, yes, the government of Sudan was conducting a genocide. The U.S. government did not do too much else, but the American people, as they always do, helped a lot, as did the people of Europe and many other places. The proof of a democracy is surely whether or not a government represents the hearts of its people.

Using the stipend I received from the genocide investigators, I got a cell phone. I wanted a cell number to leave in the camps and with my cousins in case there was news of my family and especially of my missing sister. I also wanted it so I could continue to take investigators or perhaps journalists into the camps and into Darfur. I gave this number to people in the American Embassy and other places: *This is my cell phone number. I speak English, Arabic, and Zaghawa and will take reporters and investigators to the Darfur refugee camps and into Darfur. I translated for the genocide investigators, if you want to talk to them about me.*

Soon after that, I got a call from a group of journalists from South Africa and other African countries — four black men and one white. They were fearless for their stories and wanted to go everywhere to see the violence as it was happening.

I began asking my cousins, friends, reporters, and other well-connected foreigners for the phone numbers of people who could tell us how to travel safely in dangerous territory. My cell phone began to fill with the numbers of sheikhs, drivers, Chad military men, and even rebel commanders — anyone who would help a reporter get in and out alive.

The reporters were so different from the NGO workers. They didn't care about paperwork or the legalities of borders. They just wanted to write stories that would help people. Also, they drank a lot.

If the genocide investigators were like angels from heaven, these reporters were like cowboys and cowgirls coming to clean up the land. When I said goodbye to these African journalists after our trip through the camps and a little into Darfur to see a destroyed village and talk to people fleeing and to some rebel groups, I asked them to tell other reporters to please come write more Darfur stories. They agreed to contact their journalist friends around the world and send them my phone number.

One of my friends told me that some people were asking whether I was really from Chad or was in fact from Sudan. There is always someone to report on everything you do in such places. The fact that we had crossed the border and talked to rebels was soon known by many. Chad and Sudan have a love-hate thing, and at this time they were trying to cooperate. Sudan was telling Chad that I might have been taking reporters across their border. My friend suggested I find some work where I could be invisible. I asked her to call me if it looked like something bad was going to happen. When you start to worry about these things, you see people following you, even if they are not. But maybe some were.

Soon after the African journalists left, I flew from N'Djamena to Abéché in a U.N. plane with two women from New York.

Megan and Lori were not reporters, but they were adventurous. To make a difference in the world, they had taken jobs with an international agency that helps women and children refugees.

I told them about the problem with women collecting firewood near the camps and they wanted to interview as many women and girls as they could about that and also about the lack of education for the refugee children. We went to ten camps. Megan and Lori returned to the United States and shared their stories with the Congress, the State Department, and the United Nations to advocate for money for more education in the camps and to provide armed security to accompany the women. This eventually happened for a time, thanks to many others who also argued for this. There is never enough help sent to solve the problems of poor people, but this effort did help many women at some camps. And it made me feel that I could do something.

It is not enough to say we did this and that: you must let me take you into some of these tents. Here is a woman in a small shelter of wood sticks and white plastic, living with her four small children. Her husband and two other children were killed when her village was attacked. Her surviving children often go to sleep hungry because the monthly food ration from the U.N. is not enough. Even so, she always sells some of the wheat in the nearest market so she can buy nutritious foods such as milk, meat, and vegetables. She is trying very hard, but you can see that her children have patches of deep orange in their hair, which means malnutrition. She doesn't have enough blankets for the cold nights, just two thin and scratchy blankets that do not keep anyone warm. There is a big hole in the sheeting where the water pours in when it rains, despite her twig stitching to mend it. And of course she must leave her children to gather firewood.

Three young girls in another tent also must gather firewood. The eldest of these is fourteen. The youngest, maybe nine, wears a dusty black shawl that covers her head like a hood to hide her face. She never looks up and it seems she is willing herself into the sand. They have been raped many times, but they need to go back again soon for more fuel. They cry to talk about it.

Stories like this we heard from hundreds of women and girls. It might be possible for the wealthy nations or the U.N. to send fuel with the food, or to help the refugees build efficient stoves, but this was not being done.

Lori and Megan slept in a tent each night. They were so saddened by all this that I went to a market stall one evening and got some beer for us to enjoy. The weather chilled the bottles. I knew that you must keep your hawalyas going, and I was learning how to do this. You have to find a way to laugh a little bit each day despite everything, or your heart will simply run out of the joy that makes it go.

I was not always able to do this. A French reporter, and a very good one, was so moved to see the bodies of children after an attack that I could not comfort her. She had children of her own, and could not speak or eat or drink. She could only weep for these children. The sights and smells of death I cannot properly put down here, nor would I want to, except to say that some people must go to hospitals for several days after they experience it.

Later, Megan and Lori sent me books, including an English-Arabic dictionary I still have. They did not send these things because I was a bad translator, but because I told them I wanted to learn English much better. They called my cell phone sometimes to ask about my family and about my missing sister and her family. They had always interviewed me in the way I interviewed so many others, and it was good to have people around who cared to listen and who still had the ability to be outraged and sympathetic.

What Megan and Lori feared most was that I would be sent back and shot before they could hear about it and help. They were good friends now. It was interesting for me to think that I had two friends in New York. Amazing. And Dr. John in Washington. And more here and there around the world with each new group of reporters.

I had made friends with the right people in the Chad government, who could quickly approve travel permits for reporters. I bought beers for these government people in the outdoor bars of N'Djamena and Abéché. I wanted to make it as easy and safe as possible so there would be no excuses for reporters not to come. If sometimes they wanted to give money to government or military people to make things happen easier, I let them do it, but did not take any of it for myself. This gave me a good reputation with government and military people, since they would get it all. Therefore, when a new reporter arrived, everyone in the Chad government would help me immediately. I hoped that these friends were also losing any paperwork that might cause a problem for me.

One evening at an outdoor bar, a friend said there was the possibility I might be arrested as a Sudanese spy in Chad, so that I could be traded for a Chadian spy held by Sudan. I asked if this was going to happen soon, and I was told that the files on this were being routed the long way around and around, but that this could not last forever.

My brother Ahmed had taught me, with the beautiful example of his own life, how to make friends easily, and in this way he was still helping me.

13.
NICHOLAS KRISTOF
AND ANN CURRY
REPORTING

In the summer of 2006 I received a call from New York. Nicholas Kristof of *The New York Times* and Ann Curry of NBC News, along with her crew, needed my help. I soon met them in Abéché. There was a lot of fighting right along the border at that time, so this would be busy and difficult for everyone.

We went immediately to the border town of Adre, Chad, in a convoy of Land Cruisers. This is exactly on the Sudan border, due east from Abéché. Ann wanted to report on the fighting close to Adre, since her big equipment could be set up on the safer Chad side. Nick wanted to go deep to the south along the border to villages that were in the line of attack.

As we made our plans, I saw that Ann and Nick were very admirable people. She was very polite but asked more questions than any reporter I had ever met. Nick looked like a man who gets into trouble. So I went with him.

He wanted to travel first along the Wadi Kaya, the big canyon that separates Darfur and Chad, controlled in most places by the Janjaweed. Nick had a cameraman, a woman assistant, and of course we had a driver. Sometimes we had to drive a little ways down into the wadi, seeing Janjaweed camps so close we could wave to them. We didn't wave, of course; we just drove fast. The driver was very good. The wadi was filled with mango and orange trees, and the vegetable patches of the villagers who had lived there until recently. The fruit was falling unpicked.

After eight intense hours, we arrived at the village Nick most wanted to see. The surrounding villages had been or were being attacked. Nick and his two people thanked me for getting them to the village. Because there are no real roads that you might think of as roads, they couldn't believe how we had even found the place and gotten there safely. But I was thinking that any minute they might not be thanking me.

The sheikh of the village said he expected an attack that night. I wondered if these newspeople really understood that a *New*

York Times press pass would not help them unless it happened to be bulletproof. Nick was very casual when I told him we should not unpack too much, and not set up our beds too far from the Land Cruiser. He was as casual as if he always slept in villages under attack.

We could hear shooting in the distance. The sheikh warned me that the trees surrounding the village probably hid some Janjaweed watching us — shots had been fired from there earlier.

I should have mentioned that to Nick, but I didn't want him to smile at me again like I was *such a worrier.* Besides, there was nothing we could do except be ready to move quickly, which was my job, not his.

The three of them rolled out their sleeping bags while the driver and I talked to the sheikh. The Americans had little flashlights on headbands to help them get their sleeping bags just right. The sheikh pointed to the trees of the wadi again and said I should say something about the headlamps; he said the little lights were saying, *Please shoot me in the head.* Maybe I should have said something to Nick about this, but I decided they would be finished soon and lying down, which was true.

In such situations, of which this was not

131

the first, I preferred to stay awake. The driver and I talked quietly and ate sardines from tins. In the middle of the night, automatic rifles and RPG fire came very close and woke up the sleeping campers, who seemed afraid.

I looked at Nick like *You are such a worrier.* I told them to go back to sleep, that the fighting was still two villages away. Even so, the driver and I stayed awake and counted the seconds between the RPG flashes and their noise.

The next morning we were still alive. After tea we drove to the next village, which had been attacked in the night but had defended itself and survived.

One of the attackers had been captured and badly beaten. He was about fourteen. Another attacker had been shot in his back and was barely alive on the sand at the edge of the trees. His blood was flowing out around him and probably nearly all gone. He was also about fourteen. These were Janjaweed Arab boys. We talked to the boy who had been beaten. I translated.

"Why did you attack this village?"

"We are from a village just over there. We have always been friends with the people of this village."

"So why, then?"

"We were told by the government soldiers that these people were going to attack our village and kill our families if we did not attack them first. They would give us money if we did this." The money was equal to about two hundred dollars, which was a lot of money — if anyone were ever really paid it.

"Our families need this money, and we had to protect them."

So that is how it was with them. We left the beaten boy with the villagers. They would probably not be kind to him. He was fourteen, as I said.

From here we cut deep into Darfur. The fighting here was heavy and we passed thousands of fleeing women and children as we drove toward the fighting.

"You are crazy!" people yelled at us. "The Janjaweed are everywhere over there. You must turn around!" I should have told Nick what they were saying, but I think he understood; their frightened faces and gestures needed no translation. Somehow, I had no fear myself. Whatever it was that makes a rebel or a government soldier or a Janjaweed feel like he is already dead anyway and might as well just do his job — it was like that. But I worried for Nick and the cameraman, for Nick's woman assistant, and for our driver. For them I had to be as clever as I could not to get them killed.

We reached an abandoned NGO health clinic. Beyond it lay a grassy flat over which people now ran toward us. A village just through the trees was under attack and they were running in panic past us, stopping, remarkably, to urge us to escape with them. Next to the clinic, under plastic shade tarps, were wounded people from a prior attack who had been left behind when the clinic was abandoned moments earlier. Some of those fleeing were wounded, or held their wounded children in their arms. They screamed for medical help that was no longer there. The most seriously injured just sat or lay down around the clinic, some crying or moaning from pain or despair, waiting to die from their injuries or be killed by the approaching Janjaweed. Yet they looked at us and felt concern for us and told us to run while we could.

Nick Kristof, of course, got out his notepad and started calmly interviewing these people. Madness is the business and the method of a war reporter. I breathed deeply and knelt to translate. *This man was shot by his longtime friend and neighbor, an Arab man who had been instructed to collect the gun of this man. When he refused, his friend shot him.*

The gunshots and shouting were getting closer every few seconds. "Nick, we should leave now," I said between every few phrases of translation.

"Just a few more questions," he replied, bouncing from one wounded person to another. I could see some Janjaweed assembling among the trees, waiting for their other men to catch up before rushing the field.

"A very good time to leave," I said again.

"One more quick one," Nick said, flipping the page of his small notebook to make space for the next interview.

Okay, I said to myself, *this is my work.* I translated as the birds in the trees around us now flew away.

The last man interviewed was not wounded, but was huddled there with two small children. He said he was waiting there, hoping that his wife and his other child were alive. She had fallen up ahead. Another man had run to help her, but he had fallen, too.

"Let's go up there," Nick said to me.

Okay. This is my job. We crawled in the grass to the woman. She was dead. The man who went to help her was dead. It was hard to look at them so close.

Nick said that maybe we should get going. He was such a worrier.

As we moved low and quickly past the poor waiting husband, I told him to leave now, that there was no help for his wife and child.

After one last glance at these kindly but doomed people we were running for the Land Cruiser, zigzagging and calling to the cameraman and the woman assistant to jump in the open doors, hearing the gunfire now in the open as we sped faster and faster from the meadow. A child sitting in the grass stopped crying and waved goodbye to us.

We pushed through very deep sand, sometimes with the wheels spinning. "Drive perfectly," I said to the driver. There was no room now for one wrong downshift. We got stuck for several seconds but he calmed down and drove us out. He was too nervous to be driving, but he was in the driver's seat.

We cut through a thick jungle where the Janjaweed lived with their families. This would not be where they would fight if they could help it. Yet here we got stuck very deeply. The young Arab children, maybe one or two years too young to fight, started running over to us.

Like Mr. Thoreau said, when a dog runs at you, whistle. I jumped out of the vehicle and yelled for the boys to come faster, faster, and help! I am your uncle. Help us push this vehicle! They came in a mob and helped us. I knew their brothers and fathers could be moments away. Chug, chug, chug, and we were free and moving very fast toward Chad.

We made it back to Adre, all very tense and tired. Ann and Nick shared their stories. I brought out some Johnnie Walker, which is part of what is done after such a day. I looked at them a lot as they talked. Unlike us, these people did not have to be here. *Cheers to these people,* I said to myself as I washed out my heart for the day, thinking of the child who waved to us from the grass.

14.
ONCE MORE HOME

You have met broadcast news filmmaker Philip Cox, who saved my dear head from being shot by calling a commander on the phone. Philip had been in Darfur before and knew the dangers well.

He knew exactly what he wanted: this kind of vehicle, this kind of driver, these kinds of foods to take and bottles of whiskey — some for us and some for the soldiers he would interview.

Philip wanted to see where I had grown up and where my village had been destroyed and where Ahmed was buried. So we went there despite the dangers.

After he saved me from being shot, we went to a place inside Darfur where I told him I needed to stop. It was one of the ruined villages of my dreams, the village where the man had been tied to the tree, and his little girl had been killed by the Janjaweed with his bayonet. I found what I thought must have been the tree, the place. It was just something I wanted to do, to say a prayer there for her; after so many dreams, I felt I knew her a little and needed to pay my respects. I wanted to make sure there were not small bones there needing burial, but there were not. I would come to visit this place other times whenever I was near it.

Then we went north through Chad and crossed back into the far north of Darfur. It was a long way to my village. We watched the sky all day, hoping not to see a helicopter or a plume of smoke that would mean a village attack or a battle. When we saw dust from some trucks in the distance, we stopped and let them disappear into a mirage. I made some calls to rebel groups and was told to keep our eyes open because there could be trouble in the area.

We went through the once-beautiful town of Furawiya. Some thirteen thousand people had lived here and in the surrounding villages before everything was attacked and destroyed. This was the picture-book town of North Darfur, with huge trees along its river, and mountains on each side of the sandy bottom that held the town. The destruction had been most cruel. Villagers escaping up a hillside were machine-gunned from helicopters. Philip and I saw the hill still littered with at least thirty-five bodies — many of them children.

We slowed down while driving in the sand along the wadi that had once held the larger market town near my home village. Forgive me for not using the names of some of these villages, but it is to avoid causing further trouble for those still hiding in these areas.

In the wadi there were no bird sounds — so unlike the place I remembered. The silence was deeply spooky. We arrived at the site of the old village, and there we saw some passing rebels resting under trees and others who had always lived in the area whom I recognized.

I showed Philip where the sheikh's home had been, now a black spot in the sand with the remains of some mud-walled rooms. Other patches of black sand were visible up and down the wadi. Some of the larger trees were burned, but newer trees were green and might someday again shade village life in this place.

Philip interviewed some of the rebel troops. A few people who had been living in the secret areas of the mountain valleys, and who were in the village that day to learn what was going on from the rebels, gave me some news: my sister Aysha and my father were nearby and had been told of my arrival.

My father, now very old, was still walking great distances and taking care of animals. I had kept in touch with him. My mother had set up a place in some hidden dry stream and was finding ways to plant some millet, as women do. I wasn't sure if my father was well enough to get to her very often as he moved the animals to grass and kept himself invisible to the Janjaweed and the government troops and their airplanes. But he would have left some animals with her for milk and perhaps some chickens for eggs.

I saw him before he saw me. He was wearing a white jallabiya and a small white cap, all dangerously visible but very traditional. He was more stooped over than when last we met, and a little smaller — the big sturdy body that I had known was almost gone. He was talking to some other older men, gesturing with one skinny arm.

He turned to me as I came near. His eyes were milky and I could tell that he could barely see, but he knew my steps or somehow felt that it was me. We embraced gently. He felt thin and fragile but held me in a very strong way. It was hard to let him go.

"My father," I said.

"Daoud, we have been hearing all about

141

you. It is so good to see that you are alive. You had some trouble yesterday with some rebels."

Darfur is like that. News travels fastest where it seems to have no way to travel at all.

"Take some tea with us," my father said, leading me to a tent. We sat down with the other men, who were uncles and cousins I hadn't seen in these years.

The tent flap later pushed open and my sister Aysha entered in flowing bright green with two children holding her hands. She laughed when she saw me and then just smiled and closed her eyes to float in this moment.

"Daoud, the city man, has come to visit!" she said. "You honor us simple villagers." Everyone laughed. Aysha is the funniest of my sisters.

The tent was soon filled with cousins who wanted to greet me. It was a great joy to be surrounded by family, talking and laughing as if our world were whole again — holding tightly my father's hand, knowing my mother was alive and not far away, imagining Ahmed was out watering the camels. Yet this small tent now held the entire remnant of a once great valley of villages. This beloved world was nearly lost, but here was some of it yet. We ate well; Aysha brought smoking trays of richly seasoned goat meat for everyone. Philip sat with us as part of our family now. He had made this happen, so how could he not be my brother?

Why is it that the person from far away is always the wise expert? For no other reason than this, I was consulted regarding the problem of the day: a young girl refused to marry an older man arranged for her, and she had tried to poison herself. I told them that this girl should not be forced to marry the man, and she might try to kill herself again if this was forced. The men nodded in agreement. The old ways were perhaps bending a little, and this Juliet might be free to marry her true love instead.

That night was the first deep sleep for me in these years since the attack. This was 2005, and the attack had been in 2003 — a long time not to sleep much.

Even so, I woke up and stood in the moonlight for a time, waking not from nightmares but from the comfort of this place, which had come into my sleep like the smells of spiced tea and mint. The sands by moonlight looked as they had when I was a boy and played Anashel and Whee late into the night with children now blown far away. Sandstorms will come, covering these ashes in a few years, and who will ever know that loving people lived here, and that the mountain in the moonlight, cool and silent there, is called the Village of God and is filled with all our hopes for our people?

I would like to tell you that Philip and I and our driver made our way safely back to Abéché, but it wasn't exactly that way. It was important to get out of Sudan before dark, and because I would tell the driver to turn here or there, at this tree or down that wadi, he was never sure if we were safe in Chad or again in dangerous Sudan. "Sudan? Chad? Sudan?" the driver was always calling out to me while raising his hands in the air to emphasize his point. Philip thought this was very funny. The driver simply didn't want to be killed that night. And it actually *was* funny after a while. When you are with the British for some time, strange things seem funny. The driver kept going faster and faster as the sun went down. This is not a good idea in a darkening place with no roads. I leaned forward to tell him to slow down, but I was a moment too late: we hit a hole, spun around, and crashed badly. Philip was in front, wearing his seat belt, and was not injured. The driver was shaken but okay. I was in back without my belt, as I was lean-ing up at that moment, so I crashed head-first into the driver and broke my nose, which was bleeding furiously as we all climbed out of the wreck. We were in a bad way on the Sudan side, and all Philip could do was point at my nose and laugh. This made the driver finally laugh, also. I started to laugh but it hurt too much. We limped into Abéché and Philip paid the driver in cash for his car. We then found our way to one of the bars in Abéché, which are filled with flies and black market traders. A few drinks improved the pain in my nose and neck.

We discussed only the brighter moments of the trip: seeing my family, of course, and a moment in Furawiya when Philip had stepped close to take some video of an unexploded five-hundred-pound bomb in the sand of the wadi. He had somehow tripped and fallen headlong onto the bomb. He lay sprawled over it for a long moment, wondering if his next move would be a bad idea. I looked at him and thought, *Well, the British would laugh,* so I laughed. He whispered for me to please help him get up carefully, which I was happy to do, since the moment was in God's hands, certainly.

"If it had been me to fall on the bomb, you would have laughed," I said to him in the bar in Abéché.

"If it had been *you* to fall on the bomb, it would have been funny," he explained.

He flew away the next day and I waited for the next reporters willing to brave Darfur.

A call came soon from the BBC. The BBC is a big thing all over the world, but if you grow up poor in Africa, especially in a former British Crown colony, the BBC is a very big thing. They wanted my help. The BBC did. The *BBC*. Amazing. I went to N'Djamena to prepare to meet them. There was a little problem first, however, as the love-hate thing between Chad and Sudan had changed again and rebels backed by the government of Sudan suddenly attacked N'Djamena in Chad. I woke up in that city to RPGs exploding in the streets outside my small room. You do not need an alarm clock to wake up in that city even on a normal morning, but this morning that was especially true.

15.
WAKING UP IN N'DJAMENA

Though it is the capital of Chad, N'Djamena, a city of about three quarters of a million souls, is located exactly on the country's border with Cameroon, as if it were waiting for the right moment to cross the river and escape its own poverty.

The heat wakes you up in N'Djamena. The children playing outside your door also wake you. I had taken a small room in a low, mud-walled building of eight families, so I can testify to this. Men and boys on camels, riding along the dirt streets to market, shouting from camel to camel, wake you up, too — though it is not unpleasant to hear this as you wake, for the French and Arabic of N'Djamena blend together very musically. Little scrappy motorcycles also wake you up and you can smell their smoke. The old diesel engines of yellow Peugeot taxicabs begin their daily prowl down the mud streets, and their rumble and smoke also come into your room. Many of the women of this city begin their march to the river to wash the family clothes; they talk and laugh as they pass your window. And you might get a cell phone call from friends who want to know what you are doing today.

I normally would open my eyes to my electric fan going back and forth, plugged into the tiny gas-powered generator chirping outside my door. Everyone has one of these generators. Chad has a great deal of oil and a great deal of oil money, but somehow the people only get a few hours of electricity a week.

French fighter jets from their base by the airport fly low and fast over the city on a usual morning. This is a courtesy in case you are still lazy and need to wake up.

The land beyond the town is flat desert with sparse patches of acacia, jujube, tall palms, and, in the summer rain time, a little green grass. Everything is otherwise brown except for along the river, where women lay their bright clothes along the banks to dry after washing them in the clearest currents. N'Djamena is a trading crossroads, so camels, sheep, and goats are everywhere. Some families grow cotton near the river. Some go fishing in the Chari and the Logone rivers and in Lake Chad, once the third-largest lake in Africa — though it is quickly drying up. Tilapia, catfish, and salanga are sold in the town market and fried by women in the open-air bars. It is the best of the many smoky smells of N'Djamena.

Most women wear long, bright clothes — a few wear thin, fluttery veils. The men wear their loose turbans or linen caps. Some wear traditional white robes, the jallabiyas, but most dress Western style, with matching light brown shirts and slacks. Most people, like me, are tall — I am six feet — and are also a little thin because of all the walking, the hard work, and the dieting that is one of the many advantages of poverty.

You can walk along a mud street in N'Djamena, with old apartment houses beside you, and smoky street stalls selling richly spiced kebab lunches for your only meal of the day, when suddenly you are at the door of a four-star luxury hotel. Chad has oil wells, so there are a few grand hotels for the rich, who come to quickly take the money away before it ruins the charm of our mud and straw cities. I expected to meet the BBC at one of these hotels, but I woke up in an unexpected way and had an unexpected day.

At around three-thirty in the morning, trouble began with terribly loud RPG explosions and mortar and machine-gun fire. The rebels, who were no such thing, but rather the agents of the government of Sudan, swept in from the east, the south, and the north. The Chad Army helicopters hovered over the invasion, avoiding firing where it would hit civilians.

At about five-thirty I could not stand it any longer and went outside. If I was going to die, I did not want it to be from a stray round killing me on my mattress. Let me at least be standing on a street and watching all of it.

Chad Army Land Cruisers were speeding this way and that, and the ragged trucks of the rebels were going that way and this. Young rebel soldiers, not even fourteen years of age, would jump out of the trucks where they could and run into homes to beg for street clothes so they could hide among the civilians. They had been taken as soldiers against their will, drugged, and sent into battle. But some were wise enough to do this dodge, and everyone would help them.

RPG rounds were hitting these trucks full of child soldiers; the streets were filling with the bodies of the dead and wounded. I walked to a friend's house not far away. Trucks of men shooting would go by, but they were not shooting at me. If you were unlucky, of course, you could get hit, but otherwise the soldiers were fighting one another and not the people.

My friend knows many in the Chad Army and they began to call him on his cell phone. This guy was wounded at this address, and that guy was wounded somewhere else. Could you come give us a ride to a hospital? So we, like many other groups of friends, drove madly around the city, avoiding bullets and taking people to the hospitals, which filled quickly but still did an amazing job of helping everyone they could. By noon, all the rebels had been killed, taken as prisoners, or had run away. About 250 young boy soldiers were captured and, I pray, later sent to school instead of to their deaths.

Some 400 troops were wounded in the two hospitals. In the evening, President Déby visited the hospital. It was so loud with screaming and so flowing with blood that the sound and smell of it was impossible for all but the bravest doctors and nurses. The rest of us checked on our friends. Many people were dead, but after two or three days people found their way back to the markets and outdoor bars to talk it through.

Megan called me from New York; Philip from London; others from all over. *Yes, I am okay.*

The BBC crew arrived in time to interview many of the prisoners and to see the city as it recovered.

16.
A STRANGE FOREST

After covering the story in N'Djamena, the BBC crew wanted to go to the camps and then cross into Darfur.

They had come with huge cameras and more boxes of equipment than I thought necessary for any one nation. They would fly to Abéché and I would take their gear by road. I worried that bandits, who roamed in small groups, might rob all these very expensive cameras, lenses, recording machines, and microphones. So I was careful to keep secret my travel times and routes. I asked the passengers on a truck leaving N'Djamena to please put the boxes under their seats as if it were their own luggage, which they were happy to do for a few dollars each.

After we interviewed people in the ever-expanding camps and I made my usual inquiries to the military commanders, we crossed the border. You might think that most of the people of Darfur would either be in the Chad camps or dead, but you must remember how large Darfur is, and how many villages are tucked into every part of it. There were still many villages to destroy and people to kill, as there are even still today. We met crowds of people fleeing everywhere.

At the edge of one village, in a thickly forested place, the village defenders had made their last stand by wedging themselves high in the trees with their rifles. They were all shot and killed. It had been three days or more since the men in the trees had died, and on this steamy spring afternoon, their bodies were coming to earth. We walked through a strange world of occasionally falling human limbs and heads. A leg fell near me. A head thumped to the ground farther away. Horrible smells filled the grove like poison gas that even hurts the eyes. And yet this was but the welcome to what we would eventually see: eighty-one men and boys fallen across one another, hacked and stabbed to death in that same attack.

Reporters are so very human, wonderfully so, and they weep sometimes as they walk through hard areas. There is no hiding their crying after a time. They sometimes kneel and put their heads in their hands near the ground. They pray aloud and will often find a handful of soil to lay on the body of a child, or they may find some cloth to cover the dead faces of a young family — faces frozen in terror with their eyes and mouths still open too wide. They will help bury bodies; we buried many on the BBC journey. But these eighty-one boys and men were too much for everyone.

People vomit when they get close to any long-dead body. You have no control of this, it just happens. And again at the next body. You will soon have nothing in your stomach, but still your body will retch at the sight and smell and of course the tragedy of a life so monstrously wasted. But these eighty-one . . .

Some of the BBC people had to return to Chad, where they were in a medical clinic for three days to recover from what they saw, and smelled, and learned about the nature of what simply must be called evil.

17.
THE SIXTH TRIP

I was settling into the rhythm of this work: reporters would call, I would check with commanders in the field, we would go. My next reporter had called months earlier from New Mexico in the United States and was now waiting to meet me.

Paul Salopek is a thin man, about forty-three. For my first meeting with him, I walked into the expensive Le Meridien Hotel in N'Djamena. Its grand lobby has deep armchairs, thick carpets, and African art on the walls. The river that separates Chad from Cameroon runs beautifully behind the hotel, and can be seen through large windows.

In the busy lobby, Paul heard me ask for him at the front desk. He came up and introduced himself and we sat in a quiet corner to plan the coming journey. He had only a few days to visit the refugee camps for an assignment for *National Geographic*.

We decided to fly to Abéché where Paul would meet with NGO people and I would go to the main market to find a vehicle and driver.

The central market of Abéché contains thousands of market stalls, their tin roofs overlapping to make one great cover over the middle of town. On the south end of this great tin maze you will find about thirty yellow taxicabs waiting. There will sometimes be white Land Cruisers offering rides in different directions, or available for charter. I walked among these vehicles to find a good one, with a good, intelligent-looking driver. I negotiated a fair price and, after stopping for supplies, we picked up Paul at the NGO office. We headed to the camps in heavy rain, and were not making good time because of the deep water in the wadis.

Most Land Cruisers have added to them a snorkel tube running up beside the windshield to allow air to get to the engine when the vehicle is deep in the water. When these vehicles cross a stream, sometimes you can only see the snorkels and a little bit of roof or radio antenna above the water. If you are inside, you must roll up the windows tightly. If you do not know how to swim, you will not be at all bored when the water reaches the tops of the windows. The Land Cruisers used in Africa are larger and heavier than you will see in other places, and some are quite old. This one was old but well cared for. Paul was not worried by the high waters. As someone who does not swim, I am good at rolling up the windows snugly and reminding others to do so.

It is not good to be on these roads after dark, mostly because there are no roads, but also because of bandits and lions and other animals that hunt at night. So I told Paul we needed to find a village soon. We stopped at a Zaghawa village where the sheikh was a friend of mine. After a meal of goat meat and bread, we went outside to the enclosure. The rain had stopped, and the sheikh's people had set up our mattresses and blankets on dry plastic. I fell asleep looking at the stars. This is always the best way to sleep.

I dreamed I was with my eldest brother, who was, in reality, twenty years older than me and now dead — drowned in the Nile, perhaps from a crocodile. In my dream I had somehow fallen into a big wadi and was struggling to get across and keep my head above the water. The thick, muddy current wrapped tightly around me like rope, pulling me away from the shore and from my brother, who was yelling my name and reaching out his long brown arms. I fought the water as hard as I could but my brother's hands were farther and farther away. I woke in the middle of the night clutching the plastic ground cover beside my mattress. It took a long time watching the stars before I got back to sleep.

I woke at dawn to the usual crazy chorus of hungry donkeys, roosters, goats, and sheep, all excited for another long day. I told Paul over a breakfast of green tea that I was worried about yesterday's heavy rains on the road, and suggested we go back to Abéché to let the wadis dry out. He reminded me that he only had a few days, and that we had a job to do. I said okay, and we thanked the sheikh and his family and went on our way in the chirping dawn.

Not far ahead, we had to stop as a red torrent of muddy water filled the wadi crossing our only path. This was the normal place to cross, but it seemed too deep and fast even to trust the heavy vehicle and its snorkel. Chad Army men were on the other side; they had tied a plastic rope between trees on each side of the water, about fifty yards across. The tight line was bouncing on the top of the flood. The soldiers on the other side motioned us across; we were being invited to go hand-over-hand along the rope. "Let's do it," Paul said without hesitation. I wanted to see others do it first.

Other people, with and without vehicles, were stopped on both sides. Women and men with bundles of all sizes wrapped in colorful cloth or plastic were trying to decide if it was worth the risk to cross. Some had no choice. We watched some struggle across. It seemed to take great strength, their bodies flapping on the rope like flags as they grabbed the next handhold and the next, and pulled forward as if drawing themselves out of quicksand.

In fact, many people die each year at rain time trying to cross flooded wadis.

What to do with our vehicle and our driver? The driver could go back to Abéché, of course, and we, once on the other side, could take advantage of the shuttle trips into the next town, Tine, that were being provided by the soldiers. Paul liked this idea.

I remembered that I had some friends who spoke a little English in Tine, and suggested to Paul that I call them. They could meet him on the other side, and I would go back to Abéché with the driver. This was my fear of water talking, of course. Paul just looked at me. "Suleyman, we have a job," is all he had to say. I was Suleyman.

He said he would go first to show me. He stripped down to his shorts and was soon in the water. We found young, strong men who would take his satellite phone wrapped in plastic, and also his camera and cell phone. I could see from his arms as he struggled across that he was very strong. Even so, it was hard for him to make it, and he fell to rest on the other side. He waved me over. Okay. Yes. I would have to think about this one more time.

"You can do it, Suleyman! Hold tight! Keep going!" he yelled over the loud rushing of the flood.

Well, this work was my fate. It was all in God's hands. I could not find someone to carry my phone or little camera, so I wrapped them in my clothes around my neck. This only made the water pull me harder away from the rope. It was very cold; I thought it would be warm. Just holding on to the rope was very hard. That I had to let one hand go so I could move along was a hard idea. I slipped my hands along, inches at time, feeling the rope cutting my hands. My body was stretched out in the fury of the red water. I let my brother help me. I thought of my dream but I let his arms reach impossibly across the water to give me more strength. My phone and camera were already soaked. Paul stood and was cheering my every small bit of progress. "Come on, man, you have it. You have it. That's it. Keep going."

I made it, of course. My hands were bleeding. I had moved beyond the bad luck that had taken my first brother. I could imagine him floating away into the distance now, his long arms waving goodbye.

18.

WHAT CAN CHANGE
IN TWENTY-FOUR
HOURS?

When our clothes dried, we boarded one of the army vehicles heading into Tine and went straight to the sultan's house there. I knew him from many previous trips with reporters.

We stayed with him a short time for tea and to wash up; the sultan then drove us to the market where we could rent a car and a driver to take us to the Oure Cassoni refugee camp near Bahai, about an hour away. Reporters call it Oleg Cassini, but not because of its appearance.

We arrived after high winds had beaten down the thousands of shelters and the people. Paul asked the refugees what they thought about a new peace agreement signed several months earlier by the government of Sudan and one of the rebel groups. Most people thought it would only create more violence. This was the government's intention, of course, and the people understood. If the government of Sudan wants truly to make peace, they have to provide security for the people. As long as they attack the villages or provoke others to do so, people will resist and join new groups. This is obvious to everyone.

We sat cross-legged under a large tree with ten thoughtful refugees. They described how, since the peace agreement, more villages than ever were being burned, more people killed, more women and girls being raped. It was worse now because there was less protection for the villagers in certain areas. Some refugees wisely suggested that Paul talk to rebels who had signed, and to those who had not signed. But this was a problem, since those who had signed would be following the government's orders now, which included not allowing journalists into Sudan and arresting or shooting whomever was bringing them — like myself. But there were some rebels nearby who had not signed, and we were told how to drive over to where they were.

We called over to them and they agreed to be interviewed by Paul. By the time he finished with his interviews, it was too dark to return, so we slept in their camp.

Back in nearby Bahai the next morning, Paul ran into reporter colleagues while I went to find some spicy kebab in the market and visit with people I might know.

A few hours later, in late morning, Paul was excited to see me return. He had talked by satellite phone to journalist colleagues who had just come back from Furawiya. He learned that a few families, sick of life in the camps, were risking their lives to return to the area. This was a good story, a new twist, certainly. He said we had to interview them immediately. He was running out of time, and the same might be said of those families.

People in the market had just been telling me how dangerous the whole area had become in the last few days. Sudan government troops, Chadian rebels, Darfur rebels, Darfur rebels working for the government, Janjaweed — everyone was fighting everybody in the area just over the border, and sometimes on both sides of the border. No single group held the territory. There was no one to call for permission to come through. This is when it is most dangerous to travel.

But it would be a very short trip. Two hours to Furawiya, two hours of interviews, and two hours back. With luck, we could be back in time for dinner.

The reporters Paul talked to had been able to make the trip. Paul is a very careful reporter; he was getting encouraging information from journalists and the NGO people in town. He had carefully met with these people and even with rebel leaders back in N'Djamena to help him understand the present security situation along the border. What can change in twenty-four hours? Everything, of course. But I remembered my chosen fate. My brother Ahmed certainly did not walk away when things got dangerous.

I called the rebels we had met the night before. They said things were bad now. Nevertheless, I went back to the market to find someone to drive us over there.

A Chadian man named Ali, the son of the local omda, had a new Toyota Hilux crew cab pickup truck with air-conditioning. Ali was a little older than me, very quiet, wearing the traditional white cotton shirt to his feet and a turban around his head.

I looked over his vehicle, which was parked next to other vehicles for hire.

"*Salaam malekum,*" I greeted him.

"*Malekum salaam,*" he answered.

"*Humdallah,*" I continued.

"*Humdallah,*" he replied. This is the standard exchange.

I said his car seemed excellent and that I had heard he was a good driver. "I am very

166

good," he replied with no smile.

I explained where I wanted to go with my American journalist.

"I have never been across that wadi into Darfur," he said. "And I think I never want to go. Their fighting comes over here enough."

I explained that the American would pay well and the trip would be short, about six hours. Back before dark tonight. I added, "God willing," which is often said anyway.

"No, I'm scared to go," he said. "I have two children and a wife. It is too dangerous."

I said he would be paid the full day rate, and for two full days. Ali's friends — there is always a swirl of people in such places — began to pay attention to our conversation. "That money is very good," they advised him. "Ali, you should do this. Two days' pay just to run over there and back. You can do it, God willing." As this was hardly the first time I had chartered a vehicle and driver in this market, some of them knew me and said I was very good at all this, and would not go if it was not okay. "God willing," I added.

"No," Ali insisted. "It is not safe to go over there."

His friends now went to work on him.

Good money for your family. Back by dark. No Antonovs in the sky and not many refugees streaming across today. Finally, reluctantly, he agreed. I could tell that he was not happy. But it was three hundred dollars, American. That is a small fortune — more than half the cost of a good camel.

We had to leave right away to make it back before dark. We bought some soda, water, and bread for the trip, and went to get Paul. I tried talking to Ali to get to know him. He had served in the army as a young man. A father, as I knew. Son of the omda, which I knew. He was too nervous about the trip to teach me much about him I didn't know.

As we left, I told Paul to keep his satellite phone turned on. I didn't know whom I thought we could call, but it was somehow a comfort. When we reached the wadi that separated the two countries, Ali took us expertly down into the deep water and up the other side. *Tawkelt ala Allah,* I said. *It will depend on God.* Tawkelt ala Allah, Ali repeated. We were in Darfur.

19.
SOME BOYS UP AHEAD WITH A KALASHNIKOV

We followed the main lines of tire tracks through the desert. Ali and I glanced out the window often to see if the tracks were new or old, and whether they were from government troops or rebels.

An hour went by; we were nearly halfway there. Ali didn't talk very much. He was extremely tense. We were all very tense.

I most feared a gunman walking into the road ahead to stop us. And in a narrow wadi of a mountainous area, this is exactly what happened. A young soldier, no more than fourteen, stood in the road with his Kalashnikov rifle. A second boy stood nearby. There were most certainly other soldiers all around us among the rocks, waiting for us to try to speed away.

I spoke calmly to Ali, telling him to slow down and stop. *"Mashalla,"* he said into the plastic of the steering wheel, strengthening himself for God's decision. Paul leaned forward from the back to see the trouble. I got out slowly.

The boys wore traditional clothes and had ammunition belts across their chests. I walked toward them. "Salaam malekum," I said. They responded properly, but without warmth, as we shook hands. I pulled a pack of cigarettes from my pocket and lit one. The boys didn't move. "Is there a problem?" I asked them. "No, nothing," one replied.

Two somewhat older boys appeared on the left, also with guns.

"Okay, Daoud, we need you to stand over there by them," one of the two boys who had stopped us said. He knew my name.

The other two boys took Ali and Paul out of the vehicle and were now searching it. They took Paul's satellite phone and our soft drinks. A truck drove up with their adult commander.

"You are finally here," he said to me. This was a bad sign. It meant that there was at least one spy in Bahai or in the other rebel group who told the government of Sudan that we were coming. The government had sent these cooperating rebels to come get us. I could think of no other explanation.

They put us back in our vehicle, with a new driver and the boy soldiers as guards.

Paul asked if I was optimistic. I laughed a

little and didn't say anything. We drove for an hour and a half southeast to a place that I knew was near the government-controlled areas.

We arrived at a rebel camp, and a truck with another commander pulled up. I knew him. "How are you, Daoud?" he asked. "You know the government does not want you here with your hawalya?"

I told him that no one was in control of the area so I did not know whom to ask for permission. We would be happy to go back.

"It shouldn't be a problem," he said.

He walked over to speak to the two commanders whose soldiers had captured us. He talked with them for a long while and then came slowly and sadly back to me.

"They have some authority here. They don't want to send you back so soon." He asked me for a cigarette.

"Things have changed a lot, Daoud; it's not the same. Things are all mixed up right now." He walked away and one of the other commanders came up to tell me that Paul and Ali were to stay in our vehicle and I was to go with him. I asked him what was going on.

"Please don't argue with me," he said. "We are going to take you back to Chad."

I said that I would rather travel with my

companions, for whom I was responsible.

"If you go back to be with Ali and Paul, that is your choice, your fate."

If it had been another kind of time, perhaps I would have accepted the ride back to Chad. But my job was to get the reporters into Darfur safely, and to get them out, and nothing else seemed to matter. So it was easy to thank him and go join Paul and Ali for whatever awaited us. Soldiers packed in beside us in our own truck and we were driven a long way through the desert.

"This is not good, Paul." I explained that we were heading into the area where the government of Sudan had its army camps.

Paul wasn't happy to hear this. Ali was sullen. He was always sullen, but now more so.

We arrived at an empty, destroyed village the rebels were using as a base, and were made to sit in an open area by a mud wall. A little food and water was given to us. Ali and I had our wrists tied behind us with thin plastic rope that hurt. Paul was taken in another direction. His wrists were not tied, which I took as a good sign for him.

Ali and I sat there all day, getting hot and thirsty in the sun. In the late afternoon, three vehicles came into the village carrying three rebel commanders. I could soon see

Paul talking to one of them in English. He had his notebook out and was interviewing him. Amazing. I laughed a little and pointed with my head so Ali would notice. Paul later walked near us with the commanders and said he believed they would let us go soon. I didn't think this was true, at least not for Ali and me. The mud wall looked like a good wall for shooting people.

It got dark and Ali and I tried to sleep, but couldn't. Two more vehicles arrived late, and several men came over to visit us. They beat Ali with their fists, kicking him a long time with their boots. They did not beat me. They took our watches and our sunglasses, and our mattresses from the vehicle. They took Ali's good shoes. They tried to take my shoes but I did not let them. I said I didn't want to see my own people take my shoes. I said they could shoot me if they needed my shoes, but otherwise I would need them while I was still alive. They went away.

Late at night they pulled us roughly to our feet and pushed us into the back of another truck. Paul was somewhere else — we had not seen him all night. I would later learn that he had been taken away in Ali's truck to the village of Towé, where he would be beaten for three days by young soldiers drunk on date wine.

Ali and I were driven the rest of the night to a place in the mountains, stopping in the morning at a rocky place where tracks go off in a few directions. They made us get out there, so far from any town or village. In this kind of situation you can guess that you probably have about a minute to live. I saw Ali saying silent prayers with his eyes closed. That reminded me to say some, too.

They didn't shoot us. They sat us under a tree and we waited. We got a little sleep finally. Nine rebel commanders soon arrived for a meeting a little ways away in the rocks. I knew two of the men from previous trips, from when this rebel group had not joined with the government. It was raining and each drop of it felt good on my face.

After the meeting, they came over and one said, "There's no problem, Daoud, don't worry." Then they drove away. Two other commanders — field intelligence men — then began shouting at us and beating us with their fists and boots and the butts of their guns. I felt some bones breaking in my fingers where the gun hit me. Then some soldiers tied our ankles and threw us like big sacks into the back of the truck. We continued our journey in a new direction.

When we reached another rebel base, the truck stopped and two men took my feet and two men took my arms and they swung me back and forth high out of the truck onto the rocky ground. When you are tied you can't move to fall the right way, and the sharp rocks open your skin. This was the summer rain time, so there was not even a cushion of dust over these rocks. The same was done to Ali, and I felt so bad for having ever convinced him to make this trip — he was bounced on the sharp road from so high. From this and from the beatings, he had several broken fingers and I don't know what else, maybe ribs. I think he passed out a little after bouncing on the road.

Our lips were blistered from so long in the sun without water. Our arms and fingers were very swollen and painful from the ropes, and now our feet, too. We were dragged under a tree and water was dribbled into our mouths and we were finally untied. We were told that we were waiting for the "crazy commander."

20.
OUR BAD SITUATION
GETS A LITTLE
WORSE

After two hours the "crazy commander" pulled up in his Land Cruiser and yelled at the soldiers for untying us. He supervised the very tight tying of ropes on our wrists and behind our backs. Then he had long ropes tied to our ankles. The other ends of the ropes were thrown over high branches of the tree.

"This is very simple; I will show you how it works so you can do it whenever you need to," he said to the soldiers. Then he turned to Ali and me with a quiet cruelty in his voice:

"I want to torture you two now and you will tell me everything you have in your minds: who sent you, what is your mission, who you are meeting, everything."

Torture was the popular new thing because Guantánamo and Abu Ghraib were everywhere in the news at that time, and crazy men like this were now getting permission to be crazy.

I was first. Three soldiers began pulling the rope, and I was turned upside down hanging from the tree. I thought, *Well, this is not so bad.* After a few minutes, however, it gets very bad. Your eyes feel like they are going to pop out. Your head throbs and you can't breathe. They tightened the ropes on our wrists and ankles for extra pain. Then they tied the long ropes to the trunk of the tree and went away to smoke my own cigarettes as we dangled. The pain gets worse and worse until you finally cry out. I wouldn't have thought this would be so. Of course our injuries were making everything worse — especially for Ali. From time to time they would drop us down and ask us to talk some more.

I told them again and again that I was a translator for reporters, and that the reporters were not spies; I was not a spy, and Ali was just our driver. Ali would say he had been a simple soldier in Chad a long time ago, but he was not spy. He said he had a wife and a small son and daughter, and his only job was to drive people from village to village.

They would say they didn't believe us, and raise us upside down in the tree again. After hours of this, you cannot talk or think. That is when they finally stopped. We were dropped in heaps on the ground.

At around 10 p.m., I woke up in the darkness of the desert. Night insects were busy in our bloody cuts, and this tickling had wakened me.

"Ali. Look. We are alive." I kicked him a little. "It's not so bad." In the faint light of the stars I saw his eyes move slightly.

"Yes, thank you, thank you," he said, blowing a spider away from his bloodied nose. "This is all very good. Thank you so much for this good trip." We drifted back to sleep.

In the middle of the night two young soldiers picked me up and untied me. They walked me a few dozen steps away from Ali, who was asleep.

"Okay, Daoud," one of them said. "You should go out of here now. Ali is a spy with the Chadian military so he has to stay. But our commander says you should go. Your hawalya has already been sent back to Chad. He was taken to near Bahai and he went across to Chad, and he is waiting for you there."

"That's good about Paul. Thanks for telling me that. But what am I going to tell Ali's family if I go back without him?" I said. "I can't do that. You would not do that. If you were his brothers, what would you say to someone who was responsible for your brother but left him in a dangerous situation like this?"

"Well, you are untied and we are going back to sleep, so we have done what our commander said to do."

I was free to go, but I was also free to untie Ali so we could both make our run for freedom through the mountains. As I untied him, he asked what had been going on, as he had half heard the conversation. I explained the situation, and he insisted that I leave, especially since they had invited me to go.

"This way, you can tell my family where I am and maybe they can help get me out of this," he said. "So you should go now."

I said that I could not face his family if I left him behind, and he understood this.

"They would ask you to pay for our truck," he said, which made me laugh a little because I knew it was probably true. We considered going together, but decided that we would be quickly tracked down and, under those circumstances, killed. So we rubbed some life back into our poor wrists and ankles, and waited for what would come next.

Soon after sunrise, the commander of the base came over, expecting to see only Ali.

He saw the two of us sitting untied and talking.

"Daoud. Please come walk with me. I want to talk to you," the commander said.

We walked for a half hour or so. He knew my family and he knew that Ahmed and some of my cousins had been killed when our village was attacked. He didn't like having to kill his own people now that there was this new arrangement, but he hoped for peace someday.

"When the other rebel groups stop fighting us, the killing will stop," he said, perhaps mostly to himself.

"You think that is true?" I asked him. "Why do you think the rebel groups spring up all the time?" He looked at me but could not admit what we were both thinking. He was in all this for himself now, thinking perhaps of getting a promotion someday in the Sudanese Army. War does this to people. There would always be rebel groups as long as the government was attacking villages to push people off the land. Like these rebel groups that were now killing their brothers, he had lost his way and had forgotten his people and was thinking only of himself.

"So, you know Ahmed, my brother Ahmed?" I asked him.

"I knew of him. I may have met him once

180

in El Fasher."

"Okay," I said. I didn't want to do more than bring Ahmed's spirit to walk with us. Maybe it would remind this commander to do the right thing.

He asked if I was sure that I wanted to share Ali's situation. I explained to him the same things I had been explaining all night. He looked sad and left me to go sit again with Ali.

Five soldiers, perhaps only sixteen or seventeen years old, soon came and asked us to stand. I saw the commander drive very fast away down the wadi. He glanced at us as he passed, and he looked to be in pain.

The boys tied our wrists tightly behind us and led us down the road to a tree-lined wadi away from their base. The wadi was strewn with human bones and clumps of hair and the horrible stench of death. This smell can actually stay for many months in such a place, but these bones were new and didn't need to try hard to smell bad. I tried not to walk on these bones but it was impossible. I shuddered at each step. *So, this is where I will die,* I said to myself.

21.
BLINDFOLDS, PLEASE

Ali's prayers, usually silent, were now loud and clear as the young men took positions four or five steps from us. I recognized some of these boys, but I didn't know their first names. I had known them as small children. From the way they stared back, some of them clearly remembered me. I looked to see who was going to shoot first. A small noise to my left, a sudden movement to my right — each time I braced myself. I called to the boy who looked like their leader.

"Please," I said to him, "can you get us something for blindfolds?"

He asked why we would want that.

"I know some of you boys and I don't want to watch you shoot us. You do what you have to do, but don't make us watch you shoot your own people. We don't have to watch that, not for the last thing we see."

I knew the relatives of one of the older boys — not the leader — and had seen some of his sisters and cousins in the Touloum refugee camp. I looked hard at him.

"You know, I have seen some of your family in Touloum. Many of them are alive and are wondering where you have been for a couple of years. Some of your brothers are dead, from the same army that you now eat with. You should go find your family in Touloum and help them." I could see he was very moved by this and happy to know some of his family were alive.

The boys retreated a little ways and were perhaps talking about how to make us some blindfolds. They came back slowly, talking about other things and standing around with their Kalashnikovs.

"So you should get us the blindfolds," I said again to the main boy. He walked close to me.

"Daoud, we don't know what you are doing here or if you are spies or not, but we have talked and none of us are going to kill you right now."

"Why is this?" I asked.

"Because we already lost a lot of our Zaghawa people. And now we are having to fight them, which we don't like. We have to do that. But we don't have to shoot you. So we are just going to wait for our commander to come back and he will have to shoot you if he wants to do that."

This was very good. I thanked the boys and they smiled a little. These boys had been through a lot and they still were human beings. Ali was thinking they would shoot anyway, and would not open his eyes or stop saying his prayers, which were of course good prayers and always worth praying.

I asked if we could move away from the bones and go under a tree, and we did. I asked for the first names of the boys, and we talked for an hour about their families. I had news for many of them about their families in the camps. They found some food for us, which was our first in a long time. They untied our hands for this.

"Why does everyone think I am a spy just because I am from Chad?" Ali asked them with a great deal of food in his happy mouth.

The main boy said that Chad was not Sudan. Chad was the enemy.

"You think that?" Ali said. "And you are Zaghawa boys from Darfur?" Because he has two children, he was now talking like a father to these boys.

"Did you know that Darfur was a great country long ago, so great that it was both in Sudan and also in Chad? Did you know that the French, who later controlled Chad, and the British, who later controlled Sudan, drew a line, putting half of Darfur in each new nation? Did you know that? What do you care about this line if you are Darfur men? What business is it of yours if the British and the French draw lines on maps? What does it have to do with the fact that we are brothers?" The boys were moved by this.

"And here is something else for you. Do you know that your people in Chad hear stories about the bravery of the big army you are now a part of — you and your new friends, the Janjaweed?" The boys gathered around him a little closer.

"Yes, your brave new friends attacked a girls' school in Darfur. They raped forty young girls and their teachers. Some of these girls were eight years old. Fifteen of them had to go to the hospital for a long time, bloody with their injuries. When the nurse working in the hospital told about this, she was taken and beaten and raped for two days and nights. They then cut her seriously with knives. Would you do this?"

The boys looked at one another. "Of course not," their leader said for them. "These would be our sisters." The boys nodded. At this time a heavy rain started and the boys gathered closer under the scrawny tree.

"And if they were little Arab girls?" Ali pressed them. "Would they not also be your family?"

"How would this be so?" the boy asked.

"In the way that they are human beings, and that is also your family." Ali had opened his arms for this and the rolling thunder of the storm gave his speech a wonderful music.

"Yes, of course," the boy said, and in all these boys I could see the light of their souls come back on. The rain, now too much for this tree, washed their young faces.

These boys had not eaten well for a long time. They were discouraged by life and had started to drink bad alcohol made from dates. They had not lived long enough with their fathers to be good hunters and provide for themselves; when they went out on little hunting trips during this time, hoping to shoot a big bird or other game for dinner, we saw them come back with nothing.

Ali advised them that the camps in Chad would feed them and take care of them, and that they could even go to school and find their families, and not have to hurt anyone again. For someone who was no spy, Ali was very good at turning these little soldiers around.

I asked a boy who had been quiet why he was fighting.

"Where am I to go?" he replied. "What do I do? My family is dead, I have no money, no animals, nothing. At least I can eat every day."

"You can go to the refugee camps in Chad, like Ali said," I replied. "They will give you food and you can go to school. That would be good for you."

"No, I do not want to be in the camps and leave my land," he said. "When I die, I will die in my home."

Ali was better at this than I.

When the commander's vehicle came speeding back in the mud, he saw us having our little party and began shouting at the boys. They had not done the thing that needed to be done. He scolded them, but the head boy said to him, "We cannot shoot them. We decided that you have a gun. You are like our uncle, and you will have to do this for us, because it is not right for us to do it."

The commander was pained to hear this. There seemed to be everything in his wet face: anger, exasperation, and maybe some relief. He retied our wrists himself and then walked away, leaving his Land Cruiser running until one of the boys turned off the engine.

In the evening, I was untied and taken to the commander in a mud room that was open to the stars because it had been burned.

"Daoud, you know that if I shoot you there would be trouble between my family and your family someday, so I can't do this. I talked to my cousins and they told me it would be very bad, so here is what we are going to do . . ."

I liked this so far.

"You and Ali need to go back to Chad. So these boys will drive you to another rebel camp and they will take you back from there. So, good luck."

He shook my hand. I was taken back to Ali, and I told him the good news.

"And you believe this?" he said. "You believe they can't find some other boys to shoot us at this new place?"

"That's a good point," I said, "but maybe they believe what we said when they were torturing us and that we are not spies. Maybe they just want us to get out of here. Why waste bullets on us if we will just go?"

He looked at me as if I was very stupid.

Indeed, the more I talked, the less I believed my own words.

22.
WE CAME TO RESCUE YOU GUYS

It was hard to sleep with our hands behind our backs as usual. That night it rained heavy on us. When the rain stopped, some foxes came up to us. We were too tied up to wave them away, so it was not good; there were quite a few of them. But some other animals scared them away — probably wild dogs or jackals. Finally we went to sleep.

In the morning, four of the five young soldiers took us to a camp about two hours away. The boys played a cassette of Sudanese songs and sang along as they drove. When we arrived we were asked to sit under a tree.

Two other young men were tied there. They had been badly beaten. One had a broken arm and was tied at his ankles instead of his wrists.

When we told them our names, one said, "Oh, you are the ones! We came to rescue you guys."

I asked what he was talking about.

"You called us three times and begged us to help with your truck, and to bring food and water. You said the area was very safe."

"I never called you," I said. Gradually, we figured out what had happened.

The rebels had used Paul's satellite phone to call for some mechanics to come help, and they used my name. This was the rebels' way of stealing another vehicle.

We spent the night under the tree. The next day we were told that all four of us would soon be on our way to Chad. Again we were told that Paul was already there.

Ali had a theory: they could not let us live if they were going to keep our trucks. That would make them ordinary thieves. If we were spies and had been shot, or had been shot in a fight, then it would be okay for them to keep the trucks. So they were going to kill us and didn't want to tell us that.

The young mechanics laughed at him. In their minds, they were already eating food in the Bahai market.

Before we were moved, there was another long meeting of commanders. Afterward, a vehicle approached and Paul was taken out. He was not in Chad at all. He looked exhausted and drawn, and as if he had not eaten since our capture. His face was burned and blistered by the sun.

"Thank God you two are still alive," he said. I told him we would soon be safe in Chad. It was not so far away. Paul shook his head; he did not believe anything they said, especially this. Good reporters smell lies just as dogs smell deeply buried bones.

Paul, Ali, and I were put in one Land Cruiser with its roof cut off; the two mechanics were put in the same kind of vehicle behind us. We began our trip; we headed east instead of west.

The commanders had decided to turn us over to the government of Sudan.

"We are as good as shot," Ali said quietly.

We were driven for an hour to a Sudanese Army camp in the ancient Darfur city of Amboro, the city of my own sultan's home, where his great drum had been beaten in times of war, where good schools and a hospital built by the British in colonial days were now, like the rest of the town, in unnecessary ashes. In their place, soldiers and tanks were everywhere.

Our vehicles stopped near three tanks. When the soldiers went out of the vehicle, leaving the three of us inside for an hour, I told Paul, "I don't know what will happen to you and Ali here, but I know that I am going to die here, so, if you don't see me after this, that is what happened. This is the worst idea the rebel commanders could have for us."

Paul was too tired to say anything. The trip had not helped him.

Soon we were waiting in the sun of the parade ground, whispering to each other. A commander came up to us and stopped in front of me.

"Daoud, you are the biggest problem we have, so we are going to interrogate you first."

Paul, who knew me as Suleyman, was confused to hear me called by another name.

"What is going on?" he asked.

I explained why I used two names in the two countries, and I also told him that I had a problem in Israel that made me wanted by the government of Sudan. I explained that Ali used to be in the Chad Army.

Paul said I should have told him these things. I replied that I could not tell many people. Everything is complicated like that in Africa. Nothing is simple. No one is simple. Poverty generously provides every man a colorful past.

"But you may want to separate yourself from us as much as possible," I told him.

Even in such a place a prisoner can demand to be treated separately from the others arrested.

Paul said he did not want to do that. He said he understood about my names and the other things.

"We should stick together," he said. He didn't like the situation, but he was firm about that.

I was then taken away to an interrogation room.

23.
WE CAN'T THINK OF ANYTHING TO SAY

On the way inside, I decided that I had already talked enough. These were Sudanese Army commanders now, the kind of men who had destroyed my village and killed Ahmed, and I was finished with them. When they started asking me questions, I told them that I was prepared for them to shoot me, and I knew they would do that anyway, just as they had killed my brother and many of my cousins, but I did not want to answer their questions. I told them that I accepted my bad situation and they might as well ask their questions of my brother, as I was with him now. *I am dead; you know that is my situation and I know that is my situation, so why should I talk to you?*

Then, for Paul's and Ali's sakes, I said I would reconsider this under one condition: If they would bring some African Union troops, the A.U., in as witnesses, I would answer any questions truthfully. With the

195

mandate of the United Nations, the African Union troops were in Darfur — some barely a mile away — to monitor the peace agreement between the Sudan government and one of the rebel groups. If the government and this rebel group want to attack villages together, or the government and the Janjaweed want to attack a village, or just the Janjaweed or just the government, then that is not the A.U.'s business, though they might make a report about it. They have not been given the resources to do much more than give President Bashir the ability to say that peacekeeping troops are already in Darfur, so other nations can please stay away. Also, African troops have seen so much blood and so many killed that their sense of outrage has perhaps been damaged for this kind of situation. U.N. troops from safer parts of the world, where people still feel outrage, might be better.

Just the same, I thought the A.U. troops could help get out the word that Paul, a noted journalist, and Ali, the son of an important man in Chad, had been taken prisoner. This strategy was something I had discussed with Paul as we were waiting in the sun of the parade ground.

"Let me see an A.U. commander and I will answer all your questions with the whole truth."

They looked at one another seriously — two Sudanese Army commanders and two of the rebel commanders who had brought us in — and then burst out laughing.

"Daoud Ibarahaem Hari — or whatever your spy name is — you are now in the hands of the government of Sudan, and you will talk and tell us everything, even if you don't think so now," the older leader said through the remains of his smile. Spread out on his desk were papers describing all my trips into Darfur, and Internet printouts of all the stories that had come from all the reporters and from the genocide investigation.

"You see? We know everything about you already. We just want to hear you say it."

Paul was brought into the room. He asked me what was going on. I said I had decided not to tell them anything without the A.U. present, even though I had nothing to say that they did not already know.

"They will kill me anyway, so why should I talk?" This was what he and I had agreed to do when we were whispering in the sun. He told them that he also would not talk unless the A.U. were present. They took him away and asked me questions again, which again I refused to answer.

Then they brought in Ali.

"Ali," I said, "Paul and I have decided not to talk to these people unless the A.U. are brought in here. You should do what you think best for yourself, and I will translate for you." Ali did not speak Sudanese Arabic.

"No, I think I have nothing to say to them, either," he said. His attitude toward these people was hardening, and the idea that he would never go home to his wife and children had taken hold in his thinking.

"What did he say?" a commander demanded of me.

"I am not translating for you. Sorry," I replied.

We would all three go out bravely for as long as we could bear the pain of it.

I later learned from two young soldiers guarding us that we were going to be taken to a place where we might change our minds about talking.

"Do you think that will work?" I asked the livelier of the guards. He laughed a little as he looked at me — we prisoners were kneeling in the sand.

"I think you are a hard case," he said. "But they have some very cruel commanders."

A helicopter soon landed in the dusty middle of the camp. Five fat Sudanese generals got out and marched across the sand to meet with the local officers.

"These are the cruel commanders? It looks like they eat all their prisoners," I said quietly to our guards. This made them swallow hard as they saluted the big men.

After half an hour, two of these generals came out to where we were still kneeling in the sun. The largest of them, an Arab man with many stars on his uniform, approached me with great anger in his face. I looked up at him. His round head was like a dark moon rising over his much-decorated stomach.

"You are the problem, here. You, not us, are the war criminal. You bring reporters in to lie about us and bring Sudan down. You are the criminal." The anger that poured out of him was so great that you could see his soul knew very well that he was completely wrong. That is always when anger is the greatest and most dangerous.

He looked at my swollen, discolored hands, laughed a little, and told the guards to tighten my ropes. They saluted and went to work on my bindings, but it was clear to my tingling fingers that they did the opposite.

Paul, Ali, and I were taken to the generals' helicopter and boosted inside.

The two young mechanics who had come

to rescue our vehicle were also in this helicopter. The one with the broken arm was in pain as they lifted him aboard.

I shifted around on the hot metal floor where I was told to sit.

We were in the air forty minutes when bullets pierced the cabin with loud pops.

24.
THE RULES OF
HOSPITALITY

The bullets bounced around inside the helicopter, finding the back of a young officer. Praise God, it only gave him a good thumping and a big bruise — he laughed when he realized his luck. Perhaps other bullets hit the engine, for the helicopter swerved sickeningly in the sky and the pilot worked the engine at full throttle. The generals, somewhat panicked, shouted at the pilot, asking if he could keep it from crashing. The pilot said he could. *Thank God, thank God,* the frightened generals said to each other. A commander pulled me up from the floor and pushed my face into a bubble window so I could see straight down.

"Where are we?" he shouted over the engine. "Tell me where this shooting is coming from."

I of course knew very well where we were — close to Kutum — but I told him I had no idea. I told him that down on the floor I could see nothing and had lost track of where we were. He kept shouting at me, asking if I wanted to be thrown out; Paul was trying to get them to untie me because he could see I was in too much pain on the floor to help them, even if I wanted to do that.

When everything but the engine settled down, Ali, smiling for the first time that I had ever seen, leaned over to me from his better seat and said it would be good if the helicopter crashed, because we might survive. He asked if I knew how to use a gun. "Of course," I said. Every boy growing up in Darfur goes hunting with his brothers and father. "Me, too," he said. He had served in the Chad Army so he certainly knew how to use a gun. While this talk was a little crazy, I thought, *Well, it is good that Ali is thinking positively.* He was finally cheered by some idea — our helicopter crashing. I joined him in this hope. But within half an hour we were safely over El Fasher, our destination. Here was the town of my high school days. Here was the town of the government's most notorious prison in North Darfur.

As we circled to land, one of the commanders asked if we had been fed at all lately. The young mechanics and I laughed, knowing what he was thinking: that their lapse of hospitality might be the reason for their bad luck in the air. I said we had not been given much of anything. He said we would be properly fed on the ground. The rules of hospitality are very strong here, and sometimes they come to mind at strange times.

I had seen these government buildings often from the road. They looked frightening and imposing to me in my youth, and they looked like death to me now as we came down among them. On the ground, with our hands still tied, we were made to stand outside facing an old adobe wall, painted yellow a long time ago by the British.

A commander shouted at us, inches from our faces. Mostly he shouted at Paul. They made him sit in an old chair while they shouted at him.

"We are going to kill you right now," one of them said. "We will show you who you are dealing with now." They opened their cell phones and waved the screen image of their hero, Osama bin Laden, and the burning of the World Trade Center towers in Paul's face.

It is interesting to me that people bother to shout at you, or even to hurt you, when they are planning to kill you. What lesson will that teach you if you are going to be dead? It has always seemed like a waste of energy. If you are going to kill someone, why not let him go with as much peace as you can manage to give him? I have never understood this, unless it speaks to the mental illness or at least the crazy sadness of these men. So kill us, yes, please do. But don't hurt our ears with your screaming or show us pictures on your cell phones. Just do what you have to do and leave us or our bodies in peace.

But these tortured spirits were stirred up. When these first madmen went inside, others came out and beat us, hitting us on our backs and sides, kicking us, hitting us with their gun butts, warning us not to fall down or else we would be killed. Vehicles were coming and going, but if you glanced at them they would kick you or beat you harder, yelling, "You should not look at these things, you spies."

After a time, the beatings did not hurt as much. I was only wondering when exactly they were going to shoot us or beat us all the way to death. In the next minute, perhaps? The minute after that?

After three or four hours, I was the first to fall. They dragged me into a large cell where

I waited for what would come next. Looking through the old iron bars of the door I watched my friends just outside in the sandy yard: Ali fell next, followed by the boy with the broken arm, then the other boy. Paul was suddenly not there in the chair. When all of us except Paul had been dragged into this room, a guard untied us and gave us a little water.

"You were lucky to fall so soon," Ali whispered through his thirst, a little angry at me for taking this advantage.

The next morning we were taken out to the yard and beaten until we collapsed again. I would like to say that Ali fell first, but I have no memory of that. It is more painful to be beaten a second day, when they are beating on bruises. As before, they dragged us into the cell where we were allowed to rest through the night. The third day they beat us again, but then finally gave us a little food. It really needed salt and oil and was not good. *Acida,* sometimes called *foofoo,* should not be served mixed together with lentils, but especially not without oil and salt. This was meant to upset us. It would be like mixing a hamburger in a milkshake.

We all had terrible pain in our stomachs. It might have been from the beatings or from the hunger, but we couldn't eat much. We learned from the guard that our interrogations would begin the next morning.

I was first. As they led me past the other cells, I saw Paul in one. He looked terrible. I was taken to the office of an interrogator. My legs were tied to the legs of a chair and my hands were tied around the back of it. A large man stood by with heavy sticks and a whip.

"You wouldn't talk in Amboro, that's okay. Do you want to talk now?" he asked.

I had been beaten a lot in the last six days. It was wearing me down, and I knew I was in a place where they could cause incredible pain for me.

"Okay, I will talk," I said, "if you will agree to a couple of things."

He asked me what I had in mind.

"First, you have to tell your guards to stop beating us. Second, if you have a cigarette, you have to give it to me."

"Okay, I'll give you a cigarette. But if you don't talk, the guard here will beat you."

"No," I corrected him, "If the guard beats me, I will not talk. It works like that. I will die."

"Oh, you want to die? Do you know how many people in Darfur have died?"

"I know I would not be the first to die,

and if you want to do that, he should beat me and I will die, but I will not talk if he beats me and I will not talk when I am dead."

With this he laughed a little and he got the cigarette out of his pocket — a very expensive brand. He told the guard to untie my wrists so I could smoke.

As I smoked the cigarette, I told him how Paul had contacted me, what Paul and I were doing in Darfur, why I was bringing in reporters, everything true that I could think to say. He said I had come into Darfur six times with reporters. I told him something about each trip, what we saw, the bodies, the sadness of the people, the horrible killing that the government had done to the people.

"When I was with the BBC," I told him, "we saw where you — I don't know if it was you, but maybe it was you — lined up eighty-one boys and young men and hacked them to death with machetes. The smell of that — it was three days old — made the journalists so sick that they had to go back to a clinic in Chad for three days. So maybe that's what you like to do. What the journalists like to do is take pictures of what you do so everyone can see what the Sudan Army does to the Sudan people. We saw where a grandmother had been burned with her three grandchildren. So if you are not proud of this, you should stop doing it. Journalists do what they do all over the world and nobody calls them spies."

I may have said this a little more respectfully, but it was close to this. My memory is bad about this day because of what happened next.

"You should worry more about yourself now," he replied. "Here is what I need to know: When you were talking to the rebels near the Chad border — not the ones who stopped you — you must have seen how many men they had and the kinds of weapons they had. I am going to show you pictures of different kinds of vehicles and different kinds of weapons, and you are going to tell me what you saw."

"I told you I was no spy, but look, you are trying to make me a spy."

"Just talk please. Help me with these pictures. It will be very easy."

I told him that the rebels wouldn't let us drive through their camp, and the only vehicles I saw were some old Land Cruisers, and the only weapons I saw were some old M-14s and very old Kalashnikovs. For most of the pictures they showed me of weapons, I said I didn't think I saw that.

The commander didn't believe me. He gestured to the guard, who started beating me with a thick stick, about a yard and a half long. He then beat me with his fists. I said that they could kill me, but I still would not know about weapons. This beating went on for what seemed like a very long time. I was dragged back to the cell, and Ali was taken for his turn.

He looked at my messed-up face as they took him away. He asked me if it was going to be very bad. I gestured to say it was nothing. He rolled his eyes.

They soon came for me again, because they needed a translator. They knew that Ali had been in the Chad Army, but they were trying to learn if he had been in the intelligence arm. Maybe he had come as a spy. Why would the son of an omda take a job as a lowly driver? They had already beaten him severely before I came. I translated their questions and Ali told them that it was just his business to drive people, and that he had only been a simple soldier in the army. They beat him with the sticks, mostly on his arms and legs and his back and the soles of his feet. Finally I said I would not translate if they were going to beat him. I stopped talking and they kicked and pushed me back to the cell.

They brought me back later when Ali was lying very hurt on the floor, beaten everywhere very seriously.

They told me that I would need to translate some more. I told them that I was finished doing that. I said that I would translate if they would not beat him. They said they would beat him if I did not translate.

"You have just about killed him. You can go ahead and kill him now, but I will not translate unless you stop all your beating of him."

With that, they took me away again. Ali was soon dumped back in our cell — the poor man was only half conscious. He groaned through the night.

We awoke the next morning to nothing. We thought the beatings had stopped, but then we saw Paul coming and going from his cell. This day was Paul's turn. But, thankfully, they would treat him better than they treated us. When we talked in the hall, I did not tell him we had been beaten, as I did not want to add our troubles to his own.

They took Ali and me outside and tied us under a tree. We were almost too sore to move. Paul was later brought out, moving very slowly. He looked very weak, and could only look down. His eyes were sunken. He had refused all food for seven days, demanding that the three of us be reunited. He knew very well that our situation would be hopeless without him. Even though we were now together, he was not going to eat until they released us. I thought this plan would kill him.

That evening, I tried talking to the guards standing outside our barred doorway. I asked them how Paul was doing. One of them seemed willing to talk, so I decided to try to make friends with him. He seemed like he was probably a good man. He gave me a smoke after a while and told me that Paul was in very bad shape.

"Your hawalya is maybe going to die," he said. "Unless you can make him decide to start eating." He put the problem on me.

For several hours I thought about this. When the same guard returned after his dinner, I told him that I could probably get Paul to eat, but they must help me. Soon, a commander came and took me from the cell. We talked on the way to Paul's cell. Paul was on a mattress on an actual bed, not on the floor. It was not a filthy room, just windowless and very old like our cell. The names of prisoners from colonial times were scratched on the walls. Paul looked terrible.

Why did the Sudanese not want him to die? That is a good question. It may be true that they wanted to avoid the trouble that would come with the death of a noted American journalist. But I'm not sure if these people thought like that. I think it was because you only had to look at Paul to know he was a good person, and this brought some human feelings to them.

I had decided to tell Paul something that was not true, only because he is very stubborn and because it was the only thing I could think of to save his life. I told him that if he would accept some food, they would let him make a call to his wife in the United States. He sat halfway up and looked at me.

"Is this true?"

It broke my heart to do so, but I looked at him and said that it was so. The commander behind me said that it was so. Paul agreed to eat some food.

The commander ordered a soldier to go get him some food, but I said that he must not eat our kind of food, that someone must go into town and get him an American-style sandwich that a white man could eat, and a Coke or Pepsi. There was an argument about the cost of this, but I assured the commander that our food would kill this man, and I truly believed that he was not strong enough for anything but his own food. So two large baguette sandwiches, lamb burgers, were obtained. Even so, Paul would not eat. He instead gave the food to me and to Ali and the two mechanics. Paul would break his fast on his own terms, a day later, after they threatened to force-feed him with a tube. I realized later that Paul had seen through the trick but went along with it to get food for me, Ali, and the mechanics. A good man.

25.
OPEN HOUSE AT THE TORTURE CENTER

From that night things got easier for us. It was possible for us to talk to one another without punishment.

I told the guards about life in El Fasher. My experiences there as a high school boy were not unlike their experiences as young soldiers in a strange place. We agreed that the war and the killing was a terrible time. Some of the soldiers were from the Nuba Mountains, where they had endured their own horrors at the hands of the government they now worked for. *It was foolish for the government to kill our people,* they said. "Good point," I agreed. They were scared young men, with horrible stories to tell. I listened. They would bring me cigarettes, and I suggested that it would be so much easier for us to talk like friends if we prisoners were not tied. So they untied us and let us outside so we could enjoy the cool of the evening. I told them as much as I could about my family so they might think in a new way if they were ever sent to destroy a village.

A great joy came to us when we were allowed to shower and wash our clothes. I cannot tell you the smell we presented to one another after so many days, and the itchy discomfort of our clothes. After about six days you cannot smell yourself, but you can smell the others very well. This shower was a great thing. Paul, too, was recovering, and this helped him. Some nights they let us sleep out in the sand, so much cooler than roasting in the cells.

At around 9 p.m. on the tenth evening in El Fasher, a large, muscular colonel in his late forties arrived at the prison and I was taken into his office. He removed his name badge and covered the nameplate on his desk when I was brought in, probably because he did not want his family to have to answer angry questions someday from my family — this is always on people's minds. That he was thinking I would live to tell about him was a good sign that I might not be killed that day, but it did not occur to me then. I still woke up every morning prepared to die that day; some order would come down and overwhelm whatever little friendships I had made to make our lives easier. We would then be taken out and shot, and our friendly guards would swallow the hurt of this and keep going. They had swallowed far more hurt than this. I saw every arriving vehicle as perhaps bringing that order.

This colonel was the head of intelligence for the western regions of Sudan.

I looked at a bowl of wrapped hard candies on his desk.

"Have one," he said, and I did.

"Listen, Daoud. You hold the key to what will happen to you and your friends. You will be busy with us for maybe three hours, maybe six. We will see. If you tell us the truth, you and your friends will live. If you lie to us, you will all die. So it is in your hands." This, of course, is what they say to everyone. "Before I ask you any questions, I want to show some hospitality to you. This guard is going to show you around so you feel at home here."

With that, I was taken by the arm and led down several long hallways I had not traveled before.

In one room was a large chair with electric wires fixed to it. In another room, a chair with restraints was surrounded by medical posters on the wall, helpful torture guides to the eyes, the genitals, the nose, the muscles and nerves of hands, feet, arms, legs. Pictures of eyes, ears, and arms were painted on the walls to remind visitors how easily they could be removed from the body. Trays of steel tools were everywhere.

No person was being tortured; it was all reserved for me and perhaps my friends today. The tour was long and slow and complete, and then I was returned to the chair in the colonel's office. He was smoking a cigarette and taking snuff at the same time.

"So, Daoud, what did you see?"

"I saw the way you torture people and kill them."

"Yes, you did. Would you like to just talk like friends, and we'll stay in this room?"

Under my circumstances, I told him that I thought that was a very good idea.

"Would you like to swear on the Koran regarding what you are going to tell me?"

I told him that would not be necessary, that he could be assured that I would tell the truth, and that I had always told the truth to them. But I told him I would not talk unless he could agree to something.

He seemed surprised. "And what is that?"

I told him I would need a cigarette. He laughed and pushed one across to me, with a book of matches. He called to the guard to get some hot tea for me.

For the next hour and a half I told the colonel the long story again of how I met Paul, of our arrest on the road, everything. I told him of my other trips with other reporters. Everything I could think of that was true. I knew none of this would be of use to his murdering army.

When I stopped talking, he looked at me strangely.

"This is all the story you have?"

"Everything."

"Daoud, I told you what would happen to everyone if you lied. And you are a liar."

I told him that I didn't know what he meant, that I had told him everything I could remember.

He tossed three pictures across the desk. They were photos of me standing with rebel soldiers and rebel commanders.

"We know all about you. We know your mother's name. We know your cousins. So why would we not know that you were with these rebels?"

I explained that these were trips with Philip Cox, and the BBC, and all of that.

"Well, you didn't tell me all of that, did you? That you met with these rebel commanders?"

"We met with everybody. It was for the

news stories. The reporters want to talk to everybody on all sides."

"You didn't talk to me. You didn't talk to government of Sudan commanders, did you?"

"They would kill us, so we didn't. But we wanted to do that."

He started asking me where this rebel group was based, and what another rebel group had for weapons. None of this mattered, as things change so quickly. I told him the same useless things I had told the other interrogators. Land Cruisers. Kalashnikovs. M-14s. I didn't know where they had their bases. We called to see if we could go here or there, I told the colonel, but we didn't ask where they had their bases.

"And it seems the government of Israel asked that you not be sent to Sudan when you were in Egypt. So why do you have such friends in Israel, spy?"

I explained my attempt to find a good job and that it had gone badly.

He was not happy with me, but he had an idea that Paul would contradict me. He had me taken to a nearby room and replaced me with Paul. It was now very late at night. I could hear him interrogating Paul for a long time.

I was brought back in.

The colonel was angry but controlled.

"Daoud, your friend does not want to tell us anything until he sees that you are alive and okay. So we are letting him see you. Now he wants to see Ali. Tell your hawalya that Ali is sleeping and is okay." I told that to Paul.

"So tell Paul he has to talk now."

I told Paul he should not talk unless they gave me another cigarette.

"Yes. Tell them that." Paul made a smoking gesture and pointed to me to assure the colonel that I was not mistranslating in my favor.

"You are both in a very dangerous situation. You are in my office. Many commanders come here and are so nervous they can't eat or drink. And you just demand cigarettes like all this is nothing to you. It is very surprising to me." With that, he handed his entire pack of cigarettes to Paul, who gave the pack to me.

"Get some tea for Daoud," he said to his guards, who ran for it. "And sugar," I called after them.

When the tea and sugar arrived I stood up with the tray and said that, if he didn't mind, I was going to go outside and smoke and drink this tea. Paul stayed to answer more questions, which were of no use to the colonel. I had the guard take me back to my cell after I had drunk all the tea, maybe ten or more cups, it was so good. It was clear to me from almost the beginning of this meeting that the colonel had no power to torture or kill us, or he would have done so. This seemed like a last effort to get us to talk before losing custody of us. So we could make our demands and watch what he would do. I think he was a little glad to see some human beings he could talk to.

In the morning, Paul and Ali and I were taken from our cells. The mechanics were taken in another direction. I would never see them or hear about them again until they showed up later to testify against us, and accuse us of spying, no doubt under unimaginable pressure to do so. We were driven to a civilian court in town, our wrists tied behind us.

Our case was being transferred from the military to the civilian court. What was extraordinary was that standing in the back of the courtroom were four U.S. soldiers in their uniforms: a Marine, two U.S. Army officers, and a U.S. Air Force officer. I had some idea that some wheels were turning to do something for us. But look at these guys. My God, you have no idea what they looked like to us. They came up to us, and Paul was very moved to see them. This made the officers very emotional and everyone was wiping their eyes.

Depending on your situation in the world, U.S. soldiers may not always be what you want to see, but for the first moment in all this time, I thought that I would probably not die today. I did not think the danger was over. I knew Paul might walk out with these officers, and Ali and I might be led through another door to the gallows. But maybe not. Certainly not today — not with those guys in the back of the room smiling and winking at us. The good America was in the room.

26.
THE HAWALYA

The charges against us were read. I agreed
that I had been working with journalists and
had entered the country illegally six times.
Ali admitted to entering once with a journalist.

It was Paul's turn. He walked to the front
of the courtroom. An African Union soldier
began to translate the charges against him,
but Paul stopped the court.

"I have my own translator. Please bring
Mr. Daoud Hari back," he said.

The court was still for a moment, but this
was done.

The charges against Paul were ridiculous.
He had printed a map of Sudan from the
Internet — from the popular CIA World
Factbook public website. So he was clearly
a spy for them. That sort of thing.

After Paul had rejected all these charges,
we were returned to a prison, but a different, civil prison. It was much worse than

the military prison, but we didn't care about any of that now. People knew we were there: big people. We were told that Congressman Christopher Shays had been in El Fasher the day before to inquire about our case to the governor of El Fasher. The American Embassy in Khartoum was in high gear for us. We were transferred to the civilian court, which was very good news. The miracle behind this news was Paul's wife and a few others in America who together were making things happen. Paul's many reporter friends were calling powerful people. Reporters I had worked with from the United States, Africa, France, Germany, Japan, and other places were adding pressure. And all of that was added to what the U.S. Embassy staffers were doing.

Paul seemed happy after the court appearance, but not happy with me. He was angry for reasons I did not understand. I couldn't figure it out, so I decided to worry about this problem later.

I talked to the guards a lot. They said we were big news. They gave me a local newspaper with the headline "Three Big Spies Caught." I asked the guards if they thought that was true, and they laughed. I negotiated the use of a cell phone so that Paul could call his wife. The cost of this was

Paul's wristwatch, which somehow he still possessed. This was a big moment. He found a corner of the cell for this call and it was very emotional for him. I used the phone later to call a cousin; I asked him to contact my mother and any of my brothers and sisters he could find alive. I asked him to tell them not to inform my father that I was in prison, he would walk through dangerous territory to come see me. He needed to stay hidden where he was.

I could not stop thinking about why Paul seemed cold and angry to me. So I asked him why.

"You have called me a spy to these people. You have done it over and over again when you are speaking in languages I don't understand. I don't know why you would do this — it could cost me years in this prison."

I was amazed. I sat down on the floor of the cell to think. I stood up again and paced around, trying to figure this out. "What word is this? What word do I use to say spy?" I asked him.

"Hawalya," he said.

"My goodness, Paul, that just means 'white guy,' " I tried to explain. But he thought otherwise in his mind. He was also perhaps still a little upset about the Israel and Egypt things in my background that I had not told him when we met.

The U.S. officers interrupted my investigation of this misunderstanding. They brought us blankets and sleeping bags, Cokes, and goat burgers. So this happiness overwhelmed our little problems.

Late in the evening, the attorney general of Sudan came to correct the charges against Paul. He also had us untied; someone had ordered our wrists tied like old times.

The attorney general told the guards to untie the hawalya.

Paul jumped up: "Why do you call me a spy? You know very well I am no spy."

The attorney general corrected him with a smile: "Hawalya? Sir, it means, well, it just means 'white man.' A white fellow. It's a good word, almost affectionate."

Paul looked like a man who sees a beloved brother come home after being a long time lost to him. He came over to me and apologized and we laughed.

"You are my brother," I said to him. "I would never say things to harm you." He shook my shoulders and closed his eyes and said he knew that.

He seemed more recovered in the next

hour than in all the time since ending his fast.

It had been a pretty good day, considering that the three of us were looking at fifteen to twenty years in a very bad prison. But what, not counting family, is more important than friendship?

The attorney general told Paul that his case would be separated from ours. It would make things easier. Paul looked at Ali and me.

"Absolutely not. This will not happen, I assure you," Paul told the man. "We will demand to be tried together. I will ask my country to insist on it."

At this time, though we did not know it, letters from big stars such as Bono and from famous leaders such as Jimmy Carter and Jesse Jackson were piling up on this man's desk — copies of letters sent to President Bashir. The Vatican had even written, and the government of France. When I heard about these things several days later, I hoped that Bashir was a stamp collector, because this would be a good time for him. The attorney general looked upset, but he agreed to this demand. In this way, I knew Paul was saving our lives if they could be saved. He had made the same demand with the rebels and with the army, and saved us three times altogether.

It was good that Paul and I had faced and settled our argument. Nothing is more important than friendship in dangerous times. What I did not know until later was that the Sudanese were telling the American consul that Paul's case was something they could talk about, but the two Sudanese men captured with him would be Sudan's business only. It would have been natural for Ali and me to disappear at this point — if not for Paul's demands.

Later that night I could not sleep and I imagined Ahmed came to visit me. He would know all the guards and they would be happy to see him, and they would open all the doors for us so we could take a walk through El Fasher as we had done when I was in school.

It felt very good to imagine walking with him in our old city. I think I had been living like a dead man since he was killed. But I looked around the cell and decided I had some more brothers now, and I should think in a happier way about things.

Perhaps prison was a place for me to think about things. It was in the Egyptian prison where I realized I needed to not be so cut off from my family. Now I was seeing the whole idea of family in a bigger way.

During all my years, Ahmed was always a long step ahead of me. It was still this way in my daydream.

When I saw the guards that morning, I thought, *Oh, yes, it is the part of me like Ahmed that helps me make friends so quickly.* Ahmed has saved my life several times just from that. And if I can find some joy after all I have seen, it will be something of him, too, for you have to love life like Ahmed if you are to truly serve your people.

When I went back into Darfur with my first reporters, the African journalists, I was asked why I was taking the risk, and I told them, not trying to be too dramatic, that I was not safe because my people were not safe — and how can you be safe if your people are not safe? And so who are your people? Perhaps everyone is your people. I was wondering about that.

That next day we were to be moved to the vilest of prisons, where we would wait for trial. The U.S. officers said an American had been badly treated at that prison and a Slovenian journalist had been beaten. So they objected to the move. Arrangements were made for us to stay instead in quarters in the Justice Building. The U.S. officers brought us supplies to make the room very comfortable. They also slipped us some small cell phones in case we were secretly moved — these we were to keep hidden. They also brought us some books and a small DVD player with *Seinfeld* shows. I didn't know about that kind of show, but it was very funny, especially the way Kramer comes through doors. Ali would not watch the shows. He was very certain that we would be taken away and hung or shot at any minute, and he looked at each new day as an opportunity for this. He would jump when any news came to us.

National Geographic put three lawyers on the case and called every day, as did the American vice consul in El Fasher. This went on for two weeks, and still the case dragged on. How long had it been since we were taken at the roadblock? A month and a week or so.

Then some big news. Paul snapped closed his phone after a good call.

"Richardson!" he said.

I didn't know who Richardson was.

"Bill Richardson, governor of New Mexico, which is my home state. He is the man the U.S. often sends to negotiate, and he is very good. He knows President Bashir. He is coming just to help us. Richardson is on his way to Khartoum."

On the day when we expected Richardson

might drop by to see us, Paul's wife came instead. I will not tell you how wonderful that was for both of them, and for Ali and for me. That is a story for them to tell, but, really, it was beyond all telling. They walked together in the walled compound of the Justice Building.

That night, in the public area outside the building, where we had a very close view, a man was whipped for some infraction of sharia law. Nearby, a woman had earlier been badly whipped. Her crime was making a fermented beverage and selling it in jars so she could survive. They lashed her twenty-five times until she was unconscious.

We remembered where we were, and we remembered what we do.

"You are supposed to go somewhere now," a guard told us on the thirty-fifth morning of our ordeal.

We were taken in a bright red Land Cruiser to a large mansion, the home of the governor of El Fasher, and escorted inside. Another governor, Mr. Bill Richardson, shook our hands and hugged us. I thanked him for what he was doing. Photographers were flashing our pictures.

As it turned out, we were going home.

I hugged Ali, but he looked seriously into

my eyes and said we were a long way from Chad and we should not let them use us for such pictures, since they would kill us after the Americans left. I kissed his cheeks anyway.

The military governor of El Fasher suggested to Richardson that maybe Ali and I could be his guests in this house for a week. I said, "Thank you very much but we think maybe we should be on our way." Governor Richardson winked his eye a little as if to say "good answer."

We flew in Richardson's small jet to Khartoum. Ali was very upset to go to Khartoum, because that was where the government of Sudan could have a good last chance to take us away and shoot us. He threw up several times near Governor Richardson, who was fine with it.

27.
My One Percent Chance

A flight from Khartoum through Addis Ababa, Ethiopia, brought us finally to N'Djamena. I relaxed on this flight. But Ali was watching the position of the plane. Could not the Sudanese land the plane back in Khartoum, now that the Americans had left? What was to stop them? He would not be comforted. Even as the plane circled over N'Djamena he was tense, expecting a last-minute problem that would send us back. As the plane rolled to a stop, he could not get off fast enough. On the tarmac, he stopped to breathe the steamy air. He turned to me. "Humdallah. We are home," he said, smiling. I had not seen him smile since he thought our helicopter might crash.

We were greeted by Chadian national security officials. "Come with us," they said. After three hours of intense questions, they released Ali and told me I would have to stay in jail until my situation was cleared up. A friend in the government convinced them to let me go to my little room, which was still waiting for me. It was so good to lie down on my own mattress. So amazing.

The mud wall of my room had always reminded me of the caves we explored as children in our mountain, the Village of God. The cracks in my mud wall seemed to be drawings. The caves of home have drawings, thousands of years old. There is an inner cave with a cool pool of water where children might swim on a hot day. The cave was explored many years ago by the Hungarian man who also explored the Cave of the Swimmers, just over the border from Darfur in Egypt. The book and the movie *The English Patient* were based on his life. He was the only outsider to come see our caves, as far as we know. The caves are still there, of course. Pictures of long-horned cattle and all the beasts of Africa, women and men, children. All the life. So many nights I spent in this room, looking at this mud wall, waking and making my stick pictures of scenes I needed to get out of my head. History. History. History. The people. The little girl. The woman. The child waving.

Over the next several months I would be watched closely by the Chad security officers; several times a week I had to turn myself in for questioning, during which the officers grew ever more angry at me. They were threatening to send me to Sudan in a prisoner exchange. Sudan was telling them I was a spy who was helping the rebels prepare for a new attack on N'Djamena. My jaw had swollen to twice its size from a beating. I told some of my friends that I had fallen, for if they knew I was under the eye of national security they would have kept their distance. A closer friend in the government told me that several groups of prisoners were being exchanged over the next few weeks and I would probably be in the third group.

Despite the way they seemed happy to talk to each other about me, Chad and Sudan were getting close to war again. "Rebels" who were actually proxy troops for Sudan were gathering inside Chad; heavy fighting was going on east and southeast of N'Djamena, where everyone believed an attack would come soon. People packed the bridge to Cameroon; families herded animals and carried bundles of all sizes; honking cars and buses with household goods piled on top and held from windows pressed the crowds along the bridge. Overloaded boats filled the river. Most of the small shops in the city closed, and the sound of the city now was of window shutters being nailed closed.

At this time came the news of my father's death. He had heard about my imprisonment and could not eat. By the time I was free, it was too late for him. The rebels who are not rebels would advance on N'Djamena again. My friends in government would inform me that Chad would soon arrest me and send me to Sudan in exchange for a spy. Megan in New York called and said she would help. A human rights lawyer from Washington called me when he got her e-mail. I was on the phone with him when the rebels were near the city again. I considered crossing the little bridge into Cameroon, but Chris the lawyer said they were working with the U.S. Embassy and the U.N. refugee agency to get me out, perhaps to the United States, where I could continue my work in a new way, and someday return as my people returned. I told him the rebels might be in the city in an hour or so, and that could be bad for me. I said Chad security might arrest me soon. He said if I went across the bridge all would be lost legally. Ali's family threatened to imprison me unless I could pay for the truck, an expensive truck. *National Geographic* was sending a check someday for that. I finished my call with Chris and closed the phone and said to myself, *Well, so very far away — I give these kind people about a one percent chance of helping me in time.* And then I realized that, for me, that was pretty good. And it was enough.

Leaving Africa was not simple, of course. Even after being whisked from N'Djamena, I had to be interviewed by the U.S. Department of Homeland Security people in Ghana and wait for a letter of transit. A misstep landed me in jail — more waiting. The day finally came. I stood atop a tarmac stairway, looked out over Africa, and smelled the air of it enough to last me for a while. I would work now in other ways to help get the story out and help return the people to Darfur and their homes in peace. What can one person do? You make friends, of course, and do what you can.

ACKNOWLEDGMENTS

This book is in your hands because editors Jonathan Jao and Jennifer Hershey of Random House saw something about my story in a *New York Times* column by Nicholas Kristof. So if you know these people, you should thank them when you see them, as I thank them now. I did not know how to write a book, but my friends said, "Don't worry, Daoud; we will help you," and they did. So thank you, Megan and Dennis, very much. And I thank Gail Ross and Howard Yoon, who are, respectively, a literary agent and a literary editor in Washington, D.C., who warmly gave me very good advice.

This book is in your hands mostly because I was alive to write it. For this I must thank Philip Cox; Paul Salopek; lawyer Christopher Nugent of Washington, D.C.; Megan McKenna; the amazing people of the American embassies in Sudan, Chad, and Ghana; Lori Heninger; Jack Patterson; Nicholas

Kristof and my reporter friends in many countries; my friends in Cairo and an old jailer in Aswan; my cousins in Africa and in the United States and Europe; Christopher Shays of Connecticut, and Bill Richardson of New Mexico; my late father and my late brother, Ahmed; and all my friends in Africa, some of whom I pray will forgive me for mentioning them only by nicknames, which was done to protect them. How in one life can I return the blessings of all this friendship?

If I can presume some bond of friendship between us, my reader friend, let me ask you to think of the fact that tonight as I write this, and probably as you read this, people are still being killed in Darfur, and people are still suffering in these camps. The leaders of the world can solve this problem, and the people of Darfur can go home, if the leaders see that people everywhere care deeply enough to talk to them about this. So, if you have the time, perhaps you can do so. For it has no meaning to take risks for news stories unless the people who read them will act.

— DAOUD HARI
January 2008

APPENDIX 1

A DARFUR PRIMER

The Darfur situation can be very confusing without a little extra information. This is what you would know if you were almost any Sudanese talking politics with your friends in an outdoor bar or at a university.

When the British left Sudan in 1956 they set it up with a small Arab minority government ruling over a mostly non-Arab African population.

The indigenous Africans had in fact already begun a revolt in 1955, the year before independence was final. The war, mostly in the south, lasted until 1972, when a peace agreement allowed limited self-government for the southern region of Sudan. A Southern Regional Assembly was established for that purpose, and it was to have control of much of the expected oil revenue from the fields just then discovered by Chevron Corporation in the south.

In 1983, after ten years of peace, Sudan's

president, Gaafar Nimeiri, nullified this agreement, disbanding the Southern Regional Assembly and imposing federal rule everywhere. New districts throughout Sudan would be ruled by military governors. The oil revenue, still unseen, would be controlled by the federal government in Khartoum.

Rebel groups quickly formed again. To make things worse, Nimeiri decreed that harsh Islamic sharia law would be imposed throughout Sudan, even over non-Muslim citizens in the south. These laws called for the amputation of hands for minor thefts, for the stoning of women, and many other cruelties. This angered the mass of people, who are quite moderate, and it angered the rebels, who now had three issues: a return to secular government, not sharia law; better representation for indigenous Africans, especially in the south; and a fair local share of the expected oil wealth, including oil jobs and more schools, roads, and clinics.

This political anger joined with the anger of hunger, as these were years of an intense African famine. An uprising in the spring of 1985 overthrew Nimeiri and caused the election of a parliamentary government led by moderate Sadiq al-Mahdi. He suspended sharia law, although it continued to be enforced by some local Arab administrators. Because of the lingering of sharia law, and because the other political issues of representation were still not fixed, the rebel groups didn't disband.

Four nervous years followed. The oil fields could not be put into production during these years because occasional rebel attacks sent Chevron away. Sudan, sagging under heavy debt from the Nimeiri years, could not pay its loans and was cut off from further help by the International Monetary Fund. Sudan wanted to become a big oil player, but was still a poor relation among the Arab governments. So Mahdi called a new peace agreement that was expected to further subdue sharia law and perhaps reestablish self-rule in the south. That would let the oil production go forward.

Just before the conference, Mahdi was overthrown and exiled by a military strongman, General Omar Hassan Ahmad al-Bashir, who is still in power. He resumed the expansion of sharia law, shut down opposition newspapers and political parties, and imprisoned dissidents. This was a big shock to everyone. I was in high school at the time, and all of us wanted to fight it.

Under the sharia law of Bashir, a woman today cannot leave the country without the written permission of her father or husband. Men and women must sit in separate areas of public buses. The army has been purged of unbelievers. The government-attorney staffs and the courts have been cleansed of those who are not sufficiently loyal to the agenda of Bashir and his right-wing religious brotherhood. Elections have been corrupted. Men and women have been mercilessly brutalized for the most insignificant or unproved deeds. People disappear.

Bashir solved the oil field problem his own way, just as he would later solve his Darfur problem. Many Arab nomads throughout the south had been armed with automatic weapons during the two previous governments as an unsuccessful way of protecting the oil fields from rebel attacks. In the early 1990s, Bashir turned these nomads loose on the non-Arab villages, killing over two million people.

Boys who were out tending their animals far from their villages were the few survivors. They came back to find their fathers dead and their mothers and sisters raped and killed or missing into the slave trade. These boys, after incredibly difficult journeys, found their way to Ethiopia and then to other countries, including the United States, where they are still known as the

Lost Boys of Sudan. So the Sudanese government is like this. Bashir is like this.

Communities in the United States, in Britain, and elsewhere in Europe accepted many thousands of these boys and helped them find new lives. This must not be forgotten by Muslims or by anyone.

Bashir built friendly relations with Osama bin Laden and other Islamic radicals, who then opened training camps in Sudan. He turned the oil fields over to the Chinese, who brought their own security people and guns into the now depopulated areas. Here was indeed a good model for economic development without sharing or resistance.

The famine must also be understood, for the weather changes seem permanent now. Beginning in the mid-1980s, nomadic Arabs and the more settled indigenous African tribesmen found themselves in greater than normal competition for the same few blades of grass for their animals, and the same few drops of water in the wells. Arabs drifted south into Zaghawa lands; some Zaghawa drifted farther south into Massalit and Fur tribal lands.

This weather change has created a problem between tribes, and Bashir knows that one of his predecessors lost power because of famine. There are huge reserves of fresh water deep under Darfur. If the indigenous people can be removed, Arab farmers can be brought in and great farms can blossom. Sudan and Egypt have signed what is called "The Four Freedoms Agreement," which effectively allows Egyptian Arabs to move into Darfur and other areas of Sudan. New farms might be a good idea if the water could be used wisely and not consumed all at once, but why not let these farms and farmers develop alongside the returned villages of my people? If the traditional people were allowed to pump this water, which they are not, these farms and this food for Sudan would result.

Throughout these recent years, the Arab government has been promoting Arab identity at the expense of Sudanese national identity. Arabs and indigenous Africans have gotten along for thousands of years in Sudan. Even in my own childhood, we feasted in one another's tents and huts. Any disputes that couldn't be settled through negotiations between the elders were settled in ritual battles held far from any village so that women and children and the elderly would not be harmed. In addition, there has always been so much intermarriage that it is hard to see the differences between the Arabs and the indigenous Africans. Almost every person, at least in the north half of Sudan and in most of Darfur, is Muslim, so there are no religious differences, either. But the drumbeat of Arab superiority began separating the hearts of the Arabs from their indigenous African neighbors. This should remind people of what happened in Rwanda.

Negotiations between elders to resolve tribal disputes were now harshly discouraged by the government. The Arabs were instead given weapons and military support to resolve them. While Arabs were being heavily armed by the government, non-Arab villages throughout Sudan were told to give up all their weapons or be destroyed. Darfur has been thick with automatic weapons ever since the 1980s, when Colonel Muammar Gaddafi of Libya used Darfur as a staging area for his attacks on Chad in an attempt to expand to the south. The Darfuris, both Arab and African, are good traders, and they found themselves with many of those guns. An estimated fifty thousand Kalashnikov AK-47s, RPG launchers, and M-14 rifles came into Darfur and stayed. The villagers, afraid of what was coming, would not give them up.

Darfur rebel groups bristling with this firepower started talking about Darfur independence after the latest purge of non-Arabs from government, and on April 25, 2003, thirty-three rebel Land Cruisers attacked a government military base to destroy the airplanes and helicopters that had been destroying their villages. In retaliation, President Bashir let loose the dogs of war: the green light was given to armed Arab Janjaweed militia groups. Supported by government tanks, machine-gun-mounted vehicles, additional helicopter gunships, and bombers of the Sudan Army, these Arab militias began attacking and burning indigenous villages not in a sporadic way, but in a systematic way calculated to destroy every village and kill every person. Men, women, and children were killed. Village leaders were burned alive or tortured to death in front of their friends and children. Children were tossed into fires. Wells were poisoned with the bodies of children. Everything had come into place, politically, environmentally, and culturally for a genocide in Darfur.

You may remember what I told you of this situation in Chapter 2:

The problem in dealing with rebel groups is that it is often difficult to know who is on which side on any given day. The Arab government in Khartoum —

the government of Sudan — makes false promises to make temporary peace with one rebel group and then another to keep the non-Arab people fighting one another. The government makes deals with ambitious commanders who are crazy enough to think the government will promote them after the war, when in fact they will be discarded if not killed then. These breakaway commanders are sometimes told to attack other rebel groups, or even to kill humanitarian workers and the troops sent from other countries to monitor compliance with cease-fire treaties. This is done so the genocide can carry on and the land can be cleared of the indigenous people. History may prove me wrong in some of these perceptions, but this is how it seems to most people who are there.

It is also believed that the government pays some of the traditional Arab people, many tribes of whom are otherwise our friends, to form deadly horseback militias called the Janjaweed to brutally kill the non-Arab Africans and burn our villages. . . .

This is my prediction: When the government has removed or killed all the traditional non-Arabs, then it will get the traditional Arabs to fight one another so they too will disappear from valuable lands. This is already happening in areas where the removal of non-Arab Africans is nearly complete.

I tell you all this again because even though some people think Darfur is a simple genocide, it is important to know that it is not. It is a complicated genocide.

The non-Arab traditional Africans of Darfur are being systematically murdered and displaced by Bashir's government of Sudan as a part of a program to remove political dissent, remove challenges to power, make way for unobstructed resource development, and turn an Arab minority into an Arab majority.

Can you do that in this century? Can you solve all your problems by killing everyone in your way? That is for the world to decide. Deciding if and when the traditional people of Darfur can go home will also decide if genocide works or not, and therefore whether it will happen elsewhere again in the world. It seems to me that this is a good place to stop it forever.

That will require the repatriation of the Darfur people who were expelled. The camps now in Chad can be moved to Darfur as new towns, bringing schools and clinics and opportunities for personal development to a number of areas that have never had them. From these new towns, village life and some new agriculture can blossom. A zone of protection can be created by the United Nations for this, just as they can be created for other people around the world who need protection in living balanced lives on the earth. In exchange for this protection, the full human rights of the men and women of these areas, the same rights so beautifully described by Eleanor Roosevelt and others in the Universal Declaration of Human Rights, must be added to the ancient customs. The Universal Declaration has long been accepted as international law.

This can be done. What is more important for the world right now than preserving ways of living in balance with the earth?

APPENDIX 2

THE UNIVERSAL DECLARATION
OF HUMAN RIGHTS

On December 10, 1948, the General Assembly of the United Nations adopted and proclaimed:

PREAMBLE

Whereas recognition of the inherent dignity and of the equal and inalienable rights of all members of the human family is the foundation of freedom, justice and peace in the world,

Whereas disregard and contempt for human rights have resulted in barbarous acts which have outraged the conscience of mankind, and the advent of a world in which human beings shall enjoy freedom of speech and belief and freedom from fear and want has been proclaimed as the highest aspiration of the common people,

Whereas it is essential, if man is not to be compelled to have recourse, as a last resort, to rebellion against tyranny and oppression, that human rights should be protected by the rule of law,

Whereas it is essential to promote the development of friendly relations between nations,

Whereas the peoples of the United Nations have in the Charter reaffirmed their faith in fundamental human rights, in the dignity and worth of the human person and in the equal rights of men and women and have determined to promote social progress and better standards of life in larger freedom,

Whereas Member States have pledged themselves to achieve, in co-operation with the United Nations, the promotion of universal respect for and observance of human rights and fundamental freedoms,

Whereas a common understanding of these rights and freedoms is of the greatest importance for the full realization of this pledge,

Now, Therefore THE GENERAL ASSEMBLY proclaims THIS UNIVERSAL DECLARATION OF HUMAN RIGHTS as a common standard of achievement for all peoples and all nations, to the end that every individual and every organ of society, keeping this Declaration constantly in mind, shall strive by teaching and education to promote respect for these rights and freedoms and by progressive measures, national and international, to secure their universal and effective recognition and observance, both among the peoples of Member States themselves and among the peoples of territories under their jurisdiction.

ARTICLE 1.

All human beings are born free and equal in dignity and rights. They are endowed with reason and conscience and should act towards one another in a spirit of brotherhood.

ARTICLE 2.

Everyone is entitled to all the rights and freedoms set forth in this Declaration, without distinction of any kind, such as race, color, sex, language, religion, political or other opinion, national or social origin, property, birth or other status. Furthermore, no distinction shall be made on the basis of the political, jurisdictional or international status of the country or territory to which a person belongs, whether it be independent, trust, non-self-governing or under any other limitation of sovereignty.

ARTICLE 3.

Everyone has the right to life, liberty and security of person.

ARTICLE 4.

No one shall be held in slavery or servitude; slavery and the slave trade shall be prohibited in all their forms.

ARTICLE 5.

No one shall be subjected to torture or to cruel, inhuman or degrading treatment or punishment.

ARTICLE 6.

Everyone has the right to recognition everywhere as a person before the law.

ARTICLE 7.

All are equal before the law and are entitled without any discrimination to equal protection of the law. All are entitled to equal protection against any discrimination in violation of this Declaration and against any incitement to such discrimination.

ARTICLE 8.

Everyone has the right to an effective remedy by the competent national tribunals for acts violating the fundamental rights granted him by the constitution or by law.

ARTICLE 9.

No one shall be subjected to arbitrary arrest, detention or exile.

ARTICLE 10.

Everyone is entitled in full equality to a fair and public hearing by an independent and impartial tribunal, in the determination of his rights and obligations and of any criminal charge against him.

ARTICLE 11.

(1) Everyone charged with a penal offence has the right to be presumed innocent until proved guilty according to law in a public trial at which he has had all the guarantees necessary for his defense.

(2) No one shall be held guilty of any penal offence on account of any act or omission which did not constitute a penal offence,

under national or international law, at the time when it was committed. Nor shall a heavier penalty be imposed than the one that was applicable at the time the penal offence was committed.

ARTICLE 12.

No one shall be subjected to arbitrary interference with his privacy, family, home or correspondence, nor to attacks upon his honor and reputation. Everyone has the right to the protection of the law against such interference or attacks.

ARTICLE 13.

(1) Everyone has the right to freedom of movement and residence within the borders of each state.

(2) Everyone has the right to leave any country, including his own, and to return to his country.

ARTICLE 14.

(1) Everyone has the right to seek and to enjoy in other countries asylum from persecution.

(2) This right may not be invoked in the case of prosecutions genuinely arising from

non-political crimes or from acts contrary to the purposes and principles of the United Nations.

Article 15.

(1) Everyone has the right to a nationality.

(2) No one shall be arbitrarily deprived of his nationality nor denied the right to change his nationality.

Article 16.

(1) Men and women of full age, without any limitation due to race, nationality or religion, have the right to marry and to found a family. They are entitled to equal rights as to marriage, during marriage and at its dissolution.

(2) Marriage shall be entered into only with the free and full consent of the intending spouses.

(3) The family is the natural and fundamental group unit of society and is entitled to protection by society and the State.

Article 17.

(1) Everyone has the right to own property alone as well as in association with others.

(2) No one shall be arbitrarily deprived of his property.

ARTICLE 18.

Everyone has the right to freedom of thought, conscience and religion; this right includes freedom to change his religion or belief, and freedom, either alone or in community with others and in public or private, to manifest his religion or belief in teaching, practice, worship and observance.

ARTICLE 19.

Everyone has the right to freedom of opinion and expression; this right includes freedom to hold opinions without interference and to seek, receive and impart information and ideas through any media and regardless of frontiers.

ARTICLE 20.

(1) Everyone has the right to freedom of peaceful assembly and association.

(2) No one may be compelled to belong to an association.

ARTICLE 21.

(1) Everyone has the right to take part in the government of his country, directly or through freely chosen representatives.

(2) Everyone has the right of equal access to public service in his country.

(3) The will of the people shall be the basis of the authority of government; this will shall be expressed in periodic and genuine elections which shall be by universal and equal suffrage and shall be held by secret vote or by equivalent free voting procedures.

ARTICLE 22.

Everyone, as a member of society, has the right to social security and is entitled to realization, through national effort and international co-operation and in accordance with the organization and resources of each State, of the economic, social and cultural rights indispensable for his dignity and the free development of his personality.

ARTICLE 23.

(1) Everyone has the right to work, to free choice of employment, to just and favorable conditions of work and to protection against unemployment.

(2) Everyone, without any discrimination, has the right to equal pay for equal work.

(3) Everyone who works has the right to just and favorable remuneration ensuring for himself and his family an existence worthy of human dignity, and supplemented, if necessary, by other means of social protection.

(4) Everyone has the right to form and to join trade unions for the protection of his interests.

ARTICLE 24.

Everyone has the right to rest and leisure, including reasonable limitation of working hours and periodic holidays with pay.

ARTICLE 25.

(1) Everyone has the right to a standard of living adequate for the health and well-being of himself and of his family, including food, clothing, housing and medical care and necessary social services, and the right to security in the event of unemployment, sickness, disability, widowhood, old age or other lack of livelihood in circumstances beyond his control.

(2) Motherhood and childhood are entitled

to special care and assistance. All children, whether born in or out of wedlock, shall enjoy the same social protection.

Article 26.

(1) Everyone has the right to education. Education shall be free, at least in the elementary and fundamental stages. Elementary education shall be compulsory. Technical and professional education shall be made generally available and higher education shall be equally accessible to all on the basis of merit.

(2) Education shall be directed to the full development of the human personality and to the strengthening of respect for human rights and fundamental freedoms. It shall promote understanding, tolerance and friendship among all nations, racial or religious groups, and shall further the activities of the United Nations for the maintenance of peace.

(3) Parents have a prior right to choose the kind of education that shall be given to their children.

Article 27.

(1) Everyone has the right freely to participate in the cultural life of the community, to enjoy the arts and to share in scientific advancement and its benefits.

(2) Everyone has the right to the protection of the moral and material interests resulting from any scientific, literary or artistic production of which he is the author.

Article 28.

Everyone is entitled to a social and international order in which the rights and freedoms set forth in this Declaration can be fully realized.

Article 29.

(1) Everyone has duties to the community in which alone the free and full development of his personality is possible.

(2) In the exercise of his rights and freedoms, everyone shall be subject only to such limitations as are determined by law solely for the purpose of securing due recognition and respect for the rights and freedoms of others and of meeting the just requirements of morality, public order and the general welfare in a democratic society.

(3) These rights and freedoms may in no case be exercised contrary to the purposes and principles of the United Nations.

ARTICLE 30.

Nothing in this Declaration may be interpreted as implying for any State, group or person any right to engage in any activity or to perform any act aimed at the destruction of any of the rights and freedoms set forth herein.

ABOUT THE AUTHOR

Daoud Hari was born in the Darfur region of Sudan. After escaping an attack on his village, he entered the refugee camps in Chad and began serving as a translator for major news organizations including *The New York Times,* NBC, and the BBC, as well as for the U.N. and other aid groups. He participated in the Voices from Darfur tour for SaveDarfur.org. He now lives in Baltimore.

To learn more about the author and the conflict in Darfur, please visit: www.the translator-book.com.

The employees of Thorndike Press hope you have enjoyed this Large Print book. All our Thorndike and Wheeler Large Print titles are designed for easy reading, and all our books are made to last. Other Thorndike Press Large Print books are available at your library, through selected bookstores, or directly from us.

For information about titles, please call:
(800) 223-1244

or visit our Web site at:
http://gale.cengage.com/thorndike

To share your comments, please write:
Publisher
Thorndike Press
295 Kennedy Memorial Drive
Waterville, ME 04901

1942

"ISSUE IN DOUBT"

Symposium on the War in the Pacific
by the Admiral Nimitz Museum

EDITED BY WAYMAN C. MULLINS

EAKIN PRESS ★ Austin, Texas

FIRST EDITION

Copyright © 1994
By Wayman C. Mullins

Published in the United States of America
By Eakin Press
An Imprint of Sunbelt Media, Inc.
P.O. Drawer 90159 ★ Austin, TX 78709-0159

ALL RIGHTS RESERVED. No part of this book may be reproduced in
any form without written permission from the publisher, except for
brief passages included in a review appearing in a newspaper or magazine.

ISBN 0-89015-968-8

Library of Congress Cataloging-in-Publication Data

Mullins, Wayman C.
    1942 : issue in doubt / by Wayman C. Mullins.
        p.   cm.
    Includes bibliographical references and index.
    ISBN 0-89015-968-8 : $29.95
    1. World War, 1939–1945 — Campaigns — Pacific Area. 2. World War,
1939–1945 — Personal narratives. I. Title.
D767.M84   1994
940.54'26–dc20   94-5234
                                                                  CIP

Dedicated to

all who have paid the ultimate price

for freedom and peace.

Contents

Foreword

The reader will find this book fascinating and uniquely informative. In the first place, it deals with the beginning of United States participation in World War II halfway around the world in the southwest Pacific. The vastness of the Pacific Ocean imposes difficulties of all kinds, and distance factors turned out to be the Achilles heel for the Japanese, particularly when they were faced with problems limited by time. Few people realize that if one drills a hole through the center of the earth somewhere in the South China Sea and emerges from the other side he will still be in the Pacific Ocean.

As stated in the preface, this document is an assimilation of eyewitness accounts by those who participated directly in the combat action, in addition to opinions and statements of distinguished writers and those who were present in staff meetings and conferences before and after the action in question. Consequently, there are circumstances related herein that may be challenged by a reader who also was present and has a different impression of the way events unfolded. I have found in my review that even if we take combat reports of the Japanese commander and the American commander and lay them side by side, there are bound to be differences.

The initial phase of the war in the Pacific was short, taking only about four months for the Japanese to reach their objectives. The reason is simple. The Japanese had specific objectives for which they had trained. They conducted their planning operations by messenger, taking no chance of United States electronic intercept. On the other hand, the U.S. forces were not prepared. Although war was raging in Europe and involvement seemed inevitable, some people, particularly the Congress, were not very excited. For instance, the draft was passed by only one vote, and fortification of the Pacific Islands, such as Guam and Wake, was not funded until it was too late. This was a classic case of the fact that peace is only maintained with adequate strength.

The Japanese planned the initial phase in the greatest of detail. They had reached the moment of truth. With no raw materials inside their country to feed a large buildup of their military forces and no major export program, they could not expect to become a world power without ready access to raw materials elsewhere. They concluded that with the British practically on their knees, and with the United States likely to be forced into the war with Germany, it was time for Japan to expand its empire. The key plan of the Japanese became known as the Greater Southeast Asia Co-Prosperity Sphere Plan. Through execution of the plan the Japanese expected to acquire critical resources, all of which were in short supply. They had their eyes on rice in the Mekong Valley, oil in Borneo and Sumatra, and rubber and tin in both Sumatra and Malaya. The rubber was particularly valuable because synthetic rubber was not yet developed. Once having supplied their defense industry, they planned to turn east and secure the area west of a line drawn from the Aleutians, to Midway, and to the Fiji Islands. They planned for this line to act as a forward defense line against the United States as well as a means of controlling sea lanes from India, China, and Japan when and if required.

Although the British quickly lost the HMS *Repulse* and HMS *Prince of Wales* off the coast of Malaya to major air attack, the primary American defensive effort against the Japanese was focused on the Philippines. Army forces under General MacArthur were deployed in the vicinity of Manila, and ground forces were in the Bataan Peninsula and Corregidor. Naval forces under the command of Adm. T. C. Hart were known as the Asiatic Fleet. That fleet consisted of the heavy cruiser USS *Houston*, a flagship, several old four-stack destroyers, a squadron of submarines, and a patrol wing of PBY aircraft. In about three months that entire fleet, including the aircraft, was lost in battle. From the very start, Admiral Hart correctly judged that the situation was hopeless and suggested that American forces be withdrawn and saved for the battles that were to follow. In this he was overruled for political reasons. It was felt in Washington that since the Dutch had already been forced out of their homeland in Europe they should not be deserted at this time.

During the initial stages of the operations in the vicinity of Manila, there was little coordination between the army and the navy. General MacArthur declared Manila an open city, and shortly thereafter Admiral Hart ordered the Asiatic Fleet south to join the ABDA command, which was headquartered in Batavia. General Wavel was designated commander of this American, British, Dutch and Australian joint command. With limited combat capability, particularly fighter aircraft, the outcome would arrive quickly. After the Battle of Java Sea a mass evacuation was ordered by the remnants of the Allied force. Fleet Air Wing Ten, with about forty aircraft after reinforcement from Hawaii, finally made it to Perth, Australia, with only two flyable aircraft left. Ship losses were equally as high and included the old U.S. carrier *Langley*, recently converted to a seaplane tender. *Langley* was the first carrier in the United States Navy. The Japanese victory was complete. With the fall of the Dutch East Indies, the Greater Southeast Asia Co-Prosperity Sphere became a reality.

Intercepting and decoding radio communications throughout the war proved to be of overwhelming benefit to the United States forces. Vital information was picked off prior to Pearl Harbor as well as Midway, and the interpretation of these signals became a fine art. The intercept and shootdown of Admiral Yamamoto is another very important event that affected the course of the war.

At the very beginning, hours before Pearl Harbor was attacked, many messages were received that clearly indicated action was imminent. There has been a vigorous dispute over whether Admiral Kimmel and General Short were denied information that was available in Washington and the Philippines. If this is so, then Admiral Kimmel and General Short should have their original ranks restored to them. I am one who believes that to be the only fair thing to do. On that fateful, tense morning, why didn't Admiral Stark pick up the phone and call Admiral Kimmel? He said that he was waiting to clear the message with General Marshall. And where was General Marshall? He was out riding his horse. And why didn't General Marshall phone General Short? He finally sent the message by Western Union, and as the Western Union boy pedaled up to Admiral Kimmel's office with this vital message the sky was already filled with Japanese aircraft.

In four short months the Japanese had wrought major damage to the U.S. Naval Forces and seized thousands of square miles of ocean territory filled with critical raw materials. Furthermore, they accomplished this with minimum losses. As a matter of fact, they lost only three destroyers during the extended operations from

Pearl Harbor to Darwin, Australia, to the Indian Ocean, back to Japan. War games conducted before the war showed that they could expect to lose one-third of their fleet in the first four months. The interesting thing is that they were ready to accept such losses to acquire the territory they felt they must have. They were surprised at their success and concluded forthwith that they could go anywhere and defeat any foe. However, from the seizure of the southwest area to the remainder of the war, everything was downhill. Many of the Japanese military commanders became arrogant and overly confident, which became disastrous as the United States produced vast quantities of war material and learned to fight their determined enemy.

The year 1942 was a pivotal period in the Pacific war. It is hoped that as noted historians review the battles and engagements, invaluably aided by recollections of veterans of those actual engagements, history will not repeat itself.

— Adm. Thomas Moorer (Ret.), USN

Preface

New Year's Eve is a time of revelry. People celebrate with parties and toasts to the anticipated good fortunes of the coming year. Fireworks are sent high into the night sky, glasses are raised in toasts of health and prosperity, and voices cheerfully sing out the refrains of "Auld Lang Syne." Revelers fill the main streets of America, and the country enjoys one big party to bring in the new year with a bang.

On December 31, 1941, the new year was received with a different kind of bang: the sound of enemy guns resounding throughout the world. In Europe, Adolf Hitler and the Axis powers were close to the conquest of three continents. Fascism had enveloped most of Europe and was threatening to swallow Russia and Africa. All that had saved England from the expanding grasp of Hitler's minions were the valiant pilots of the Royal Air Force (RAF) and the Lend-Lease program whereby a battered and bloodied England and Russia received vital war materials and supplies from the United States.

In the Far East, Japan had accomplished several goals toward becoming a world superpower. Through military might, she had totally overwhelmed and defeated several nations, including Thailand and Manchuria. Her armies were gobbling up territory in Burma, China, Korea, and Russia. The air corps, army, and navy were poised at the throat of Singapore, Malaya, and the rest of the Dutch East Indies. In one of the most daring and audacious acts in modern history, Japan had unilaterally and unequivocally declared war on the United States by attacking the United States Pacific Fleet at Pearl Harbor, Hawaii, the United States Army in the Philippines, and had brought to submission the United States Marine Corps garrison on tiny Wake Island. The Empire of the Rising Sun had turned an eye toward Australia and was preparing to launch a strike against Darwin and other Australian holdings and British colonies and influences in the South Pacific.

Every inhabited continent and virtually every country in the world was at war. Peoples of all nations were fighting and dying on the battle lines of freedom, and no nation, no island, no population on earth was safe from the vice-grip of Hitler, Mussolini, or Tojo.

New Year's Eve of 1941 was not a time of rejoicing and exchanging wishes of health and prosperity for the coming year. The only thing promised for 1942 was despair, death, and a grim struggle to stop the fascist monsters.

Agreements to assist our European Allies were still being discussed, debated, and argued by leaders in Washington. British Prime Minister Winston Churchill was in Washington to try to sell the United States on supplying men and more material and equipment to the European theater. To what degree the United States would commit to a war in Europe was far from resolved.

But one fact was certain. Japan had drawn a line in the sand, and the United States was fully prepared to cross that line. Roosevelt moved ships, planes, and men to the Pacific with lightning speed. Ships were transferred from the Atlantic and from bases within the United States. Planes were located, repaired, salvaged, and immediately deployed to Pacific installations by any means possible. Men were moved west just as fast as trains, trucks, buses, cars, and ships could load them and head for the Pacific. Civilian production facilities were given government contracts overnight and retooled to supply the American war machine. It may not have been a year of joy and elation, but in 1942 Americans were going to damn sure guarantee that it would not be a year of defeat and domination.

The year 1942 was one of sacrifice, suffering, and bloodshed, but it was also a year of hope and optimism. It would be the most significant year in World War II. On all fronts, the Allies stalemated, and in some cases defeated, the Axis powers. Rommel's powerful Afrika Corps was stopped in North Africa, the Russians held the line at Stalingrad, and the Allies regrouped and began to shrink the Rising Sun. For the United States, 1942 was significant in several regards, most having to do with the war in the Pacific. The military learned how to fight. The air, land, and sea forces honed their skills and learned their lessons in the Pacific. These lessons would reap dividends in later crucial battles in the war, including the Normandy invasion in France. The United States (because of victories against the Japanese) changed from attitudes of defensiveness to attitudes of optimism and victory. These victories meant more than the mere gaining of ground. They showed the Japanese to be beatable, they opened vitally needed routes for supplies, equipment, and men, they taxed and wore down the Japanese war machine, and they prevented the Japanese from obtaining needed supplies and food to sustain its military machine. The United States forced Japan to significantly alter war plans and strategies.

By the end of 1942, Japan was no longer intent upon domination but wanted to merely retain what it had. The United States was on the offensive for good. America, not Japan, dictated the course of the war in the Pacific. And victories in the Pacific in 1942 allowed the United States to place a greater emphasis on the European theater. Actions in the Pacific made it possible for the United States to truly commit to a two-theater war.

The advantages gained in 1942 had a price tag attached. The Battles of Java and Coral Sea, the dissolution of the Allied joint command in the Pacific, the Battle of Midway, the invasion of New Guinea, and Guadalcanal were all fought at a premium price. These faraway places became household words and military legends. The public learned a new vocabulary with strange spellings and sounds. Corregidor, Bataan, Papua, Buna, Java, Balikpapan, Midway, Vella Lavella, Tassafaronga, and the Louisiades were just a few of the names permanently etched into American consciousness by American fighting men. The Pacific was no longer the idyllic white-sand beaches with hot, sunny days and star-filled nights. The Pacific became a proving ground and tomb for those Americans forced into the rites of passage. Japanese soldiers, sailors, and airmen also found their manhood tested in those places, for war touches all men equally. For every promise made by Imperial Japanese Headquarters, thousands of Japanese military men made good the marker with their lives.

The year 1992 marked the half-century point since those bleak days. Contained in those fifty years were two more wars, more evolutions in the techniques of warfare, the replacement of propellers with jets, floating ships that were larger than city blocks (and carried more men than small cities), and man's first walk on the moon. The black days of 1942 were long ago but seemed like yesterday. The survivors of those battles of the faraway places and strange-sounding names aged and went away with time, until there remained only a handful to pass on the tale of what happened in the Pacific.

At San Antonio, Texas, in March 1992, some of those survivors gathered to pass on that legacy. At a symposium co-sponsored by the Admiral Nimitz Museum, the Admiral Nimitz Foundation, the Texas Parks and Wildlife Department, the United States Naval Institute, and Pennzoil, men and women who played the hero's role in the momentous events of 1942 told of life in the Pacific in 1942. Titled "1942: 'Issue In Doubt,' " this symposium brought together the combatants of 1942 from all over the world. Soldiers, sailors, marines, and airmen from the United States, Australia, England, and Japan met, remembered, shared, and related their legacy of what fighting in the Pacific in 1942 was like.

This book is about that symposium. It is the book of those men and women, friend and foe. It is a book of their life in the Pacific theater in 1942, in their words. It is a book of the historians who provided the framework for the actions of 1942. Veterans and experts of virtually every major military action which occurred in the Pacific during 1942 are represented in these pages. They tell of the ABDA command, Battle of Java Sea, the fall of the Philippines, Wake Island, Battle of Coral Sea, the Doolittle raid on Tokyo, the Battle of Midway, the New Guinea campaign, and the fight for Guadalcanal. There are also the side stories of 1942, some of which have received very little attention and others of which have only come to light within the past few years. The reader will learn of the new form of naval warfare first seen in 1942, the agony of Death Railway (fictionalized in the novel and movie *Bridge on The River Kwai*), the saga of PatWing 10, and the ongoing controversy over cryptanalysis and its role at the Battle of Midway. No other book provides such an integrative view of the historic events of 1942. Many of the oral histories have been added to and expanded by the veterans and historians. This book will ensure that the legacy of the past is not lost to our future.

Can we afford to lose that legacy? Many have said (in one form or another) that the past is the key to our future, that what we have learned by history is that which will guide us in all the days to come. If we lose the past, we lose part of the future. The teachers of history are not those who write about it but those who live it. Historians may analyze, condense, summarize, and even revise our history, but they cannot teach us history. Only those who have lived history can do that.

This book is unique in regards to World War II in several respects. It is not a history book; it is a book about people who lived history. It is about the human dimension of 1942. Generals and admirals place pins on maps, historians use lines and arrows, to show the ebb and flow of battle. For every pin, line, and arrow, thousands of men and women fought, suffered, bled, and died.

The lessons to be learned from war are not the strategies and tactics. It is the individuals who pay the price to make the strategies and tactics work. In these pages reside that human drama, played out in military actions and victories won and lost. The reader is urged to read slowly in order to read the emotions of war. To the individual, war is emotions. It is dread, fear, terror, uncertainty, hope, joy, relief, and elation. The careful reader will see that range of emotions repeated endlessly within these pages.

Every person who fights a battle leaves a part of themselves on the battlefield and brings a piece of that battlefield home. In 1992, we know quite a bit about post traumatic stress disorder (PTSD), including causes, symptoms, and cures. We did not know about PTSD in 1942. For many of the veterans of World War II, they have suffered in silence for almost fifty years. The motivation for some of the veterans who participated in the symposium and this book was to experience the cure for PTSD, to exorcise some of the demons they have been carrying for half a century, and ultimately to return pieces of the battlefield to the Pacific. I hope they were successful.

A unique feature is the saga of the women caught in the South Pacific by the war. Histories, documentaries, and other references to the Pacific war have all but ignored these brave women. They were as much a part of 1942 as were the men who fought. Even today, with the emphasis on equality of the sexes and equal rights, the women who blazed this trail have been ignored. We do not remember the valiant women of that period who "broke the mold" to begin the long and hard process of assuring women an equal place alongside men. It is my hope that this book contributes to and helps resolve the ongoing battle.

Another unique feature of this book is the Japanese perspective. Of the very few oral histories available, the Japanese perspective has been ignored. It is not only interesting but vital to see and understand the picture of warfare from the viewpoint of the enemy combatant. The reader will see that the Japanese picture of the military actions is different from that of the Allies, but the emotions and agonies of war are the same. The Japanese soldier paid the price for the fallacies and idiocy of their commanders. The reader may be surprised to discover that the Japanese combatant, at least emotionally and psychologically, was no different from his Allied counterpart.

I am not a historian. In fact, I probably know less about World War II than any person who contributed to this book. I was neither a participant nor, as John Costello says, a rewriter of history. I am a reporter of the human drama which unfolded in 1942 and a collector of what the veterans and historians related. There will not be a complex array of footnotes and citations within these pages. The purpose is not to make the reader an expert in the tactical and strategic actions of 1942, but to make the reader aware of the human element of 1942. I have contributed little to this book. Some may argue that I have contributed anything to this book. I do not take that as an insult, rather as a compliment.

My job was twofold. I pulled together in a coherent manner the recollections of the participants of 1942 and the historians which provided the context for the experiences of the veterans. Some veterans' experiences needed contextual information supplied to make those experiences fit into the overall *gestalt* of 1942. Any errors of fact or omission are mine and mine alone.

It has been said that heroes are those who are afraid to go but go anyway. The veterans within these pages were heroes twice over: once in 1942 and again in 1992. To relive the horror of 1942 and share one's soul with a world of strangers takes a special kind of person.

Acknowledgments

This book would not have been possible without many other people whose names do not appear within these pages. My deepest gratitude is extended to Rear Adm. (Ret.) Charles D. Grojean (executive director of the Admiral Nimitz Foundation), Bruce H. Smith (superintendent of the Admiral Nimitz Museum), and the entire staff of the Admiral Nimitz Museum and Admiral Nimitz Foundation. They dropped other projects to assist, to collect and gather material, to answer an endless stream of ignorant questions, and performed numerous other tasks to make this book possible. I would especially like to thank Paula Ussery for her patience in assisting with the photos used in this book, Ruth Peeters for helping insure the proper spellings of place names, and Nancy Inman for assisting with the myriad small details (and for the bread). Thank all of you for making a difficult task infinitely easier. I would also like to thank Wayne Gordon, who teaches Japanese in San Antonio, Texas, for transcribing Mr. Shiro Hashimoto's presentation.

One person at the Admiral Nimitz Museum deserves special mention. Mrs. Helen B. McDonald deserves as much credit as I for bringing this book to publication. She was tireless and selfless in her efforts to assist me. She spent hours on the phone, talking to me and veterans around the world. She pushed, cajoled, encouraged, and occasionally placed a well-aimed boot at me to keep this project moving forward. Helen went "above and beyond" the call of duty to insure the completion of this project, including the feeding and TLC toward myself when I visited Fredericksburg. Helen provided guidance where necessary and inspiration when needed. I consider Helen a good friend and colleague and wish to thank her from the bottom of my heart for her assistance.

A special thanks also goes to all those who participated in making the pages of this book come alive with the drama of 1942. The veterans and historians who gave their time, effort, tears, fears, and joys to relate what 1942 was about deserve a special place in our hearts and minds.

I. 1942: The Pacific at War

The World at War: Overview of 1942

Dr. Walt Whitman Rostow was special assistant for National Security Affairs for both Presidents Kennedy and Johnson. During World War II, he served as a major in the Office of Strategic Services, the precursor to the Central Intelligence Agency. In 1969 Dr. Rostow returned to teaching at the University of Texas.

Dr. Walt Whitman Rostow

In my memory, the Second World War didn't turn around in a particular year, but on a particular day. On Sunday morning, November 8, 1942, nearly a half century ago, I played touch football in London with a group of friends who were also working with OSS, the Office of Strategic Services (forerunner to the Central Intelligence Agency). The place was Hyde Park, some distance down from the corner where all matter of opinions were being aired, war or no war. The weather was memorably mild with a slanting autumn sun. I don't remember any brilliant forward passes, long twisting runs, or other heroics. But I do remember that after the game, before heading back to our respective bachelor flats, that we talked a bit about recent events, and agreed that for the first time we were sure that, sooner or later, our side would win the war, for there were indeed heroics at work that week, from one end of the world to the other, from New Guinea west to North Africa.

The events that convinced us the Allies would ultimately make it were the fact that General Montgomery, having broken the German line at El Alamein on October 23, was on November 8 pursuing the remnants of Rommel's army at the Libyan border. The Anglo-American landings in Northwest Africa also took place on November 8, and the Russian counterattack at Stalingrad had begun and was going well. The naval victories in the Coral Sea and Midway in April and May, 1942, foreshadowed the turning point in the Pacific, which came about a week after our touch football game, when Guadalcanal was firmly held (around November 15), and the Japanese were stopped short of Australia, an outcome which was by no means inevitable. Nevertheless, the remarkable first page of *The New York Times* of November 8 reported that MacArthur was moving on Buna, in northern New Guinea. On the front page, in the left-hand corner, was MacArthur and Buna, and you got successively the Russians at Stalingrad, Rommel being chased, and over in the right-hand corner, the landings in North Africa. And that was the day that we played touch football.

After a war militarily won so decisively, it's easy to forget the tragic disarray in the global arena of battle, between the German assault on Poland in the late summer of 1939 and the great turnaround of 1942. With one exception, but only one, the grotesquely unprepared targets of Hitler and the Japanese military bought time by surrendering space and by surrendering people. It was an ugly, gut-wrenching process to endure. And in fact, the Second World War as a whole was a much closer and precarious affair than it appears in hindsight.

In Asia, the Allies, in a series of humiliating defeats, surrendered to the Japanese virtually all of Southeast Asia down to and including Singapore, and the critical Malacca Straits. The Chinese, having already fallen back on ChungKing, had surrendered the heavily populated coastal areas. In 1940 all of continental Europe was overrun, except Sweden, Switzerland, Spain, and Portugal. In 1941 and 1942 all of eastern Europe was consolidated by Hitler, and his forces stood before Leningrad, Moscow, and Stalingrad. In the Mediterranean, Greece was taken in 1941 and Rommel pushed the British out of Tobruk in June 1942. The British were backed up against Alexandria, Cairo, and the Suez Canal. The whole of the Middle East was up for grabs.

The one exception to this panorama of apparently ignominious retreat was a battle on which future Allied global victory depended, the Battle of Britain. Aside from keeping Britain in the war, that battle turned Hitler's ground forces to the east and above all it heartened and at long last unified America, making Lend-Lease possible and the ambitious American war production goals set in mid-1941. Early in 1940, about seventy percent of Americans indicated they supported aid for the Allies, if such support did not involve the risk of war. By the time of the November 1940 election, about seventy percent supported aid to the Allies at the risk of war. The gallant young men of the RAF and the stubborn performance of the British people under Churchill's leadership in the face of heavy and protracted area bombing attacks were largely responsible for this shift.

I said these retreats were apparently ignominious because, on the whole, the time they bought was well used to prepare the stage for the turnaround of 1942 and the subsequent Allied offensives, which drove to the heart of Germany and Japan. Consider the following four factors.

First, and perhaps most fundamental, was the full mobilization of American industrial power for war production purposes, a process in which the great Frenchman Jean Monnet, working with the British supply mission in Washington, having also gained the confidence of Franklin Roosevelt and Harry Hopkins, played a critical role. The surge of American production over the next year and beyond made possible the survival of Russia and the British forces in the Middle East, as well as the dispatch in mid-1942 of the first elements in the United States Eighth Air Force to be based in Britain.

Second, there was also the far-sighted gamble of Winston Churchill. A remarkable gamble, really, to send major armored forces to the Middle East in the summer of 1940, when the German invasion of Britain seemed a real and imminent danger.

Third, there was the build-up of methods to protect convoys as well as radically to expand merchant ship production, which permitted Anglo-American forces to hold the German submarine offensive at bay. Although it was an extraordinarily later combination of baby aircraft carriers, British flying boats, and ultraintelligence that definitively set back the submarine threat, which had been mortally dangerous, the convoys at first braved the German U-boats to deliver desperately needed supplies to the Allies in Europe.

Finally, there was the survival of sufficient Chinese nationalist and communist forces in the Asian interior to pin down considerable Japanese forces despite preparations by both Chinese factions for the postwar showdown they knew would come.

The stalemate created by these holding actions permitted the 1942 turnaround, which will forever be associated with El Alamein, Algiers, Stalingrad, and Guadalcanal.

It took more than two and a half years of hard and bloody fighting beyond November 8, 1942, to achieve the victory foreshadowed on that day.

In the Pacific, the offensive against Japan was launched in earnest in July 1943, and thereafter sustained until Japanese surrendered. It was an offensive with three major dimensions: Nimitz's brilliant island hopping; progressively more effective submarine attacks on Japanese shipping; and a devastating strategic bombing campaign climaxed by the attacks on Hiroshima and Nagasaki.

In Europe, against the background of heavy attrition of German forces and Russian forward movement on the Eastern front, the Allied counteroffensive was gradually developed by air power and the Mediterranean campaigns to the point where the direct assault on western Europe mainland could at last be undertaken. This preparatory stage was concluded in the final week of 1943, when daylight air supremacy over central Germany was established, guarantying full air control over the Normandy beachheads in June and permitting the use of the Anglo-American air force to support the ground offensive with attack on German oil and transport facilities, notably the Seine-Loire bridges.

The defeat of Germany was accomplished in the spring of 1945, after the western Allies failed to seek a decision in 1944, thus permitting Soviet forces to hold the territory of Poland and much land further to the west on V-E Day, laying the basis for the cold war.

As victory against Japan was completed, the Soviet Union moved into a commanding position in Manchuria and moved down to the 38th Parallel in Korea.

The moment of American assumption as role of senior partner in Europe can clearly be dated from January and February of 1944, although American forces engaged in western Europe were outnumbered by the British until sometime after D-Day. With the movement of General Eisenhower's headquarters to Britain from North Africa, in preparation for Operation Overlord, and the rapid buildup of the American forces for the invasion, the central fact became apparent that the United States, which up to that time had been distinctly a junior partner in the Allied enterprise in western Europe, and to a lesser degree in the Mediterranean, was assuming unambiguous primacy in the Allied effort. This position was reinforced by the success of the American air forces in achieving daylight supremacy over Germany in February 1944, a result many British and some American experts believed to be impossible.

Such was roughly the framework of the Second World War. It left the United States an unchallenged leader of a coalition which dominated the seas, western Europe to the Elbe, and the colonial empire of western European states. But it left the fate of central and eastern Europe and of China not merely unsettled, but already dangerously embroiled with communist power.

At the beginning of 1943, at Casablanca, Admiral King had said, "In the European theater, Russia was most advantageously placed for dealing with Germany in view of her geographic position and manpower. In the Pacific, China bore a similar relation to the Japanese, and it should be our basic policy to provide the manpower and resources of Russia and China with the necessary equipment to enable them to fight." In fact, the American roles that emerged were not as insular and naval as King's 1943 prescription for victory. Large American ground forces were engaged, as well as the navy, and the American battles were fought deep within Eurasia as well as on the island approaches. But the timing of the American build-up and the instinct to conserve American lives converged with ambiguities about the conditions for postwar peace, to grant the nation only a dilute victory, from which the cold war quite promptly emerged.

Now I turn for a few lessons for the present and the future. Military historians so minded are likely to argue indefinitely over whether the cold war could have been avoided had Eisenhower insisted firmly that Montgomery capture and open the port of Antwerp, or backed a single united thrust across Germany in 1944, or approved the air attack on German oil installations in March rather than May 1944.

I would not deny my fellow academic historians their innocent sport. But the issues posed for reflection by the story of the Second World War are more profound and will bear on the nation's future.

First is the extraordinary delay before the American people accepted the fact that the emergence to power of the Japanese military and of Hitler posed mortal dangers to the American national interest. The illusion that there could be safety in isolation persisted for some down to Pearl Harbor itself. The history of the United States in the twentieth century suggests strongly that all of us, and especially those who will live a good part of their lives in the twenty-first century, should come to national consensus on the nature of our national interests if we are to transit the decades ahead successfully. For there may not again be a Great Britain to hold the line until we come to our senses and rearm.

In fact, if we run the twentieth century over without the soundtrack, no rhetoric, no speeches, no newspaper editorials, or even academic books on foreign policy, and if we simply observe when the United States acted, with purpose and vigor to defend the national interests, a quite clear and consistent *de facto* definition of the national interest emerges.

We have acted consistently to assure that no single nation or coalition dominate the balance of power in Europe or Asia, and thereby gain control of the Atlantic or Pacific; that no major external power emplace itself in this hemisphere with substantial military force; and that we deter the use of weapons of mass destruction against ourselves or others. We're also committed ideologically by the very nature of this society to advance the cause of economic and social development of human rights and political democracy.

When the chips were down, when we were under acute threat, we acted to defend these interests. But we have not been notably forehanded. We have tended to live by Samuel Johnson's great principle, which he stated in the eighteenth century, "Depend upon it, sir. When a man know's he's to be hanged in a fortnight, it concentrates his mind wonderfully." Indeed, we even resisted accepting the fact that like other nations we had abiding interests. When Churchill said, as he often did, that the Second World War was "the unnecessary war," he had in mind above all that there would have been no war had the United States recognized its interest in the mid-1930s, as it saw them in, say, 1942.

This is not the occasion to describe my conception of the post-cold war world and the task of protecting our interests in that environment. I confine myself to a few simple propositions.

The world around us, with power and technological skill defusing away from Moscow and Washington, is evidently capable of chaos and violence. We can see it in many parts of the world right now. But there are also hopeful possibilities on every continent, which could in time lead to a state of reasonable order.

Stable order in the regions requires that the major political problems be settled; that effective arms control levels be set, which render grossly irrational any thrust for regional hegemony; and in this setting, that concerted measures be undertaken in support of economic and social progress, human rights, and democratic political practice. To move in these directions, the United States must evidently work steadily and stubbornly with others who share our conception of world order, for we are not, and will not be, a superpower which can decree these results from Washington. What we are is the critical margin. And without the strength and will and coalition leadership of the critical margin, order is not likely to be established.

And, of course, we must also reverse aggression, as we did at great cost in Korea and the Persian Gulf. But the measure of success from now forward will be the prevention of aggression. That is the greatest lesson of the Second World War and indeed the lesson of the twentieth century as a whole. If you look back at the twentieth century, it consists in very large part of the struggle to defeat the Kaiser's effort to establish hegemony in Europe. Then we had a miserable and ineffective interwar period. Then we had to deal with Hitler and his effort to do the same, and then the Japanese military after Pearl Harbor. That war ended in such a way that it led directly to a cold war in which we had to deal with the Soviet and communist efforts as global hegemony. It took forty-five years. And that's a hell of a way to spend a century. And we ought to do better.

To prevent aggression, we must not only be clear about our national interests, not only effective in helping move a world of diffuse power toward order, but we must also remain reasonably well armed — not extravagantly, but reasonably. For we must never again let ambitious leaders judge the United States irrelevant, as did the German Kaiser, Hitler, and the Japanese military.

The Empire Expands

Adm. (Ret., United States Navy) Thomas H. Moorer graduated from the Naval Academy in 1933 and was at Pearl Harbor on December 7, 1941. He served in a PBY squadron. Later he served throughout the Pacific during World War II. He is the only officer in United States Navy history to serve as both chief of naval operations and as chairman of the Joint Chiefs of Staff. He is also the only navy officer to have ever commanded both the Atlantic and Pacific fleets. Admiral Moorer was heavily involved in those events in the dark days of early 1942.

Retired Admiral Moorer will provide a brief overview of why Japan entered the war and why they took such a large gamble by attacking the American Pacific Fleet at Pearl Harbor. Many have questioned why a small island nation such as Japan would have the audacity and elan to take on not only the United States but the entire Allied combine in the Pacific. From his first-person interviews and work with key Japanese government officials and military planners, Admiral Moorer provides an answer to this question.

Adm. Thomas H. Moorer, USN (Ret.)

I think it is very important that we go very carefully through what has occurred during the last fifty years in order that history will be correct. And we must do that at a time when we can have access to the people that actually made the history, because today there are many people who are trying to rewrite history and the effect of it is to demean and degrade, in some cases, what the United States has done over the years as we have progressed. So it's very important that history be accurate.

I decided I will review a very interesting and, I think, challenging experience that I had after the war, which relates to the beginning of the war. I was appointed as a thirty-two-year-old commander as a member of the Strategic Bombing Survey. The Strategic Bombing Survey had been created by President Roosevelt to look at Europe. But then President Truman took it up and sent a group to Japan, and I was a member of that group. Our staff included industrialists, military personnel, and social and medical experts. We were about 300 strong and were supplied with a large staff of interpreters and excellent typists. We lived aboard the USS *Ancon*, which during more peaceful days had shuttled between Panama and New York. We conducted most of our meetings in the Mejii Building. We were charged with looking at just about every aspect of their society — the military, economic, industrial, health, the food situation, and so on. Paul Nitze, later the secretary of the navy and deputy secretary of defense, was the executive director. We had people like Ambassador Galbraith, who was an economy specialist and used to be at one time ambassador to India. He looked at their economy. We studied the whole panorama of Japanese life.

Now we were also, in the military group, told to ask the Japanese why they got into war, why they attacked Pearl Harbor, how they went about planning such an operation, and additional details such as that. While we were doing this investigation, we were provided with subpoena power and were given number-one priority on all airlines. We were therefore able to bring credible witnesses from Singapore, the Philippines, Hong Kong, anytime during the course of the studies we came across an individual's name. If he was alive we sent for him. That was, I think, one of the most interesting things I did during my entire career.

We began our interrogations by looking at the prewar planning. In the first place, the Japanese noticed that the British were heavily involved in other parts of the world, and that in the United States we had many isolationists. They didn't think too much of what we would do in the event they got in the war.

The Japanese were vitally in need of four commodities: namely oil, tin, rubber, and rice. And consequently, they set up a plan to literally seize the source of those commodities in Southeast Asia. The Japanese had not one single oil well and consequently were interested in Java, Sumatra, and Borneo. The rubber from Malaya was vital for a military machine, there being no synthetic rubber at that time. The Mekong Valley in Vietnam at that time was producing six million tons of rice, which Japan needed to feed its population.

The Japanese were going to do this by a three-pronged attack: one to the east, to the Celebes down through the Makassa Straits, and then to the west, where they were going to take French Indochina, Singapore, etc. They wanted to control the sea lanes between the Pacific and Indian oceans. So far as the attack on Pearl Harbor was concerned, they were going to use a force of six carriers. They planned the Pearl Harbor attack in a briefcase, which meant that the Pearl Harbor attack was never mentioned on the radio.

There was much dispute within the Japanese high command over going to war with the United States. However, General Tojo had complete political control and he overrode Yamamoto, who insisted that it would be impossible to defeat the United States. He did agree, however, to go forward with the plan and put together the details for the Pearl Harbor attack.

Pearl Harbor as it appeared on the morning of October 30, 1941. Few people realized the maelstrom in the Pacific would originate here in just over one month. *Photo source unknown, print courtesy of Admiral Nimitz Museum*

The attack force left the inland sea of Japan on the second day of November, went north to the Kuriles to an anchorage called Hitokapu, and from there proceeded to the east, north of the shipping lanes, and then turned south to a point 200 miles due north of Pearl Harbor. We did find out that they had orders that if they were discovered anytime two days before the attack, they were to turn around and return.

In the meantime, the other force, the invasion force, headed south. The Japanese set up so that they could take their aircraft with them and only make short advances, stop and build an airfield, move the fighters in, and then move to the next step. They were successful, and by March they had control of these resources. They went into such detail that they had, in effect, designated *quislings*, or directors of each country, in advance. They had gone down and made arrangements with these individuals so that the whole operation would move smoothly, and they didn't have to spend all their time trying to set up a government control of the area that they had captured.

It is interesting what the Japanese did with the carriers that attacked Pearl Harbor after they had left from the attack. They sent two of them to Wake Island to assist in the capture of Wake. The Japanese had made some unsuccessful attempts to capture Wake, so they provided additional air support for that invasion. The other four proceeded south to attack Darwin, Australia. In addition to that, they were then to proceed south of Java and Sumatra, which they did, and support these invasion operations in the event support was needed. Support was not needed. However, in the process, they did spot ships that were being evacuated from the Dutch East Indies area and sank, among others, the USS *Langley*, which was our first aircraft carrier. As a matter of fact, I was assigned to the *Langley* as my first duty assignment after I finished flight training in 1936. But she was sunk and there was a great loss of life. She should not have been sunk.

The Japanese carriers then proceeded to Ceylon [what is now Sri Lanka] and they sank the *Hermes* [British carrier] and also the *Duke of Glouster* [cruiser]. Many people will ask the question, "Well, why didn't they keep going?" Don't forget that now we are in April [1942] and they had commenced operations in November the preceding year, in 1941. The admiral [Yamamoto] turned the task force around, and they headed back through the Malacca Straits and then on into Japan.

They were all ready to certainly give a rousing welcome to this successful effort. The Japanese were in a state of euphoria as to what they had done. They were real great at war-gaming. When they war-gamed this entire operation, it worked out that they were going to lose one-third of their fleet. As a matter of fact, they only lost three destroyers, sunk by Dutch submarines, plus maybe a hundred aircraft, maybe sixty or seventy of those at Pearl Harbor. So you can see that they had the idea that they had unlimited strength and that they were going to succeed in everything they had planned.

Well, about that time, when they were getting into this mindset, along comes Mr. James Doolittle with the B-25s that were launched from the *Hornet*. Colonel Doolittle's planes overflew the Japanese mainland and caused psychological and political havoc. Now, Admiral Yamamoto and General Tojo were always having a little difference of opinion. General Tojo's entire experience had been in China, and consequently he judged the entire world, and particularly the industrial complex, as just like that in China. Admiral Yamamoto, on the other hand, had been to Germany, Italy, the United States, and England, and so that is why he tried to prevent, I think, the war. But once the decision was made to go ahead with it, he went into it with vim and vigor, and of course was in charge of this big naval operation.

In any event, they had lost very few aircraft. They had certainly been successful, and so they returned and were ready to move east to a line extending from the Aleutians to Midway and on down to the Guadalcanal area.

When Colonel Doolittle came over, that kicked off the Midway operation, because Tojo said that was the island where the planes came from. Admiral Yamamoto said they came from an aircraft carrier. But Tojo was determined to capture Midway and the plans were made. In their haste to attack Midway, the Japanese were forced to resort to radio transmissions which the United States intercepted. Admiral Nimitz called all forces back from the Guadalcanal area to Pearl Harbor to obtain necessary repairs, and then to the Midway area to engage the enemy. An interesting fact at that time concerned the USS *Enterprise*. The *Enterprise* had been so heavily damaged at the Battle of Coral Sea that it was necessary to place navy yard workers aboard to ride the ship as far as French Frigate Shoals.

What were the lessons learned? Certainly, Japan must have learned that it's fatal to plan a short war. They made no effort whatsoever to train replacements. This meant that if you were on a Japanese destroyer at the beginning of the war and the destroyer survived until the end of the war, you were still aboard the same ship. Consequently, when the first group was killed (pilots in particular) at Midway, that finished them. And Japan did not set up any stockpile of critical material, either. So toward the end of the war, their production, for all practical purposes, was zero. The other thing they learned was quality control, and they've certainly put that into effect in recent years.

From the point of view of the United States and the Allies (Britain, Holland, and Australia), they certainly learned a bitter lesson, and that is that peace only comes from adequate strength. It was my observation that only a small force with adequate air cover would have been capable of thwarting the Japanese invasion to the south, and as the Japanese themselves said, the perception of a weak United States perhaps would not have prevailed.

This perception was based upon the Japanese observation of three things. First, the Congress refused to fortify Wake and Guam islands. Second, the United States passed the Draft Law by only one vote. And third, the United States Army was training in Louisiana with wooden guns. Consequently, the Japanese came to the conclusion that they could get away with a short war simply by attacking the United States Fleet in Pearl Harbor and preventing it from interfering with the seizure of the raw materials in Southeast Asia.

Setting the Stage: Avalanche of Disaster

The early days of 1942 in the Pacific were some of the darkest a free world has ever faced. Even the German Blitzkrieg in Europe could not compare with Japanese victories in the early months of 1942. Every move by the Allies, every line of defense, and every military movement was easily thwarted by a relentless Japanese push to obtain their objectives.

John Costello has summarized the darkest days of World War II. He encapsulates the power of the Japanese against an ineffective and politically blundering Allied force. His narrative covers the period from December 22, 1941, through May 7, 1942, when at last the Allies gained a small measure of victory at Coral Sea.

John Costello was educated at Cambridge as a historian. He is a former producer for the BBC and has written several books on the War in the Pacific, including *The Pacific War*, *Virtue Under Fire*, and with Adm. Edwin Layton and Roger Pineau, *And I Was There*. He is an expert on Allied intelligence gathering.

John Costello

Once again I represent the British position in the Pacific War, which we in Britain have conveniently forgotten about, and which I've spent the last ten years trying to remind the United States about. I'd like to take you back to the hours immediately after Pearl Harbor, which is where the avalanche of disaster began. Churchill, that night, as he recorded in his memoirs, said he went to bed and slept the sleep of the "saved and thankful," because we had won after all. He was confident that the shotgun marriage forced by the Japanese, of British grit and United States resources, would quickly establish military dominance over the Axis powers. But when Churchill and his entourage arrived in Washington on December 22, 1942, there were no victories to chalk up, none in sight, and only the somber prospect of disaster to survey. The only cheer amidst the grim reports from the Far East was the news that the Red Army had halted the German advance on Moscow with the Panzer divisions twenty miles from the snow-covered towers of the Kremlin.

December 22 happened to be the very day that Wake Island was finally forced to surrender. This lonely outpost in the Pacific had been the sole holdout against an initial wave of Japanese conquest initiated on December 7 by the Pearl Harbor raid. In quick succession, Malaya had been invaded, and the decimation of Gen. Douglas MacArthur's air power at Clark Field had doomed the Philippines. Guam had fallen next day. Within hours of the Japanese assault, Hong Kong was under heavy siege, and the Japanese had moved into the Gilbert and Ellice islands.

On the morning of December 10, shortly before the Japanese bombers set out to seal their initial triumph by sinking the British battleship *Prince of Wales* and her consort, the battlecruiser *Repulse*,[1] off the east coast of Malaya, the unbroken tide of victory had been shaken by the small Wake garrison. Against overwhelming odds, Maj. James Devereux's sharp-shooting marines had set a cruiser ablaze, and incredibly blasted a destroyer in two. The Japanese were forced to retire. The small marine garrison had racked up an astonishing victory which gave a badly needed boost to the morale of the American nation in its hour of national calamity.

Holding on to Wake, Midway, and Samoa became the linchpin of the Pacific Fleet strategy, and a relief expedition set out from Pearl Harbor supported by two carrier task forces. But it was delayed by command confusion and caution after Adm. Husband E. Kimmel was relieved as CINCPAC in mid-operation. The relief force was still a day's hard steaming short of Wake on December 22, when the Japanese arrived to land a force of over a thousand, which rapidly overwhelmed the 200-strong marine garrison. "The heroic defense," as Roosevelt called the marines' stand at Wake, had demonstrated that the Japanese were not nearly so invincible as the early reports coming in from the Philippines and Malaya and Hong Kong made them seem.

That day, Gen. Mashaharu Homma's 14th Army had pulled ashore at Lingayen Gulf, routing three divisions of Philippine infantry and a cavalry regiment[2] MacArthur was counting on to execute his ill-judged beach defense strategy. As the Japanese advanced rapidly toward the Philippine capital, MacArthur cabled a dire warning that unless he received more fighter planes and American regulars, not only the Philippines but the whole Allied position in the southwest Pacific would collapse. "Councils of termidity based upon theories of safety first," he predicted, "will not win against such an aggressive and audacious adversary as Japan."

The newly appointed director of war plans, Gen. Dwight D. Eisenhower, however, cautioned the U.S. Army chief of staff, Gen. George C. Marshall, that trying to fight any reinforcement through to the Philippines would take months now that the navy was so hard-pressed in the Pacific. He feared that this might be "longer than the garrison could hold out with any dribble of assistance if the enemy committed major forces to their reduction."

MacArthur was left in no doubt about the ominous scale of the Japanese assault next day when he toured the front. With his Luzon Army being rolled back to Manila at an alarming rate, he swallowed his pride and resurrected the original war plan that he had overturned in November, which called for fighting retreat to the Bataan Peninsula. News that another large Japanese force was coming ashore at Lamon Bay, in the west of Luzon, persuaded him to evacuate the Philippine capital and transfer his staff to the fortress island of Corregidor in Manila Bay.

It was against this grim background of defeat and looming disaster that the British and American chiefs of staff assembled in the White House on December 23 to set the strategic priorities for the Allied war effort. Churchill had chosen *Arcadia* as the code name for this first joint war council, hoping that its illusion to the land of pastoral tranquility of Greek myth would be symbolic of the harmony of their joint endeavor.

It was to prove a bitterly ironic title, for though the president and the prime minister enjoyed a remarkable affinity of purpose, the newly allied military leadership did not. Unlike Adm. Harold R. Stark, the chief of naval operations who had been the architect of the so-called Europe First U.S. Rainbow 5 Strategic War Plan, Adm. Ernest J. King, the newly appointed commander in chief of the United States Fleet, was no Anglophile. His experiences in World

War I had taught him to distrust the British, and he was determined not to capitulate to dictated strategies that would downgrade the Pacific. Winning the war against the Japanese, he saw, would depend upon naval operations.

The army staff were no less partisan in appreciating that winning the war against Nazi Germany must inevitably call for a land campaign. They were therefore disposed to concentrate on the Atlantic theater as called for in the 1940 war plan. United States Army Chief George C. Marshall was broadly in agreement with the British priorities, whereas King and the United States Navy were very sensitive to seeing any of their forces committed to the propping up of the Imperial British possessions in the Far East.

The United States chiefs of staff were also sensitized that the British prime minister had moved into the White House, lock, stock, and traveling map room. From his second-floor bedroom he was exercising a powerful influence on their commander in chief, Roosevelt, in late night "tête-à-têtes," as he called them. Churchill and his staff had taken the precaution of working up a strategic plan, which was based on getting American support for a Mediterranean campaign to meet Stalin's demands for opening up a second front in Europe. He wanted American troops to garrison northern Ireland, thereby releasing British forces to fight in North Africa, while American bombers would join the RAF [Britain's Royal Air Force] in laying waste the industrial heartland of the Third Reich. Whatever resources were left over, and there were precious little, could be deployed to assist the "stand on the defensive" in the Far East. British forces in Singapore, he assured Roosevelt, could hold out for six months, thereby denying Japan access to the oil supplies of the Dutch East Indies and winning time for reinforcements to be sent through to Burma to defend the overland supply route to China.

The president, to the dismay of his own military staff, appeared to agree with Churchill's broad strategic vision of how the war should be fought. As Gen. Joseph Stillwell, then with Army War Plans, acidly observed of Roosevelt's posture, "The Limeys have his head while we have his left tit." On Christmas Eve the British were delighted, therefore, to hear Admiral Stark reiterating the Europe First commitment: "Our view remains that Germany is still the prime enemy and her defeat is the key to victory. Once Germany is defeated, the collapse of Italy and the defeat of Japan must follow."

But the furious protests of the secretary of war [Henry Stimson], however, insured that Churchill did not get the strategic Christmas present of MacArthur's diverted troop convoy that he had hoped that he had persuaded on Christmas Eve should be sent to Malaya. His Washington Christmas was filled with the news that Hong Kong had fallen. But when the prime minister addressed a joint session of Congress on December 26, he succeeded brilliantly in what one spectator called "the reading of the banns" on the Anglo-American nuptials. Churchill's inspiring rhetoric may have carried the day, but hammering out the terms of this marriage contract was to take more than three weeks of arduous staff work, while the president and prime minister turned to drafting the euphonious "Declaration of the War Aims of the United Nations." In deference to Stalin's refusal to declare war on Japan, any mention of the third member of the Axis was left out of the declaration.

After kicking "like bay steers," the British finally gave in to the American demand of a single unified Allied command. On February 5, when Gen. Sir Archibald Wavell was informed that he was to head up ABDA [American, British, Dutch, Australian] forces against Japan, one British commander in India stoically commented, "I have heard of men having to hold the baby, but this is quadruplets." Not only was he faced with the impossible task of defending a front of over 2,000 miles against a well-oiled Japanese military machine with disgruntled and inadequate forces of four nations, but he also had to create a liaison with Chiang Kai-shek, the nationalist leader who had been designated the supreme allied commander in China, Siam, and Indochina.

When Wavell arrived in Singapore on January 5, en route to take up his command at the ABDA headquarters in Java, Gen. Tomoyuki Yamashita's were pedaling down the arterial highways that the British had built to service the Malaya rubber plantations in a "bicycle blitzkrieg" that was already advancing southward at a rate of over twenty miles a day.

Across the South China Sea and the Philippines, MacArthur's forces were also in full, but a rather more disciplined, retreat. MacArthur was redeeming his disastrous earlier failure with a brilliantly executed "Far Eastern Dunkirk" that extricated his two Luzon armies from the Japanese pincer movement. By the end of the first week of January, 80,000 American and Filipino troops were digging into the first of the prearranged Bataan defense lines. But because of MacArthur's earlier dispersal of their supplies in support of his beach defense strategy which had failed, they were left with the resources to hold out for only a month, instead of the six months invisaged by the original Orange War Plan.[3]

Ensconced in the fortified military tunnel on Corregidor, MacArthur began bombarding Washington with urgent appeals for an American sea thrust to get munitions and food through to the troops on Bataan. But the Asiatic Fleet, now part of the ABDA command, such as it was, had already written off the Philippines to concentrate on the defense of what was called at the time the Malay Barrier. The chief of naval operations advised the president there were just not enough transport ships available to send more reinforcements to MacArthur, even if the Pacific Fleet could muster the carrier task forces to fight a convoy through to the Philippines. But this did not stop Roosevelt from radioing Manuel Quezon on Corregidor that "every available vessel is bearing . . . the strength that will eventually crush the enemy."

Marshall also reassured MacArthur that "the rapid development of an overwhelming air power on the Malay Barrier will cut the Japanese communications south of Borneo and permit an assault in the southern Philippines." His wishful thinking appears to have ignored Eisenhower's January 3 report that fighting a relief convoy through would be completely unjustified. After reading this report, Secretary of War Henry Stimson solemnly observed, "There are times when men have to die."

"Help is definitely on the way. We must hold out until it arrives," MacArthur declared to his troops on Bataan after being buoyed up by these empty promises from Washington. It turned out to be his first and last visit to the front. When the promised stream of ships and aircraft failed to materialize, he eventually realized that he had been misled and betrayed by Washington. The general was so ashamed at having let his men down that he never faced them again and became the target of their excoriations in the famous dirges that began "Dugout Doug."

To reassure the Australians, Roosevelt promised to send 20,000 troops across the Pacific and 50,000 more if the Philippines fell. Churchill had assured Roosevelt that Singapore, the so called "Gibraltar of the Far East," could withstand a six-month siege. But it was now obvious that this was not going to happen.

The first operational phase put Japan's plan to drive the Europeans from Southeast Asia, now the Philippines and Malaya, firmly in its grip. On January 11, invasion forces landed on the northern coast of Borneo and paratroops dropped by air on Celebes. By the beginning of February, the exploratory tentacles of the Japanese octopus were being pushed out north from Thailand into British-ruled Burma. They encountered little resistance. Only a single Indian army division, trained rather appropriately for desert warfare when they were actually fighting in jungles, stood guard over the strategic highway of the Sittang Valley, along which the Allied supplies moved up to the mountain passes and into China. Japan's 15th Army quickly started rolling back these demoralized and badly coordinated defenders. The Japanese army advanced over a hundred miles in just two weeks. "The Japanese were in top gear and overdrive," the British commander said as he described his own fighting operation as a nightmare campaign.

With the Japanese forces on land and sea advancing on all fronts, communications bedeviled the ABDA naval operations, which began on January 24 with a night attack on the oil port of Borneo at Balikpapan. Two United States Navy cruisers and four destroyers missed a golden opportunity to wipe out an enemy invasion fleet, and the Japanese campaign on Borneo rolled ahead without hesitating for a single day.

Any inclination for ABDA to celebrate the sinking of three troop transports that night was wiped out the next day by the news from Malaya that Gen. Arthur Percival had ordered the final retreat to Singapore. Troopships carrying a British and Australian division had just docked, but even these reinforcements did not reassure Churchill, who claimed to have just discovered that the vaunted "Gibraltar of the Far East" had no landward defenses. With the enemy pushing forward toward the muddy waters of the Johore Strait, a shocked prime minister claimed that "the possibility of Singapore having no landward defenses no more entered my mind than that of a battleship being launched without a bottom."

The prime minister immediately ordered that the city of Singapore must be converted into a citadel. Everyone was to take up picks and shovels. They were to fight to the death. The prospect of "a British scuttle while the Americans fought so stubbornly on Corregidor," the prime minister told the chiefs of staff, was "terrible to imagine."

The Japanese were in fact marching across Southeast Asia on a veritable trail of broken promises. "Help is on the way from the United States. Thousands of troops and hundreds of planes are be-

ing dispatched," MacArthur continued assuring GIs on the Abucay
Line (Bataan) from the safety of his bomb-proof shelter in the
Malinta Tunnel on Corregidor. But when no friendly planes and no
additional food arrived to supplement the starvation rations, the resistance began caving in. A sustained offensive of 5,000 Japanese
troops on January 20 punctured the first line of MacArthur's defense line. And before it collapsed, he had ordered a fighting withdrawal to the Mariveles Mountain Line.

"I have personally selected and prepared this position, and it is
strong," MacArthur radioed Marshall. "I intend to fight to complete
destruction." But the general's declaration was to echo less than valiantly two weeks later when he supported President Quezon's request for a declaration of Philippine's neutrality. Washington's failure to send reinforcements, Quezon told Roosevelt by cable from
his sickbed in the Malinta Tunnel, had doomed the Philippines to
almost total extinction. The suggestion of surrender, which
MacArthur had tacitly backed, came only a month after he'd received a half-million-dollar honorarium from the Philippine trea-
sury, in recognition of his "magnificent defense." Therefore, this
new message landed like a bombshell in the White House. The president responded immediately by emphatically denying Quezon's request, while Marshall reminded General MacArthur in no uncertain
terms that there was "to be no talk of surrender so long as there
remains any possibility of resistance."

But the United States chiefs of staff were now resigned to the
eventual loss of the Philippines. MacArthur's stand was seen as a
way of forcing the Japanese to commit more resources to the battle,
and thereby delay the southward advance long enough to try and
prop up the defense of the Dutch East Indies and the approach to
Australia. What forces the United States Navy was able to muster
had to be concentrated on keeping open the lifeline for the United
States across the Pacific.

On February 1, 1942, the Pacific Fleet delivered its first coun-
terpunches, six months earlier than the Japanese had predicted. Carrier air strikes against the Marshall Islands, from Rear Adm. William
F. Halsey's *Enterprise*, turned Kwajalein Atoll into a miniature Pearl
Harbor, while 300 miles to the south, Rear Adm. Frank Jack Fletcher's *Yorktown* task force hit Makin. These raids, as we shall see,
threw Admiral Yamamoto's strategic calculations off balance, but
they did nothing to halt the relentless tide of Japanese conquest.

The day after the Marshall Island raid, the last British soldiers retreated from Malaya and the causeway linked to Singapore was dynamited. A week later, when Tomoyuki Yamashita's troops came swarming across, supported by tanks and heavy artillery, they found that the charges of dynamite had been miscalculated and they could walk across at low tide. By dawn on February 8, 30,000 enemy troops had overrun the front line of the Singapore Island defenses, though they were manned by more than twice the number of British and Australian troops. Overhead, waves of unchallenged Japanese bombers rained destruction down on the defenders and sank evacuation vessels carrying civilians out from the harbor.

"The battle must be fought to the bitter end and senior officers should die with their troops," Churchill cabled Wavell on February 10. But it was too late. General Percival did not learn until Yamashita had bluffed him into surrendering on February 14 that Singapore's defenders had not only outnumbered their attackers by more than two to one, but the Japanese had actually run out of ammunition. The bayoneting of prisoners and the rape of the city by Japanese troops added to the humiliation and disgrace of what Churchill called "the greatest disaster and capitulation in British history."

Taking stock of what the prime minister had categorized as the "cataract of disaster" engulfing ABDA, Wavell had sent the prime minister a grim strategic prognosis predicting the imminent loss of Java, which was only defended by a single Dutch division. He recommended that no attempt be made to reinforce the Dutch East Indies, since this might compromise the defense of Burma and Australia.

The fate of Burma had already been decided by the Australian prime minister, who recalled a division of troops that had been on its way to Rangoon. When the news reached Canberra of the fall of Singapore, panic set in, and the retreating Indian army division in Burma was routed on the Sittang River on February 21. This collapse was followed in short order by the February 18 bombing of Darwin, Australia, by the carrier-based planes of the Kido Butai, and a naval skirmish in the Bandung Straits by the ABDA forces that failed to interfere with the Japanese invasion of Timor.

Defeat piled on defeat. On February 25, six cruisers of the ABDA fleet were trounced in the Battle of the Java Sea. All were to be sunk, including the gallant *Houston*, which went down in the night action in the Sunda Strait with her guns still firing. Next day, Japanese planes caught the fleeing British cruiser *Exeter*, which had helped to put an end to the German pocket battleship *Graf Spee* eighteen months earlier. This naval disaster sealed the fate of the crumbling ABDA command. Wavell flew from Java to India, leaving the Dutch to make a final stand against this avalanche of disaster.

When Halsey's *Enterprise* raided Wake Island on February 21, it was another annoying gnat bite for the enemy and was a minor story in the American newspapers, compared to the continuing saga of MacArthur's last stand in the Philippines. His Republican supporters on Capitol Hill were already lobbying for him to be recalled to Washington to take charge of what they saw as a badly flagging United States war effort. The general, however, let it be known he intended to fight out to the finish, and his wife and young son refused to leave Corregidor in the submarine that arrived to evacuate the American governor of the Philippines and President Quezon on the night of February 21, 1942.

Roosevelt knew that it would be politically disastrous for him if MacArthur perished like a latter-day General Custer. He'd been elevated to heroic status because he was the only American commander battling against the Japanese at the time, although the ability to hold out by his forces had been severely curtailed by his own strategic miscalculations. With the collapse of the ABDA command and the Malay Barrier strategy, the political repercussions of what were perceived in Washington to be a looming threat to Australia were also being felt in London and Canberra. Prime Minister Curtain of Australia moved to recall the two Australian divisions essential to the British attempt to hold Egypt against the advancing Afrika Corps. He blackmailed Roosevelt, in effect, to send more American troops across the Pacific to garrison Australia. The political price for this was that the new supreme commander in the theater had to be an American, and MacArthur was the obvious talent available.

At first MacArthur resisted the telegram of February 21 from Washington, signed by the president's secretary of war and General Marshall, ordering him to leave at once for Melbourne, where he was to assume command of all United States troops. After melodramatically offering to resign to fight to the end as a private alongside his men, MacArthur finally agreed to break his earlier pledge, on the direct orders of the commander in chief and on the condition that he could choose the right "psychological time" to leave Corregidor.

On the night of March 11, 1942, Gen. Douglas MacArthur, accompanied by his wife and small son, together with his entire seven-teen-strong staff, embarked on four United States Navy PT boats. After a 600-mile dash through enemy-held waters, which the sixty-two-year-old general characterized as "like a ride in a concrete mixer," he arrived in northern Mindanao and then transferred to an American bomber and flew to Australia to deliver his famous Ceasarean utterance, "I came through and I shall return."

MacArthur's ringing declaration buoyed up the American public and increased the pressure on Roosevelt to reverse the Europe First direction of the United States' war effort. A powerful factor influencing public opinion on Capitol Hill regarding the reassignment of American priorities to the defeat of Japan over Germany was the compelling image of a "Hero on Ice," as *Time* magazine portrayed MacArthur. He had arrived in Australia expecting to find a full army instead of two ill-equipped American divisions. He was hoping to lead a crusade to make good his promise to relieve the Philippines. Encouraged by a jittery Australian prime minister, MacArthur delivered a speech to the Canberra Parliament calling for more United States forces to defend Australia. Deploying a flair for media strategy that at least equaled, and some might argue exceeded, his military prowess, General MacArthur embarked on a public relations campaign to rouse the Pacific First lobby in Congress.

He found an unlikely ally in Admiral King, who on March 12 had replaced Stark, the architect of the Europe First strategy, as chief of naval operations. But one of the staunchest defenders of the Europe First strategy was the head of Army War Plans, General Eisenhower, who resisted demands for a change from the acerbic Admiral King, whom he found to be "an arbitrary stubborn type with too much brain and a tendency to bully his juniors." King, however, was not motivated by any particular affection for the United States Army, or wish to help MacArthur extricate his forces from the grave he had helped dig for them in the Philippines. King simply found it offensive that the navy should be kept standing on the defensive in the Pacific at a time when he believed, from information supplied by his intelligence staff in Washington, that Japan's next move would be to smash through the Philippines to land in Australia and then move on to invade the American islands in the southwest Pacific and attack Hawaii.

The conflict over these rival theaters came to a head in March 1942 as the Joint Chiefs of Staff were forced to reconsider their strategic priorities in the light of Japan's continuing avalanche of military victories. "Hold Hawaii, support Australia, and drive northward from the New Hebrides," became King's strategic rallying cry. But army fears of being sucked into what Secretary of War Stimson scornfully referred to as "King's creeping movement to New Caledonia" was set to rest, at least temporarily, by a March 7 cable from Churchill, warning Roosevelt of a coming German spring offensive in Russia. This allowed Marshall to regain the initiative and argue that the war against Hitler really had to be given priority over the war against Japan. This was the basis of the case he set before the president and Joint Chiefs of Staff at their March 16 conference. He argued persuasively that the collapse of Germany must inevitably rule Japan, while the reverse would not be the case. So the United States Army chief of staff advocated sending every available reinforcement to Europe and Russia, even if it meant losing Australia.

The compromise that was finally hammered out by the United States Joint Chiefs of Staff, in fact, left the Europe First defense strategy essentially intact. But as a concession to the chief of naval operations, it was agreed that a limited reinforcement might be sent to the Pacific theater to secure Australia and Hawaii.

The army and Europe First may have prevailed over COMINCH's call for a naval offensive against Rabaul, but to Ernie King this was only a temporary truce and not a surrender. His stubborn campaign to effect a shift of the strategic priority of the United States Chiefs of Staff to the Pacific theater was to have a potentially disastrous influence on the intelligence estimates of Japanese intentions in the Far East. King's pigheadedness and that of his subservient intelligence staff very nearly brought about the Pacific Fleet's defeat at the Battle of Midway.

Yamamoto and the Japanese high commander were also having their knockabout strategic debate over priorities as their so-called first operational phase of their grand strategic plan approached its fulfillment in March 1942. The momentum and magnitude of their easy victories bred a complacency and overconfidence that led to a major strategic overreach that the Japanese attribute to "Victory Disease." The American carrier raids had been a goad, but they had not interfered with achieving the Japanese objectives of the first operational phase. But now, Yamamoto knew that he would have to take account of the Pacific Fleet during the second operational phase. This had originally called for consolidating the island perimeter to establish "a strategic situation of long-term invincibility," by taking control of New Guinea and the Solomon Islands. The Japanese navy set sail for Midway in a bid to lure the Pacific Fleet out to smash it once and for all, and seal the fate that the Pearl Harbor raid had not done. The combined fleet would then be free to move toward the objectives of the third operational phase, which called for, and I quote, "the capture of Hawaii and the outlying islands, an attack on the United States, Panama and Canada, as well as against the central Pacific, until the United States loses its fighting spirit and the war can be brought to a conclusion."

As the strategic debates continued at Imperial General Headquarters, Japanese forces continued to push their way up through Burma and down on the American forces holding the mountain redoubt at the foot of the Bataan Peninsula. The fourth month of successive Japanese victories began with a smashing blow the Kido Butai delivered to the British Far-Eastern Fleet. After raiding Ceylon, the Ceylon port of Trincomalee, and sinking an aircraft carrier and two cruisers on Easter Sunday, their success obliged Vice Adm. Sir James Summerville to withdraw his fleet to the safety of Mombasa on the African coast. This was the worst humiliation that had been inflicted on the Royal Navy since before the days of Nelson two centuries earlier!

Two days later, the United States suffered its worst defeat when the Japanese finally captured the commanding heights of Mount Natib and the Mariveles Line on Bataan collapsed. In less than forty-eight hours an entire army "vanished into thin air," as Maj. Gen. Edward P. King desperately signaled Corregidor on the afternoon of April 6: "We have no further means of organized resistance." At dawn next day he ordered the flags of truce to be raised.

"No army has done so much with so little and nothing became it more than its last hours of trial and agony," was the epithet delivered by MacArthur, its erstwhile commander, appropriately at an Australian press conference that afternoon. But for more than 70,000 American and Filipino troops who had surrendered, the trial and agony was only just beginning.

Under Japanese bayonets, the survivors were to be herded like cattle back up the sixty-five miles of Bataan's thick jungles that they had fought themselves to exhaustion defending. Starved by their captors, whose Bushido warrior code taught them that a soldier who surrendered was not worthy of human respect, straggling prisoners

were clubbed unmercilessly and those dying from disease and malnutrition were bayoneted or buried alive by their companions at
gunpoint. The Bataan Death March earned an awful place in the
grim record of Japan's wanton atrocities, alongside the sack of
Singapore and the rape of Nanking. More than 7,000 Americans and
Filipinos never survived the terrible ordeal and of the 60,000 who
did, most were little more than walking skeletons, whose only relief
to the interminable march was that it had ended. They now faced the
war of continuing misery of brutal prison camps where meager rice
rations, disease, and humiliation relentlessly extracted their toll of
human life. Conditions like these were shared by the more than
150,000 Allied soldiers and civilians that the Japanese had captured
in their unstoppable four-month-long rampage of conquest through
Southeast Asia.

Yet, within a week of the capitulation of Bataan, the United
States delivered an air attack on Tokyo, which while its military impact might be compared to a flea bite, its psychological impact was a
rhinoceros-like blow to Japan's pride.

On April 18, 1942, the unthinkable occurred for the Japanese,
when the Tokyo air raid sirens blasted off and the twin-engined
American B-25 bombers roared in from the sea to drop high-explo-
sives on Japan's sacred soil. In a brilliantly executed display of
Army–Navy cooperation, Admiral Halsey's two-carrier task force
had launched a fifteen-plane strike against Tokyo, Nagoya, Kobi,
and Osaka. This attack was led by Col. James H. Doolittle. Though
the physical damage inflicted was slight, the loss of face at Imperial
Japanese Headquarters was terrible.

Yamamoto retired to his cabin, mortified by the thought that
the navy had failed in its duty to prevent the violation of the sacred
air space above the Imperial Palace. After it was discovered that the
American pilots had parachuted over the mainland, the Japanese
army in China embarked on a wanton rampage. They slaughtered
upwards of a quarter of a million peasants in Chengkiang and
Kiangsu provinces in revenge for the assistance given to Doolittle's
fliers in escaping. But the April 18 token air raid on Tokyo evapo-
rated any doubts that the army still had about the necessity for the
Midway operation to deal and ally with the Pacific Fleet once and
for all. In their determination to avenge the American air attack,
Imperial General Headquarters not only gave their go ahead to
Yamamoto's new strategy, but agreed to advance his ambitiously

complex operation to the first week of June. The introduction of the new naval code books was once again delayed by the switching around of forces. This enabled the United States Navy's proficiency, which had been gained penetrating the year-old combined fleet code, JN-25B, to continue until the salient elements of both of Yamamoto's operations had been assembled.

Nimitz's skillful exploitation of his radio intelligence advantage allowed him to commit two American task forces to the Coral Sea at the beginning of May in time to derail the first installment of Yamamoto's grand strategic bulldozer. The carrier battles of May 6 and 7 off the Solomon Islands in the Coral Sea, although a tactical victory for Japan in terms of tonnage sunk, forced the Japanese to call off the invasion of southern New Guinea and became a strategic victory for the United States.

The Battle of the Coral Sea provided an important boost to Allied morale because it happened to coincide with the last days of Corregidor and the final stages of the ignominious British defeat in Burma, as well as the China army's withdrawal from the upper Burma highlands. Japan's conquest of Southeast Asia had come to a halt. The carrier action had succeeded in stopping the avalanche of strategic disaster for the Allies. In the aftershocks of this battle, the way was open for the Pacific Fleet to seize the initiative, which it did a month later at the Battle of Midway.

The Pacific Boils: The Japanese Juggernaut

World War I saw the first use of aircraft in combat. These airplanes had a limited role during World War I and played no role in assuring any tactical or strategic victories. At the beginning of World War II, the Japanese used the airplane as the principal strike force for its land and sea units. Without the airplane, the Japanese would not have achieved the success it did during that grim period of history. Covering the same time frame as John Costello (December 1941 – May 1942), John Lundstrom describes how Japan used a different type of warfare to rapidly spread their tentacles of power in the Far East.

John B. Lundstrom, curator of history at the Milwaukee Public Museum, has a master's degree in diplomatic and military history from the University of Wisconsin–Milwaukee. He has written several books, including *The First South Pacific Campaign: Pacific Fleet Strategy December 1941 – June 1942* and *The First Team*.

John B. Lundstrom

In Valhalia, a special place is reserved for those ill-fated souls exposed on the front-lines in a war suddenly launched by a far-stronger foe. Savage attacks end the illusion of peace and security. The defenders pay the price for their country's neglect. Their only strategy is to delay the enemy until reinforcements could arrive. It is a desperate race against time. Certainly one of the classic holding campaigns occurred from December 1941 to May 1942 in the Far East, where a motley array of Allied soldiers, sailors, and airmen tried bravely but unsuccessfully to stem the Japanese tide. Air power played a crucial role in the loss of the Philippines, Malaya, and the Dutch East Indies.

Spurred by its desire for oil and raw materials, but denied normal trade because of its aggression in China, the empire of Japan looked longingly southward at the riches seemingly within easy reach in the Dutch East Indies. Barring the way were the forces from Britain and her commonwealth, the Dutch colonial forces, cut off from their homeland, and the United States. Distracted by the war with Nazi Germany, the British neglected the military and economic development of their East Asia possessions. Although not yet in a shooting war, the United States also regarded Europe as the decisive theater for future operations. Ultimately, the leaders of neither power thought Japan to be much of a threat. The Allied forces were lightly spread over 4,000 miles of ocean and tropical islands from Burma to the Philippines. In fact, Imperial Japan amassed not only the Pacific's most powerful navy and eleven divisions from a brave and experienced army, but, more importantly, an air arm superior to anything the Allies could then bring against it.

Japanese planners opted for a strategic offensive conducted in stages set to begin on December 8, local time. First they targeted the Allied strongholds in Hong Kong, Malaya, and the Philippines for simultaneous assaults. After these bastions had fallen or had been neutralized, Japanese forces would converge on the Dutch East Indies from both flanks and also capture Burma. After that, they expected to sit tight behind a formidable defense perimeter, utilize their looted resources, and build up to meet a long-delayed counteroffensive.

For the initial phase of their Southern Operation, the Japanese allocated around 1,200 aircraft. Of these, the Imperial Japanese

Army Air Force furnished 700, organized into two air divisions. The principal fighter was the Nakajima Ki-27, later dubbed NATE by the Allies. Although sporting fixed landing gear and lightly armed with only two 7.7mm machine guns, the Ki-27 was highly maneuverable. The army also allocated fifty of its newest fighters, the Nakajima Ki-43 Hajabusa, or Oscar, which closely resembled the Navy Zero fighter. The Japanese Army Air Force's principal offensive weapon was its regiment of medium bombers, mainly the Mitsubishi Ki-21, or SALLY. The Japanese army aviators were reasonably well trained and had benefited from combat operations against China and against the Soviets over Manchuria.

Unlike the United States Navy, the Imperial Japanese Navy created a large land-based air force, almost the twin in strategic terms to that of the Imperial Army. The Japanese navy air contribution to the Southern offensive comprised some 480 land-based aircraft and thirty-four from the light carrier *Ryujo*. An armada of six carriers with 414 aircraft embarked and set sail eastward to execute the surprise attack on the United States Pacific Fleet base at Pearl Harbor. After the carriers returned from the Hawaiian operation, they, too, would support the southward advance. The Imperial Navy was impressive not only in quantity but also in the quality of its aircraft and aviators. Their training was the equal of any in the world, and in the last few years they likewise had gained much valuable combat experience over China. The average amount of flying time in one of the land-based fighter groups was 1,000 hours per pilot. In contrast, some of the United States Army Air Corps pilots in the Philippines had as few as fifteen hours in fighters, and the British were not much better off.

The Imperial Navy's pilots were outstanding, and their aircraft were excellent, particularly the fabled Mitsubishi A6M2 Type O fighter. Both carrier and land-based air groups flew this superb machine. Not only was the Zero fast, highly maneuverable, and heavily armed, but it enjoyed a radius of action far superior to any single-engine fighter in the world. It outclassed every other fighter in the Far East. The principal Japanese naval strike aircraft were their medium bombers, or "land-attack planes," the Mitsubishi G3M3 Type 96 NELL, and the Mitsubishi G4M1 Type 1 BETTY.

For the opening phase of their offensive, the Japanese deployed their air forces into two main groupings. Against Malaya, they concentrated some 500 army and 180 navy aircraft in southern Indo-

The USS *Arizona* becomes the focal point for an America bent on revenge following the Japanese attack of December 7, 1941. *U.S. Navy photo, National Archives, print courtesy of Admiral Nimitz Museum*

china. Packed on Formosa, directly north of the Philippines, were 200 army planes from the 5th Air Division and 300 navy planes, including about 100 Zeros, of the 11th Air Fleet. The Zero's excellent combat radius permitted it to cover the 500 miles from southern Formosa to Manila. By comparison, this was farther than the distance from eastern England to Berlin, Germany. The Zero's excellent range permitted the Japanese to dispense with the need for aircraft carriers just to put fighters over central Luzon.

What did the Allies have in the way of aircraft to match against their formidable foe? The British Far East Command in Malaya counted 158 first-line aircraft, many of them obsolescent or already obsolete. The principal fighter was the Brewster Buffalo, the export version of an American carrier fighter being phased out of operational units. Its nickname "Buffalo" pretty much summed up its sorry performance as a fighter. Burma's garrison included another squadron of Buffaloes and also part of a rather unique fighting force,

Claire Chennault's American Volunteer Group, or "Flying Tigers." Intended for the defense of the Burma Road supply line to Nationalist China, the AVG's Curtiss P-40B Tomahawks were preparing to leave central Burma for southern China. Dutch Army Air units in the Dutch East Indies numbered about 200 aircraft, many obsolete cast-offs from other countries. The fighter force included Buffaloes, some Curtiss P-36s, and another Curtiss product known as the CW-21B, but most of the bombers were antiquated Martin B-10s.

Most exposed to the Japanese onslaught was the Philippines, garrisoned by Gen. Douglas MacArthur's United States Army Forces, Far East, and Adm. Thomas C. Hart's Asiatic Fleet. The aviation components of these two commands were Maj. Gen. Lewis H. Brereton's Far East Air Force and Capt. Frank D. Wagner's Patrol Wing 10. For many years the Philippines largely was ignored as an isolated strategic backwater, almost certain to fall to a sustained Japanese offensive. The only American defensive plan was to hole up in fortresses to await a possible counteroffensive across the Pacific. However, beginning in the summer of 1941, MacArthur argued passionately for more than just a defensive posture. He wanted the Philippines to be greatly reinforced. Not only was the archipelago to be a bulwark to thwart any Japanese advance, it would also unleash a powerful offensive blow against the enemy's heartland. The principal weapon was to be strategic air power in the form of Boeing B-17 Flying Fortresses. Ranging out far from Luzon, these heavy bombers were expected to cut the shipping lanes to Japan and ultimately set her patchwork cities ablaze. MacArthur needed until April 1942 to assemble the necessary forces. Of course, the Japanese would tamely oblige.

Aside from these flights of fancy, what did America's air resources in the Philippines comprise in December 1941? Only that summer and fall did some modern planes, including P-40 fighters and the first contingent of B-17 Flying Fortresses, begin reaching MacArthur. As of December 7, 1941, the Far East Air Force numbered about 125 first-line fighters and bombers. The 24th Pursuit Group controlled the fighters, including about 72 P-40Bs and P-40Es, and 18 older P-35s. The 19th Bombardment Group had 34 operational Fortresses, but they were the older C and D models without tail gunners. Also present was the 27th Bomb Group, but none of their Douglas A-24 Dauntless dive bombers had yet reached the islands. The navy's Patrol Wing 10 comprised about 30 Consolidated PBY Catalina Flying Boats used for long-range searches and strikes. The tiny Philippine Army Air Corps possessed a dozen cast-off Boeing P-26 fighters and three B-10s.

Caught in the midst of a rapid build-up, the Far East Air Force worked to create the infrastructure of airfields and depots necessary to support the increase. Sufficient fields necessary to disperse the aircraft did not exist. The fighters operated from a few sites in and around Manila and central Luzon. The B-17s could only operate from Clark Field north of Manila and from the auxiliary field at Del Monte on Mindanao. On December 7, only one newly installed radar was functioning, that at Iba Field northwest of Manila. The air warning network was primitive, and communications were poor. Only Clark Field had a semblance of anti-aircraft protection. For example, the air defense of Nichols Field, near Manila, relied only on a couple of .30-caliber Lewis machine guns.

To Allied commands in the Far East, war with Japan appeared imminent in early December, because search planes tracked a Japanese convoy obviously bound for Malaya. Before dawn on December 8, the Philippines received word of the Japanese surprise attack on Pearl Harbor. Unfortunately, MacArthur's headquarters apparently failed to authorize a bombing raid by the B-17s against Formosa. Things became more confused after daybreak when Japanese raids failed to show up as expected. In fact, the Imperial Navy had prepared a massive dawn strike by 108 land attack planes and 92 Zeros against Philippine airfields, but the weather prevented their takeoff. Fearful of being caught on the ground themselves, the Japanese finally got away six hours behind schedule. The Philippine air warning network proved ineffective, and the Japanese destroyed half the B-17 force on the ground at Clark Field, while they were arming for a dusk strike against Formosa. Worse were the slashing, strafing attacks by free-lancing Zeros. Despite the bravery of the defenders, the Japanese raids on December 8, 9, and 10 ripped the Far East Air Force to shreds. By the evening of the tenth, effective United States fighter strength had been reduced to thirty planes. Nowhere had they been able to intercept the oncoming Japanese with any real concentration of numbers.

However, numbers alone did not stop several intrepid fighter pilots such as Lieutenants Boyd Wagner and Russell Church, or Capt. Jesus Villamore of the Philippine Army Air Corps. Unescorted B-17s and PatWing 10's PBYs flew valiant, but largely ineffective, penny-packet strikes against Japanese war ships and troop convoys. Certainly the issue in the Philippines was not long in doubt. The Far East Air Force could do nothing to halt the convoys approaching Luzon. With justice could a staff officer of the Imperial Navy's 11th Air Fleet write of the situation on December 15: "Enemy air power in the Philippines has been smashed." The cost was twenty-three Zeros, ten land attack planes, and one flying boat.

During the rest of December, while strong Japanese invasion forces converged on Manila, American air strength was gradually whittled down until a few surviving B-17s and PBYs were withdrawn, leaving only a few fighters used for reconnaissance flights. The ground echelons joined MacArthur's troops, now largely confined to Bataan and Corregidor. The Japanese pointed with great pride to the superlative performance of their wide-ranging Zeros as their key to victory. It seems that the Far East Air Force, thinking it was out of range of any land-based fighters, discounted enemy fighter escorts except those which might have come from carriers. For Japan, the Zero fighters in the Philippines were indeed both sword and shield.

The pattern of Japanese air domination was repeated in Malaya. Almost from the very beginning, the Japanese established air superiority over the invasion beaches in northern Malaya and struck hard all over the peninsula. On December 10, NELL and BETTY landattack planes from the Imperial Navy's 22nd Air Flotilla stunned the world by sinking the British battleships *Prince of Wales* and *Repulse*. During December, Japanese air power supported the Imperial Army's relentless advance through the jungles of the Malay Peninsula to the great prize of Singapore.

The Flying Tigers had scored their first victories on December 20 over Kunming, China, but after December 23, they would see their heaviest combat over Burma. That day, while Japanese ground forces crossed Thailand, aiming toward the Burmese border, the Japanese Army Air Force flew its first raid against Rangoon. That began a series of fierce air battles over Burma, valiantly defended by the Royal Air Force and a majority of the American Volunteer Group.

By the end of December, with Allied air power in the Far East either largely destroyed, as in the Philippines, or pinned-down defending Singapore and Rangoon, the Japanese shifted into phase two of their Southern offensive. Much of the Japanese army air strength in the Philippines prepared to move west to Bangkok to assault

Burma. Hopping over Luzon, Imperial naval air units leap-frogged south from Formosa to Davao on Mindanao. From there, they supported further southward advances, both along the east coast of Borneo and down the Celebes toward Ambon and Timor. Outnumbered, the valiant counterattacks by the 19th Bomb Group's B-17s and PatWing 10's PBYs could do little to slow the Japanese tide. By January 24, the Japanese had seized Balikpapan in Borneo and Kendari in the Celebes. They were vital points in the continuing strategy of isolating eastern Java.

While the Japanese ravaged the Far East, the Allies attempted to counter by unifying the defenses of the so-called Malay Barrier. At the Arcadia conference held in late December in Washington, Roosevelt and Churchill set up the ABDA command under Gen. Sir Archibald Wavell. The idea of ABDA (which stood for American, British, Dutch, and Australian) was to "secure points of vantage," from which an eventual Allied counteroffensive might be launched. The Allied planners counted on a massive infusion of air power to hold the Japanese in check until naval and ground reinforcements could be sent. Whether this was even feasible, given limited Allied resources and the physical difficulty of getting aircraft to the Dutch East Indies, let alone Japanese opposition, is to be considered. The experiences of some of the United States Army Air Corps replacements bound for Java certainly illustrate the point. Most of the heavy bombers, the B-17s and Consolidated LB-30 Liberators from the 7th Bomb Group, started out from Florida, flew down to Brazil, hopped the Atlantic, crossed Africa and the Middle East, and stopped off at Karachi and Ceylon, before the long last leg across the Indian Ocean to Java. Beginning about mid-January, only thirty-eight B-17s and a dozen LB-30s reached Java.

The 7th Bomb Group made its first strike on January 16 against Menado in the northern Celebes and lost three of five planes to fierce Zero counterattacks. Hurriedly formed at Brisbane, the 17th Pursuit Squadron (provisional) flew 17 P-40s across Australia and then over water from Darwin to Timor to Surabaya in Java. Ultimately, of another 124 P-40s being sent to Java, only 26 ever landed at an airfield ready to fight. On February 3, masses of Zero fighters and land-attack planes operating from newly acquired bases in Borneo and the Celebes descended without warning on Surabaya and other key sites in eastern Java. They virtually obliterated the defending Dutch fighters and destroyed numerous aircraft on the ground. By the next day, the United States Army Air Corps units retained only nine operational heavy bombers and 11 P-40s. Over the next several days the Japanese strike groups ranged at will over Java.

By mid-February, the third phase of the Japanese operations against Java had begun. In the west, the imminent fall of Singapore permitted the Japanese to land paratroops at Palembang on Sumatra and capture not only important oil fields but the only major airfield between Singapore and western Java. To the east, preceded by a massive raid on Port Darwin by four carriers and also land-based planes, the Japanese invaded Bali on February 19 and Timor the next day. Now the Allies had no way of flying short-ranged aircraft from Australia to beleaguered Java. Zero fighters soon moved up to Bali and nearby islands. From there, the Japanese ranged far south of Java and effectively isolated it. Neither the weak ABDA naval command nor dwindling air power could prevent Japanese convoys from reaching both ends of Java on March 1. The only recourse was evacuation, and those bombers within range flew out to other Allied bases. Vessels fleeing the region had to run a gauntlet of enemy aircraft and warships. The Dutch formally surrendered Java on March 9.

The last goal of the Southern Operation was Burma on the western flank of the Greater Southeast Asia Co-Prosperity Sphere. Ever since December, the British and the Flying Tigers had tried to hold off increasingly strong Japanese air attacks. Unfortunately, the Allied success in the air could do little to prevent Japanese advances on the ground. Finally, after the disaster at the Sittang River in February, the way to Rangoon was open. During March and April, the AVG fought a series of rear-guard actions as the British and Chinese troops retreated to India and China. Finally, by May the Japanese had achieved their strategic aims in the entire theater.

The effective application by Japan of air power ensured strategic success in the Far East. Using well-trained pilots, often with superior aircraft to the Allies, the Japanese applied overwhelming air strength in key sectors. They looked for every opportunity to move their air units ahead and support advancing spearheads. Nowhere could the outmatched Allies concentrate enough planes to do more than temporarily slow the Japanese juggernaut. In 1941 and early 1942, raw courage was simply not enough to allow the American, British, Dutch, and Australian airmen to defend the Far East. But courage, strength of numbers, and the intelligent employment of air power would bring them back in 1945.

II. A Different Kind of War: Goliath on the Seas

From Wooden Ships to Stout-hearted Men

As long as men have been going to the sea in ships, the oceans have been an important battleground. Opposing navies first positioned ships side-by-side, sailors jumping gunwales to battle hand-to-hand. Fists, clubs, knives, and swords were used to conquer the oceans. The victors gained ships and important trading routes. Ships not wanted or needed were set afire and left as a funeral pyre.

With the advent of gunpowder and the knowledge to form iron into barrels, clubs and swords gave way to pistols, rifles, and cannons. Ships would close to a side-by-side position and blaze away at one another. Cannons were used not to sink ships (the cannon balls would only bounce off the heavy hull timbers), but to disable the enemy's vessel by splitting the masts and spars. Once the enemy ship was disabled, pistol-shot would be used to kill the crew and force submission.

Steel hulls of the mid and late nineteenth century made cannon fire even less effective. The introduction of steam power nearly made the cannon obsolete as ships no longer had to rely on the wind for position. A captain could easily maneuver and adjust his ship to achieve optimum firing position.

In the late nineteenth and early twentieth centuries, navies essentially put artillery pieces on their ships. Greatly modified for naval use, these new guns employed explosive shells which could travel for thousands of yards. When adequate range-finding and target-solution technology was developed, no ship was safe in the open ocean. Once within distance of human eyesight, an enemy could be fired upon and sunk. The "cannons" could cover long distances, could be accurately placed, and were large enough and carried enough of an explosive charge to penetrate steel hulls and then detonate.

36

The development of the airplane brought a new set of eyes to the navy. Airplanes could search for and find enemy ships and notify the navy, who could then bring its battleships to bear on the enemy. In some cases, the planes could assist the battleship by firing their machine guns at the enemy ships. This tactic was designed not to sink the ship, but to hit crew members and possibly hamper defensive maneuvering efforts. When planes began carrying bombs, the plane could be used to drop bombs on the enemy ship. Horizontal bombing, as it came to be called, was one of the most wasteful and ineffective military techniques ever developed for naval warfare. Pilots discovered it was virtually impossible to hit a moving ship by dropping a bomb from an airplane. (This would change in the 1960s and 1970s with the development of the "smart" bomb.)

Battleships carried one or two float planes, which could be launched and recovered using a crane. The float plane could only search limited areas and had only limited effectiveness for naval uses. Naval fleets needed far more planes than could be carried on the battleships for the plane to become a viable naval weapon. In the 1920s and 1930s, the aircraft carrier was developed. This allowed the navy's eyes-in-the-sky to travel with the fleet. In short order, specialty planes began to be developed for carrier duty. Dive-bombers, torpedo planes, and fighters for fleet protection were developed.

To the navy, the battleship remained the main attack weapon and the aircraft carrier was useful only for scouting planes. The carriers were not seen as an integrated part of the fighting capabilities of the fleet. The planes could spot the enemy and harass the enemy by strafing, horizontal bombing and/or torpedo attacks, but it was still the job of the battleship to defeat the enemy. As John Lundstrom will relate, this perception drastically and rapidly changed in 1942 in the war in the Pacific.

Carrier War in the Pacific

John B. Lundstrom

The character of naval warfare changed drastically on December 7, 1941. Two massive waves of 360 Japanese aircraft surprised and smashed the battleship force of the United States Pacific Fleet at Pearl Harbor. Such awesome offensive power arose from the decks of the six large aircraft carriers of Vice Adm. Chuichi Nagumo's Kido Butai, or Striking Force.[1] Nothing the Allies currently possessed in the Pacific could stand up to it. No longer could navies reckon their might primarily in the number of their battleships and the weight of their big naval rifles for a conventional gun duel. Able to strike hard from long distance, aircraft carriers came to the fore and, so long as they lasted, would dominate naval operations in 1942.

In simplest terms, the aircraft carrier was a floating airfield fitted on a huge hull and designed to maintain, protect, and transport the airplanes making up its air group. Developed by the Royal Navy during World War I, the concept of aircraft carriers appealed strongly to the Japanese and the Americans, who confronted each other across the broad expanse of the Pacific. In 1922, Japan completed the *Hosho*, the first carrier designed from the keel up, while the United States soon followed with the converted collier *Langley*. On these small vessels, naval aviators considered the problems of operating land-type aircraft (as opposed to seaplanes) and experimented with likely solutions.

The first United States navy aircraft carrier, USS *Langley*, in the Panama Canal (circa 1930). *Navy Department Photo #NH62905, United States Naval History Division*

In the late 1920s, both navies took a quantum leap forward with the addition of huge new carriers converted from battlecruiser or battleship hulls. The next decade proved to be a golden age of aircraft carrier development. The third generation of carriers appeared in the form of the *Soryu* and *Hiryu* for Japan and the American *Yorktown*-class. They led to the two *Shokaku*-class carriers, commissioned in late 1941, and the first of the superlative *Essex*-class carriers scheduled for early 1943. Embroiled in their war against China, the Japanese committed their carriers off the Chinese coast and also utilized their aircraft from shore bases. As with the German Luftwaffe in Spain, the Imperial Navy's aviators gained valuable combat experience against a weaker opponent.

Examining the carrier forces of Japan and the United States at the outbreak of the Pacific war, one is struck more by the similarities between the two competing programs rather than the differences. In fact, they resembled each other far more than the pioneering British. Control by the Royal Air Force over the Royal Navy's carrier aircraft design and pilot training stultified British carrier development in the 1920s and 1930s. Such can be the perils of unifying the services.

Both the Japanese and the United States formed their carrier air groups around the same types of radial-engined aircraft: single-seat fighters capable of dealing with land-based opponents, two-man light bombers designed for steep diving attacks, and slightly larger three-seaters capable of lugging ship-killing torpedoes or carrying bombs. The British, for example, eschewed dive bombers in favor of torpedo planes and initially preferred two-man fighters, such as the Fairey Fulmar.

In 1942 the respective categories of Japanese and American carrier aircraft matched up surprisingly well. The fabled Mitsubishi Type O carrier fighter, or Zero (later dubbed ZEKE by the Allies) outperformed its American counterpart, the Grumman F4F-3 Wildcat, in terms of climb rate, maneuverability, and range. Yet United States Navy fighter pilots, drawing from their prewar tactical training, utilized the Wildcat's firepower and protection to blunt the Japanese advantage. The two dive bombers, the Aichi D3A1 Type 99 carrier bomber (or VAL) and the Douglas SBD-3 Dauntless performed similarly. However, the Dauntless carried twice the weight in bombs (1,000 pounds as opposed to the 550 pounds carried by the VAL), and the Japanese bombs could pierce more armor.

The Japanese excelled in torpedo attack capability. Although old by 1942 standards, the Mitsubishi B5N2 Type 97 carrier attack plane (or KATE) and the superb Type 91 aerial torpedo proved far superior to the Douglas TBD-1 Devastators and the Mark XIII torpedoes used by the United States torpedo squadrons through June 1942. The Japanese dropped their fish while traveling over 200 knots and above 250 feet, while the Americans had to drop down to 100 feet and release at 110 knots. Even the fine new Grumman TBF-1 Avenger torpedo bombers did not tip the scale in favor of the Americans, because they continued to use the abysmal Mark XIII torpedoes. If one thing really differentiated Japanese from United States carrier planes, it was protection. The Americans enjoyed armor and self-sealing fuel tanks, whereas Japanese planes, lighter and generally longer-ranged, were especially vulnerable to gunfire.[2]

Tactics also played a role aside from the aircraft themselves. The Japanese held the advantage in terms of tactical coordination among squadrons within individual air groups and between those of different ships. Customarily drawn from two, four, or even six carriers, a smoothly integrated Japanese strike was beautiful to behold. The aircraft swiftly joined together under one command for a massed attack. Much sooner than the Americans, the Japanese experimented with deck load strikes and multiple attack waves. Even from the multi-carrier task forces, American carrier air groups seldom tended to operate together and seldom achieved coordination even at that level.

The Americans moved out ahead in technology, particularly electronics. Radar and fighter direction techniques adopted from the British offered invaluable early warning of Japanese search planes and strike groups. American radios and homing devices performed better than the Japanese, although communication failures continued to bedevil the United States Navy throughout 1942 and adversely affected a number of battles.[3] In addition, the Allies gained the incalculable advantage in the first seven months of 1942 from reading portions of the Japanese secret naval message traffic. But it was still necessary to go out and vanquish a formidable enemy.

The last topic in this brief comparison of the two carrier navies in early 1942 concerns the aviators themselves. Fundamental differences existed in the procurement of flying personnel. The Imperial Navy relied heavily upon a thin cadre of regular naval officers, the Etajima graduates, to command a force of enlisted flyers. They recruited only a small number of college-trained reserve officers, none of whom flew from carriers in 1942. Aside from sailors transferred to the aviation branch, the Imperial Navy enlisted increasing numbers of boys as young as fifteen or sixteen and trained them as aviators. Although senior noncommissioned officers reached warrant rank or even special duty ensign, the burden of command remained with the dwindling band of experienced regular officers.

In contrast, the United States Navy, having a much larger pool of college-educated men upon whom to draw, depended strongly on its reserve officer program. By 1942, enlisted pilots made up less than ten percent of the total, and soon after most of them were commissioned. Annapolis graduates continued to command groups and squadrons, but reserve officers assumed increasingly important roles.

Flight training for the two navies was generally comparable, but in early 1942 the Japanese aviators on a whole were more seasoned than their American counterparts. This is reflected in a significantly lower accident rate. Interestingly, Japanese carriers did not employ landing signal officers to coach incoming planes. Instead, the pilots lined up their approach using a system of lights and deck markings to stay in the groove. They also excelled in night carrier operations. The Japanese also operated under a different philosophy regarding command in multi-seat aircraft. Often, the observer/navigator, rather than the pilot, commanded the aircraft. In the United States Navy, the pilot was always the senior member of the crew.

In late December 1941, the Japanese carrier strength amounted to six fleet carriers, the *Akagi, Kaga, Soryu, Hiryu, Shokaku,* and *Zuikaku* (which had attacked Pearl Harbor) and three light carriers.[4] The total nominal strength in aircraft was about 447 planes. By the end of summer 1942, three more light carriers with an additional 104 aircraft were expected to join the fleet. At the same time, the United States Pacific Fleet comprised three large carriers, the *Lexington*, the *Saratoga*, and the *Enterprise*, nominally equipped with 220 planes. Reinforcements which could be made available in 1942 from the Atlantic fleet numbered another three flattops, the *Yorktown, Hornet,* and *Wasp*, with 220 more planes. The potential for the United States to expand its pool of naval aviators and aircraft was much greater than for Japan. However, the advantage in carriers and aircraft at the outset lay strongly with the Japanese. The question became what they would do about it.

The course of the carrier war in the Pacific during 1942 falls into three distinct phases. The first phase could be characterized as the "raiding stage," with numerous attacks against land targets, either islands or harbors. What transpired became almost a concerted effort by both sides to avoid confrontations between opposing carrier forces. This was made possible by the decision of the Imperial General Headquarters to reorient the powerful Kido Butai from the east to the south to support the advance into the Dutch East Indies and the South Pacific. Despite the failure to find and destroy the American carriers during the Hawaii operation, the high command no longer considered the shattered Pacific Fleet to be much of an immediate threat. In the process, Adm. Isoroku Yamamoto, commander of the combined fleet, divided the carriers into separate task forces. Never again after mid-December 1941 would the six big flattops operate together. Commanders Minoru Genda and Mitsuo Fuchida, the two key architects of the Kido Butai's massed air power, strongly disagreed with this strategy. They considered the American carriers to be their prime opponents and wanted to draw them into battle and destroy them.

In January 1942, Nagumo's four carriers pounded small Australian bases on New Britain and New Guinea in support of the landings at Rabaul. Leading ninety planes against almost no opposition at Rabaul, Fuchida assessed the whole operation as "wasteful and extravagant," and equivalent to using "a sledge-hammer to crack an egg." At the same time, the other two flattops of the Kido Butai attacked Allied positions and ships in the Dutch East Indies.

Consequently, none of the Japanese carriers could intervene when the Pacific Fleet's carriers launched their first counterattack. That was precisely what Adm. Chester W. Nimitz, the new fleet commander, intended. His offensive power rested with three small task forces, each built around a single carrier and escorting cruisers and destroyers. In January 1942 the carrier *Yorktown* reached the Pacific, but a Japanese submarine damaged the *Saratoga* and negated the increase. For a month, Nimitz contemplated offensive operations against the enemy's outlying defensive perimeter. He found it difficult to select targets which might meaningfully divert the Japanese without being more than his force could handle. Combat intelligence and the ULTRA code-breakers helped estimate when the Japanese heavy ships would be occupied elsewhere. Thus, on February 1, 1942, Vice Adm. William F. Halsey with the *Enterprise* and

Admirals Chester W. Nimitz, Ernest King, and William "Bull" Halsey in 1942. *U.S. Navy photo, Naval History Division, print courtesy Admiral Nimitz Museum*

Rear Adm. Frank Jack Fletcher with the *Yorktown* surprised Japanese bases in the Marshalls and the Gilberts.

Somewhat flustered by the unexpected American response and fearful of a possible nuisance raid on Japan itself, Yamamoto detached the carriers *Shokaku* and *Zuikaku* to patrol off the homeland. Nagumo took the other four carriers southwest into the Dutch East Indies to cut off the beleaguered Allied forces on Java. On February 19, Fuchida's 188 planes crushed Port Darwin in northwest Australia. He considered the effort against these meager targets to be, in his words, "hardly worthy of the Nagumo force," particularly as a strong Japanese land-based air strike followed closely on the heels of his raiders.

In February, with the Japanese carriers again conveniently out of the way, the Pacific Fleet carriers kept harassing exposed Japanese bases. On February 20, Vice Adm. Wilson Brown's *Lexington* force threatened Rabaul and withdrew after a spirited air battle in which Lt. Edward H. "Butch" O'Hare became the first navy ace of

World War II. Four days later, Bull Halsey's *Enterprise* attacked Wake Island. Ten days later he penetrated deeply into Japanese-controlled waters and raided tiny Marcus Island, only a thousand miles east of Tokyo.

Adm. Ernest J. King, commander in chief of the United States Fleet, looked to the South Pacific as the first location of the Allied counteroffensive and set Rabaul as its ultimate objective. Consequently, he concentrated two-thirds of the available carrier strength in the region by adding Fletcher's *Yorktown* force to Brown's command. In timely fashion, Brown struck back against the Japanese advance, when on March 10, 104 *Lexington* and *Yorktown* aircraft stunned the invasion forces off Lae and Salamaua in eastern New Guinea. They inflicted the heaviest loss yet as suffered by the Imperial Navy during the war. The sudden appearance of Brown's carriers set back Japanese plans to leap forward to Port Moresby and the Solomon Islands until their own carriers could offer support.

In March, Nagumo's carriers rampaged off Java, which fell to the Japanese that month, then regrouped for a massive foray into the Indian Ocean. In early April, his five big carriers (less *Kaga* under repair in the homeland) raided Colombo and Trincomalee on Ceylon. Almost effortlessly, they destroyed the old British carrier *Hermes* and two heavy cruisers who were unable to escape, along with the rest of the British Eastern Fleet. By mid-April, the Japanese had achieved virtually all of their initial war objectives. With astonishingly little loss, they had conquered Southeast Asia and the oil-rich Dutch East Indies, leaving only isolated American garrisons, particularly Corregidor in the Philippines. Fall was expected there shortly. Under the circumstances the Japanese might be excused their arrogance and contempt which they obviously felt toward the Allies. However, according to the old saw, "things change."

April 18 saw the most celebrated of all the 1942 raids: Lt. Col. Jimmy Doolittle's Tokyo strike. It would impact greatly upon Japanese and American operations. Originating with Admiral King's staff, the idea of utilizing medium bombers on a carrier to attack Japan mesmerized President Roosevelt and the high command. At Alameda, the newly arrived carrier *Hornet* embarked with sixteen army B-25 Mitchell bombers, manned by hand-picked army crews who had secretly practiced short distance takeoffs. North of Hawaii, Halsey and *Enterprise* joined the *Hornet* force for the approach to the target. Thus, Nimitz had committed half his available carrier strength to the operation. Doolittle planned to attack Tokyo and other Japanese cities on the nights of April 18 and 19, then reach Chinese airfields after dawn. Detected prematurely the morning of April 18, Halsey launched the B-25s at 650 nautical miles. Expecting a conventional carrier strike the next morning, the Japanese were stunned when the Mitchell B-25s roared low over Japan that afternoon. Unable to find any airfields, fifteen B-25s crashed in China and the remaining crew flew to the Soviet Union.

Deeply embarrassed by the Doolittle raid, Admiral Yamamoto pressed forward with a plan approved only two weeks before, one which greatly altered Japanese strategy. It was designed to lure out and crush the troublesome American carriers once and for all. The bait was to be the invasion of Midway Island, only 1,130 miles northwest of Oahu. An agent of destruction would be the six big carriers of the Kido Butai, supported by the majority of the combined fleet. Yamamoto's planners looked to the anticipated victory as a springboard for the eventual capture of the Hawaiian Islands. The only thing pending before the grand Midway offensive scheduled for June was a sort of sideshow set for early May in the Coral Sea. It was a local offensive against Port Moresby and also Tulagi in the Solomons. On loan from the Kido Butai were the *Shokaku* and *Zuikaku* and joining them was the light carrier *Shoho*, with a total of about 140 planes to support the invasion forces. Counting on surprise, they did not expect much opposition, probably only one American carrier.

At the same time, Yamamoto sought a head-on confrontation with the enemy carriers. So did Admiral Nimitz. By April 22, ULTRA had revealed much of the Japanese Port Moresby plan, which looked like only the beginning of a much wider offensive in the South Pacific. Now with the enemy carriers emerging for the first time beyond their defensive perimeter, Nimitz decided to strike back with all four of his flattops to defend the key South Pacific island bases. Victory would give the United States the initiative. Unfortunately, the Doolittle raid had tied up half of his carriers (*Enterprise* and *Hornet*) which could not even reach the Coral Sea until mid-May. In the meantime, Frank Jack Fletcher's *Yorktown* and *Lexington*, with 138 planes, would deal with the initial Japanese thrust against Port Moresby.

The battle opened on May 3, with Japanese landings on Tulagi. Fletcher, with the *Yorktown*, counterattacked the next day. Luckily, for him, the *Shokaku* and *Zuikaku*, having been delayed, were not in position to intervene. On May 7 and 8, the opposing carrier forces clashed for the first time in naval history. Like many first-time events, the Battle of the Coral Sea was not a thing of elegance, as the frustrated antagonists groped around seeking each other. Rear Adm. Samuel Eliot Morison rather uncharitably described the result as the "Battle of Naval Errors." On May 7 both sides loosed strikes on the basis of erroneous contact reports and misidentified targets. Fortunately for Fletcher, his planes pulverized the *Shoho*, while Japanese Vice Adm. Takao Takagi had to settle for the oiler *Neosho* and the destroyer *Sims*. While the invasion forces scurried north out of the way, the two carrier forces exchanged blows on May 8. Not all of the seventy-five American planes found the target, and those that did attacked in piecemeal fashion. All sixty-nine Japanese attackers executed a coordinated assault on Fletcher's carriers. When the smoke cleared, three heavy bombs had torn up the *Shokaku's* flight deck, but the Japanese had done worse to the Americans. The gallant *Lexington* succumbed to fire started by two torpedoes and two bomb hits, while the *Yorktown* ran southward with bomb damage deep in her vitals. Yet the Japanese had taken such severe plane losses that they called off the Port Moresby invasion. Coral Sea became the first Allied strategic victory of the war.

Later in May, despite losing the services of both the *Shokaku* and *Zuikaku*, the latter due to a shattered air group, Admiral Yamamoto confidently proceeded with his Midway plan. Out in the lead was Nagumo's Kido Butai, with the *Akagi*, *Kaga*, *Soryu*, and *Hiryu*, with about 230 planes, plus another 21 Zero fighters intended for Midway once it fell. Behind them were the invasion forces and a powerful battleship group supported by the light carriers *Zuiho* and *Hosho*. Dispersing his carrier strength even further, Yamamoto allocated two light carriers, the *Ryujo* and newly commissioned *Junyo*, to a diversionary attack against the Aleutians. The fleet sailed in late May and anticipated attack in the Aleutians on June 3 and Midway on the following day.

At Midway, the Imperial Navy expected to surprise their opponents and force them to dance to their tune. However, as in the Coral Sea, Nimitz knew from deciphered Japanese radio messages and brilliant deductions on the part of his code-breakers that the enemy was coming east. He still had to fight them. The loss of the *Lexington* severely reduced his strength and the newly repaired

Saratoga would not be ready in time. Despite bomb damage, the proud *Yorktown*, only patched up and not repaired, joined her sisters *Enterprise* and *Hornet* for battle. The three flattops wielded some 221 operational planes. Fletcher exercised tactical command over the carrier striking force poised northeast of Midway.

Midway certainly turned into the decisive carrier slugging match everyone seemingly had sought. Unaware of the lurking American carriers, Nagumo launched a powerful air strike against Midway. Rear Adm. Raymond A. Spruance unleashed a massive counterblow from the *Enterprise* and *Hornet*, followed an hour later by the *Yorktown's* contribution. Midway's gallant attackers and the sacrifice of Spruance's two torpedo squadrons, VT-8 and VT-6, kept Nagumo too busy to respond immediately when his search planes sighted an American carrier. With unforeseen but incredibly fortunate timing, the *Yorktown* strike group and the *Enterprise* dive-bombers converged on Nagumo's carriers. The *Yorktown's* torpedo planes and escorting Grumman Wildcats drew most of the defending Zeros down and away from the incoming Dauntless SBD dive bombers. They made the most of the opportunity. A superb display of dive-bombing left the *Akagi*, *Kaga*, and *Soryu* as doomed, burning hulks. Only the *Hiryu* survived to wreak havoc on the *Yorktown*, later finished off by a submarine. Brave *Hiryu* did not savor her success, for that afternoon *Enterprise* and orphaned *Yorktown* dive bombers set her afire and left her to sink.

After losing his carrier air power, Yamamoto had no recourse but to retreat with his armada of battleships, cruisers, and destroyers. Defeat at Midway cost Japan four carriers and transformed the course of the Pacific war.

Midway ended the short phase of "decisive" carrier battles. There simply no longer were enough carriers to expend recklessly in that fashion. Now the two navies took time to regroup and reassess strategy and doctrine. In May and June 1942, the Imperial Japanese Navy had lost five carriers and 300 aircraft, with severe aircrew casualties, particularly among leaders. Most of the surviving aviators had fought all the way since December and desperately needed rest. Nagumo's Kido Butai now comprised two big and three light carriers, with another light carrier nearing completion. Total plane strength amounted to 300, but lacked replacement crews and aircraft. The six carriers which had assailed Pearl Harbor had wielded no fewer than 414 aircraft. Things certainly had changed. In turn, the Pacific Fleet now controlled four carriers, the *Saratoga*, the *Enterprise*, the *Hornet*, and the *Wasp*, just arrived from the Atlantic. Their plane strength came to about 315, with steady replacements altogether not yet assured. Other than the *Ranger*, considered unsuitable for carrier war, the fleet could not count on the first *Essex*-class carriers until the spring of 1943 at the earliest.

Delay was the last thing considered at Washington and Pearl Harbor. King and Nimitz moved quickly to forestall a big Japanese build-up in the Solomons. Centered around an airfield on Guadalcanal, the big island eighteen miles south of Tulagi, they orchestrated the first Allied counteroffensive of the war. On August 7, only two months after Midway, marines landed at Guadalcanal and quickly gained a foothold around the precious Lunga Airstrip, which they dubbed Henderson Field.

To the Solomons, the Pacific Fleet committed Fletcher's three carriers, the *Saratoga*, the *Enterprise*, and *Wasp*, with 237 operational planes. Initially, they provided vital air support for the landing forces. Yet Fletcher realized that the tables had turned, so to speak. Now, by supporting invasion forces of his own, he confronted the same problem faced by the Japanese carriers at Coral Sea and Midway. Now his flattops had to brave strong enemy land-based airpower and submarines to be followed by counterattack by Japanese carriers. Yet his efforts to preserve his carriers for that struggle met with strong disapproval.

Shortly after the Guadalcanal landings, Yamamoto sent down from Japan a powerful force which included the *Shokaku*, *Zuikaku*, and the *Ryujo*, along with 177 planes. Before Nagumo could arrive, a most important event took place. On August 20, marine aircraft began operating from Henderson Field. That set the pattern for the entire campaign. The Japanese planned to build up their ground forces on Guadalcanal, cut off the marine garrison by sea, and then reconquer the island. However, before Japanese naval forces could safely approach the island in daylight, it became vital to neutralize Henderson Field through land-based air attacks or ship bombardments. No longer would Nagumo rush blindly in just to take on an island air garrison. He had learned his lesson at Midway. He considered the American carriers his principal opponents and looked for Japanese attacks on Guadalcanal to flush them out. For Japan, the marines and Henderson Field turned out to be far tougher than expected, and Allied naval and air support was just sufficient to keep them going.

For the American carriers, the principal problem became supporting Guadalcanal without unduly exposing themselves to attack. Given limited resources, they had to fight from where they could do the most good without being drawn away from their own shore-based air support. Unlike Coral Sea and Midway, the surface navy bore the brunt of naval action off Guadalcanal. Unfortunately, ULTRA, which proved to be so valuable to Coral Sea and Midway, almost completely disappeared from mid-August to early November. Indeed, United States naval intelligence could not even say how many Japanese carriers had come south, let alone any specific reading of their plans. The American carrier commanders had to depend solely on sightings by aircraft and submarines to locate their opponents. This meant considerable apprehension and heartburn.

The two big carrier clashes during the Guadalcanal campaign were the battle of the Eastern Solomons on August 24 and the battle of Santa Cruz on October 26. The *Enterprise* suffered heavy damage during both battles, while the *Hornet* went down off Santa Cruz. In both engagements the American carriers had to retire, but not before they had bloodied the Japanese ships and air groups sufficiently to deter them from advancing further toward Guadalcanal. Also during the campaign, submarines sank the *Wasp* and crippled the *Saratoga*. Yet United States aircraft losses were generally light, and most of the planes ended up fighting at Guadalcanal.

The Japanese were not so fortunate. Although the Guadalcanal campaign cost Japan only one carrier, the *Ryujo*, sunk on August 24, their losses in skilled veteran crews, particularly at Santa Cruz, were devastating. Indeed, Santa Cruz became the death thread of the old Kido Butai aviators. The Imperial Navy never saw their likes again. Fully half of all the dive bomber crews and forty percent of the torpedo plane crews perished. Corresponding United States losses were two and ten percent, respectively.

Nowhere is there a contrast in fortunes better than that shown during the crucial naval battle at Guadalcanal. By November, attrition had reduced each side to one operational carrier in the region. Japan retained the *Junyo*, with a shattered air group, and the United States had the battered *Enterprise*, but with a strong air group. On November 13 and 14, while the Japanese attempted to force a large convoy into Guadalcanal, the *Junyo* flyers played almost no role. However, Bill Halsey committed the big "*E*" to the battle and her Air Group 10 proved invaluable in insuring the Japanese defeat.

After Guadalcanal, the American carrier navy soared with vastly increasing numbers and quality. Incessant combat ashore ground down their Japanese counterparts, who were burdened by inferior aircraft and too little training. After Santa Cruz, in October 1942, the next carrier battle did not occur until June 19 and 20, 1944, during the invasion of Saipan. Although officially called the Battle of the Philippine Sea, its unofficial title, "The Mariana's Turkey Shoot," speaks eloquently of the contrast between 1942 and later carrier battles.

III. The Demise of the Asiatic Fleet

Java Sea

The ABDA command was the great experiment that failed. Commanded by Gen. Sir Archibald Wavell, the forces of ABDA were strung out over a 2,000-mile line in the South Pacific. Dated and limited equipment problems, lack of communications, and political issues plagued ABDA from the start.

Ground troops were armed with dated equipment and did not have enough. The mainstay ships of ABDA were worn-out four-pipers, antiquated World War I destroyers. Naval ammunition did not function properly. It was common for shells to misfire or not explode on contact. Torpedoes did not run true or failed to explode on contact. Repair facilities were few and far between, and there were acute shortages of maintenance personnel and spare parts. ABDA had a critical shortage of airplanes, leaving naval vessels with little or no air cover.

ABDA commanders did not keep their people fully informed of ABDA movements, nor did they pass on available communications intelligence to keep their people apprised of enemy plans and actions. This was due to the different nations' lack of experience in joint operations, not maliciousness. ABDA lost the *Houston* and *Perth* for this reason. The Dutch had intelligence information on the Japanese Fleet in Bantam Bay (Java Sea), but did not inform Captain Rooks (*Houston*), who could have then avoided the Sunda Straits. ABDA forces retained the communications system of their home countries, thus having four different signaling systems and communications systems, which often led to misunderstood or misinterpreted communications.[1]

Each nation in ABDA had its own agenda, interests, and concerns regarding the war in the South Pacific. These "turf wars"

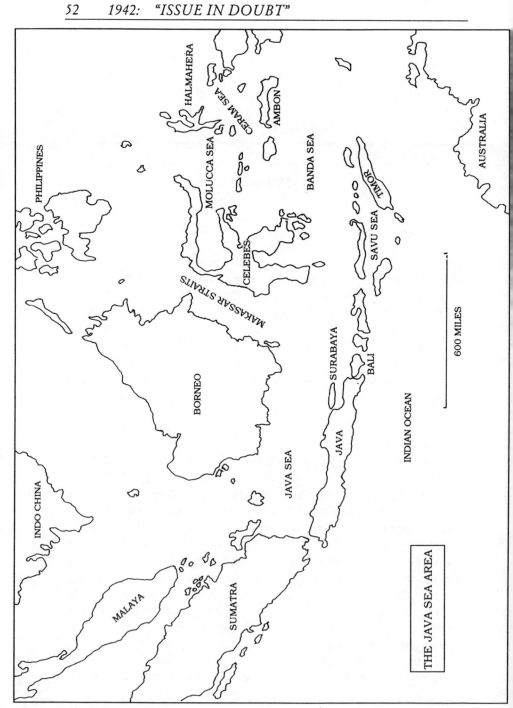

THE JAVA SEA AREA

HMAS *Perth* wearing her camouflage paint scheme. *Royal Australian Navy, print courtesy Admiral Nimitz Museum*

served to destroy whatever cooperation and joint decision-making had been developed.

In February and early March 1942, the Japanese, commanded by Vice Adm. Takao Takagi, effectively brought an end to ABDA in the Java Sea. In a series of actions covering that one-month period of time, the Japanese sank the *De Ruyter, Encounter, Electra, Evertsen, Exeter, Houston, Java, Perth,* and *Pope*. The HMS *Jupiter* struck a mine and sunk.

Following the Battle of Java Sea, the remaining ships of ABDA were taken from naval Commander Conrad Emile Helfrich and returned to command of their rightful countries. ABDA was finished as a military command.

Beginning and End: Overview of the Asiatic Fleet

No one factor can be assigned blame for the ineffectiveness of the Allied efforts to slow Japan's relentless march in early 1942. Several of these factors do involve the ABDA command and actions surrounding the Battle of the Java Sea. Some factors, including dated equipment, disorganized command, and impaired communications, have already been mentioned. In an overview and analysis of the ABDA command, Dwight Messimer will mention several other factors which played a significant role in the demise of the ABDA command. He will also discuss how the Allies tried their utmost to stop the Japanese, and will provide an overview of the actions engaged in by the Asiatic Fleet.

Dwight Messimer has written three books on the war in the Pacific. His books are *No Margin for Error*, an account of the United States Navy's first transpacific flight, the *Pawns of War*, about the loss of the USS *Langley* and USS *Pecos*, and *In the Hands of Fate*, about the early operations of Patrol Wing 10. He is a former tank commander in the United States Army and presently teaches history at San Jose State University and is a sergeant on the San Jose (California) Police Department.

Dwight Messimer

Let's start with what the Asiatic Fleet was not and what it was. It was not a battle fleet as we came to understand battle fleets in the First or the Second World Wars. It was a fleet designed to protect American interests in the Far East, and to show the flag. For that mission it was equipped with old ships. In fact, Adm. Thomas Hart once remarked that "they were old enough to vote."

The two cruisers assigned, the USS *Marblehead* and the USS *Houston*, were both older ships. They were not radar-equipped. The thirteen destroyers were all flush deckers, called "four-pipers," that had been built at the end of the First World War. The submarines assigned to the fleet on the eve of the war were six old "S" type boats, based on World War I designs. Those were the real fighting units of the fleet.

The rest of the fleet was composed of the vessels in the Yangzee patrol, five river gunboats that could not operate offshore, and two coastal gunboats that were of little use in surface warfare.

The fleet's air arm consisted of Patrol Wing 10 (PatWing 10) made up of twenty-eight PBY-4s. The PBY-4 was a preamphibious version of the Catalina flying boat. To get it out of the water, you had to put wheels on it (a sort of dolly affair) and pull it up on the beach. The PBY-4 could only land and take off on the water. Pat-Wing 10 also had some small utility aircraft assigned to it.

Supporting the fleet were a couple of oilers, tenders, and auxiliaries. As the war drew near, the fleet was reinforced with twenty-three modern Fleet-type submarines and six motor torpedo boats.

There is a misunderstanding that needs to be set aside immediately. The Asiatic Fleet, along with the entire United States military, has been accused of being unprepared for the Japanese attack on December 7, 1941, and the fighting that followed during the next six months. With respect to the Asiatic Fleet's material preparedness, that accusation is true. But to accuse the Asiatic Fleet of being unprepared with respect to organization, training (they were extensively trained), and deployment is a disservice to those people.

Admiral Hart believed the war warning he received on November 20, 1941, and he acted on that warning. He deployed his fleet southward in accordance with the war plan in effect at that time, and dispersed his on-shore stocks of fuel, munitions, and spare parts.

Through no fault of Admiral Hart, the fleet was not prepared for joint operations with the British and the Dutch. There had been very little discussions with the three European powers in the Far East about joint command, and no agreement had been reached on that issue. Each fleet was left to fight the Japanese according to its own national interests. The common effort was to be accomplished through the vaguely defined doctrine of "cooperation."

Nor was there agreement between Admiral Hart and Gen. Douglas MacArthur about how the Philippines was to be defended. The critical issue was air power, and how army aircraft were going to be used to support and protect the fleet. In MacArthur's view, they were not going to be used for that purpose. He apparently held the view that the navy had its job and he had his. This may sound overly harsh, but I have the impression that MacArthur's attitude toward Admiral Hart was, "You have your boats. You go play with them. I have a war to fight here."

When the war started, the fleet was deployed southward according to plan. But the fleet's headquarters was based in Manila, and Manila quickly became untenable. By December 14, the Asiatic Fleet had fallen back to bases in Ambon and Java. What was left behind in the Philippines were the submarines, a couple of tenders, the auxiliaries, and a lot of navy personnel who could not be lifted south. They fought as infantry, and were killed and captured as infantry on Bataan and Corregidor.

Along with the surface ships, PatWing 10's remaining PBYs flew to Sarabaja on December 14. By that time, PatWing 10 had lost half its aircraft.

Once the fleet had been forced out of the Philippines, there was a renewed effort to coordinate the naval activities of the three European powers. The British main interest was in the defense of Singapore, and they wanted the Americans to provide ships for convoy escort into Singapore. The Dutch were primarily interested in the defense of Java, and the Americans were desperately anxious to support the troops in the Philippines. As a result, there was no concerted effort made to stop the Japanese southward advance.

It is unfortunate that during this time Admiral Hart came under criticism for indecision and lack of initiative. He is accused of sending his ships wandering around aimlessly, accomplishing nothing. People were demanding to know why he was not coming to grips with the Japanese fleet as it drove south.

But he did try to come to grips with the Japanese. The problem was that every time he sent ships north, they did so without air cover. And the Japanese controlled the skies. The outcome of those desperate attempts was predictable, and the inevitable result was that Hart's forces were driven back.

The first attempt to strike the Japanese was made by PatWing 10's PBYs. Six of them set out on December 27, 1941, to attack Japanese shipping at Jolo. Unescorted, the slow, poorly armed PBYs were quickly destroyed by Japanese fighters. Only two PBYs returned to Ambon. The raid was completely ineffectual.

But the disaster at Jolo had positive results. From that time forward, the vulnerable PBYs were used for reconnaissance and rescue — two jobs at which they excelled.

The next attempt to hurt the Japanese was made by a task force composed of the *Marblehead* and the newly arrived USS *Boise*. They were escorted by four destroyers with the submarine S-36 scouting ahead. The mission was to attack the Japanese at Balikpapan. But the *Marblehead* developed shaft problems and had to drop out. The *Boise* ran on a rock, tore her bottom out, and had to limp back to Australia. The S-36 grounded on a reef and had to be scuttled. That left the four destroyers to carry out the night attack on January 23–24, 1942.

Their attack achieved tactical surprise and they sank four Japanese transports. The skirmish was heralded as the "first American victory." I guess it was a victory, though a very small one, and one that did not even put a dent in the Japanese drive south.

Criticism of how Admiral Hart was conducting the war reached a peak on January 28, 1942. In effect, he was relieved of his command, but for the record, Adm. William Glassford was made commander, United States Naval Forces, Southwest Pacific. Hart still commanded the Asiatic Fleet, but in effect that command had been inactivated.

The change in the American command structure coincided with the creation of a unified command called ABDA. But by that time the situation in the Southwest Pacific had reached the point where there was no hope of saving Java. Once Singapore was lost, the British quickly concluded, along with the Americans, that defending the Netherlands East Indies was no longer possible, and they started making plans to get out.

Though the Asiatic Fleet had essentially ceased to exist as an organization, its ships still had to fight and die. On February 4, the crippled *Marblehead* and the *Houston* were sent north to stop the Japanese. Without air cover, the ships came under Japanese air attack and were badly damaged. The *Marblehead* was rendered inoperative for the remainder of the campaign, and the *Houston*'s after-turret was destroyed.

The retreat from Java was in full swing, and there was a sense that it was every man for himself. The Dutch fought the pointless and futile Battle of the Java Sea, and the survivors tried to run for safety. The *Houston* stumbled into the Japanese invasion fleet and was sunk.

Despite the hopelessness of the situation, a last-ditch effort was made to supply the Dutch with thirty-two P-40 fighters. The attempt was politically motivated and made no sense militarily. The seaplane tender USS *Langley* was sent from Australia to Tijilijap, Java, with a deckload of P-40s. She never got there. One day out from her goal she was attacked by Japanese bombers and sunk.

The attempt to deliver ready-to-fly P-40s to Java was, given the situation at the time, absurd. Even if the *Langley* had arrived in Tijilijap, there was no way the fighters could have been unloaded and towed through town to the hastily prepared airstrip in time to get them into battle. The Japanese were already ashore in Java.

Another freighter, the SS *Seawitch*, did make it to Tijilijap, and did offload her disassembled and crated fighters onto the wharf. But every one of those fighters, still crated, was dumped into the harbor. The sending of those ships and their fighters to Java deprived the army of aircraft that could have been used in India. As it was, when the 51st Fighter Group arrived in Karachi, they had only one fighter plane.

The sidebar to that ill-advised attempt to reinforce Java with fighters was the loss of the USS *Edsall*. She had been sent, along with the USS *Whipple*, to pick up survivors from the *Langley*. After the *Langley* was sunk, the two destroyers rendezvoused with the *Pecos*, and most of the survivors were put aboard the oiler. But the pilots who were going to be desperately needed in Australia and India were put aboard the *Edsall* and sent back to Java to fight as infantry! The *Esdall* never made it. She ran into the Japanese fleet and was sunk with all hands by gunfire.

Other *Langley* survivors had been taken aboard the fleet oiler USS *Pecos*. The next day *Pecos* was also attacked by Japanese aircraft and sunk. Nearly 800 men were killed.

The last dramatic operation was the Operation Flight Gridiron, the attempt to rescue key military personnel and army nurses from Corregidor. Two PBYs were sent north on April 27, 1942, and both arrived at Corregidor safely. But when they landed on Lake Lanao to refuel, one of the PBYs flown by Tom Pollock struck a rock and sank.

The other PBY continued on to Australia while Pollock and his crew tried to salvage their plane. In the meantime their passengers, figuring the plane was a total loss, went inland. They were captured by the Japanese. Using canvas, burlap and pitch, Pollock and his crew patched the hole, took aboard anyone who wanted to go to Australia, and took off. They reached Australia safely on May 2, 1942.

In conclusion, I can tell you that the Asiatic Fleet was hopelessly outgunned when the war started. They did everything they could to stem the Japanese tide, but in fact, they had no effect on the Japanese advance. By January 1942, the Asiatic Fleet had ceased to exist as an organization on paper and as a fighting unit. Despite the Allied victory in 1945, the fleet's purpose for being had been swept away by the changes that followed the war. It was never reconstituted.

Adm. Thomas H. Moorer also took part in the actions surrounding the Java Sea. Here is his analysis concerning those bleak days in the Pacific.

Adm. Thomas H. Moorer, USN (Ret.)

I will go into some detail about my personal experiences, which if I wasn't a Christian when they happened, I am now. Before the war, Mr. Roosevelt and Mr. Churchill made an agreement, and that was that the United States would send B-17s to Clark Air Force Base in the Philippines and the British would send the *Repulse* and the *Prince of Wales*, two big battleships, to Singapore. In their discussions, they believed, apparently, that those forces deployed in the Asian area would deter the Japanese from making their assault on that particular area to get raw materials. Of course, the B-17s were lost at the outset. They did not in any way support the navy, as was the concept at the time. I think people had far too much confidence in the effectiveness of horizontal bombing on a moving target, like a ship. And secondly, as you know, the *Repulse* and *Prince of Wales* were immediately sunk off of Singapore and never did really get involved in any kind of support of the ground forces. So, the Asiatic Fleet as well as our Allies were lacking the support that people had thought about for a long time before this happened.

General MacArthur told Admiral Hart to go play with his ships and don't bother me. He had declared Manila an open city on Christmas Day, I believe it was, in 1941. He never advised Admiral Hart he was going to do that and Admiral Hart, of course, was then moved by submarine, which put him out of contact for a week or so, to join this command that had been hastily set up with General Wavell[2] as the commander of ABDA. The American, British, Dutch, Australian command was really the ultimate in disorganization — at least my experience with them happened to be that way.

We had a young pilot in my squadron named Bob Dede, and he shot down a Japanese Zero on a patrol up in the Makassar Straits and came back and claimed a kill. So they had a little conference in the office staff and gave him a probable. That really burned Dede up because he saw the Zero hit the water. On a patrol about two or three days later, the same thing happened to Dede. He shot down another Zero, and it hit the water with the tail out of the water. So he promptly landed alongside it, got in his rubber boat, went over, climbed up, cut this rising sun out of the tail, and brought it back down to Surabaya and asked them what they thought of that. Well, they finally, reluctantly, gave him a one kill and a one probable.

But seriously, it was just nothing but unadulterated murder to put the World War I forces, what the majority of the Asiatic Fleet was composed of, into that kind of a combat situation where they had very little, if any, intelligence. We had limited weather information and the task assignments were done on a willy-nilly basis. Admiral Hart was a fine officer, I thought. He, of course, recognized what the odds were, so he began to recommend that the forces be withdrawn before they were destroyed and be available for the war he recognized was bound to follow.

That was certainly not politically expedient because the Dutch had been chased out of Holland, and the Dutch East Indies was their last home. So the Dutch leaders were determined to fight to the death. That placed the United States in the position where certainly the people in Washington did not want to fade away in that context. As a result, most all the Asiatic Fleet was destroyed in about two months' time. That's one of the sad stories of that war.

I will say that the reason I would like to thank the Admiral Nimitz Museum Foundation for this is because it's very difficult to find many books about this action we've been talking about here today. You ask somebody on the street about it and they've never heard of it. I think that this is going to do a lot of good and make the public aware of what these people really went through — the army, navy, army air corps, the whole group. We should let this be a lesson, to never again let our people, both military and civilian, get caught in that situation. In my view there is no excuse for it.

Three Strikes and You're Out

As was mentioned, Admiral Hart escaped the Philippines aboard a submarine. Admiral Hart did not want to leave by submarine, complaining that the trip would keep him isolated from his duties for too long a period of time. Had he known what was in store for his staff members who were not lucky enough to board that submarine, he might not have complained. Cecil King, Jr., was one of those who were not able to leave the Philippines by submarine. His escape was much more eventful.

Chief Warrant Officer (Ret.) Cecil King, Jr., was assigned to the Flag of the Asiatic Fleet under Adm. Thomas Hart. He left the Philippines for Java and then to Australia. Three of the ships he served on were subsequently sunk: the USS *Houston*, USS *Perry*, and USS *Langley*. Before retiring to his home in Texas, King served under three successive chiefs of naval operations. King believed in the old sailor superstition that one should have a pig tattooed on one foot and a rooster on the other to save oneself from shipwreck and drowning. The tattoos must have worked for him.

Cecil King, Jr.

The Asiatic Fleet was indeed a kind of French Foreign Legion operation. It was an outpost with the tour of duty an absolute mandatory thirty months. Some of the sailors were a bit eccentric. I will confess to that. But nonetheless, when the chips were down, they were there. Admiral Hart moved his staff off the *Houston* in November of 1941, and that was an unprecedented step to those of us involved. We had an idea of what was about to happen. We were waiting for the other shoe to drop, so to speak, which it did in the Philippines on December 8, when we were attacked simultaneously with Pearl Harbor. Two days later, the navy shipyard at Cavite was pretty well wiped out and with substantial casualties. It was pretty much downhill from then.

Manila was declared an open city on December 25. All military had to leave the city on that day. I was in a small group with Admiral Hart that boarded a PT boat on the Manila waterfront to go out to Cavite to get on this PBY that was going to take us south. But on the way out to the plane, we watched it being destroyed on the water by fighter planes and we headed on to Corregidor. Admiral Hart left there on a submarine, and after a day or two several of us on the staff were scheduled to board the USS *Peary* (DD-226), an old four-piper that had been very heavily damaged in Cavite. Her topside was beat up, but her engines were sound and she was essentially seaworthy. We were going to make a run for it. The *Peary* was painted green, with swabs and palm leaves tied around the topside and canvas strung between the four stacks to break up that typical four-piper silhouette. The idea was to come alongside an island during the day and then run like hell at night.

We left Corregidor about dark and in a few hours ran into some incoming Japanese ships who apparently thought we were one of their stragglers. This went on for quite a while. To use an understatement, we were lucky to clear from the Japanese ships just before dawn. We came alongside land on the island of Panay. Unfortunately, a formation of BETTY twin-engine bombers passed directly overhead, testing our camouflage, I suppose. To make matters worse, the chief engineer put out some black smoke about that time. The planes kept on but we didn't know whether or not we'd been sighted. So we pulled out.

I was stationed as a lookout on the flying bridge on top of the regular bridge, and was given a piece of smoked glass from the galley to stare into the sun for carrier planes, our worst nightmare. In midafternoon that day we were sighted and were engaged in a torpedo attack by a Japanese Emily flying boat. We were able to outmaneuver the torpedoes and we also fired our three-inch forward deck gun for effect only. We had only surface ammunition and star shells, and the gun could only be trained up forty-five degrees, but we fired away. Also about that time, my group had custody of some classified material in bags with grommets in them. We were in deep water, so we dropped them over the side. Our immediate future was a little murky at the time.

We then set course for the town of Menado on the Celebes Island to take on fuel, and about an hour out saw and were seen by a navy PBY. We were happy to see a friendly for a change, and not knowing who we were because of our camouflage, he reported us as a Japanese light cruiser on the way into Menado to unload some troops. Luckily we couldn't hear this. We sighted Menado. We got fairly close to it and discovered that it was entirely in flames. So we took a left inside a channel alongside Celebes. In this channel we sighted three Lockheed Hudson bombers with Allied wing markings: red, white, and blue circles. We were delirious with glee and waved our tin hats and so on, but only very briefly. These Australian planes were in response to the PBY's contact report. They began an immediate, very-well coordinated bombing and strafing attack. We were not flying our colors at the time and in trying to hoist them they fouled and all you could see was red and white stripes, which didn't much help our identification problems. We were maneuvering as best we could inside this channel and one bomb struck the fantail and knocked the rudder out and it also struck the depth-charge racks. I could see this bomb coming through the air — it took about two hours to get to us. I could see it was headed toward the fantail. That's where our depth charges were and, as a matter of fact, it struck that area but didn't set off the depth-charges. I guess they weren't fused. But one of them was smoking and was dropped over the side. We didn't have any use for it at the time. By that time it was pretty dark and those three Australian planes left, we were happy to see.

We set hand steering by voice communication to get control of the ship. We were spinning out of control in the channel. The decision was made to beach the *Peary* on a remote island, Mindoro Island in the Halmahera Group. Most of the crew spent the night ashore. The next day emergency repairs were made on the rudder and a PBY came in and landed some critical repair equipment. Contact was also made with the Dutch troops and the Dutch people on this island, and they came in with a lot of people carrying quarts of Heineken beer. I would say that this cold beer was warmly received by those of us who were the happy recipients.

The *Peary* was refloated and then we went on to Ambon to refuel. We were running on fumes. We were escorted part of the way to Ambon by the same three Australian planes. They came aboard in Ambon, and there were no hard feelings. That was a mistake of war; we understood and they understood. We certainly appreciated their coming to see us. That was a decent thing to do.

We went on to Port Darwin. Our group went aboard the USS *Langley*. We were given some clothes and some personal gear and then we got orders to leave the *Langley* and to board the cruiser *Boise* to go back to Surabaya, Java, where Admiral Hart's staff, or the remnants of it, were setting up a headquarters. We got to Java, which turned out to be a carbon copy of the Philippines.

Incidentally, I should remark that the *Peary*, which offloaded us in Port Darwin, was around for a couple of weeks. On February 19, and at the time of the 100-plane Japanese carrier attack on Port Darwin, the *Peary* was unmistakably sunk. About fifty lives were lost, which was about half her crew. When Java was going downhill and the enemy finally landed, I was sent over to the Tijilijap side to go aboard the USS *Sturgeon*, a submarine which was carrying some forty-odd wounded off the *Houston*. They took us to Fremantle. About this time the *Houston* was sunk in a night surface engagement. Because my records were aboard the *Houston*, I was reported as missing in action. A little later I was able to call home, not knowing I was dead. My call caused some little commotion in my hometown of Aransas Pass, Texas. I guess some were glad and some were not. So I spent a little time in Australia and then went back to the United States to return to the Pacific aboard the USS *Hornet*, which was a welcome change from the *Peary*.

The Japanese Perspective

Although the Japanese seemed invincible in the early days of 1942, they were not without their problems. Personnel and material problems affected the Japanese as they did the Allies. Local commanders covertly questioned the strategy of Imperial Japanese Headquarters, and Japanese torpedoes failed to operate properly. Teiji Nakamura will discuss these and other issues from the Japanese navy perspective.

Teiji Nakamura attended the Japanese Naval Academy at Etajima, where he learned the principles of the Samurai warrior and the devotion to country. He served on the destroyer *Yudachi* and in a number of the early campaigns in the Pacific during World War II. When the *Yudachi* was sunk at Guadalcanal, Mr. Nakamura was reassigned to the battleship *Nagato* and later back to Etajima as an instructor.

Teiji Nakamura

The *Yudachi* was a modern destroyer completed in 1937. Her displacement was 1,685 tons, and she was equipped with five 5-inch guns, two 40mm guns, and eight 24-inch torpedo tubes. Her crew complement was 209. She joined the war and from the beginning had the highest level of training and her crew morale was very high.

Before the war, it was considered that a decisive sea battle in the western Pacific was the key task of the Imperial Japanese Navy. The destroyers were expected to attack the enemy main force with torpedoes, our best weapons against a superior enemy fleet. Another manifold task was to serve as escort, or a screen for the main body or of a convoy, as well as patrolling and minesweeping duties, anti-aircraft defense, and anti-submarine warfare. The latter gradually became the most important, but the torpedo attack remained the primary role of the modern destroyer.

In the actual war, however, a decisive fleet battle with battleships as the nucleus, the battle for which we had trained, never happened. Surface actions occurred in some cases, but in most cases,
destroyers undertook such tasks as defense against air attack, anti-
submarine defense, and harbor patrol. In the first phase of the war,
that is the Japanese Invasion Phase, *Yudachi* belonged to the 2nd
Destroyer Division of the 4th Destroyer Squadron. She joined in
the raid on Vigin in the northern Philippines and later took part in
the invasion of Lingayen. As the Japanese thrust to the south, she
took part in the operations at Tarakan, Balikpapan, and Surabaya.

The *Yudachi* then moved to the north and joined the blockade
of Manila Bay. Anti-submarine patrol, escort duty, and picket duty
was done along the way, as well as anti-submarine sweeps and patrol
after she arrived. These were normal tasks during the invasion. It
was usual to have air raids and sometimes submarine contacts were
reported, upon which attacks were made. In Balikpapan, we were
surprised by United States destroyers, and to our chagrin, lost four
transports without knowing what was happening.

A highlight of these operations was the Battle of the Java Sea.
On February 27 we received a report from one of our aircraft that
five enemy cruisers and six destroyers (there were actually nine)
were sighted at a point about sixty miles south of Surabaya. The
escort commander hastened to the enemy with most of the escort
ships, including the *Yudachi*, and joined the support force. Our
strength altogether was four cruisers and fourteen destroyers. When
I sighted the enemy about two hours before sunset, I recognized
that three destroyers were leading five cruisers in column. The leading cruiser was identified as the Dutch *De Ruyter*, but she looked
much bigger than a heavy cruiser, and some Japanese wondered if
she might not be a new kind of battleship. After closing, our escort
force launched four torpedoes each, with bearings intended to give
good torpedo dispersion, at ranges of 12,000 to 14,000 meters. Our
ships were firing shells at the enemy ships at the same time. At this
moment, big columns of water shot up one after the other near the
point where the torpedoes had been launched and it seemed to us
that they could have been impacts of shells from the enemy
battleship's main guns. After launching torpedoes, each Japanese
ship retired westerly to lure the enemy ships into the torpedo field.

About twenty minutes later, a seaplane reported the sinking of
one enemy ship by torpedo and the senior commander ordered all

ships to charge the enemy force. Then each ship turned immediately to make a charge. *Yudachi* was the last ship in the division column and launched four torpedoes at a distance of 9,000 meters in the face of heavy enemy fire. Again, big columns of water were shot up just after each ship had launched its torpedoes. *Yudachi* could not avoid a water column and ran into the water column and was showered with metal pieces, which were later found to be parts of a Japanese torpedo. Shortly after sunset, the escort force took the night battle station, and after searching for the enemy without result resumed the original mission.

In my opinion, the Imperial Japanese Navy disclosed two important defects in this battle. One was the lack of fighting spirit generally at the close hard fighting on the command level. The idea of a decisive sea battle was one of the main reasons for this tendency. It was not easy for senior officers to adjust to the new aspect of war when they had good reason to try to preserve their forces and prepare for a decisive sea battle in a later stage. Combined with the psychology of the battle, this desire to preserve their forces made the battle indecisive. Cruisers fought at long distance, more than 20,000 meters, and only two destroyers dashed to launching position of 5,000 meters as instructed as the standard daytime duel.

The second defect was the self-explosion of the torpedoes. It became clear that the columns of water were shot up as a result of the self-explosion of the torpedoes as a result of parts that we found recovered by the *Yudachi*. Later it was found that the inertia exploder equipped in our torpedoes was too sensitive, and steps were taken to improve on this defect. Even then it was reported that half the torpedoes launched by two cruisers were exploded in the wake of enemy ships. As such, the result of the torpedo attack in this daytime action of the Java Sea battle was a miserable failure. In total, 137 torpedoes were launched, and there was only one hit.

The Death Railway

By early 1942, the Japanese occupied almost the whole of Southeast Asia. Japan's military was spread from Singapore to Bangkok to Rangoon, India. They had overextended their reach and were forced to slow their expanding empire because of the lack of supplies and munitions. To supply their far-flung troops and regain their early initiatives, Imperial Japanese Headquarters decided to build a railroad linking Singapore, Bangkok, and Rangoon. They would use POWs and conscripted laborers in the construction of this railroad. Captured Allied soldiers were shipped to Thailand and Burma to build a labor force for the Japanese.

The first POWs began work on Death Railway in June 1942, at Ban Pong and Nong Pladuk, in southern Thailand. This was where the railways from Bangkok and Singapore converged. Other POWs began work on the northern section of the railway at Thanbyuzayat, Burma, beginning at the established railway which ran between Moulmein and Ye. The two groups were to work toward each other and were to meet between Taimonta and Konkoita, Thailand.

The southern section of the railway started easily enough. POWs rapidly constructed the first fifty-five kilometers of railway from Nong Pladuk to Kanchanaburi (or Kachanabuan). They followed the Kwae-Noi River, a tributary of the Mae Khlaung River. At Tha Makham, just outside of Kanchanaburi, the POWs began experiencing the difficulties which would ultimately give this railroad its name — Death Railway. Before ascending into the mountains, a bridge had to be built across the Kwae-Noi River. In a project lasting almost six months (October 1942–February 1943) and costing thousands of lives, the POWs finally finished the construction of a wooden bridge across the Kwae-Noi River.[3] As construction moved farther north, the arduous work, jungle, and climate began claiming their tolls of POWs. Malnutrition, illness, disease, and the inhuman treatment by the Japanese were killing hundreds of POWs and conscripted laborers for every meter of track laid. Malaria, dysentery, insect bites, 100-degree-plus temperatures, along with humidity high enough to produce a physical presence, worked in concert with the brutality of the Japanese to claim POW lives.

POWs working on the northern section of the railway were faring no better. Although there were no major river crossings, the jungle and mountains were proving to be more than formidable. From the start, workers fell behind schedule. Approximately 100 kilometers south of Thanbyuzayat, at the Burma/Thailand border, a solid wall of mountains had to be cut through. Known as Three Pagoda Pass, this obstacle further slowed work. No amount of pushing, prodding, goading, or torture by their Japanese captors could keep the workers on schedule.

Table 1. Allied POW work camps and distances on the route of Death Railway.

Camp Name	Distance	Camp Name	Distance
Nong Pladuk	000	Rindato	198
Komma	002	Brankassi	208
Ban Pong	005	Takanum	218
Rukke	013	Namajon	229
Taruartoi	026	Tomajo	237
Tamuang	039	Tamuron Part	244
Tung Tung	041	Krian Kri	250
Kao Dih	047	Kutikonta	262
Pak Prage	048	Konkoita	262
Tung Na Talea	049	Teimonta	273
Kanchanaburi	051	Nikki	282
Tha Makham	055	Sonkurai	294
Chungkai	057	Three Pagoda Pass	298
Wang Lan	069	Changaraya	301
Won Yen	078	Anganan	311
Bankao	088	100 Kilo Camp	315
Takiren	098	Kyando	320
Arrowhill	108	Aparon	332
Lum Sum	110	Aparain	337
Wang Po	114	Mezari	343
Chong Cab	121	Kami-Mezari	349
Wang Yai	125	Konsi	354
Tha Soe	130	Tanzun	358
Nam Tok	130	Tanbaya	362
Tonchan	139	Anakuin	369
Tampi	147	Bekitan	375
Hin Tok	155	Repo	385
Kanyu	166	Konnokoi	391
Kinsaiyuk	168	Rabao	396
Kinsaiyuk Main	172	Tettoku	401
Rin Tin	181	Wegare	406
Kui Yong	190	Thanbyuzayat	414

Note: All distances given in kilometers.

As POW deaths continued to mount and the mountainous jungle terrain proved to be a near impenetrable environment, the Japanese kept replenishing the expendable supply of construction laborers. The influx of POWs and conscripted laborers began to grow, with two to fill the spot of every one who died. This made the already inhuman living conditions even worse and the death rate grow even faster. Laborers were worked from sunup to sundown, with less than a cup of water and one bowl of rice per day for sustenance. Any minor cut or illness, falling by the wayside or passing out from the heat, or failing to work because of exhaustion, illness, or malnutrition, was a death sentence. Neither the Japanese nor the jungle showed mercy.

With work on the railway lagging far behind schedule and the Imperial Japanese Headquarters pushing ever harder for completion, POWs were moved inland to temporary work camps. For months at a time, POWs would live at these ill-provisioned camps until a section of the railway was completed. They would then be moved to the next camp to begin the process anew. (Table 1 lists the work camps along Death Railway.) When prisoners died, they were left where they fell, for there was a steady stream of replacement POWs.

In October 1943, the Death Railway was completed when the northern and southern sections joined at Konkoita, Thailand. The POWs were removed to camps at Tha Makham, Kanchanaburi, Tamuang, and Nakhon Pathom, where they were given food and medicine, were allowed to recuperate somewhat, and were then transferred to POW camps in Japan. This must have seemed like heaven for the emaciated and exhausted POWs.

Very few POWs who began work on the Death Railway lived to see it completed. The average POW life-span was only a few months. Life had been reduced to surviving the next yard of track. POWs did not think in terms of surviving the day, but in surviving the next piece of track laid. Faces changed so rapidly that every day saw strangers working together. Friendships were not formed because one did not live long enough. The POWs who did live to see Death Railway completed suffered long-term illness, disease, and disability. Many of the survivors have recurrent bouts of malarial fever. Worse, most suffer permanent disability due to vitamin shortages suffered during construction of the railway. Many of those survivors are nearly blind due to vitamin deficiencies. The Allies did not know of this brutality until it was too late. One can only imagine

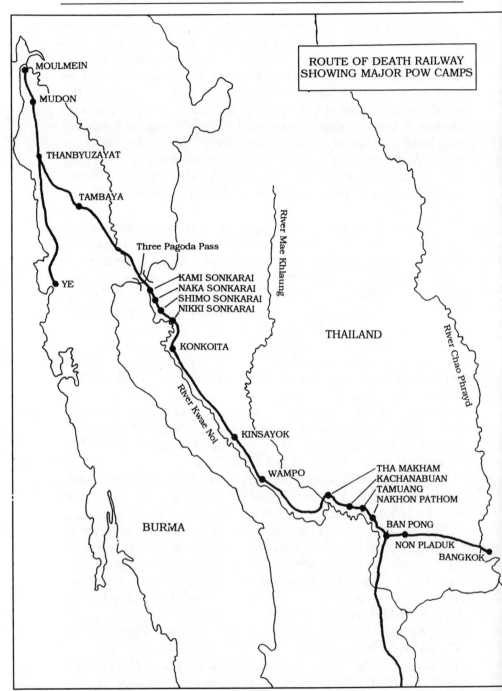

how the course of 1942 might have changed had the Allies been aware of the degradation, deprivation, torture, and misery suffered by these brave POWs.

More than 30,000 British, 13,000 Australian, and 700 American POWs worked on the Death Railway (Japanese estimates place the number of POWs closer to 70,000). Almost 500,000 conscripted laborers were used in the construction of the railroad. Conservative estimates indicate that more than 18,000 POWs and more than 100,000 Asians died building the Death Railway. We will likely never know the true numbers.

In one of the great ironies of World War II, the Death Railway never performed its function of supplying the Japanese military. Almost from the start of construction, the Allies kept the railway under constant bombardment. Allies were trying to build the railroad, while other Allies were trying to stop construction. No train ever completed a journey on the railway.

The Lost Battalion

Few people realize that American POWs worked and died on the Death Railway alongside Australian and British POWs. The story of the American POWs in Thailand gets lost among the story of Bataan and the Philippine POW ordeal. In terms of human degradation and suffering, claims that one group of POWs had it rougher than another would be ludicrous. But neither can we allow the agony and death of one group of POWs to overshadow the other. Frank Ficklin was one of the American POWs assigned to work camps in Thailand. His story of life in Thailand speaks eloquently for all American POWs who were forced to construct a railroad for the enemy in a hostile jungle.

Frank Ficklin joined the 131st Field Artillery in 1939 and traveled with his battalion to Java in January 1942. His unit surrendered to the Japanese in March 1943. He spent time in prison camps in Java, Singapore, and Thailand, and worked on the Death Railway.

Frank Ficklin

I'm Frank Ficklin, 1992 president of the Lost Battalion Association. The Lost Battalion Association is a fraternal organization formed in 1945 and whose members are survivors of the cruiser USS *Houston* and the personnel of the 2nd Battalion, 131st Field Artillery in North-Central Texas National Guard Unit. The two units consisted of 904 men. There were 336 navy, 33 marines, and 535 army personnel. They seemingly disappeared from the face of the earth following their capture by the Japanese in March 1942.

The cruiser USS *Houston* and the Australian cruiser *Perth* were sunk in the early hours of March 1, 1942, when they engaged a large Japanese landing fleet consisting of one aircraft carrier, five cruisers, eleven destroyers, several PT boats, and forty transports in the Sunda Straits off west Java. After a tremendous battle in which the two Allied cruisers inflicted heavy losses on the Japanese fleet, the two Allied cruisers were sunk. Only 369 of the total complement of 1,163 of the USS *Houston* managed to reach shore. All survivors became prisoners of the Japanese.

The 2nd Battalion of the 131st Field Artillery, less Battery E, went into combat in support of an Australian Pioneer Infantry group in Leuwilleng near the central Java city of Bandoeng. The men of the battalion became prisoners on March 8, 1942, after the Dutch commands unconditionally surrendered on the same day.

Battery E had remained behind in the east end of Java to guard an airfield at Malong, and to support the Dutch troops and the Surabaya area, which is at the east end. Battery E was engaged in heavy ground action prior to their unconditional surrender. Battery E remained in the Surabaya area until removed to Nagasaki and other areas in Japan via Batavia and Singapore in November and December of 1942.

For the American POWs in Java, there began an unbelievable string of events which would last three and one-half years, and was to weld the two military units together in a bond that is closer than blood. The day-to-day suffering throughout forty-two months of starvation, physical and mental torture, degradation, and tropical diseases with no medical help, and watching their friends die slowly, built a close relationship which still exists today.

Moving by ship from Java to Singapore and then to Burma, Thailand, or Japan, the men were packaged like cattle in the lower holds of the ship, taking turns sitting, squatting, standing, or lying down, all the while suffering from seasickness, dysentery, malaria, and other tropical diseases, at the same time standing in their own filth or that of their neighbor's. It was impossible or not permitted to go to the ship's side latrine on the main deck.

The men then worked twelve to eighteen hours a day in the steaming jungles and monsoon seasons of Burma and Thailand, felling trees, building roadbeds, bridges, and laying ties and rail with primitive tools in building the infamous Burma–Siam Death Railway. Some of the men were mining coal or working on the docks in Japan while living in substandard housing without heat or sufficient clothing during the cold Japanese winters.

Death Railway is a prime example of Japanese military brutality and inhumane treatment of POWs and Asian conscripted laborers, where over 105,000 died constructing 260 miles of jungle railway. Allied POWs who worked on Death Railway numbered 60,000, and 15,000 died. This was in a two-year period. Approximately 270,000 Asian conscripted laborers were recruited through deception and trickery to help build the railway. More than 95,000 died during the construction. There's no accurate figure of subsequent deaths of Asian laborers after their release from labor camps. The deaths of Allied POWs and Asian conscripted laborers were listed as caused by various tropical diseases, malnutrition, tropical ulcers, beriberi, cholera, and various other diseases. However, the true cause of death was brutality, starvation, and lack of medical attention. The famous movie, *The Bridge on the River Kwai*, portrays some of the brutal treatment and suffering of the British POWs in building one bridge on the construction of the 260-mile Death Railway.

The Allied World War II cemetery in Kanchanaburi, Thailand, honors British, Dutch, Indian, and Australian soldiers who lost their lives during construction of the notorious Death Railway. However, there is no mention of the 133 Americans who died during construction of the railway. The Lost Battalion Association felt that a similar honor should be afforded the Americans and in 1989 began inquiries to the U.S. State Department, Senator Phil Gramm, and the U.S. Embassy in Thailand.

The U.S. Embassy obtained permission from the Thai Department of the Interior, with the understanding that the governor of the province of Kanchanaburi had the final authority for the site of the monument. In mid-1990, the governor of Kanchanaburi appointed a commission composed of fifteen government agencies to study our memorial proposal. After several months of meeting and discussions, I requested permission to meet with the commission to assist in choosing a memorial site. On December 14, 1990, the first secretary of the U.S. Embassy and I met with members of the commission and the chief civil engineer of the Thai National Railroad and agreed on a site and a procedure for constructing a concrete base and landscaping. A bronze plaque was cast containing the names of the 133 Americans, and a dedication was scheduled for February 23, 1992, with forty Lost Battalion members to attend in Kanchanaburi, Thailand. A letter was received from the chief civil engineer, Thai National Railway, dated July 7, 1991, altering the agreement and changing the concrete base to an elaborate marble base with a cost increase of approximately $17,000. Our reply on August 21, 1991, thanked the railway for their time and effort in designing and upgrading the monument base, but requested that they reconsider their verbal agreement, as we were unable to finance the additional $17,000. We have not received a reply as of this date. We are still in contact and hope to resolve the situation to the satisfaction of all.

By the way, that bronze plaque sits in my garage today and we hope one day to have a memorial service to honor those 133 Americans who paid the ultimate price.

IV. Situation Grim

The Fall of the Philippines

At 0340 on December 8, 1941 (December 7 in Hawaii), Gen. Douglas MacArthur was notified by Gen. Leonard T. Gerow, chief of the Army War Plan Division, of the Japanese attack against Pearl Harbor. At 0530, General MacArthur received a communique from Washington, D.C. to execute the Rainbow 4 War Plan. At 0600, in the Gulf of Davao in Southern Mindanao, the seaplane tender *William B. Preston* was attacked by Japanese fighters. Gen. Richard Sutherland (chief of staff to MacArthur) and Maj. Gen. Lewis Brereton (commander, Army Air Corps, Philippines), for the second time that day, requested a photo reconnaissance flight to Formosa. For the second time, MacArthur rejected the request. At 0900 hours, Japanese bombers struck northern Luzon, bombing the United States airfields at Baguio and Tuguegarao. From 1200 to 1337 hours, a flight of 192 Japanese bombers struck Iba, Clark, and Mindanao Air Fields, destroying all but seventeen of Brereton's B-17 heavy bombers. In one fell swoop, Japan began the war against the Americans in the far Pacific and gained control of the air.

On December 22, 1941, under the command of Gen. Masaharu Homma, the Imperial Japanese 14th Army landed troops at Lingayen Gulf and Davao, and by the next day had advanced to within 100 miles of Manila, with only token resistance from the Allies. On December 23, the Japanese 16th Division landed at Lamon Bay. Realizing the hopelessness of attempting to hold the Philippines, MacArthur implemented War Plan Orange and declared Manila an open city on December 25, 1941. At the same time, MacArthur removed himself from the mainland and reestablished his headquarters in the Malinta Tunnel on Corregidor.

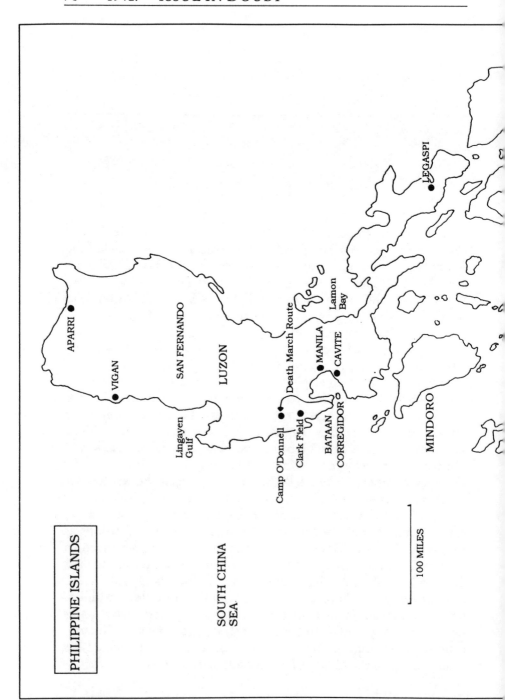

PHILIPPINE ISLANDS

SOUTH CHINA SEA

LUZON

SAN FERNANDO

APARRI

VIGAN

Lingayen Gulf

Camp O'Donnell

Clark Field

Death March Route

BATAAN

CORREGIDOR

MANILA

CAVITE

Lamon Bay

MINDORO

LEGASPI

100 MILES

As the Americans retreated to Bataan, General Wainwright's army slowed the Japanese advance to Bataan by destroying over 180 bridges and helped insure that General Parker would get his South Luzon Forces (15,000 strong) safely to Bataan. Just before the new year, the last American and Filipino troops crossed the Layac Bridge into Bataan, destroying it behind them, effectively sealing the Peninsula.

During the first week of 1942, the Americans (15,000 troops) and Filipinos (65,000 troops) formed two defensive lines on Bataan. The primary defensive position stretched from Abucay to Mount Natib. The secondary defensive perimeter was established in the Mariveles Mountains. The first Japanese advance onto Bataan on January 7, 1942, was stopped at the Abucay and Mount Natib line. On January 14, General Homma was reinforced; on January 20, the Japanese took Mount Natib; and on the 21st they broke through the American and Filipino lines at Abucay. By January 23, the Allies had retreated to the secondary defensive position in the Mariveles Mountains. The Japanese slowed their advance on Bataan to await reinforcements, and by the end of March they had received ample reinforcements and decided to take Bataan. On April 3, the Imperial Japanese Army took Mount Samat. Allied forces fled Mariveles City for Corregidor, and on April 9, at Lawao, Maj. Gen. Edward P. King surrendered the remaining Allied forces trapped on Bataan.

For the next month, the Japanese were content to try to blast the Corregidor defenders out by using heavy artillery. The majority of remaining United States forces (about 4,000 personnel) sought refuge in the Malinta Tunnel. Most were suffering from malaria, dysentery, and starvation.

A 2,000-man Japanese force invaded Corregidor on May 4. The attack was preceded by an artillery barrage of over 16,000 artillery shells. The 1st Marine Battalion fought a fight to the death, blunting but not repelling the Japanese forces. The marines had battled valiantly, but the Japanese still managed to land 600 troops on Corregidor. They controlled the eastern end of the island, which allowed them to bring in more troops, supplies, equipment, and heavy artillery. Within hours, the Japanese landing force began moving inland, overwhelming the American defenders.

On May 5, with the end in sight, General Wainwright raised the white flags of truce and ordered "Execute Pontiac," the code for the surrender of Corregidor. At 1600 hours, General Wainwright mo-

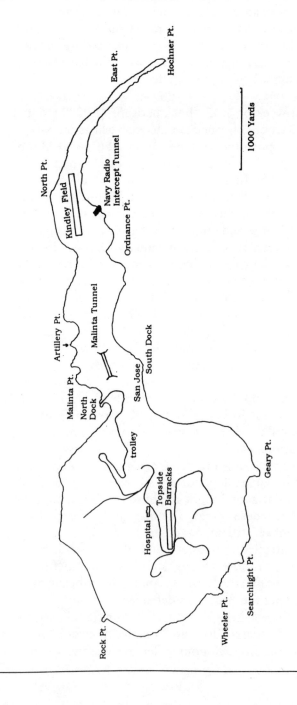

CORREGIDOR ISLAND
January 1942

tored to Cabcaben on the mainland and met with General Homma to work out the details for the surrender of the island. General Homma wanted Wainwright to surrender the entire Philippine Islands and Wainwright refused. Homma refused to accept Wainwright's "partial" surrender and sent him back to Corregidor, and in a final act of submission, ordered him to surrender to the local commander. On May 6, Wainwright acceded to Homma's demand, was taken to Manila, and over the local radio station he formally surrendered the Philippines to the Japanese. The message was read at 1200 hours. The Philippines belonged to the Japanese, although there were still pockets of resistance to wipe out. For example, General Sharp continued the fight on Mindanao for another two days before surrendering.

The Philippine Ordeal

The fall of the Philippines and the American surrender on Corregidor was more than the end of a military struggle. For the defenders on Corregidor, the war was just beginning. Fighting the Japanese was easy; surviving amid the Japanese as a POW was the real battle. Not until the recapture of the Philippines in 1944 did the Allies and American public learn of the true nature of the Japanese soldier.

Steeped in a deep tradition of the Bushido, the Japanese soldier saw surrender as the ultimate disgrace. To them, the soldier who surrendered was not worthy of being called "human." Accordingly, they treated POWs as subhuman, subjecting POWs to atrocities beyond imagination, refusing to care for, feed, or provide medical attention to the POWs. Whether a POW lived or died simply did not matter to the Japanese.

Few who endured the humiliation and suffering in the Philippines are willing to discuss their ordeal. Donald Wills is one who will discuss those dark and horrible days.

Donald Wills graduated from the Virginia Military Academy in 1940. He joined the 14th Horse Cavalry and was transferred to the 26th Horse Cavalry in the Philippines. After the surrender of Bataan, he spent two years as a prisoner of war before managing to escape. After his escape, he served with the guerrilla forces on Mindanao until the island was liberated by the United States. For his efforts and his heroism, Donald Wills was awarded the Silver Star, the Air Medal, the Bronze Star, and the Purple Heart.

Col. Donald Wills, USA (Ret.)

The events of December 8, 1941, upset many of our plans at Fort Stotsenberg, adjacent to Clark Field in central Luzon, the Philippines. Units of the 26th Cavalry (Philippine Scouts) were getting ready to go on maneuvers at Camp O'Donnell. Many of us were wondering how we were going to train and exercise our polo ponies for the upcoming season. Subsequent events solved that problem!

The 26th Cavalry was the last horse cavalry unit of troops in the United States Army. It consisted of about 850 Filipino enlisted men and about 34 American officers. The 26th Cavalry was made up of a headquarters troop, seven horse troops, a machine gun troop, a scout car platoon of eight scout cars, and the regimental trains consisting of about 65 vehicles. I was the newly appointed regimental motor officer.

At 0600 hours on December 8, 1941, we were at breakfast in our officers' mess when we heard via commercial radio that Pearl Harbor had been bombed. We quickly finished our breakfast and reported to our units. I reported to our regimental headquarters building. Events then moved swiftly. The regimental units were moved to concealed bivouacs along the Bamban River north of the post, leaving only the regimental headquarters staff and motor elements on the post. General MacArthur had designated the 26th Cavalry as a reserve for the North Luzon Forces.

Clark Field was bombed at 1230 hours by Japanese dive bombers. The damage was heavy. Most of our planes were caught on the ground and destroyed. The United States Army Air Corps suffered heavy losses.

Japanese troops landed in far north Luzon on December 9 and 10, and in southern Luzon on December 12. On that day, heavy bombers hit Fort Stotsenberg and Clark Field. I remember looking up from my slit trench in front of the headquarters building and counting thirty-four twin-engine bombers, their silver bodies glinting in the bright sun. They were flying in perfect formation with their bomb-bay doors open. We could see the black bombs fall out. This occurred at about 1030 hours. In the bombing, we lost forty horses, two enlisted men were killed, and six were wounded. My motor pool and many vehicles were badly damaged along with some empty barracks buildings. My personal automobile had over 200 shrapnel holes in it, but it would still run after all the tires were patched!

On December 13, the regiment evacuated the post and started its march to Lingayen Gulf. We arrived at Damortis on the coast on December 22, 1941. Japanese troops had already begun to land along the east shore of Lingayen Gulf on December 22. They continued landing troops through December 24 at Agoo, just three to five miles north of Damortis.

I remember making a reconnaissance trip via motorcycle north from Damortis on the coast road to try and contact Lieutenant George, who was in one of the scout cars. Along the way, I counted sixty-eight Japanese troop ships and vessels lying offshore. Landing barges were coming ashore less than a mile up the coast. I was not able to contact Lieutenant George and returned to Damortis. Our first casualties came that day on that same road when we lost Lieutenant George and his scout car to Japanese dive bombers. They were continually scouting the road and shooting at anything that moved. That day we lost two more officers killed and thirty enlisted men missing.

The Japanese had complete air superiority. We should have known that with the advantages the Japanese had, the fall of the Philippines was just a question of time.

The regiment was ordered to withdraw to the Bued River line. During this confusing time, Japanese tanks broke through and mixed with the American tanks and the 26th Cavalry horses on the fenced road. The Japanese advance was stopped for a time at the Bued River. During the night, the regiment reorganized and withdrew to Pozarubio, arriving at 0200.

On December 24, at 0800 hours, the regiment pulled back to Binalonan, arriving at 0100 hours. The Japanese pressured us all the way. Japanese troops attacked at dawn with tanks and infantry. I evacuated the trains shortly before dawn. By 1230 hours, the Japanese troops occupied the town and we lost several officers and a number of enlisted men.

The 26th Cavalry was ordered to withdraw to Tayug and lure the Japanese away from Highway 3 and delay their advance south. This was to allow the South Luzon Forces, who were being driven west by Japanese forces who had landed at Lamon Bay on the east coast of Luzon, to get into Bataan. General MacArthur had reverted to War Plan Orange #4 (withdraw into Bataan), as he estimated he had only about 40,000 effective troops against approximately 100,000 Japanese military. It now became a race to get all Luzon forces into Bataan before the Japanese captured the Calumpit or the Lubao bridges over the Pampanga and Culo rivers.

The 26th Cavalry spent Christmas Day of 1941 in Tayug fighting a delaying action with the Japanese. We fought through Umingen, Munoz, San Isidro, and Mexico, arriving in Mexico at 0130 hours on December 28. In Tayug, our Christmas dinner had been a can of sardines with rice. I sent a telegram home reporting all was well with me. I still have the copy of that telegram, which my parents saved.

By January 6, 1942, the last bridge into Bataan was blown. These were the Calumpit and Lubao River bridges. Bataan was closed off!

The Battle for Bataan now began. The 26th Cavalry suffered heavily in the action around the Layac Junction on the road into Bataan. We lost ten enlisted men and twenty-five horses to artillery fire. On a trip along the dirt road from the front back to the regimental trains, I had to cross a field under artillery attack and my motorcycle was hit by shrapnel. It was hit on the back fender and I was able to keep going. The 26th Cavalry also lost three scout cars, two officers, and eighteen enlisted men when they tried to move down that same road later in the day. By then, the Japanese had broken through the 31st Infantry defensive line.

We were cut off and had to work our way south through the jungle. It took until January 9, 1942, 1400 hours, to reach the road at Hacienda Abucay. By then, we had been reduced to eating wounded horses to survive. On January 16, the horses were sent to the rear quartermaster area to be used for food for the troops on Bataan. The regiment would now have to move by commercial buses.

Actually the horses had been a liability during the entire campaign. Time had passed them by and the use of horse-mounted troops was an antiquated procedure. At the end of a long day, the men had to curry, feed, and water their horses before they could eat and relax. We would have been better off moving by motor.

For the troops on Bataan, the outlook was grim. Food supplies had only been stocked for 40,000 troops. There were about 100,000 people on Bataan (80,000 military and 20,000 civilian). MacArthur made his only visit to Bataan on January 10 and assured the troops that help was on the way. My only glimpse of MacArthur was when his car swept past my motorcycle on the west coast road and I was smothered in a cloud of red dust!

By March 1942, the last of the 26th Cavalry horses were slaughtered and eaten. By that time, we were reduced to eating leaves, monkeys, pythons, wild pigs, and almost any other thing available. One day I was spear fishing off the west coast. I was strafed by a Japanese plane but managed to elude the machine gun fire by diving down about ten feet and hanging on to the coral until he had departed.

On Bataan, we were waiting for the United States forces to "blacken the sky with planes." Little did we know that would not happen for another three years, long after many on Bataan had been killed in battle or had died in prison camps as POWs. Japanese troops were also decimated by sickness and in March, an additional 100,000 troops were brought to the Philippines for a final push on Bataan.

Japanese attacks increased and in March, MacArthur left for Australia, leaving General Wainwright in command. By early April, it was all over. The United States and Filipino forces surrendered on April 9 at 1300 hours. From April 4 until the surrender on April 9, the troops had very little rest. I calculated that I had been able to sleep for about ten hours in a period of 106 hours. We had been moving day and night during that time. By the time of the surrender, the 26th Cavalry had lost twelve officers and approximately 500 men.

On the day after the surrender, I came down with malaria and Colonel Vance, the regimental commander, sent me to Hospital #2 in his staff car.

The Japanese moved approximately 75,000 persons out of Bataan on the infamous "Death March" in the next week or so. Approximately 62,000 Filipino soldiers and 10,000 Americans were moved out of Bataan. At the same time, the Japanese built up their artillery to about 600 pieces to use to assault Corregidor. The guns were all around Hospital #2. The American guns on Corregidor were firing back. Many shells exploded in the hospital area and a number of patients were killed.

On May 6, the Japanese stormed ashore on Corregidor with tanks. The United States and Filipino forces surrendered. Between May 6 and May 25 (the period after the surrender of Corregidor), the patients in Hospital #2 had very little food in our barbed-wire enclosed hospital. The Japanese had to let some of us who were ambulatory go out on foraging details to try to find food. We were able to find some, but we also saw the devastation. Dead bodies were everywhere, on the jungle trails, in wrecked vehicles, and even on

Near the end of the Bataan Death March, a thinning file of prisoners approaches Camp O'Donnell carrying fallen comrades in improvised stretchers. *National Archives, print courtesy Admiral Nimitz Museum*

the roads (some flattened into dark leather masses by the traffic of Japanese trucks). We even observed bodies being eaten by the giant Monitor lizards that live on the peninsula.

On May 25, the 12,000 troops from Corregidor were moved by barge to Manila and Bilibid Prison. At the same time, the prisoners from Hospital #2 were transferred by truck to Bilibid Prison.

On May 29, we were all moved out of Bilibid by train to the town of Cabanatuan. I came down with infectious hepatitis, but was able to make the trip by taking Nembutol, aspirin tablets, Paragoric, and some bismuth sub carbonate. I did not want to be left behind at the prison. We all marched out to POW Camp #2 on May 30. There was no water at that camp, so we had to march six kilometers back toward Cabanatuan to Camp #1 where there was water. In early June, all prisoners from Camp O'Donnell arrived and Camp #1 reached a population of 6,000 men.

Water was scarce. There was one faucet for every 2,000 men and it was turned on for a half-hour per day. Food was scarce (we got rice and greens soup twice a day) and disease was rampant. Dysentery, malaria, hepatitis, diphtheria, and malnutrition ran through the camp. POWs were dying at forty to fifty per day, and there was no medicine to help the sick.

In August 1942, all American officers with the rank of colonel and above were moved to Japan. By October, deaths were still running about fifteen to eighteen per day, or about ten percent of the camp population per month. We were reduced to eating grass, frogs from the drainage ditches, and the blood from carabao we had to butcher for the Japanese troops. We heated the blood in a canteen to congeal it so we could slice it and eat it with rice.

In October 1942, a 1,000-man detail was made to go south to Davao Penal Colony on Mindanao Island. I made sure I was on that detail, as it was 750 miles closer to Australia and any place would be better than Cabanatuan. The trip was made on a rusty 5,000-ton former American tramp steamer named the *Erie Maru*. The trip took thirteen days, from October 27 until November 8.

Davao Penal Colony was an improvement over Cabanatuan. The twenty-one months I spent there were at least survivable. There were 2,000 men at the camp and we worked on the self-sufficient prison farm or at an Abaca plantation down the coast. We raised food which was shipped to Japanese troops elsewhere. Our rations, however, were better than they had been at Cabanatuan. I stayed in good health except for a couple of bouts with malaria. I was always looking for a chance to escape. By April 1944, the American camp commander, Colonel Olsen, had me confined to barracks to prevent me from escaping.[1] Someone had reported me when they overheard some plans being discussed while we were working at the rice mill.

The months slid by until June 1944, when the Japanese decided to move all POWs north to Manila and Japan. On June 11, 1944, we left Davao in a two-ship escorted convoy. After stops at Sarangani Bay, Parang, and Zamboanga City, I was finally able to escape on June 10, 1944. Before that, I was frustrated by the gunboat escorts which had floodlights over the sides and Japanese guards all over the ship.

Moving up the west coast of Zamboanga, I was able to dive over the side of our boat at about 1930 hours on a dark, rainy night. I did this just before our boat moved out into the South China Sea and away from the coast. The Japanese machine gun fire and grenades were wasted in the black of the night. I did receive one small wound from a grenade fragment, but it was not serious.

After a tiresome and at times confusing four-mile swim to shore, I landed on a small sandy beach between some rocky points. My sole possessions were an underwear shirt, underwear pants, and two socks tied around my waist containing a compass, a burning glass, a few medicines and two chocolate bars from our only Red Cross package given to us by the Japanese. I was barefoot and did not even have a knife.

In the next few days, I walked down the coast and was contacted by some friendly Moro natives. They took me to the Moro guerrilla soldiers, who took me to their headquarters. I weighed 125 pounds. My normal weight was 185 pounds. I was in fair health. I walked barefooted for sixteen days across the Zamboanga Peninsula to join other American guerrillas in the hills.

Radio contact was made with MacArthur's headquarters and they said they would pick me up by submarine. I decided to stay with the guerrillas and even a few scores with the Japanese. I stayed with the guerrillas and operated against the Japanese. I became the assistant chief of staff (G-3) for the island of Mindanao.[2] I was in charge of plans and operations. By June 1945, Mindanao had been liberated by our actions and by the American landings.

By that time, I decided I had settled my score with the Japanese and I returned to the United States. I had been away for five years and it was good to get home. I had risen to the rank of major and had been awarded the Silver Star, Bronze Star, the Air Medal, the Purple Heart, and a number of Filipino decorations. I was offered a promotion to lieutenant colonel and a regular army commission. I decided instead to get out of the army but remained in the reserve. I retired as a colonel in 1978.

On December 8, 1941, Japanese air attacks on the Philippines destroyed most of the Army Air Corps planes and equipment. A few pilots and aircraft did manage to escape that initial attack and carry on the fight. One of those pilots who did manage to carry on was Lt. Gen. (Ret.) Joseph H. Moore, who will describe American air efforts in the early days of the war in the Philippines.

Lt. Gen. (Ret.) Joseph H. Moore joined the Army Air Corps in

1937, and was trained as a fighter pilot. In December 1941 he was in command of the 20th Pursuit Squadron at Clark Field. Later in the war he was transferred to the European Theater of Operations and took part in the Normandy invasion. General Moore served at the Pentagon, as a fighter-bomber commander in the United States and France, as Air Operations commander in Vietnam, as vice commander-in-chief of the Pacific Air Forces, and as tactical air commander for NATO in Turkey.

Lt. Gen. Joseph H. Moore, USAF (Ret.)

My participation in this life, my participation in World War II, started at Clark Field in the Philippines. I commanded the 20th Pursuit Squadron. A year before, fourteen months actually, we departed Hamilton Field as an intact squadron, as the first air reinforcements for the Philippines. When we arrived there by ship about thirty days later, we found that they had a composite group composed of one pursuit squadron, one observation squadron, and one bombardment squadron. The pursuit squadron had P-26s, which my unit had used at Barksdale Field about six years before and had subsequently been passed on down through Hawaii and then into the Philippines. It was a fun plane to fly, but it had no combat capability whatsoever. It could turn inside of a Zero and outclimb a Zero, which we found out in the early days. But the P-26 had very little firepower and could not cope with the Zero.

They evacuated all of the families in May and June of 1941 and began a serious build-up to bring in more forces to the Philippines. By the time the war began in December, we had five pursuit squadrons, four not fully equipped with P-40s and one squadron with P-35s, which were planes that had been sold to Sweden. When the Germans had taken over Sweden, those planes had been embargoed and sent over to us. They had some capability, but were not as good as the P-40s.

Two weeks before the war began in the Philippines, we stopped all training flights and went on a constant state of alert. We knew that there were over 200 Japanese airplanes on Formosa and that the only American targets in their range were the Philippines. We expected to be hit. We had been told we were going to be hit in the opening phase of the war. About five days before the war started,

Gen. Hal George, who was our pursuit commander, assembled all of the fighter pilots at Clark Field and briefed us on the situation. Adm. Saburo Kurusu had just passed through the Philippines to Hawaii on his way to Washington.[3] General George said, "He's only buying time. We've got to be prepared. We've got to absorb the first blow." And he ended up by saying, "You gentlemen are not exactly a suicide squadron, but you're goddamn near one." That raised the hackles on our necks. And then he said, "I want to see my squadron commanders." Everyone else was dismissed and we sat around the table, the five squadron commanders with the general, and figured out what we were going to do on the opening day of the expected attack to defend Clark Field.

Clark Field was the only field in the islands of the Philippines which could support B-17 operations. B-17s could land on a couple of others, but this was the only one they could operate from fully loaded. We had thirty-four B-17s at Clark Field at that time. They had been arriving in complements of six, to maybe nine, over a period of six weeks or two months. They were commanded by Lt. Col. Gene Eubanks.

My pursuit squadron, in those days, was stationed at Clark. About five days before the war started, we decided we ought to keep our one radar, located at Iba on the China Sea coast, which was a little sand strip we used for a gunnery camp, operating twenty-four hours a day rather than cutting it off as we had been doing. During the first night it was operating, we discovered a flight of twelve-plus planes coming down from the north about fifty miles offshore. One plane would peel off about Lingayen and come down inland over Clark Field and Manila and then turn and go back. The others in the formation stayed together, went down opposite Corregidor, made two complete circles, and went back north. This went on for three nights, and it did not take a highly intelligent person to realize that this was a flight from somewhere around Formosa. They were probably working out time, distance, and fuel consumption problems.

We asked permission to intercept them.[4] The second day we were told to take one airplane and go out and see if we could identify them. We had one airplane take off. It was flown by Hank Thorne, commander of the third squadron, which was at Iba at the moment. He took off on a heading which he expected to make an interception. The unidentified flight progressed a little faster than Hank expected and he missed them. We could see this on that one radar. The only communications we had with Hank were by a radio taken out of a P-40 that was located in the tower at Iba, and its range did not allow the correction of his course, so he went out flying time-distance. He didn't see a thing and came back. We analyzed the problem. The next morning permission was requested to send more planes up and permission was given to send six out in a spread-out formation to cover more area to try to identify them. That was Sunday morning. Nothing showed up.

Around midnight on that Sunday, we got orders to have the entire squadron report to the flight line. I had a flight on duty all night anyway, but we brought the entire squadron down. We milled around trying to find out what was going on, and at about 4:30 in the morning we got news that Honolulu was being bombed by Japanese airplanes. Well, Colonel Eubanks immediately bombed-up (loaded with bombs) his thirty-four B-17s and requested permission to go to Formosa to strike the fields we knew were bases for the Japanese planes. This permission was denied by MacArthur's headquarters.

At first light, my squadron scrambled. The other pursuit squadrons that were in various other bases, mostly around Manila, scrambled to take the positions we had planned on to defend Clark Field. The B-17s took off fully loaded and flew south to get away from the expected target and just disperse themselves in the air. Nothing happened. No enemy planes came in. At the limit of our endurance in the pursuit planes, we had to go back to land.

We had built revetments around the north and west sides of Clark Field, and our planes were always parked in those. We refueled and prepared for the next scramble. We had a procedure for such scrambles, which worked out quite well in many practice runs. With all pilots on the alert, Group Headquarters would give us an order, over the telephone, to prepare to scramble. All pilots ran to their planes parked in the revetments and prepared to take off when ordered. I remained on the telephone, so my crew chief ran to my plane. A white signal flag was flown on a pole that was visible to all pilots sitting in their planes. When Group gave me the orders, on the phone, to take off, they would tell me the heading to fly and the altitude to reach. At this point a red flag was run up the pole and all pilots started their engines. My crew chief would start the engine of my plane so that it was running by the time I reached my plane. It was always parked near the end of the runway, so all I had to do was jump in the cockpit and begin my takeoff roll. The other planes would take off behind me. We would fly the heading and reach the altitude ordered, then check in by radio and be vectored to intercept our targets.

This procedure worked quite well in practice, but on this day, when we received the order to prepare for scramble, the pilots ran to their planes but never received an order to scramble. The pilots sat waiting in their cockpits for about an hour and a half. Finally, one of our crew chiefs standing near our operations tent saw a flight of planes coming in from the west over Mount Pinatuba,[5] which has been prominent in the news recently, and I looked up and saw a line of planes. They looked small to me and were coming from the direction of the China Sea. My first reaction was that they were carrier-based, small planes coming off a carrier. We rushed out and I got off the ground. The two pilots behind me got off. The next four pilots in my squadron, taking off one at a time because the field was quite rough (we did not take off in formation), were killed by bombs blanketing the field. My intentions were to catch these carrier planes on the way back to their carrier, so we climbed up toward the west, away from Clark Field, to a height of about 22,000 feet. We leveled off and ran into nine Zeros who were coming in to strafe Clark Field. I had never heard of a Zero before. I learned more in thirty minutes of flying in combat then than I had learned in the past four and a half years of practicing our pursuit training.

Those of us who got back learned that it was impossible to turn and dogfight with a Zero. We could outrun it, we could absorb more punishment than it could, and we had pretty good firepower. Once you got a burst into the Zero, the Zero had a tendency to explode because it had no leakproof tanks like ours had.

After I got back on the ground, I found that twenty of my squadron's airplanes (I had twenty-three) had been destroyed. We did salvage one later. There were twenty B-17s that had drifted back in, one and two at a time, during the hour and a half we were sitting on the ground. All twenty of them were destroyed. We had a pretty rough time for the next two or three weeks.

On Christmas Eve we were evacuated from Clark Field to Bataan. My squadron was assigned to Mariveles, which is on the very southwest corner of Bataan, where a road through a rice paddy had been widened to fifty feet to make an airstrip. My instructions were to build revetments around this airfield for the reinforcements we expected to come in any day. Ed Dyess had the only other squadron which was operational, and he was over on the Bataan strip, which was on the Manila Bay side of Bataan Peninsula. We had a total of five flyable P-40s. We were instructed to avoid all combat and only use those for reconnaissance flights that MacArthur's headquarters directed us to do. That was the principal action we had for the first two months on Bataan. All the other air corps people, Army Air Corps people in those days, were assigned to ground duties, as were the navy's PatWing 10 personnel. There was a concerted effort made by the Japanese to land way down south of our front lines on the China Sea coast. They put Ed Dyess' squadron over on Longoskaw-yan Point. My squadron was put in next to him as his left flank, and PatWing 10 was down to my left flank to ward off these attempted landings. We all fought for six weeks on the ground as infantry troops. The Japanese were knocked out, not so much by our valiant ground fighting as by the Filipino Scouts and the 30th Infantry, which were the only real ground troops we had on Bataan.

Eventually I went back to my duty on Mariveles to prepare for incoming reinforcements. I operated two of the remaining five airplanes off that strip and there were three over at the Bataan strip. We had a golden opportunity when we found some enemy transport ships coming into Subic Bay. We got permission (it turned out later that we really did not have permission) and loaded everything we could and made several concerted attacks during the day against these ships and sank two of them. Ed Dyess had experimented with hanging a 500-pound bomb under the belly of a P-40, which did not have bomb racks but it did have a bomb bay tank, external tank. He hung that 500-pound bomb on the tank rear, and he was credited with sinking a troop ship with one of these.

Coming back from the last strike late that afternoon, just after dark, Japanese planes had taken off from Manila to intercept us. We had to land my two planes in the dark, pretty fast, to get them down, and they ran off the end of the runway and were both destroyed. We lost one plane on the early first flight at Subic to ground fire. The other two landed at Bataan strip, and that airfield sloped downward toward the water. We took off toward the water and landed the other way, going up the hill. Coming in at dusk with a strong wind, one of our planes ground-looped and tore a wing off, so we had one flyable airplane at the end of the day. About this time we discovered a J2F2, a navy amphibian float plane. It was a biplane that had been strafed in the early days of the war near Mariveles Harbor, where we were building the strip. We got that patched up and I received permission to fly my pilots down to Mindanao and Cebu so that we could get them fattened up by eating good food, and therefore enable them to fly the airplanes we expected to come in as reinforcements.

We had been put on two rations a day as soon as we got to Bataan in late December. My flight surgeon figured out that the nutritional value of both of those meals was about one-fourth of what a normal American pilot needed to eat per day. So we were all getting pretty malnourished and our strength and stamina were disappearing pretty rapidly. I sold my bosses on the idea that if I could get my pilots down there where there was plenty of food (and there was plenty of food down there because the Japanese had bypassed the southern islands), they could get back to fighting strength.

The Philippine Archipelago extends 1,500 miles north and south, and there are more than 7,000 islands in that archipelago. The biggest islands are Luzon to the north and Mindanao to the south. Panay is about halfway. The Japanese had just bypassed everything from Panay south when they went down toward Borneo and toward Java. They had an iron blockade around Manila Harbor and Luzon. That's all they cared about at the time. So we had lots of food and supplies down south. I flew this old navy amphibian at night because it only made 90 knots and I didn't want to get caught in the daytime by the Japanese. We started flying this back and forth. We hauled in food on the return trip, as much as we could put in that great big boat hull, and then took pilots down the next night trip.

I was on Cebu when Bataan fell. I received orders from Colonel Grover, who was on Mindanao, to report to him immediately, so I flew down there that night. The enemy made a surprise landing on Cebu at daybreak the next morning. I stayed on Mindanao until a flight of three B-17s and ten B-25s, led by Gen. Ralph Royce, came up from Australia to take part in a grandiose scheme to get some food into Bataan and Corregidor. The plan was to fill about twenty small inter-island boats with food and make a run through the Japanese naval blockage into Manila Harbor. The bombers were to distract the enemy navy ships forming the blockade by repeatedly bombing them, while the small boats slipped by close to shore until they reached Manila Harbor. We believed that, by sheer surprise and audacity, the plan would be successful.

Unfortunately, the bombers did not arrive until after Bataan had fallen, so it was too late to attempt the resupply mission. But they stayed three days, bombing targets of opportunity, then flew back to Australia. I rode out in one of the B-25s.

Things were then beginning to pick up a little bit down there. We were getting more aircraft, but the pilots were quite young and inexperienced. It took a little while to pick up what you needed to learn, to cope with the more experienced Japanese pilots and the better combat capability of the famous Zero. Eventually we did turn in some pretty credible work on New Guinea. Then the tide turned at the Battle of Coral Sea and we began forging back.

I came back to the States late in the fall, stayed a year, and then I joined the last air force unit going to England for the build-up of the Ninth Air Force for the invasion of Germany. And I went across to Normandy on D-plus-10 and went on up through France and Germany before coming back home again.

When the Japanese began the war in the Pacific, the United States was short of replacement equipment, replacement pilots, and air-fields from which to operate. The Americans had to rely on mainte-nance, material, and facility support from the Allies, particularly the Australians. Officially designated on paper as Army Air Corps units, this "rag-tag" group of replacement pilots and Australian Al-lies often combined and formed their own unit designators. Both the official and unofficial designators were used to identify unit membership.

Lt. Col. Wallace Fields was one of the first reinforcement pilots to be assigned to the South Pacific. He was a pilot in a B-17 and performed a variety of functions during his tour as a bomber pilot. As he will recount, his squadron was involved in the evacuation of General MacArthur, Philippine President Quezon, and their respec-tive staffs before the fall of the Philippines.

Lt. Col. Wallace Fields joined the Army Air Corps in 1940 and flew in the first heavy bombardment of the Japanese stronghold on Rabaul in February 1942. He flew fifty-one combat missions in B-17s, most with the 435th Reconnaissance Squadron and the 19th Bombardment Group.

Lt. Col. Wallace Fields, USA (Ret.)

On December 17, 1941, crews from the 9th, 11th, 22nd, and 88th squadrons, 7th Bombardment Group, departed from Hamilton Field loaded with spare parts, ammunition, and great expectations for their flight to PLUM, which was the code name for Del Monte on the island of Mindanao in the Philippines. They were going to join the other six crews who had preceded them to Hickam Field and who had landed during the middle of the attack at Hickam Field. Some of them did not survive that attack, but some of them landed on golf courses and did survive the attack. We went with ammunition, as opposed to the first six crews who went without ammunition and were caught in the middle of the raid with no way to fight back. Some of these crews had cadet navigators and others had young pilots who were hastily trained as celestial navigators. When they landed at much damaged Hickam Field, these crews were stripped of their planes and spare parts and were assigned to fly reconnaissance missions for the navy and Hawaiian Department.

Three crews had been ordered to pioneer a new route to Australia via Christmas Island, Canton, Fiji, and New Caledonia. On February 12, 1942, twelve crews were dispatched for Australia, being lovingly assigned some of the older B-17Es, with few of the spare parts which they had carried to Hawaii. Those crews arrived in Townsville, Australia, on February 19. The twelve B-17 crews were welcomed with open arms by the small cadre of Australian Air Force, keeping in mind that most of the Australian air force and army personnel were already committed to the British effort in Europe and Africa. The American crews were assigned quarters on Garbutt Field in Townsville, with additional housing in a nearby wooded area for makeshift parking of aircraft, tent housing, tent mess hall, plus a small wooden building used to house operations and headquarters. The quarters provided sturdy steel cots and mosquito nets and were within reasonable distance from the dispersal area and squadron mess hall. The Australians were really great to us, and we quickly became a part of the local populace and economy.

The arrival of the twelve well-used B-17s with no maintenance personnel and few spare parts provided the force with which plans were formulated for an American B-17 raid to Rabaul on February 23, 1942. These plans were coordinated with the Australian Air Force, with the B-17s still bearing the red and white rudder markings denoting their assignment as reconnaissance ships for the United States Navy. Two ships were involved in a taxi accident, taking the crews of Ralls and Bostrom off the mission. A weather front and some engine troubles further cut into this mission, allowing only three ships to make it to Rabaul. One of these, flown by Fred Eaton, was damaged by Zero fire, forcing a landing in Agaiambo Swamp in Papua, New Guinea. Thanks to Allen Champion, an Australian resident magistrate and coastwatcher in New Guinea, the Eaton crew was rescued and returned to squadron duty after six weeks.

This ship has become known as the "Swamp Ghost" and is pictured in the March issue of the *National Geographic.* An effort to recover this aircraft has been ongoing for eight years by the Travis Air Force Base Historical Society. This plane is an early E model and the only known surviving example to have the remotely operated lower turret.

At this time, Port Moresby was the only advanced staging base in New Guinea, with the Japanese occupying Rabaul, Gasmata, Cape Gloucester, Kavieng, Bougainville, Tulagi, Faisi, Buka, Lae, Finschafen, and Goen, and soon to occupy a strip at Buna. A strip was prepared at Buna by Allied forces, and on the day of completion the Japanese moved in and occupied it as a fighter haven for their Zeros. An effort was also under way by the Japanese to take Milne Bay. All these bases gave the Japanese complete fighter air control along with their virtually unchallenged naval forces. This overwhelming power was opposed now by eleven B-17s, a few Australian Beaufort Bombers, Lockheed Hudsons, and Wirraways. The Wirraway was a converted AT6, one of our advanced trainers with machine guns on it. Those were some of the fighter planes the Australians had to work with, particularly at Rabaul.

Following the Rabaul mission, the 435th Kangaroo Squadron performed squadron maintenance with combat crews, using one of the taxi accident casualties for spare parts. This squadron was born in Australia and made up from crews from four different squadrons. A squadron patch was designed within the squadron as follows: The squadron was formed in Australia, hence the kangaroo. It was a reconnaissance squadron, hence the spyglass held by the kangaroo. It was a bombardment squadron, hence the bomb in its tail and the cloud background portraying the only defense the lone ship missions provided except for the plane's own armament. There was no nose art on any of the ships, nor were any of the ships permanently assigned to any crew. They flew whatever plane was in commission at the time.

On March 16, 1942, three 435th Kangaroo Squadron crews were designated to fly General MacArthur and members of his family and staff from Mindanao. The pilots of these crews were Bostrom, Lewis, and Chaffin. General MacArthur was flown by Frank Bostrom to Darwin, where he boarded a civilian plane to Alice Springs, then switched to rail car, arriving in Melbourne four days later. On March 26, three planes, flown by Harry Spieth (with me as his copilot), Dubose, and Faulkner, flew an evacuation flight to Mindanao for Philippine President Quezon, his family, staff, and some maintenance personnel. This flight was timed for a night landing at Del Monte Field on the island of Mindanao. This was necessary because the Japanese had the field virtually surrounded. The field was defended by Air Force pilots, maintenance personnel, and anyone able to carry a gun. The landings were made with only lighted smudge-pots lined up on the pilot's side of the landing strip. The pots were extinguished immediately upon touchdown. Time on the ground was used for a hasty refueling and a quick and meager meal. Selection of the passengers had been previously determined, and it was hard to see those wanting to be evacuated but for whom there was no room. We also were approached by persons who tearfully wanted to stow away with no parachute on this evacuation trip. After departing Mindanao, the flights landed at Darwin, refueled, and then flew on to Alice Springs for the night.

Here we had the chance to visit with General Valdez and General Romulo. They related an incident at which President Quezon, being driven into the airfield at Mindanao, saw an ice cream parlor and called out, "Stop the car! Stop the car! We must have ice cream." The convoy stopped for ice cream, even though this move was extremely sensitive and it was vital to the war effort to prevent the president and his followers from falling into Japanese hands.

In late March, the maintenance personnel from the 22nd Squadron of the 7th Group were reunited with those of the combat crews in the 435th Squadron, and with this move the 435th maintenance took a sharp turn upward. The 19th Bomb Group had lost most of their planes at Clark Field but were able to evacuate personnel, but had nothing to work with. In the process of the reorganization of the 19th Bomb Group, they had units assigned at Mareeba and Longreach, plus a newly acquired squadron, the Kangaroo Squadron, at Townsville. All unit locations were in Queensland, Australia. With this reorganization, the 435th Squadron continued their assignment of reconnaissance and bombardment for the Fifth Air Force, with pertinent information being funneled to the Allied Navy and Australian commands.

On April 10, General Royce led a three-ship mission to bomb Nichols Field in the Philippines. This mission flew out of Darwin with the B-17s leading ten B-25s. This proved to be the last mission to the Philippines until the war was drawing down near the end of the conflict. The 435th pilots were Bostrom and Ralls, with the other B-17 flown by Teats from the 30th Squadron of the 19th Group. This mission became known as the Royce Mission, with General Royce riding on the mission with Bostrom.

Reconnaissance planes were continuing to note a build-up of Japanese shipping and naval activity. On May 6, my diary noted that we had dropped bombs over a carrier escorted by six escort vessels. Admiral Goto of the Japanese Navy noted in an interview for the book *Zero*, by Martin Caidin, that with this B-17 discovery, the chance for secrecy was lost and the Battle of the Coral Sea was imminent. The 19th Bomb Group sent their only two combat-worthy planes to Townsville, temporarily joining the 435th Squadron. These two planes were flown by two brothers, Fred and Al Keys from Meridian, Mississippi. This addition gave the 435th a total strength of twelve airplanes, all B-17Es, if all were in commission. The twelve B-17s, plus a newly arrived squadron of B-26s, comprised the total bomber strength of the Allied air forces in Australia. The epic Coral Sea Battle that ensued is now naval history.

Beginning in late June through early July 1942, the 435th Squadron flew many mapping missions, photographing the progress of airfield construction and movement by the Japanese prior to Marine landings on Guadalcanal. These missions were staged from Port Moresby and were approximately 2,000 miles round-trip and eleven hours or more in duration.

One check-off LB-30 mission on July 10, with Dick Ezzard as pilot, stands out in particular. This plane, the LB-30, had no turbo-superchargers and was limited to 11,000 or 12,000 feet altitude. Our photo mission to Guadalcanal had been completed when we were attacked by two Zero float planes. Our number-three engine was shot out, but our camera operator got pictures of the two planes in one frame. This picture was believed to have been the first one taken confirming the Zero float plane in operation. An effort was made to salvo an empty bomb bay tank with an existing "Rube Goldberg salvo system," but the salvo system failed and the trip back to Moresby was made on three engines with an empty bomb bay tank protruding from the bomb bay. The flight engineer had his shoe sucked off in the slip stream while trying to kick the tank out.

For several days in September, B-17s were utilized to ferry troops of the 32nd Infantry Brigade to Port Moresby, reinforcing the Australian and United States infantry units necessary to repel Japanese units coming over the Kokoda Trail in an overland effort to neutralize Port Moresby and its several operational strips. A few Japanese troops did cross over the Owen Stanley Range, and some were captured just outside the combat crew billets at 7 Mile Strip.

These billets were native-built grass huts furnished with the conventional steel cot and mosquito nets. Outside were the essential slit trenches in which we took refuge from the bothersome sporadic night bombers and the very real threat of Zero strafers. An austere mess hall was also provided from which we were served the usual Spam concoctions using powdered eggs, dehydrated onions, potatoes, powdered milk, and well-paraffinated butter as the blue plate bill of fare. No other comforts were available or expected.

A brief recap of the 435th or Kangaroo Squadron follows. Between February 23, 1942, and November 15, 1942, the 435th Squadron flew 385 reconnaissance missions and 145 bombing missions. Most of these had the presence of fighter escort, *all Japanese.* Not a single mission of the 435th squadron was made with the pleasure of friendly fighter escort. Most sorties involved a single ship only. This recap will compare favorably with the other three squadrons of the 19th Bomb Group following their reorganization in Australia. Beginning in November 1942, the 19th Bomb Group was rotated to the United States for reassignment.

This discussion would not be complete without acknowledging the expression of love and respect for those great enlisted crew members and maintenance personnel who kept our planes flying through truly adverse working conditions. This is also true for all of our Australian Allies who received us so willingly and helpfully during our stay in their country. They are a great people and loyal friends.

★   ★   ★

Often overlooked and/or ignored in the official histories of World War II, in the historical anthologies of battles and campaigns, in media and news reports of Allied actions, and in the popularized fiction of books and movies is the role of the female soldier. In the 1940s, women in the military were assigned "noncombat" roles. They were staff aides, public relations specialists, typists, and nurses.

These female "noncombatants" were assigned billets supposedly safe from enemy attack. The best laid plans, however, often go awry, as was the case with one army nurse, Hattie Brantley. Her safe and secure "noncombat" billet became four years of war and captivity. Today, when we argue and debate equal opportunity and equal rights for the sexes, we would be well advised to remember the lessons taught and the roads paved by the Hattie Brantleys of the 1940s.

Hattie Brantley graduated from the Baylor School of Nursing and became an army nurse in 1939. She was a member of the first medical group assigned to Bataan, on Christmas Eve of 1941. She became a prisoner of war when Corregidor fell and continued to provide care for Americans until her release in 1945.

Hattie Brantley

We never had any doubt whatsoever that help was not on the way. We knew it was and that it would get there and we would come out all right. "Help was on the way" was our daily greeting. Today we say to each other, "Have a nice day." That's a very common cliché now, but we said, "Help is on the way," or "Any day now we'll see those Americans coming back."

At the news of Pearl Harbor, I was on duty in the Philippines in an outlying post outside Manila. It was December 8. We went to breakfast. The chief nurse had the radio on and we heard the news of Pearl Harbor. She said, "Now girls, nothing's going to change. Those Japanese are not coming here. We're going to just go along and operate as normal." One of the nurses and I had the morning off, so we went out and played golf. Talk about stupidity and belief that help was on the way. Shortly we moved into Manila. Everybody congregated in Manila, where the bombing was going on, and we set up hospitals in public buildings. But very quickly, by December 24, we were sent to Bataan. Twenty-five army nurses and some Filipino nurses were sent to Bataan on December 24. Our commander said, "Take your white duty uniforms. Take your white duty uniforms." And this was even before the days of drip-dry. These were starched, poplin uniforms, and we got on the bus in that white uniform and our barracks bag packed with only our white duty uniforms and went to Bataan.

"The hospital is all set up," he said. Well, baloney. We didn't even have any baloney to eat. It was a Filipino Army training post. There were some native buildings. We dug the cots out from World War I storage areas of the buildings and set up those cots ourselves. They were about twenty-four inches high, and it isn't easy to take care of a patient at that level. This was all pre-MASH (Mobile Army Surgical Hospital) period. We had no facilities as the *M*A*S*H* series shows you or that they have today. Shortly, our Hospital #1 was full of patients and they took bulldozers down into the jungle and scraped out paths along the riverbed and made Hospital #2. At the end there were 3,000 at our hospital and 5-7,000 in the other hospital. We had many tropical diseases as well as the horrible casualties. At #2 Hospital, the nurses lived in gutted public transportation buses. They bathed in a stream that ran through the area. Immediately, we were on two meals a day and they were not very substantial meals. The patients were on cots under the canopy of the jungle. We had injuries, malaria, dengue fever, and all sorts of insect bites. Everything got infected, and all the time we worked as hard as we could and did what we could. I will never forget a patient, a quadruple amputee, and I think he worried more about what we girls were having to endure than what he was having to endure.

We moved our Hospital #1 further down the peninsula as the line fell back in January. We were on a hillside in an old garage, just a corrugated tin roof over our heads, and we soon filled this area and had to set up beds under the jungle as they had at Hospital #2. But one of the first things we did was take white bedsheets and nail them, stick them on the high side of a hillside in the form of a cross so that the area would be marked as a hospital. Every morning this little Japanese reconnaissance plane came over, and we would say, "Here comes Tojo." They would observe our area.

In late March, our hospital was bombed. A 500-pound bomb hit one of the areas, one of the wards in the hospital. Two nurses received shrapnel injuries, and many patients were killed. Several of the medics were hurt at that time and many killed. At Bataan, as the situation continued to deteriorate and injuries and battle casualties increased, we often worked around the clock. I can't say that everybody did their duty, but everybody did the best they could. We worried about running out of supplies. Supplies were getting awfully low, even ether to give a patient a little anesthetic to do surgery. Dressings were becoming nonexistent. Every day somebody would climb a tree and look out toward the bay to see if that convoy was coming.

As Bataan was going to be surrendered on April 9, we were herded into buses as darkness fell on April 8 and were evacuated to the end of the peninsula as the enemy literally came over the hill. All nurses were successfully evacuated to Corregidor. Not one nurse was lost in this operation. We went to Corregidor and lived in Malinta Tunnel. We took over the tunnel hospitals. There had been nurses on duty there, of course, and now there were about 112 of us that were on Corregidor. General MacArthur was evacuated, and as transportation became available about forty-five nurses were evacuated from Corregidor. There were sixty-seven of us left there. After the fall of Corregidor on May 6, 1942, we remained there taking care of our patients. We had no interference from the Japanese, except our food supply was even less than before.

We were transferred into Manila in late June and were interned in Santo Tomas Civilian Internment Camp with Allied civilians. I think there were about 5,000 civilians interned at the end of the war. We army nurses provided the care for the patients in this hospital. We didn't do much surgery except life-saving surgery, but there were medical diseases. We had about a total of 100 patients at all times.

We had an educational system set up for the children. These were families of Allied people who lived in Manila, business people, and so forth. Three years we were there, so three groups of students graduated from high school from the University of Santo Tomas. It was terrible to watch the children as the starvation process proceeded. They became like little old men and women. They would sit on the sidewalk and had absolutely no energy to accomplish anything.

We did receive during our period of internment three Red

Malinta Tunnel, Corregidor. *From the Sharlot Hall Museum collection (Photo #91.551.002B), Admiral Nimitz Museum*

Cross packages and some vitally needed medication, mostly vitamins, and this did make a great difference. When Manila was recaptured, they found tons of Red Cross supplies stored in Manila that the Japanese had not released to us.

We received very little news and absolutely no mail. We found out later that three men in camp had a radio, which they kept disassembled, of course. At night when there was an opportunity they would assemble the radio and get some news. And then they could pass along the news to us in sort of a code. We had a loudspeaker system in camp that announced the work details. We did have duty in camps. We nurses did four hours' duty each day in the hospital. But all the camp internees had to do two hours of duty. They had vegetable detail, pick the worms out of the rice detail, clean the latrine detail, and that sort of thing. Every morning these details would be announced by the radio announcer on our loudspeaker system and when this radio heard the news that Leyte had been invaded, the next morning the announcer used that in his announcement and said, "It's better Leyte than never." So we got that clue. Then when the American bombers came in September 1944 and dropped bombs on the pier area, the music that woke us up next morning was "California, Here I Come" and "Pennies From Heaven."

We had absolutely no indication that help was about to arrive, except we kept saying every day, "Well, help is on the way." And it was a complete surprise when on the night of February 3, 1945, a Sherman tank rumbled through the bamboo gate and came into the prison camp and up to the main building. It was dark, of course. We had had blackout for all of those years, and we were all huddled inside wondering what was happening, thinking we were being invaded again, when this turret came up and a strong American voice said, "Aren't there any Americans here?" And we said, "Yeah, what took you so long?"

And so we were rescued. And as I said, there were sixty-seven army nurses and eleven navy nurses who served as prisoners of war — and we all came home!

★   ★   ★

As did any country at the time, the Philippines had a large complement of non-Filipino civilians. These civilians owned businesses, worked for foreign corporations which had branch offices in the Philippines, were military dependents, or who merely enjoyed the Filipino lifestyle. As Margaret Gillooly will explain, the Japanese offered no special treatment to these civilians.

Margaret Gillooly was sixteen years old when the Japanese invaded the Philippines and took her parents prisoner. After hiding in the mountains for six months, she turned herself in to the Japanese and was eventually reunited with her parents at the Santo Tomas Internment Camp. She graduated from the Internment School.

Margaret Gillooly

I've discovered for many years that most of the people I've met, including the news media, are stunned to realized that the Philippine Islands, and indeed the whole South Pacific, was occupied by civilians long before the war. We were a rare breed, apparently, in this country. So we've been in the process of trying to educate people about what happened to civilians during that war. The army, navy, marines, and air force were not the only occupants of that part of the world.

We were residents of the city of Cebu. My dad was a department store manager for the H.E. Hecock Company. We lived in Manila for the first year, and then in 1940 we moved to Sabu City, where he had the whole assigned southern group of traveling salesmen and a few smaller stores under his management. On December 2, my parents decided that they would go to Manila to pick out Christmas stock for the store and also take the small orchestra, which was famous for having recorded for the first time Philippine folk music, to Manila to fulfill a contract with Decca Records, to record this for the first time. They all went to Manila, and were of course caught there on December 8 with the bombing of Pearl Harbor and the Philippines, and were forced to stay.

They were able to finally get passage on the inter-island steamer, which was the only one going to the southern islands. On December 16 they boarded the steamer and were waiting and waiting for the captain to start up the ship and go through the bay. It turned out that the army would not give him a pilot to go through the mined bay in Manila. He got angry about midnight and said he was going to take it through himself. He did. He proceeded to go. He was stopped in the center of the bay in the open channel by Corregidor. The navy wanted him to identify himself and he was signaling back and forth to the Corregidor fortress. They eventually cleared him, but the ship had drifted in the channel. When he started it up, he hit a mine. The mines had never been taken off contact pending his identification. So the bottom was blown out of the ship. It sank in two or three minutes. The oil from the ship covered the water and all of these people were thrown into the water, those who could get out of cabins or who were on the deck. My parents were on the deck. They would not go below deck because it was such a risky situation.

My dad was in the waters of the bay for about five hours before PT boats which were sent out by the navy picked up those survivors they could reach. There had been empty 55-gallon drums that floated off the top of the ship and were hitting people in the head and knocking them out. A Filipino jumped on my father's back and was trying to undo his button on his wallet pocket, to pick his pocket in the midst of all this, and my father instantly was furious and did a round-house with his fist and hit the man in the face and knocked him off his back. Whether he survived or not, I don't know. They were very fortunate because the sharks that are ordinarily around there were feeding on garbage on the other side of Corregidor Island, so they were not right there to attack people who were in the water.

My mother, however, was not picked up and she floated with the current past Corregidor out into the open sea. One PT boat decided it would make one very wide, final sweep, and they went way out beyond Corregidor and cut their engines and floated for a while. They heard one lone voice screaming, "Help, help." They took a megaphone and were calling out and saying, "Keep screaming, we're coming toward you." They followed her voice until they found her. Of course, everybody that went into the water was covered with black oil and very hard to see at night. It was about seven hours before she was rescued. The fish had been sucking on her. She had black and blue marks all over her body. They eventually pulled her clothing off in the course of this, and so she was just in her undies when the navy officer, Lieutenant Ross, picked her up. She was brought to Corregidor, to the hospital, and my father eventually found her. After they were there for perhaps twenty-four hours or so, they were removed to a hospital in Manila, on the shore side.

This was a great tragedy because the steamer had a capacity of about 400. It had been loaded with some 1,200 people, all trying to get back to their homes. There were only 285 that survived, my parents among them.

I was in the city of Cebu. I'm an only child, so this was a very difficult separation for me. On December 16, there was a cable through the army that informed me that my parents had been rescued, that there had been this disaster, but that they were okay. I never, in all the course of time through 1942, heard directly from my parents nor did I receive any mail. They were subsequently interned at the end of January 1942, in the Santo Tomas Internment Camp. Everyone had been rounded up by that time.

This was the beginning of the year of my growing up. I was very independent and I was really excited about it. I worked for the army for a little while helping to plot submarine movements in the Philippine Islands. We moved a number of times. The Japanese put us in different internment camps and we were able to exist in a very primitive way. We lived on practically nothing. We had to buy our own food because the Japanese kept telling us we were only in protective custody. They had no reason to feed us and they did not have to follow the Geneva Convention rules. So it was all very difficult. In a period of seven months I learned two years of Latin.

We were not invaded until April 10, and the Japanese found out we were there. On May 1 we surrendered. We were put in a provincial jail. At this time I was called to the front by one of the officers and was told that there was someone there to see me. I couldn't imagine this. In this horrible jail and the conditions that we were living in, which were just filthy, I went up to the front and here was a navy man, all shot up, bandaged, walking on crutches. He said, "I'm Lieutenant Ross. I rescued your mother." And that was just a stunning realization and also quite remarkable to me that he would have found me in that prison camp.

We were moved to a junior college site for a few months, then in October of '42, we were taken to a Filipino country club for a second prison camp. There we experienced a locust plague, which was one of the most remarkable things I've ever seen, but very frightening, to be inundated by millions and millions of these little flying beasts. Some people attempted to boil them, fry them, and roast them to see which form of cooking made them taste better. Our food was very scarce. We lost a lot of weight, as you can imagine. We were in the early stages of malnutrition. We had some schooling available because we had some textbooks. We tried to keep up with studies as best we could. I learned how to draft patterns to make clothes for myself out of any kind of yardage that I could scrounge. I learned how to treat my ailments, because we did not have medicines with us, by doing healing prayer and getting myself well again. I experienced tonsillitis on a chronic basis. We were very able to do primitive cooking. I learned how to adapt the recipes that I had learned at fourteen to feed 150 people, cooking over open fires, stacked laundry pans, which were all the cooking gear we had, and learned a lot in that first year. And one of the things that was so interesting to me at the time was that I was secretly glad, though terrified about what was happening to us in the war years, but secretly glad that I was independent, that now I could be on my own. It was a surprise to other people, I think, because they expected me to cling to other families since my parents were not there.

We were eventually put on a ship and taken to Manila. We didn't know our destination to start with, but we were loaded on

December 15 to go to Manila, and in this year of independence, nobody messed with Margaret. When we were taken off the ship, we were put on buses and driven from the pier to the Santo Tomas Internment Camp, where I anticipated (since I knew they had survived) that I would see my parents. My mother stood back in the crowd, but my dad went up, had gone to every bus to see where I was and when I was getting off. Well, I happened to be the last person on the last bus and he was just frantic that maybe something had happened to me. I walked up to the door of the bus and I stood on the step looking around to see if I could see them. This man came toward me with long, shoulder-length gray hair and a beard, and he held out his arms to me, and I doubled up my fists and I was ready to let him have it. And he said, "Baby," which was his pet name for me. And when I heard his voice I knew it was my father, so I just collapsed in his arms, sobbing for all I was worth, and we had a very joyful Christmas that year.

The Battle of Wake Island

On December 7, 1941, the Japanese struck Pearl Harbor and in a matter of minutes had destroyed (at least temporarily) the United States battle fleet. America needed a victory to give the country a psychological lift. A small island at 19 degrees 18' 40" north latitude and 166 degrees 35' 22" east longitude would provide that psychological victory, although it was not likely most of the country had ever heard of the island before December 10, 1941. By December 23, 1941, everyone knew the name of that small island — Wake.

Wake was discovered in 1796 by schooner Capt. William Wake. On July 4, 1898, the United States claimed the island as a United States possession, and in 1935 the island was first used when PanAm built a terminal and hotel for its transatlantic flights.

In the late 1930s the United States military determined that Wake Island would be ideal as part of a defensive ring of islands to protect Hawaii from possible Japanese attack. The other islands in the defensive perimeter were to be Johnston, Midway, Palmyra, and Samoa. In January 1941 construction of the Wake military garrison began. The USS *William Ward Burrows* arrived with the initial load of men and equipment of the Morrison–Knudsen Company, who had been contracted to construct an airport, seaplane base, and submarine docking facilities.

At 0650, December 8, 1941 (December 7 in Pearl Harbor), Wake Island received a message announcing the attack on Pearl Harbor. At 1200 hours the Japanese began their attack against the marines stationed on Wake Island. Their initial attacks were unsuccessful.

In the early morning hours of December 23 the final assault on Wake began. Members of the Maizuru Force landed on Wilkes and Wake, rapidly overwhelming the outnumbered defenders. At 0500 Commander Cunningham radioed Pearl Harbor: "Enemy on island. Issue in doubt." By dawn, the Japanese had landed over 1,000 men on the three atolls and had surrounded Wake with twenty-seven ships. After fierce hand-to-hand fighting in the early dawn hours, Major Devereaux surrendered the island.

For the gallant defenders of Wake Island, however, the war was far from over. Civilians and military alike were kept sitting outdoors on the Wake Island airfield for two days with no food or water. All American personnel except 118 civilians were evacuated on January 12, 1942, in the hold of the *Nitta Maru*. The American POWs were interned at different POW camps in Asia, including Woosung and Kiangwan outside of Shanghai; Fengtai outside of Peking; Fusan, Korea; and Hokkaido, Japan. Another twenty Wake POWs were transferred to Zentsuji, Japan, in May 1942. On October 17, 1942, Admiral Sakaibara, Japanese commander of Wake, executed the 98 Americans remaining on the island. For this, Sakaibara was tried, found guilty, and hanged on June 18, 1947, on Guam. Of the 1,462 American POWs, 261 died in POW camps, on board ship, or escaping; five successfully escaped the POW camps; and 98 were executed on Wake Island.

On September 4, 1945, Wake Island was surrendered to the United States. In a bitter twist of fate, Maj. Walter Bayler, the last American to leave Wake Island before Japanese occupation, was the first American to set foot on the island when it was liberated.

In the battle for Wake Island, the Japanese lost 820 men with 333 wounded. Four of their warships were sunk and six were severely damaged. The Americans lost 120 killed, 49 wounded, and two missing in action.

Col. (Ret.) Arthur Poindexter was a part of the marine garrison on Wake Island in December 1941. He was captured following the epic-like defense of Wake Island and spent the remainder of the war as a prisoner of war in Japan. Colonel Poindexter is retired from the United States Marine Corps.

Col. Arthur Poindexter, USMC (Ret.)

Wake Island is actually a coral atoll formed by a submerged volcano with only its top above the surface of the ocean. The atoll consists of three slender islets (Peale, Wilkes, and Wake proper) in the configuration of a wishbone, with a coral reef which arches across the open end to enclose a shallow lagoon. Although the circumference of the atoll is almost twelve miles, the total land surface is less than three square miles, which is less than New York's Central Park.

Situated in the mid-Pacific, Wake Island is approximately 1,034 miles west of Midway Island and 2,004 miles west of Hawaii. Wake Island is, in fact, roughly 600 miles closer to Tokyo than to Pearl Harbor.

Owing to its location, part of the Japanese *grand* strategy for conquest in the Pacific called for the immediate seizure of Wake as an essential link in their defensive perimeter. Only by holding Wake could the Japanese prevent the United States from launching air attacks on their bases on the Marshall and Gilbert islands to the south.

Capture of Wake and Guam would also block the American supply line to the Philippines. In addition, possession of Wake would provide a base for reconnaissance and a stepping stone for the invasion of Midway.

Although such considerations must have been apparent to United States military planners, the construction work to develop Wake as an advanced naval base was not undertaken until January 1941. It was not until August of that year that Admiral Kimmel, commander in chief of the Pacific, was authorized to provide a military garrison for the island.

The troops assigned to proceed to Wake and provide a "limited defense" of the island consisted of a detachment from the 1st Defense Battalion of the Fleet Marine Force, Pacific. The original detachment comprised five officers and 173 men, but in November the detachment was reinforced, bringing its strength to 15 officers and 378 men under the command of Maj. J.P.S. Devereaux, United States Marine Corps.

The armament of the defense force consisted of six 5-inch naval guns manufactured for the broadside batteries of World War I naval vessels, three batteries of 3-inch anti-aircraft guns (some without fire control equipment), 18 M1918 .50-caliber machine guns with pedestal mounts, and 30 M1917 .30-caliber water-cooled machine guns for beach defense. Communications gear and individual weapons and equipment of the troops were also of World War I vintage.

The weapons enumerated above provided armament for an entire defense battalion with a T/O&E strength of 980 officers and men, yet the detachment assigned to emplace and man these weapons had less than half that strength. In addition to the critical shortage of personnel, the other glaring discrepancy was the lack of radar equipment for early detection of approaching aircraft.

On December 4, 1941, just three days before "all hell broke loose," a skeleton squadron of fighter aircraft (VMF 211) consisting of ten officers and 49 men with 12 Grumman F4F-3 Wildcat fighters, under the command of Maj. Paul A. Putnam, landed on Wake. There was also a small Army Air Corps communications detachment consisting of an officer and four men. Also present were small detachments of naval personnel, including Cmdr. Winfield Scott Cunningham, United States Navy, who had been assigned to assume command of the naval air station at such time as the station was ready to be commissioned. In the meantime, Commander Cunningham was the senior officer present, and nominally in command. However, the defense force, including the aviation element, functioned under the control of Major Devereaux.

In summary, the defenders of Wake comprised what some military veterans would consider to be a bastard-type unit equipped with hand-me-down weapons, which were mostly of World War I vintage, and assigned a bastard-type mission. It is, therefore, somewhat ironic that this unlikely aggregation of the prewar military establishment would give the nation its first victory of the Second World War.

Starting the day that the fighter squadron arrived, Major Putnam had set dawn-to-dusk combat air patrols consisting of four Wildcats flying at an altitude of 12,000 feet to conduct 360-degree surveillance of the ocean areas surrounding Wake.

Hence, four Grumman Wildcats were airborne on the morning of December 8, 1941, at the time Major Devereaux received the report that Pearl Harbor was under attack. The major ordered the field music to sound "General Quarters," and all hands proceeded to their assigned battle stations.

Shortly before noon the garrison came under attack by thirty-six twin-engine medium bombers of the Japanese Navy's 24th Air Flotilla. The attackers came in at an altitude of only about 1,700 feet, concealed from the patrolling Wildcats by a low cloud cover. Owing to the lack of radar and the constant roar of pounding surf that drowned out the sound of their engines, the bombers emerged from the cloud bank and were over the island, executing their bombing and strafing runs before the anti-aircraft guns of the defenders could respond effectively.

The principal bombing and strafing targets were the Pan American Airways facilities and the airstrip, which they plastered with closed-pattern bombing while strafing the area viciously with 20mm machine guns. Seven of the eight planes on the ground were destroyed and the eighth was badly damaged.

Other damage was extensive and casualties were numerous. Several of the pilots, including Lieutenants George Graves, Frank Holden, and Robert Conderman, were killed or mortally wounded while attempting to get to their planes in order to take to the air. Casualties amounted to at least eighty-four killed and many more wounded, including Lt. Henry "Spider" Webb, Capt. Frank Tharin, and Major Putnam, who remained ambulatory and carried on as squadron commander. So far as is known, all the enemy planes returned to base, although some sustained damage from anti-aircraft machine gun fire.

In the grisly aftermath of the disastrous first strike by the enemy, tasks consisted of evacuating the wounded to aid stations, clearing away burning debris, repairing the surface of the runway and apron, constructing covered revetments to house the planes that were still operational or salvageable, and burying the dead.

On each of the days of the siege that followed, there were more bombing raids, some involving even more enemy aircraft than were involved in that first devastating attack. Although the casualties inflicted and damage resulting from subsequent raids were severe, the enemy also sustained losses. After the first day, approaching bombers were intercepted by combat air patrols (of never more than four fighters) which attacked the flanks of the formation and each time downed one or more of the incoming bombers. The fighters would break off when the bombers were over the island, and the anti-air-

craft batteries would begin registering an effective barrage. Although flak was not heavy, the anti-aircraft fires were accurately delivered and sent several bombers on a final descent into the sea or
leaving the island as "smokers" that probably failed to return to
their bases in the Marshalls. When bombers were beyond range of
the anti-aircraft guns, the pilots of VMF 211 harried the retreating
bombers as they droned their way back to base at their 160-knot
cruising speed, and were able to down at least two more bombers
from each day's raids. The morale of the defenders soared as they
discovered that they were able to fight back effectively.

According to war diaries in the archives of the Imperial Japanese Navy, the first Wake Invasion Force sortied from their Ruotta
anchorage at Kwajalein Island in the Marshalls on December 8,
1941, and arrived at a point south of Wake Island two days later.

The force consisted of three cruisers, six destroyers, two converted destroyers used as assault transports, and two maru-type
transports. Also supporting the operation were two or more fleet
submarines assigned to conduct offshore surveillance for amphibious reconnaissance prior to the assault landing at Wake.[6]

Soon after midnight on December 11, the amphibious task
force entered an assembly area five or six miles south of Wake about
0100 and began debarking the landing force in choppy seas. The assault transports carefully lowered large landing craft, each capable of
carrying eighty armed men to the shore. However, when the maru-
type transports attempted to lower the landing craft, the boats
banged dangerously against the sides of the ship, rendering the de-
barkation of the landing force nearly impossible and extremely hazardous. Some of the landing craft capsized and swamped. When this
was reported to the task force commander at 0230 hours, H-hour
was postponed until after daylight.

While this was taking place, the defenders of Wake began to
observe blinking lights offshore to the south. "General Quarters"
was sounded and all hands stood to at-battle stations (as per Alert
Condition 1) although strict blackout was maintained.

Shortly before 0500 hours the invasion force began its final approach to their objective on a northwesterly course with Admiral
Kajioka's flagship, the *Yubari*, at the head column followed by the
other two cruisers. The six destroyers followed in two columns. The
two assault transports followed the column on the starboard side of

the formation while the two maru transports took up positions astern of the portside column.

In the early morning light, all ships of the invasion force were visible from the island as the formation changed course and opened fire at 0522 from a range of approximately 8,000 yards. Steaming parallel to the south shore of Wake, they began their naval gunfire preparation for the landing. Initially, Camp Number 1 seemed to be the primary target, although the bombardment caused little damage. Owing to the low silhouette of the island, most shells passed overhead and exploded in the lagoon.

The two gun crews of Lt. C. A. Barninger's Battery A on Peacock Point, at the southeastern tip of Wake proper, and the two gun crews of Lt. John A. McAllister's Battery L, at Kuku Point on the southwestern tip of Wilkes Island, had the lead ships of the passing columns in their scopes and were already tracking their targets. However, all the guns on the island remained silent because Major Devereaux had issued emphatic orders to hold their fire until he personally gave the order to open fire. The major had calmly and quite shrewdly estimated the situation and concluded that his 5-inch coastal defense guns were no match for the heavier armament of the attacking ships, either from the standpoint of effective range or in weight of metal (caliber). Hence, his best tactic was to rely on the element of surprise and allowing the enemy to conclude that the coastal defense guns had been put out of action by the air raids.

After completing their first firing run, the lead vessels closed the range to 6,000 yards and executed a 180-degree change of course and commenced another firing run from the opposite direction. Still there was no response from the shore batteries as the Japanese ships steamed parallel to the southern shoreline of Wake with all the guns belching fire. Naval shells passed overhead with a hollow hissing sound followed by explosions in the lagoon to the rear.

Tension continued to mount as the bombardment continued. Some oil tanks between Camp Number 1 and the channel were hit and set ablaze. Major Devereaux remained firm in his injunction. Battery commanders as well as the gun crews were becoming impatient and frustrated as they awaited the order to open fire. The situation had taken on shades of Bunker Hill and the "don't fire until you can see the whites of their eyes" bit. Admiral Kajioka and his officers may have been quite puzzled by this lack of reaction by the defenders. Perhaps they expected to see the colors flying from the water tower in Camp 1 hauled down and replaced by a white flag. Nevertheless, the ships of the attack force continued the bombardment of the island.

After completing the second run, the lead ship reversed course again, closed the range to approximately 4,500 yards, and began the third firing run. Major Devereaux had finally achieved his objective of luring the enemy ships within effective range of his coastal defense guns. Now he could inflict substantial damage to the amphibious task force. Accordingly, at 0615 hours, quite calmly in the tradition of Commodore Dewey at Manila Bay with his legendary command, "You may fire when ready, Gridley," the major issued his order to open fire.

Both batteries at the southern extremities of the atoll roared into action. Owing to the destruction of the rangefinders of both batteries as the result of bombing, range had to be estimated without reliable data. Hence, the first salvo fired by Lieutenant Barninger's Battery A directed at the flagship *Yubari* splashed into the ocean beyond the target, sending water high into the air. However, the deflection was perfect. Barney ordered the gun captains to reduce elevation by 200 yards and resume firing. The result was that rounds of the second salvo struck the cruiser amidship close by the waterline. Smoke (or steam) spewed from a hole in its side, as the *Yubari* turned away from the island on a zigzag course. One of the converted destroyers maneuvered into a position between the cruiser and the shore battery and attempted to lay a smokescreen to conceal the withdrawal of Admiral Kajioka's stricken flagship. This vessel was hit and seemed to change into a ball of fire and sank in a matter of seconds, apparently with no survivors.

While Battery A was engaged in its gunnery duel with the *Yubari* and its escort, Battery L at the western tip of Wilkes Island engaged the other two cruisers, which had shifted their fires to the coastal batteries. John McAllister's crews quickly scored hits on both the *Tenryu* and the *Tatsuta*. Even the transport *Kongo Maru*, which remained a comfortable 9,000 yards from the island, suffered some hits.

At this point, the three ships of Destroyer Division 29 began steaming in column directly toward the Battery L position. The *Hayate* was in the lead and closely followed by the *Oite* and the *Matsuka*. The *Hayate* became the priority target and was hit squarely by three salvos. There was a monstrous explosion amidships and the bow and stern of the vessel seemed to separate as it disappeared below the surface, leaving a spot of foam where a ship had been just seconds before. There were apparently no survivors from its crew. The *Oite* then came under fire and was also hit. However, it managed to change course and lay smoke to cover its withdrawal, along with the *Matsuka*.

While this was taking place the ships of Destroyer Division 30 had ranged to the west of Wilkes, where the two guns of Lt. Woodrow Kessler's Battery B on Peale Island could be brought to bear. Battery B quickly scored hits on the *Yayoi* and the *Kisaragi*. Both ships continued to return the fire of the batteries on Wilkes and Peale islands until they, too, were obliged to reverse course and lay smoke to cover their retreat to the southwest.

Prior to 0700, Admiral Kajioka decided that his plan of operation for invading Wake Island had been thwarted, not only by unfavorable weather but also by the stout and accurate firing by the shore batteries. He ordered a general withdrawal of his task force toward Kwajelein, and by 0720 all of the enemy vessels had retreated beyond the effective range of Wake's shore batteries.

The four F4F Wildcats that were still in operation after the destruction wrought by enemy air raids were ready to scramble prior to dawn, but had been ordered to remain on the ground until after the coastal defense batteries had answered the enemy fire. As soon as this had occurred, Major Putnam took to the air, along with his three most experienced pilots, Captains Henry T. Elrod, Frank C. Tharin, and Herbert C. Freuler.

The first mission was to seek out and engage any enemy aircraft supporting the invasion force. But since the enemy's original plan called for a ship-to-shore movement during hours of darkness, there were no carrier aircraft on station at the time. When this had been verified by a 360-degree sweep of the area at an altitude of 12,000 feet, the pilots of VMF 211 were ready to pounce on the ships of the attack force as soon as the gunnery battle was concluded.

When the ships of the would-be invasion force had retreated beyond the range of the coastal batteries, Major Putnam and his daring cohorts zoomed down upon the enemy cruisers executing "smokestack" bombing and strafing attacks. Both ships of Cruiser Division 18 sustained damage. The torpedo battery of the *Tenryu* was put out of action, and part of the superstructure of the *Tatsuta* was destroyed.

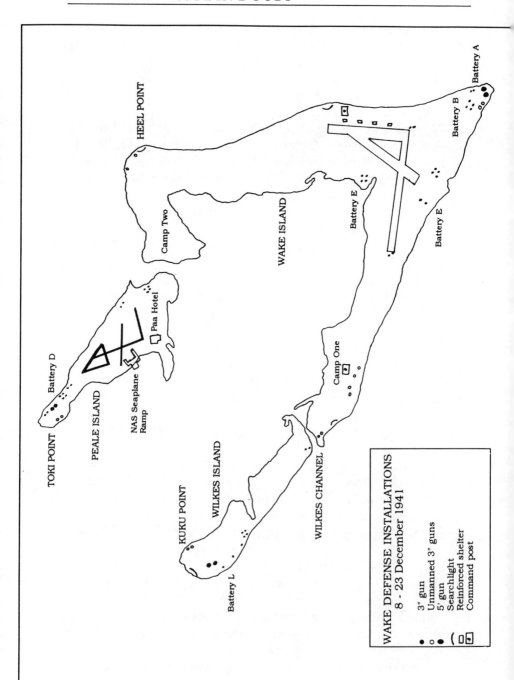

WAKE DEFENSE INSTALLATIONS
8 - 23 December 1941

● 3" gun
○ Unmanned 3" guns
● 5' gun
(Searchlight
□ Reinforced shelter
▣ Command post

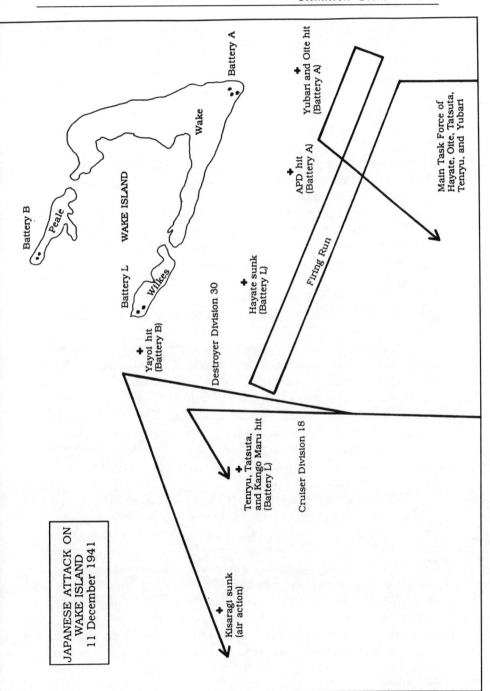

JAPANESE ATTACK ON
WAKE ISLAND
11 December 1941

Battery B

Peale

WAKE ISLAND

Wake

Battery A

Battery L

Wilkes

Yayoi hit
(Battery B)

Destroyer Division 30

Hayate sunk
(Battery L)

APD hit
(Battery A)

Yubari and Oite hit
(Battery A)

Firing Run

Main Task Force of
Hayate, Oite, Tatsuta,
Tenryu, and Yubari

Tenryu, Tatsuta,
and Kango Maru hit
(Battery L)

Cruiser Division 18

Kisaragi sunk
(air action)

Captain Freuler attacked the transport *Kongo Maru*. One of his 100-pound bombs struck its stern, igniting gasoline fires that ravaged topside equipment on the ship. After each pilot had expended all of his .50-caliber ammunition and the two 100-pound bombs were released from improvised racks on the belly of their planes, they would return to the island to refuel, rearm, and return to the fray.

The most spectacular achievement of the air operations was the "smokestack" dive bombing attack by Capt. "Hammering Hank" Elrod, which dealt the fatal blow to the already damaged *Kisaragi*, thirty miles southwest of Wake at 0731.

All together, VMF 211 pilots, now with only four planes, flew a total of ten sorties, dropped twenty 100-pound bombs, and fired 20,000 rounds of .50-caliber ammunition. Although all of the pilots had managed to return alive, their success had not been without cost. All of the planes had sustained damage from the anti-aircraft fire by the ships they had attacked. Captain Elrod's plane was so badly damaged that he was obliged to make a crash landing. There were now only two F4F Wildcats still operational to oppose attacking enemy bombers.

Just before noon on December 11, Lieutenants John F. Kinney and Carl R. Davidson were at the controls of the two Wildcat fighters that were still serviceable. They were conducting a combat air patrol when they sighted a formation of thirty shore-based bombers approaching from the northeast at 18,000 feet. They intercepted the attacking bombers and unhesitatingly tore into the formation, with their machine guns spewing out a hail of .50-caliber projectiles. Davidson knocked two of the bombers out of the sky, while Kinney sent another limping back to base, emitting a trail of black smoke.

The anti-aircraft batteries on the atoll reacted swiftly and delivered accurate barrage fires that caused one of the bombers to plummet into the water just off Wilkes Island. In addition, they accounted for three more "smokers." Batteries D and E fired a combined total of 225 rounds, which was a remarkable feat considering that each of the batteries had only three guns that were operational.

That afternoon, Lieutenant Kinney was able to report to Major Putnam that he and his engineering crew had three of the Wildcats patched up well enough to fly combat air patrols. This was another remarkable accomplishment, achieved by salvaging and interchanging parts of wrecked F4Fs, as well as using a considerable amount of ingenuity.

Owing to difficulty in starting the plane's engine, there was some delay before Lt. David D. Kliever lifted off the runway to join the other two pilots of the combat air patrol. As he was gaining altitude he spotted a completely surfaced submarine approximately twenty-five miles offshore on a bearing of 225 degrees from Wake. After ascertaining that it was an enemy sub, he pushed over and dove at the sub from an altitude of 10,000 feet, with his machine guns blazing. Just before pulling out of his steep dive he released both of the 100-pound bombs. When he pulled out of his dive he was so close to the surface that fragments of the exploding bomb ripped holes in his wing and tail surface.

Although Kliever could not be sure that either of the bombs had been a direct hit, he was quite sure that both bombs had landed within a very few feet of the pressure hull. He circled to the right and watched the submarine sink below the surface. Later, he and the other pilots circled overhead and observed a large oil slick.

Just after dawn on the morning of December 12, two four-engine patrol bombers strafed and bombed Wake and Peale islands without causing significant damage. Captain Tharin, who was already in the air at the time, managed to intercept and shoot down one of the huge flying boats. This definite kill occurred just after 0500.[7]

Following the triumph of the defenders of Wake on December 11–12, the siege of the atoll continued unabated until December 23 with daily bombing attacks by as many as forty-four enemy aircraft. During the latter part of this period, the incoming bombers were escorted by carrier-based fighter planes.

The intrepid pilots of VMF 211 took turns at the controls of the two remaining Wildcats and continued to effectively challenge the attacking enemy formations despite the appalling odds, until December 22, when their last two planes were lost.[8] The remnant of the squadron then reported for assignment as marine infantrymen.[9]

Also on December 22, the island commander was informed by CINCUS that there would be no ("repeat no") friendly forces operating in the vicinity of Wake Island and that any air or sufrace craft sighted were to be regarded as hostile and taken under fire without hesitation. When this word was passed to the defense force, it became abundantly clear that there was no prospect whatever of relief or reinforcement, and that the high command in Hawaii and in Washington had written Wake Island off the list of viable military resources.

The second amphibious assault by the Japanese was launched

under cover of darkness on December 23, 1941, by an attack task force consisting of more than twice the number of ships and personnel allocated to the attack force which had been repulsed by Wake's defenders on December 11. This force, which was supported by carrier aircraft, overwhelmed the sparse beach defenses of the atoll, and after several hours of ferocious combat, reduced the defense force to several more or less isolated pockets of resistance.

Since Major Devereaux had lost contact with most of the elements of his force, Commander Cunningham decided to surrender the island to preclude the slaughter of the unarmed civilian construction workers.[10]

Although the battle at Wake Island was minor in scale when compared to subsequent operations in the Pacific, it did have a significant impact on the war in two respects. First, the defeat of an enemy task force which had been assigned a priority mission was a setback which upset the timetable for the Japanese campaign of conquest in the Pacific. It created a delay that bought time for the United States Armed Forces to prepare for the assault on Midway and thereby achieved a major American victory. Secondly, by providing even a small victory during a time of gloom and uncertainty, the episode served to bolster the morale of a dazed and apprehensive nation, and to galvanize the resolve of the American people to strive for and achieve victory.

In the context of military history, the fierce action at Wake Island on December 10–11, 1941, was not only the first American victory of World War II, but it has been accorded a number of other firsts, including (1) enemy surface ship was sunk by American forces, (2) enemy vessel was sunk by American aircraft, (3) Japanese fleet submarine was sunk by American forces, (4) amphibious operation was aborted, (5) Medal of Honor was awarded to a marine aviator (Capt. Henry T. Elrod), and (6) Presidential Unit Citation was awarded by personal direction of the president and signed by President Roosevelt.[11]

And finally, the "Saga of Wake Island," as it has been called, provided an abundant harvest for the grist of the propaganda mill. Along with the slogan "Remember Pearl Harbor," "Remember Wake Island" became one of the often repeated phrases of war propaganda.

The episode has been likened to such epics of American military history as Belleau Wood, Bunker Hill, and the Alamo. However, the Wake Island battle, when placed in a more modest perspective, is another story of a small group of Americans, men and boys, determined to give it their best shot for God, corps, and country. Their efforts, their achievements, and their sacrifices add another small bit to the heritage of future generations of Americans.

V. A Ray of Hope in a Stormy Sea

The Defenders Continue the Fight: PatWing 10

There were thousands of stories of bravery during World War II. There were an equal number of stories with unusual, comic, or crazy overtones. There were stories of men taking the initiative, acting on their own to perform acts of valor, bravery, or daring. There were stories of individuals standing apart from the crowd and distinguishing themselves from the group and the ordinary. Very seldom did all of these factors come into play at one time and with one group of people. Such was the story, however, of PatWing 10, a group of navy pilots who flew amphibious PBYs in the early days of the war.

The saga of PatWing 10 began in an ordinary manner. The men and planes of PatWing 10 were stationed in the Philippines in December 1941, based at Cavite, Olongapo, Sangley Point, and Manila. On December 8, when the Japanese attacked the Philippines, the ordinary saga of PatWing 10 began to take on all of the elements of the above mentioned attributes. In early and mid-December, as the Japanese moved through Luzon toward Manila, PatWing 10 began moving south, to Laguna de Bay and out of the Philippines into other bases and islands in the South Pacific. Using several seaplane tenders, and relying on Dutch, British, American, and Australian units to refuel their planes, PatWing 10 began to distinguish themselves in acts of bravery and valor by flying mission after mission back into Japanese-held territory in the Philippines to rescue trapped American military and civilian personnel.

By the end of December, PatWing 10 was stationed over almost the entire territory of the South Pacific, with planes located in Manila, Balikpapan, Borneo, Surabaya, and Ambon. Their patrol area ranged from the South China Sea in the north, to the Philippine Sea in the east, to Malaya and Sumatra in the west, and Australia and the Indian Ocean in the south. In January, VP-22 from Hawaii joined PatWing 10, bringing twelve new PBY-5s, which were divided among bases in Surabaya, Ambon, and Darwin. As the Japanese marched through the South Pacific, PatWing 10 was continually forced to retreat farther south, until in March 1942, all that was left of PatWing 10 was on the Pelican River (Swan River Yacht Club) in southwestern Australia. Before the remnants of PatWing 10 were taken out of the South Pacific in mid-1942, they had lost forty-one of forty-five planes (fourteen shot down, twenty-four destroyed on the ground, and three to accidents) and well over half of the personnel assigned to the squadron.

PatWing 10 was the first complete and organized aviation unit to fight back against the Japanese in the South Pacific. For fighting a war, they flew the worst of all possible airplanes. The PBY was big, strong, and rugged and was able to lift heavy loads off the water and fly for long distances without refueling. It was primarily made of wood and fabric. The frame was made of metal, but the rest of the aircraft was fabric and wood. The fabric was stretched over the frames with "dope," a glue-like compound that was extremely flammable, even when dry. When hit by enemy shells, the plane was prone to burn rapidly. It was a slow-flying plane, making it an easy target for enemy gunners.

There were three significant advantages of the PBY which played a crucial role in its success in the early days of the war. One, it did not need a permanent home for fuel dumps. A seaplane tender could be used for refueling or the PBY could land along an island coastline or in a river and refuel from previously deposited fuel drums. Two, the PBY was a fuel miser. It could (and did) cover distances other airplanes and crews could not hope to. Three, the PBY could carry heavy cargo loads. This made the PBY ideal for the rescue and evacuation of personnel.

The crews of PatWing 10 were given a variety of missions, many of them suicidal. PatWing 10 participated in photo reconnaissance and surveillance missions, rescue and recovery missions, and horizontal bombing raids on enemy ships and ground facilities. Most PBYs shot down by the enemy were engaged in this last bit of foolishness. The PBY made for such an inviting target as it was almost impossible for enemy gunners to miss, whether firing from a ship or from another airplane. But whatever the assignment, mis-

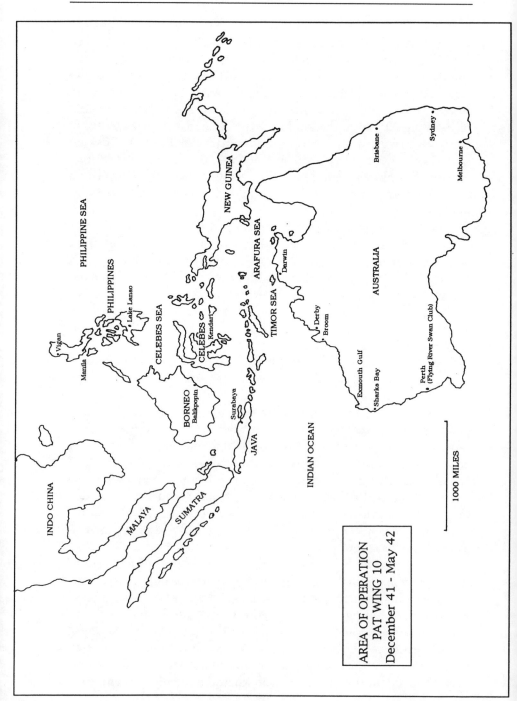

AREA OF OPERATION
PAT WING 10
December 41 - May 42

sion, or odds, the crews of PatWing 10 flew the missions without question, developing a panache and laissez faire attitude unparalleled by combat crews in World War II.

With a crew complement of seven or eight members, the PBYs were often a welcome sight to those captured by the ground. The crews of the PBYs usually consisted of three pilots, one more than likely being an enlisted pilot (naval aviation pilot, or NAP), two radiomen, and two or three machinist mates. The crew was often crosstrained in other functions, any being able to perform all other functions on the ship. In addition, the crew members could repair the ships from the ground up. No task was beyond the capabilities of a crew member.

To illustrate the versatility and adaptability of the crews, after arriving at Pelican Point, PatWing 10 found there was no way to heat-soften the rivets used to repair the seams in the hulls and wings. To Joseph Antonides and his maintenance crew, that presented little problem. Scavenging aboard the USS *Wright*, a floating derelict, they found an old salt bath which Antonides and his team repaired and converted into a machine to heat-treat the rivets. It was not unusual for crews to repair bullet holes with pieces of tin cans, tree branches, clothing (in one instance a crew used the petticoats of a female passenger), and even pieces of pencils.

Nothing was beyond the ingenuity of PatWing 10. In the retreat from the Philippines, Gordon Ebbe had the job of placing buoys on Lake Lanao for the planes of PatWing 10 to tie-up to when they landed. Ebbe had a unique way of placing the buoys, "We put the buoys and anchors in a Moro banca, and they damn near sank the boat. At first we had the Filipinos dive down and estimate the depth, but that took too long. So we used the pragmatic method of throwing the buoy and anchor over the side. If the buoy stayed on the surface, it was OK." (Messimer, 1985; page 71.)

Almost every crew of PatWing 10 was shot down at one time or another. The case of Lt. Jack Dawley and the crew of P-6 was not a rarity for PatWing 10. On December 26, 1941, Dawley and P-6 were stationed in Ambon and had been assigned as part of an air group ordered to fly a horizontal bombing mission against Japanese ships at Jolo Harbor, Jolo Island. Even before beginning his bombing run, his PBY took numerous hits from Japanese Zeros and anti-aircraft fire. Dumping his bombs, Dawley landed the shot and burning plane several hundred yards off the southern coast of Jolo. Two crewmen,

AMM1c Earle Hall and RM3c James Scribner, were killed by the enemy fire, and one crewman, AAM2c Everen McLawhorn, was seriously wounded. The survivors swam to the shore of Jolo, where they were picked up by some Moro natives. Dawley's crew joined with four other survivors of the Jolo raid, and together they made it to Siasi, Jolo. Obtaining a wooden boat, Moro paddlers, and some provisions, the nine survivors headed south into the Pacific. On New Year's night, with McLawhorn suffering terribly and everybody half-sick from exposure and fatigue, Dawley still found reason to celebrate: "Having no way to tell time exactly, it was agreed that when the moon could be seen by sighting up the sail mast, it would, arbitrarily, be midnight. At 'midnight' then, with toasts (of brandy they had aboard the raft) to loved ones, to shipmates, to ourselves, and to the hope that we would all be able to toast again in 1943, and with the time-honored custom of singing 'Auld Lang Syne,' we dropped the hook for 1941 and weighed anchor on 1942." (Messimer, 1985; page 132.)

Making their way to Tawitawi the next day, Dawley and his bedraggled band located a hospital where McLawhorn could be treated. On January 4 they made their way to Sitangkai, Sibutu, where Deputy Governor Amirhamja Japal gave them a customs launch and they made their way to Tawau, British North Borneo, on down past Boenjoe Island, and on to Tarakan on January 8. From Tarakan they were flown back to PatWing 10 at Balikpapan, Surabaya, and finally Ambon.

This small band of fearless pilots and crews went over and above what was required, and in doing so gave new meaning to the concepts of courage, adaptability, and ingenuity. Their actions also served to raise the morale of other retreating Allies, and to give other soldiers, sailors, and airmen the verve and elan to continue the fight.

Survival and Rescue

The experiences of Adm. (Ret.) Thomas H. Moorer while serving with PatWing 10 were unusual experiences for most aviators. For PatWing 10, his experiences were within the realm of the everyday and mundane. It could probably be argued that PatWing 10 crews should not have been called aviators; they should have been called swimmers. Most spent more time in and on the water than they did in the air.

Adm. Thomas H. Moorer, USN (Ret.)

Before I get started on my personal experiences, I would like to make a couple of comments, particularly to the young people that read history. I have found here, and in Washington in particular, that people cannot resist assuming that in the days we are talking about we had the same technology that we have today. For instance, there was no radar on the aircraft, which significantly enhances search capability. We had very poor communications. As a matter of fact, General Moore just mentioned they had to take a piece of communications equipment out of an airplane and put it up in the control tower. The weather predictions were very limited. And so when you start thinking about why didn't you do this and why didn't you do that, don't unconsciously assume we had all the things that they have today. That was fifty years ago, when technology was an entirely different animal.

At the beginning of the war, I was assigned to a VP squadron, VP-22. We had already sent two of these squadrons out to the Philippines, where they were designated as Fleet AirWing 10. They were in the Manila area at the outset of war. There was one major bombing attack made by Fleet AirWing 10 on the island of Jolo, south of the Philippines, where they lost four of the six planes and learned right away that horizontal bombing was not the way to go.

My squadron conducted reconnaissance. We had, as a matter of fact, been on Midway Island for two months and we searched 600 miles north of Midway, which would have possibly located the Japanese strike fleet which was coming on an easterly course about 600–700 miles north of Midway. But of course, as I said, we had no radar and had to rely entirely on our eyes in order to find a ship at sea. We finally managed to get two aircraft in commission by, I think, about 2100 or 2200 hours the night of December 6, 1941. I went up with my copilot and the other pilots to talk to Admiral Kimmel's staff. He said, "Well, we don't have enough aircraft to really conduct an intelligent operation."

Once you got out a thousand miles, you could only handle a ten-degree search, go out, come across about twenty miles, and come back. You would go across twice the distance that you could see in the current weather conditions and then come back. The idea was to head for Kwajalein. Admiral Kimmel and his staff thought the Japanese carriers would head for Kwajalein after they made the attack on Pearl Harbor. The idea was to be out far enough at day-light, knowing the speed of the ships and so on, that the Japanese had to be between you and Pearl Harbor. That's what I did, and that was the mission I had the night of December 7. Of course, the Japa-nese were north and they went elsewhere, as I will describe in just a minute.

We managed to get a complete new squadron of replacement aircraft from the States. The big advantage of these aircraft was that they had the R-2800 engine. They were called PBY-5s and were much easier to take off with a heavy load than the one we had been using (PBY-4) for a long time.

About that time we got orders to send a squadron to reinforce Fleet AirWing 10 (PatWing 10) in Manila. Consequently, we loaded-out for that. I was the operations officer. I saw to it that we put one spare part of everything in every airplane; one airspeed meter, one vacuum pump, one generator, one starter, and so on. We practically exhausted all the supplies in Pearl Harbor. On top of that, we took 600 pounds of canned goods because we didn't know whether we were going to have a chance to get anything to eat in Manila. There was no airfield on a direct route between Midway and the Philippines. The Japanese were attacking and capturing Wake and were also after Guam, so we had to go roundabout. We went down to the Fiji Islands, then to Noumea, then to Townsville, then to Port Moresby, then to Darwin, and then to Java. We began to operate in conjunction with Fleet AirWing 10 in search operations as the Japanese came down from the north.

Also, the Dutch had prepositioned jet fuel, or rather I should say 100-octane fuel at that time, in many, many places around the islands. Every plane had a long hose and a fuel pump that was run by a lawnmower engine. When we got low on fuel, we knew where these places were so we would just beach the plane up on the sand and go ashore and look through the jungle. We would find a 55-gallon drum and stick the hose in the drum and pump the PBY full of fuel. Generally speaking, we never came back to the same place we had left because the Japanese were following us back.

We operated throughout that area, all the way from Darwin to Sumatra. Just nip and tuck. We had lost many planes. We finally, as a matter of fact, wound up in Perth with just two out of the thirty planes we started with. Many of them were, of course, destroyed on the water.

While I was operating out of Darwin we got word that the Japanese carriers were in the vicinity. The six carriers that were at Pearl Harbor were divided and two carriers were sent to support the Wake Island operation. The Japanese had failed in their first effort, and the admiral [Kajioka] was ordered to capture it the second time or not come home. They significantly reinforced his operation, beginning with the two smaller of the six carriers that were at Pearl Harbor. The other four came down to attack Darwin. I was detailed to go and see if I could find them.

We were at that time operating from one of the tenders, which was a converted four-stack destroyer, the *Willie B. Preston*. I took off from Darwin and headed toward Ambon, which was halfway between the Philippine Islands and Australia. I was successful, all right. I found them. The carriers had launched a very large flight to attack Darwin. We had in our planes no leak-proof tanks, although we had supplied the British and the Dutch with new PBY-5s that did have leak-proof tanks. When I got attacked by the Japanese and got hit, of course, the plane immediately caught fire. It was streaming fire about 100 yards behind. It looked like a shooting star. The trailing edges of this airplane were fabric, so they began to burn off. Nevertheless, I managed to get the plane down on the water with some effort. The fighters, which had normally been following the practice of strafing people on the water like that, did not because I figure the bombers kept going and the fighter people realized that pretty soon the bombers were going to get over their target and not have any escort. They all formed up and went on and rejoined their regular position.

After I went down, we got out of the aircraft and launched our liferafts. We had two rubber boats, one of which was full of holes, so we all got in the other one and got clear of the plane because it was obvious that it was going to burn fiercely for some time. When we hit the water, there was a ship about fifteen miles away that I had seen and the ship turned and headed toward us. This ship [SS *Florence D*] was flying the Philippine flag. It was a very large ship. It headed over and picked us up.

I found out after I got aboard that it was carrying ammunition to Corregidor and was stacked from stem to stern with ammunition of all kinds. Well, I knew what that meant. I told my crew to all go aft, and when I saw the first attacking plane I was going to jump over the side and I wanted them to follow me. About 1400 hours that afternoon we looked up and saw nine enemy dive bombers and I did just that — I jumped over the side. So did my crew, except for one, who had become impatient and tired of sitting back there (we were on the equator and the temperature was 120 something) and he had gone forward to talk to the captain. We never saw him again. Incidentally, he had a twin brother in our squadron. That was before the day that the navy no longer permitted brothers to be in the same unit.

The first bomb blew the bow off the ship. The ship went down at about a 45-degree angle. It was a big ship, I think about 500–600 feet long, and the stern was left above the surface of the water. We were in the water with a large number of Filipino sailors who got off the ship. We managed to climb back aboard the stern with the help of some of the Filipinos and cut loose two lifeboats. I put my copilot in one and I got in the other and we proceeded to pick up our own crew and the surviving Filipinos. There were about eighty in the Philippine crew, and I think about forty were in the water. Some of them were terribly burned and they died later. But we did manage to pick them up. About the time we got them in the boats, the Japanese came over and strafed the boats again. The Filipinos were the first to jump out the second time.

We picked them up again and I set sail for what I hoped was going to be Darwin. The lifeboats typically had no compass and no water, which are the first two things you put in a lifeboat if you're going to have a lifeboat. Fortunately, two things saved us. There were three or four cases of condensed milk, and also the Southern Cross was sitting out there just as pretty as you please. We raised the sail and ran with the wind on a southeasterly course.

Finally, we heard some surf. It was at night when we hit the beach. As soon as we grounded the two lifeboats, doused the sail and grounded the boats, the Filipinos (who were youngsters or actually kids) jumped out of both boats and ran into the jungle. Some day when I have more time I'm going down there and tell them the war's over. They had had enough of the war. We investigated the next morning, found out that it was an uninhabited island called Bathurst. It had two rivers. We could not move. I had the crew build large letters in the sand that said, "Water, medicine." After a few days we were there sopping up that condensed milk with nothing else to eat, and an Australian Hudson plane came over. He circled and dropped a note that said, "I'll be back." He came back in about two hours and said we would be picked up at daylight. Sure enough, at daylight there was a corvette [HMAS *Warranambool*] out there and they sent in a lifeboat and picked us up. Some of us had been injured and could not swim out to the ship. The radioman had a broken ankle and I had been hit in the left leg. We were in pretty good shape, though, considering what had happened. A young ensign they had on the corvette pulled me aboard when we came alongside. The captain then headed for Darwin.

We were attacked on the way in by an Emily flying boat making horizontal attacks. This captain was a captain in the Australian reserve. He had just come from Crete, where Lord Montbatten's destroyers had sunk. This was the first place that German paratroopers had ever been used to try to capture territory. There was a hell of a fight down there and this captain said, "After all, I've been fighting the Germans. These Japanese, they're no good. They're just amateurs compared to the Germans." He was a little disdainful, but I think they got his attention a little later on in the war.

He took us into Darwin and put us ashore. There wasn't a human soul in town, not one. No man, woman, or child. They had all put to the bush as a result of this attack. We went into the hotel. I had been there once before that previous fall, so I knew about the hotel. The Australians had left so fast they had left whiskey on the bar and steaks in the icebox. We just set up shop. Two days later the MPs came back into town (they were the first ones to reappear), and we managed to get off a message to come pick us up.

Well, there's a sequel to that story that I think is interesting. There was a book that was written entitled *Australia's Pearl Harbor*, which described the Japanese attacks on Darwin, February 19, 1942. Included in the book was the statement that I had been killed. At that point I was chairman of the Joint Chiefs of Staff, so I wrote the author a letter and told him that he had made a small mistake. There was a great roar and hoopla about that. Len Vickridge, who had pulled me aboard the Australian corvette, read the book and we immediately began to correspond. He will visit me in Washington in the fall of 1992. He was very much involved in the America's Cup Race at Newport, when the Australians licked us. He was crowing all over the place, sending me all of the newspaper headlines, and made me a member of the Fremantle Yacht Club. He really rubbed it in. Of course, we got even the next year.

Desperate Measures: The Doolittle Raid

Early 1942 was a grim period for the United States. Pearl Harbor and the Pacific Fleet had been hit hard in a surprise attack, Wake had been captured, and the Japanese were steamrolling the Pacific and Allied forces. The Japanese were making plans to invade the shores of California, Oregon, and Washington.[1] Something had to be done. At the urging of General Arnold (chief of staff, Army Air Corps), Admiral King approved possibly the most daring plan ever given the go-ahead by the United States military: a bombing raid on Japan.

Capt. Donald B. Duncan, air officer to Admiral King, was assigned to plan and execute a bombing raid on Tokyo. He determined that B-25s were the only planes which could execute such a daring move, and that the only possible way to accomplish the mission was to modify the planes for carrier operations. Sixteen B-25s were specially modified to handle an increased weight and fuel capacity. Col. James Doolittle was selected to lead this mission against the Japanese mainland.

The B-25s and flight crews were sent to Eglin Air Field, Florida, for training. The outline of a carrier flight deck was painted on the runways at Eglin and the crews trained from dawn to dusk, taking off in the allotted distance. Landings were not practiced as the flight was not expected to return to the decks of the carrier. None of the mission personnel were informed of the actual mission.

From Eglin, the planes and crews were flown to Sacramento, California, where training continued. At the end of April, the specially modified B-25s were flown to San Francisco and loaded aboard the aircraft carrier *Hornet*. On April 2, 1942, the *Hornet* left San Francisco for the Pacific en route to Tokyo. As the carrier left San Francisco, the crews were finally informed of the mission they were to fly.

Between Midway and the Aleutians, Adm. William "Bull" Halsey and the aircraft carrier *Enterprise* joined Task Force Mike. During the early morning hours of April 18, 1942, Task Force Mike reached the designated takeoff point approximately 600 miles west of Kyushu, Japan. At 0725, the first B-25 took off from the deck of the *Hornet*.

Doolittle's raid accomplished far more than believed possible. It completely changed American attitudes toward the war in the Pacific. For Japan, the Doolittle raid was the impossible. For a nearly defeated enemy to strike the very homeland of Divine Providence was unbelievable. Imperial Japanese Headquarters hastily convened and changed their entire strategy for the continuation of the war. One result of the Doolittle raid was Imperial Japanese Headquarters advancing the date for the invasion of Midway, a rash decision which was to have implications reaching to the USS *Missouri* in Tokyo Bay in 1945.[2]

★   ★   ★

"We don't expect anyone to come back alive" is a popular line in fictional spy stories and movies. The suicide mission is a popular theme for fiction because it holds the reader's interest. In real life, very seldom are suicide missions undertaken. The raid on mainland Japan by the Doolittle raiders comes as close as one can get to the popular fiction premise. The Doolittle raid was real-life. The men selected for that mission knew (even though the mission was not revealed at the time of selection) they had been chosen for an extremely dangerous and daring mission. They were well aware that this might be a "suicide" mission. One of the last survivors of that daring raid is Brig. Gen. (Ret.) Richard A. Knobloch.

General Knobloch became a pilot in the Army Air Corps in 1940 and volunteered for the Doolittle raid on Tokyo in 1942. He then flew fifty additional missions against the Japanese and was awarded the Distinguished Service Medal, the Distinguished Flying Cross with clusters, and many other medals.

Brig. Gen. Richard A. Knobloch, USAF (Ret.)

The time was 0600. The date was April 18, 1942. It was a date that shall go down in history because of its impact on the war in the Pacific. At that hour, there were sixteen B-25 medium bombers, overloaded way beyond the recommended gross weight, sitting on the deck of the *Hornet*, whose bow was pointed directly at Tokyo. The distance from the *Hornet* to Tokyo was 812 statute miles. The sixteen aircraft on the deck were manned by eighty men, five men to a crew. The word came from Adm. Bull Halsey's flagship, the *Enterprise*, to man our planes. That was at 0600 hours. We had, in effect, been manning the planes before that time but didn't start the engines. We were just topping off full tanks, putting five-gallon cans into the back end to give us extra fuel because it appeared we would be taking off early and would need the extra fuel. At 0800 hours a signal came. The whistle sounded that a message had been received and was going to be passed over the loudspeaker. The message came from Admiral Halsey: "Army crews, launch your planes." So we crawled into the cockpit at this time and started engines.

The carrier deck length was 809 feet, but we only had about 465 feet that we could utilize because we weren't permitted to take off aft of the superstructure. We were just a little bit near the lower end of the superstructure. They were afraid that in case something happened it would set the superstructure on fire and set the whole carrier on fire. As each airplane took off another airplane would roll up to the same takeoff point. Colonel Doolittle used 467 feet, as I recall. That's the amount of deck space he had. The rest of us were placed anywhere from 460 to 470 feet from the end of the deck, within five feet plus or minus of Colonel Doolittle's deck space. The distance required for his takeoff was about 300 feet. His wheels were off the deck at about 300 feet from the point he gave it full throttle.

The deck was pitching. Occasionally we would take spray over the bow, and the brake release signal was given to the crews when the deck was pointed down toward the water. It didn't look very appealing. You could look out through the windshield and there was the water, dead ahead of you. It was an overcast day, so it wasn't a beautiful blue or beautiful green of the ocean. It was dirty looking and not very appetizing. Then the bow would come up and you would get a little lift, and with the power from your engines you were airborne. Almost everybody got off without any problem.

Two had a minor problem. One, Trav Hoover, forgot to neutralize his trim to give his plane a slight nose-up. Instead, he had his elevator trim tab all the way back, which gave him nose-high altitude. He took off and almost stalled. It looked like he was going to fall on the deck. He managed to get the nose down and took off. Ted Lawson taxied into position. Everything looked fine. He'd run up his engines to full power and the brake release was given. We all noticed that his flaps were moving up. He rolled to the end of the deck and disappeared off the end. We thought, "Uh-oh, there goes number one into the drink." But he came staggering up and was able to recover with a zero flap takeoff in 465 feet distance. It took pretty good piloting to do that.

The aircraft were overloaded. We had four 500-pound bombs, three 500-pound demolition bombs, and one 500-pound incendiary cluster, and extra fuel tanks all throughout the airplane including where the rear lower turret had been.

As we headed toward Japan, the weather got steadily better. We had a little difficulty finding our targets. A pilot never gets lost — a little disoriented once in a while, but never lost. It looked like there were airplanes coming from all directions over that part of Japan because we were trying to find landmarks. We finally all found our landmarks. We were flying at treetop level, as low as we could get. We didn't know whether the Japanese had radar or not. We suspected they might have some land-based radar, so we were staying as low as we could. The tactic we used was when you had the target in sight, you'd pull up to about 1,000 feet or 1,200 feet (so the demolition wouldn't blow you out of the sky), drop your bombs, make a left or right turn out, and head out to sea as if you were going to some secret destination. Then when you'd get just out of sight of land or it was in the distance behind you, you'd make a right turn and head out down along the coast of Japan, around the southernmost island, and head across the Yellow Sea to China.

As we approached the coast of China, about halfway across the Yellow Sea, the weather started to deteriorate. Of the sixteen aircraft, eleven of the aircraft decided to pull up into the soup, and as it got worse, we gradually got closer and closer to the water. Pretty soon we said to heck with this noise, because we didn't know where we were. We had no way of taking sun shots.[3] It was on pure dead reckoning with a drift meter on the white caps on the water. So the margin of error was pretty high and we thought we might fly into a hill along the coast. So the majority of us pulled up to about 6,500-7,000 feet and flew along, in the rain and miserable.

We tried our homing radio. It didn't work. The reason it didn't work was because no one was transmitting down on the ground. The airplane that was supposed to fly in this equipment for us had crashed in the storm and had destroyed all the equipment, and we didn't know this. We tried to tune in on a simple homing radio, and it didn't work. We didn't get contact with anybody.

But one thing that was progressing very well — very fine, very efficiently — was the gas running through those engines. You've seen the peg on your car where it goes "flicker." Some of you have, which indicates that it's empty. Well, in our airplane when we got the flicker against the peg (the indication of the amount of fuel we had aboard), we had put the airplane on automatic pilot, gathered around the escape hatch in the back, pulled the handle and kicked it, and it dropped out. The hole, by the way, is about two by two and a half feet. We were all real slim in those days. We got through that hole, the escape hatch, without any problem. But also it was a little bit shaky to look at that hole. It reminded me somewhat of the black hole of Calcutta. Vapors were coming up from it and the whistle of the wind and, of course, the constant pressure on you to get out of that thing because the engines were going to quit at any minute.

Of the sixteen airplanes, eleven crews bailed out, four ditched or crash landed, and one went to Vladivostok and landed gear down on a Soviet airfield, where the crew was interned for fifteen months. Losses of the raid were a total of seven as a direct result of the raid. The Japanese captured eight crew members, of which they executed three, one died of beriberi and malnutrition, and four survived the war in a POW camp. There were two who came down in a lake and got tangled up in their parachutes and drowned before they could be rescued. One crew member didn't get out of the airplane, or did just get out of it before it hit the ground. His body was found immediately adjacent thereto.

The results of the raid had a great impact on the Battle of Midway. There was some material damage. You couldn't miss going into a target at that low altitude. We had a very simple bombsight that was developed by one of the fellows. It was just like a GSAP gunsight aiming point type of device, but based on the speed and altitude you were at you dropped your bomb when the target came through the sight. The damage was material damage. Second was the psychological impact. It was good for the United States and the Allies and bad for the Japanese. They realized they could be attacked. As a result of this, many Japanese war plans were changed. They withdrew many land, sea, and air forces from the extended perimeter they had around Japan so they could protect Japan from further attack of this nature. At the same time, it helped implement the Japanese establishing a fleet to get to Midway and Hawaii, and they were intercepted by a great number of the United States force that whipped them soundly.

Battle of the Coral Sea

As far as World War II battles go, Coral Sea was not the largest, deadliest, costliest, or most renowned. Coral Sea has a special place in naval warfare, however, as it was the first battle that pitted the aircraft carriers of two nations against each other and was a portent of things to come in the Pacific War.

In late April 1942, the Japanese were assembling a task force to invade New Guinea. Admiral Fletcher, commanding Task Force 17 and steaming the South Pacific, had the carriers *Lexington* and *Yorktown* (flagship) at his disposal. On May 6, 1942, he received communications intelligence that Admiral Goto (Task Force commander) and the New Guinea invasion force would be traversing the Louisiades on May 7, 1942. Fletcher directed Task Force 17 to the Jomard Passage to set an ambush for Admiral Goto's force.

On May 7, 1942, United States and Japanese forces met. Planes from the *Shokaku* and *Zuikaku* severely damaged the *Neosho* and sank the *Sims*.[4] Later that day, a *Lexington* strike force sank the Japa-

The Japanese carrier *Shoho* sinks during the Battle of the Coral Sea.
National Archives, print courtesy Admiral Nimitz Museum

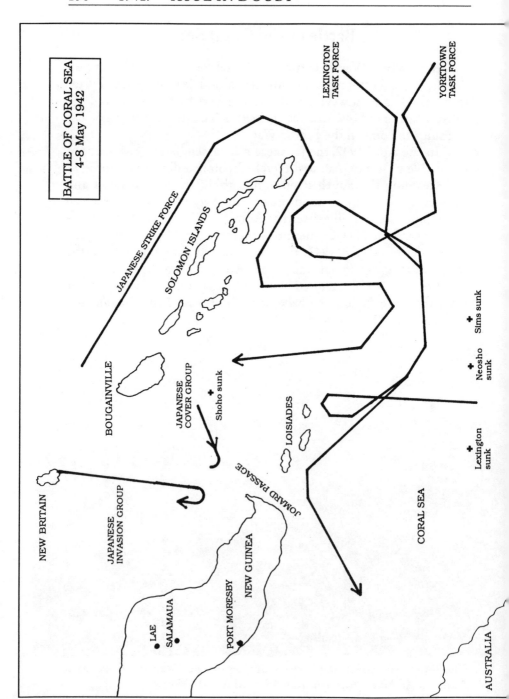

nese carrier *Shoho*, and one of the *Lexington* pilots, Lt. Cmdr. R. E. Dixon, radioed his now famous message, "Scratch one flattop. Dixon to carrier. Scratch one flattop."

At this point in the battle, two unusual events occurred. One, a flight of B-26s attacked the HMAS *Australia*, thinking the ship to be Japanese. Second, because of the bad weather and darkness, a flight of nine Japanese Zeros believed the carrier *Yorktown* to be their home carrier. As they attempted to land, and before the Japanese realized their error, the Americans had shot down one of the Japanese planes.

On May 8, both sides did damage to the other. Air strikes from the *Lexington* and *Yorktown* did severe damage to the *Shokaku*, forcing her to retire from the Coral Sea and retreat to Japan for repairs. This attack cost the United States forty-three planes. Japanese torpedo planes and dive bombers attacked the *Lexington* (two torpedoes in port side) and *Yorktown* (bomb explosion on the fourth armored deck). On the *Lexington*, Lieutenant Commander Healy, in the Damage Fire Control Center, sent a message to the *Lexington*'s Captain Sherman: "We've got the torpedo damage shored up, the fires out and will soon have the ship back on an even keel. But I suggest, sir, that if you have to take any more torpedoes, you take them on the starboard side." Just as the fire control party was getting things under control, an internal explosion rocked the carrier. Destroyers *Hammann* and *Morris* were called in to take the crew off the *Lexington*. At 2000 hours, on May 8, 1942, the destroyer *Phelps* torpedoed and sank the USS *Lexington*, the first aircraft carrier lost by the United States in World War II.

Because of the strong American resistance, Admiral Inouye canceled the Port Moresby invasion and postponed the Papuan Peninsula invasion. To avoid further damage (and the United States could hardly afford the loss of another carrier), Admiral Fletcher ordered Task Force 17 to retreat to Noumea, far out of range of the Japanese.

The Battle of the Coral Sea had been won by the Japanese. The United States had lost a mainstay of her fleet, the *Lexington*, and a second ship, the escort *Sims*. The *Neosho* had been heavily damaged and forced to withdraw. In addition, the United States Navy lost sixty-six aircraft, a significant loss in the early days of 1942. The Japanese lost the carrier *Shoho* and seventy-seven airplanes. The Japanese, much more than the Americans, could afford the loss of an aircraft carrier.

While the Japanese won the tactical victory, the United States had won the strategic victory on three fronts. Because of the Japanese withdrawal, the Allies controlled the Coral Sea, a vital area in the South Pacific. The Japanese advance toward Australia had been stopped and the Japanese three-phase war plan had to be significantly altered. Finally, the *Shokaku* missed the Battle of Midway because of damage received at Coral Sea, and the *Zuikaku* missed the Battle of Midway due to lack of pilots and aircraft lost at Coral Sea.

★   ★   ★

The Battle of the Coral Sea was unique in several respects. It was the first carrier naval battle of World War II, it was the first time main forces of the United States and Japan squared off face-to-face, and it was the first time aviators fought a sea battle. One naval aviator who distinguished himself at the Battle of the Coral Sea was Rear Adm. William N. Leonard. As he makes clear, Admiral Leonard was a fighter pilot.

Rear Adm. (Ret.) William N. Leonard graduated from the Naval Academy in 1938. He served as a fighter pilot in the Pacific War and participated in the Battles of the Coral Sea and Midway. He served aboard the USS *Yorktown*.

Rear Adm. William N. Leonard, USN (Ret.)

The name *Yorktown* comes into navy conversations rather frequently. That's always music to my ears because she was a fine packet, as we used to laughingly say in the nautical sense. I was a member of the *Yorktown* fighter squadron CV-5 for almost a year. We joined her in June of 1941 and stayed with her until, at Midway, her deck was stilled and she sank into the sea. Most of our people had to swim away from it. Fortunately, I didn't have to do that. I had landed my fighter on the *Enterprise*. The kind of a ship it was has a lot to do with what she was able to do, and it was a happy ship run a good part of the time by a rather strict disciplinarian known as Jocko Clark. He was the executive officer, later a war-fighting air admiral.

Being a fighter pilot in a navy squadron meant that you flew fighters. That's what we called those things. They were not pursuit airplanes, as the Army Air Corps called theirs. They were pursuit pilots, not fighter pilots. This is a distinction which has been blurred in recent times.

In the *Yorktown* we found ourselves victims of what you might call "mobile capability." The ship could go a long way pretty quickly, and she could get a long way into trouble quite fast. We left the happy shores of the Atlantic and steamed into the Pacific at the speed of light, as far as I was concerned. We got there awfully quickly. The commander in chief [Admiral King], COMINCH, had ideas about what the *Yorktown* itself should do. That was to beef up seapower consistent with and responsive to his theories of the next direction of the Japanese onslaught, which would be over toward the Coral Sea, once they had finished up in the East Indies. The Coral Sea then became our beat, and we ended up with a battle there. But we did a lot of other things in the Coral Sea before we had the Battle of the Coral Sea.

We made the first heavy attack on the Japanese as we joined the *Lexington* and flew over the Owen Stanley Mountains in New Guinea to attack the ports of Salamaua and Lae, that were just in the process of being invaded by the Japanese. We had a rather mild exposure to combat in that incident. One of my favorite authors has described what our fighter squadron did to celebrate that event: "We amused ourselves strafing Japanese landing craft in the water." Well, the amusement aspect was maybe a little bit overdone, but we felt we were earning a little keep and we did try. The Owen Stanley Mountain pass that we flew over was 10,000 feet high. That's not the mountain tops — that's the low spot that you go through. Well, a fighter could do that quite well. However, there is the weather factor which can mask the peril. If you don't see the mountains, they are very permanent and still very much there. You cannot move them with a fighter or any other airplane I know about.

I mentioned New Guinea because that's at the northwestern end of the Coral Sea. Most of the fussing we got into was in the southeastern end of it, in the vicinity of Guadalcanal and south of that island. After our attack at Salamaua and Lae on March 10, we didn't see dry land again until a short stop at Tonga Tabu in late April 1942. Well, that's not really unusual for somebody flying from a carrier, especially in those days when we were doing many things for the first time. I do think that it's one of the longest times a carrier was out of sight of land or its planes were out of sight of land. We were maybe establishing a record. As a matter of fact, the only people who saw land on May 4 were in those planes that *Yorktown* launched to attack the Japanese who were setting up a base in the Guadalcanal area on Tulagi.

Tulagi was a little island just across the channel from Guadalcanal itself. It was my pleasure to be assigned the first fighter sweep in which we made an all-fighter attack on whatever we could find over there. We were told, though, that if we didn't find those airplanes that were bothering our attack airplanes that we had better not come back. So we went over there with that as our objective and we indeed shot down everything that was menacing our attack. In the process we got a good look at the island of Guadalcanal. It's a very steep island. It has 8,000-foot mountains, and if you approach them from the south they are almost like a cliff. However, on the northern side it sloped off into a nice savannah. Some enterprising people had planted coconut palms there until hell won't have it, which means there is no place to land. This was before the Japanese had come in there. This was May 4, a prelude to the Battle of the Coral Sea.

Bad weather is a serious factor we fighter pilots encountered flying and fighting over the Coral Sea. The weather can be ninety percent beautiful and ten percent terrible, a place where forecasting was primitive and the imperatives of combat permitting little choice as to when and where to operate. We got one of those ten percenters on May 7, when, fortunately, in the morning we got off a good attack and sank the *Shoho*. I was flying CAP (combat air patrol) over the ship. CAP would mean my mission was to protect the ship and not go on the strike. After the strike planes returned, we got into bad weather. It got worse and worse until finally they canceled all flight operations except for a few fighters that were sent off to chase snoopers, the Japanese search planes that were trying to locate us. All the way from 800 feet to 26,000 feet in one of those fighters, I can tell you there was nothing but solid clouds. If there were snoopers in there they didn't see me and I didn't see them. It was a dull, bad day for fighting or flying, or for doing anything else except trying to get away from trouble.

That evening, however, in spite of all this bad weather, we had the terrible sound come up on the announcement system. We were still at general quarters. The pilots were in the ready room all suited up. We had life jackets and joked that if the ship went down we were all set. We were all ready to go and they said, "Fighter pilots, man your planes." We all looked at each other and said, "Somebody is nutty here. What are we going to do?" Well, the word came down, "We have detected (our radars were working) a flight of hostiles." Short word for trouble ahead. They launched us in this terrible weather. But it was for a good cause. The Japanese had been trying to find us in the terrible weather and had not been able to do it. But here was a strike that was out there. It was after sunset, getting dark quite quickly. And here we were, launched to attack these guys. Our radar was telling us where they were.

My particular flight was not vectored out. They didn't vector everybody out all at once. They would send out selected flights to handle certain parts of the attack. It turned out that it wasn't an attack. That was one thing we found out very happily. These airplanes were in transit. They were going by and they were not headed in toward us. So they kept me over the ship, and my wingman and I just flew round and round and round. We flew over two hours up there.

Some of the other guys that went out had very fine opportunities, at low altitude, because everybody was squashed down close to the water beneath the terrible weather. We really cut up this flight of dive bombers and torpedo bombers, which apparently had been hunting for us all afternoon and had not found us. Ultimately they had to throw away their bombs and their torpedoes and try to get back home as best they could. While they were in this unhappy state, who should make life even more troublesome for them but our little all-fighters' launch. The *Lexington*, next to us, launched all her fighters too. Now this was not all fun. We lost some people in that one.

That Friday evening wound up with some rather interesting events with the Japanese actually getting into our flight patterns in the dark because they thought they had arrived over their own ships. Our ships did a lot of shooting at them and at us fighters. In the dark, anything with wings on it is bad news, so they'll shoot the hell out of it and ask questions later.

It was a terrible way to get ready for the day of the battle which came on May 8. We finally all got aboard in various stages of dilapidation. We counted our losses. We lost two in our squadron and there were one or two lost over on the *Lexington*. We were faced with a grand battle the next morning, so you can imagine what a frame of mind we were in. But we did all right the next day. I won't describe the battle, except that for fighters, it was either patrol over the ship to defend the ship or to escort attack airplanes and help them fight their way through as they attacked the Japanese carriers.

I happened to draw escort duty and was the boss of the escort flight of four fighters that took our torpedo planes in to attack the *Shokaku*. The torpedoes again did not function. The early torpedoes were slipping into disrepute for failing to do the job. The torpedo planes went right up to their launch points. We were opposed by a few Zeros and we managed to distract them and keep them from firing at our torpedo planes, and we absorbed a little bit of damage from them but didn't see any troubles dished out on our torpedo planes. As an escort fighter, you get a mark of credit for saving your torpedo planes and you measure that by seeing how many got hit. And here the answer was zero.

We rendezvoused with our torpedo planes after they had made their launches against the *Shokaku* and headed back to "home plate," as we called it. Nine torpedo airplanes went in and nine came out. I counted again and I had ten. This is not counting my fighters. I was short one fighter. But the tenth airplane turned out to be one of our dive bombers who had absorbed a bit of damage and could not climb and keep up with his squadron mates. He could match the speed of the torpedo planes, so he just hooked on to that squadron and we all came home happily, missing just one fighter. This one got home after a fashion. He landed on the *Lexington* and managed to rendezvous with a lot a trouble over there and had to swim away from it. But the rest of us got back on our ship.

When you count the pluses and minuses of it all, it is pretty terrible when you see the *Lexington*, which represented the biggest, meanest, most capable carrier we ever could expect to have, blowing up and blowing away. That's pretty depressing, and it remained quite depressing for the next several months until we found out what were really the issues in the Coral Sea. We had knocked off the capability of two of the best Japanese carriers. We had injured one so badly she could not operate aircraft for months afterward. We had depleted their air groups by the action the night before, when we carved up that wayward attack that could not find us, and by the attrition we had inflicted on them as they attacked our carriers the next morning. They actually had lost the use of two of their most valuable carriers along with their aircraft. We had lost one but had ended the threat in the Coral Sea. Those two Japanese carriers were not able to rendezvous at Midway to dish out more trouble. On the other hand, the good old *Yorktown* got patched up promptly and off it went to more glory at Midway.

VI. The Tide Turns: Midway

The Controversy Continues:
Cryptanalysis and Midway

The most closely guarded secret the United States held during World War II was the ability to read Japanese communications. Most people are familiar with MAGIC (Japanese code machine) and our possession of MAGIC. Most people are aware of the general role code-breaking played in the early days of the war, especially at Midway. The full story, however, of code-breaking and the role played by the code-breakers in the Battle of Midway is even today replete with loose ends, secrets not yet revealed, and issues remaining unresolved.

Two of the world's leading experts on COMINT (communications intelligence), Fred Parker and John Costello, debate some of these remaining issues. As an introduction to this stimulating debate, Paul Stillwell recalls an interview with one of the leading code-breakers of World War II.

Paul Stillwell is editor-in-chief of *Naval History Magazine* and director of the oral history program for the United States Naval Institute in Annapolis, Maryland. He is the editor of *Air Raid Pearl Harbor!* and the author of *Battleship Arizona: An Illustrated History.* His recollections of Capt. Tom Dyer provide a fitting introduction for this section.

Paul Stillwell

The Naval Institute oral history program has the recollections of both Capt. Joe Rochefort and Capt. Tom Dyer, who were instrumental in the code-breaking done in Hawaii. Captain Dyer proclaimed himself, and probably correctly so, as the greatest pure code-breaker *per se*. It was a mind-boggling effort, requiring supreme mental effort. He said he had never worked so hard before or after in his life, trying to be able to read something the Japanese had deliberately made so hard that it couldn't be read. He said that he took the equivalent of No-Doze medicine even at the risk of his health because he knew that people were out fighting and dying, and he was willing to risk his own health to make things better for them.

He said that Rochefort was not the great code-breaker *per se*, but his gift was in analysis. He could read a message that had maybe thirty to fifty percent of the code groups broken and be able, through a combination of knowledge, intuition, and analytical skill, to figure out what went in those remaining blanks and to divine the Japanese intentions.

I asked Captain Dyer what the satisfaction was of being able to read a Japanese code, in effect being able to look through a window and see those things you weren't supposed to see after months of staring at a blank wall. He paused for a moment, and then with a twinkle in his eye he said, "Well, the physical sensation isn't the same, but the satisfaction is the same as sex."

★   ★   ★

Fred Parker is a senior historian of the Center for Cryptologic History at the National Security Agency. His field of concentration is communications intelligence in the navy's decision-making process during the Pacific War.

Fred Parker

We will look at one of the most remarkable sources of intelligence ever developed, just as it began to emerge from obscurity and neglect, a source of intelligence like no other. By penetrating Japan's most secret communications, it provided to those who understood it precise and timely insight into the intentions of an unsuspecting adversary.

We will deal with a few months out of the year 1942, months during which the prewar efforts of a very few men and women to gain recognition for this almost magical material were completely and splendidly vindicated. If the efforts of Joe Wenger, Joe Rochefort, Edwin Layton, Tom Dyer, Jack Holtwick, Agnes Driscoll, Lawrence Safford,[1] and the analysts on Corregidor to exploit Japanese navy communications had been given due recognition and support before Pearl Harbor, the entire course of history might have been changed.

As it did in 1941, the Japanese navy in 1942 used radio communications to support their strategy and tactical operations. In our examination of the Battles of the Coral Sea and Midway, we'll explore how skilled American communications analysts exploited these communications, both in form and in substance, to provide communications intelligence, or COMINT, which strongly influenced the navy's decision-making processes at the highest levels. Through the information derived from Japanese navy communications, Admirals King, Nimitz, Fletcher, Fitch, Spruance, and Theobald were truly given a priceless advantage over their adversaries — an advantage all but Theobald seemed to have exploited to the fullest possible extent. As a final footnote to this history of the Battle of Midway, we'll examine the impact of public revelations on the source of this intelligence, a source that will certainly be lost if we're careless of the advantage that generations of analysts have struggled so hard to gain.

Before discussing the events surrounding the Battles of the Coral Sea and Midway, it is constructive to compare Japan's reasons for entering the war with the goals that were redefined by the Japanese army and navy after only a month of successful campaigning. Taken from Takashiro Hatori's history of the Greater East Asia War, Japan's prewar goals were not too ambitious given western preoccupation with Hitler and Mussolini. In fact, they must have seemed achievable if, as Professor H. P. Wilmont says in his book *Empires in the Balance*, a total victory over the United States was never their goal.[2] According to Hatori, Asia was defined as China, Manchuria, Southeast Asia, and India. The Imperial General Staff approved the goals for a second phase very early in 1942. After their unexpected early successes against the European powers, they probably felt almost invincible. However, developing the ambitious plans urged by the combined fleet staff to prevent American and British counteroffensives seriously overloaded their planning capabilities.

The haste in which their Phase Two plans were developed goes a long way toward explaining why the Japanese Coral Sea and Midway operations failed. These objectives led the Imperial General Staff, on January 23, 1942, to publish Naval Directive #47, which outlined the order of events to be followed in Phase Two. This directive was finally implemented on March 9. The Moresby campaign, which led to the naval battle in the Coral Sea, was kicked off by seizure of the airfields and port facilities of Lae and Salamaua on the northeastern coast of Papua, New Guinea. Overall command of the campaign was assigned to Vice Admiral Inouye, commander in chief of the 4th Fleet.

The campaign had barely begun when it was interrupted on March 10 by an unexpected attack by aircraft from two American carriers, *Lexington* and *Yorktown*. The carriers were lying undetected in the Coral Sea off Moresby, and their aircraft attacked Japanese work crews who were repairing the old Australian base at Lae. This attack convinced Admiral Inouye and Admiral Yamamoto, commander in chief of the combined fleet, that the 4th Fleet must be reinforced with naval air support, and that the current Moresby campaign must be postponed until the first week in May.

Thus, as a result of American initiative, the Japanese timetable for Phase Two was disrupted slightly, although the basic strategy remained unchanged. Our success in forcing the Japanese to postpone the Moresby operation was due in no small part to intelligence reports prepared by the communications intelligence centers in Hawaii, the Philippines, and Melbourne, Australia.

Japanese preparations for Moresby required lead time, organization, and extensive radio communications. On January 29, twelve days after Rabaul was secured, a weather station established on Rabaul began to collect and report and forecast the weather for the Port Moresby area. By March, other preparatory activities were detected in Japanese navy communications. Based solely on their analysis of the activity, Hypo, Corregidor, and Melbourne routinely issued warnings of Japanese future operations in the direction of Lae, Port Moresby, and the Solomons. These warnings led the CINCPAC intelligence officer, Cmdr. Edwin Layton, and Admiral Nimitz to agree with a Hypo prediction that, in late February, a Japanese offensive was prepared for the Moresby area.

In February a major intelligence breakthrough occurred for the United States, when navy cryptanalysts in the Pacific and in Washington successfully penetrated the cipher then used by the Japanese navy in their general purpose code, designated by OP-20G as JN-25. The navy capitalized on the breakthrough by increasing the number of cryptanalysts and other key personnel working on the cipher and on JN-25 code recoveries. Within a month, they were able to read virtually all intercepted messages the Japanese navy sent in this code. The messages proved to be a treasure-trove of information concerning Japanese intentions and actions related to Japanese Phase Two goals.

A force build-up throughout the southwest and central Pacific was linked to the forthcoming campaign against Moresby and to another undefined campaign later. Moreover, a diagraph trigraph designator system used throughout the Japanese Fleet also appeared in the message transmissions. The designators represented specific objectives and were often adapted to convey organizational information. The original designators observed by navy COMINT analysts were solved almost immediately. Digraphs beginning with "A" applied to American targets in the central and northern Pacific. British and Australian targets in the Pacific assigned designators beginning with "R."

On April 9, the designator system revealed an order of battle for a Moresby task force which included carriers. The 4th Fleet message in which it appeared also mentioned an MO striking force and an MO attack force. RXB and RY were soon identified as Tulagi Island in the Solomons and Ocean Island in the Gilberts. MO joined the growing list of accepted Moresby designators. On April 11, these developments led Layton to publish an estimate that a Japanese offensive in the Solomons, Ellice, or Gilbert Islands seemed likely.

MacArthur's intelligence staff did not believe the navy's reports about Japanese intentions, particularly against Moresby. A MacArthur intelligence staff report declared that the build-up of Japanese seapower posed more of a threat to the coast of Australia and to New Caledonia than to Port Moresby. It claimed that Moresby was more vulnerable to attack by nearby land-based air units and that a successful attack would not require the carrier task force destined for the 4th fleet. Fortunately, MacArthur and his chief of staff did not completely ignore the warnings from the navy COMINT centers.

On both the 25th and 27th of April, MacArthur warned the army commander on New Caledonia of a likely Japanese attack. One and possibly both of these messages, however, came to the attention of a newspaper correspondent. On April 30 MacArthur received a message from Gen. George C. Marshall, chief of staff of the

United States Army, concerning a story about Japanese intentions which appeared in the Washington papers under the dateline "Allied Headquarters, Australia, 27 April." The story revealed a naval concentration in the Marshalls, apparently preparing for a new operation. General Marshall pointed out that if the Japanese became aware of the story, they would be justified in believing their code was broken, which would be a disaster. MacArthur denied any knowledge of a release concerning such information, and there was no noticeable improvement in Japanese communications security.

On May 5, Admiral Nimitz advised his task force commanders, Admirals Fletcher and Fitch, how the Japanese strike force planned to enter the Coral Sea from the east, when it planned to attack Port Moresby, and from what direction it was coming. This information, which was vital to Admiral Fletcher's operational plan and his understanding of the information now being derived from reconnaissance aircraft based in Australia, was obtained from a message originated by the commander of Cruiser Division 5, Vice Adm. Takao Takagi, who was also the Moresby strike force commander.

Based on the same translation, Nimitz was also able for the first time, to develop strong speculation that X-day was May 10. Later the same day, MacArthur's headquarters sent both Fletcher and Nimitz a translation from the Melbourne center which stated, "At 0600, 5 May, the MO occupation force will be in a position 8 degrees north, 155 degrees, blank minutes east,³ speed 23, course 300." This information coincided exactly with the locations being reported by reconnaissance aircraft. Combined with the reconnaissance information received from MacArthur, one can hardly imagine what combination of information would have been more welcome or more valuable on May 5 to the commanders of Task Forces 16 and 17.

On May 5 and 6 MacArthur filled the skies over the northern Coral Sea and the Solomon Sea with reconnaissance aircraft and bombers which repeatedly sighted and attacked the vulnerable Japanese convoys and their escorts. Each sighting was reported to the American task force commanders, along with the location, makeup, and heading of each group of Japanese ships. Accordingly, as dawn came on May 7, the two American task force commanders knew far more than their enemies about the plans and dispositions of the opposing forces. Through a combination of aerial reconnaissance and communications intelligence, they knew that a single Japanese carrier and its escorts had actually been sighted west of

Bougainville and that the Japanese convoys carrying troops for the invasion of Moresby and their protecting covering forces, including a single carrier, were loitering in the Solomon Sea west of Bougainville.

From communications intelligence alone, they knew that the Japanese were devoting three carriers to the Moresby operation, *Shoho*, *Shokaku*, and *Zuikaku*. They knew that on May 7 the occupation force covered by *Shoho* planned to enter the Coral Sea around the southern tip of Papua, New Guinea, after capturing the islands of Deboyne, Salamaua, and other potential seaplane bases in the Louisiades. They also knew from this source alone that the two strike force carriers, *Shokaku* and *Zuikaku*, from Carrier Division 5, planned to pass north-northeast of Bougainville, probably to enter the Coral Sea south of Tulagi, that the carrier strike force intended to approach Moresby through the Coral Sea from the southeast, to bomb Moresby on X-minus-3 and X-minus-2, and that X-day was probably May 10, 1942.

The Battle of the Coral Sea began on X-minus-3, May 7. At 0815 local time Admiral Fletcher was informed by a *Yorktown* reconnaissance pilot of two carriers and a Japanese task force at 10 degrees, 3 minutes south, 152 degrees, 27 minutes east. This location, where the Solomon Sea and the Coral Sea meet, was consistent with communications intelligence and the sighting reports. Due to improper encoding, the reconnaissance report was inconsistent with intelligence in identifying two carriers. A little over an hour later, Fletcher launched a full air strike from both *Yorktown* and *Lexington* against what he had every reason to believe was the escort of the Moresby occupation force leaving the Solomon Sea.

At approximately 1136 local time, Admiral Fletcher received that brief but famous message from Lt. Cmdr. R. E. Dickson, a squadron commander from *Lexington*, "Scratch one flattop." During the next few hours, Admirals Fletcher and Fitch received the bulk of their COMINT support from radio intercept detachments placed aboard their carriers by Hypo. The *Yorktown* detachment, about which we know the most, closely monitored the efforts of Carrier Division 5 to recover aircraft from the carrier *Shoho*. This detachment also followed the Japanese strike forces attack against the oiler *Neosho* and its escort, the destroyer *Sims*.

The linguist in the *Yorktown* detachment reported that he used COMINT to influence Admiral Fletcher not to risk discovery of his task force by breaking radio silence to either warn or recall the two vessels. There is no indication, official or otherwise, what other considerations influenced this decision.

At 1749 local time, *Yorktown*'s radar detected approaching enemy aircraft about twenty-five miles away. Fighter protection was launched immediately, and the American aircraft quickly found the approaching Japanese. About thirty minutes later, the Japanese abandoned all radio security and the detachment reported to Fletcher a message to the commander of Carrier Division 5 that his "Attack squadron had been annihilated by enemy fighters."

Before dawn, on May 8, Hypo provided *Yorktown* and *Lexington* the new call signs, frequencies, and procedures being used by the Japanese strike force and gave new locations for the Japanese carriers. They were then located to the northeast of the American task forces. Within three hours of receiving the message, Admiral Fletcher's planes found the enemy carriers. Shortly afterward, Admiral Fletcher radioed both Nimitz and MacArthur that a Japanese naval force consisting of two carriers, four heavy cruisers, and many destroyers was located at latitude 12, longitude 156. Fletcher gave his own position as latitude 14.30, longitude 154.30.

The attack on *Yorktown* and *Lexington* lasted a little less than an hour and a half, from 1113 to 1240 local time. Immediately after the attack, as happened the day before, the Japanese pilots and radio operators aboard the carriers discarded security considerations and talked openly and freely on their radios. It was apparent immediately that something had happened to the carrier *Shokaku*, when she failed to respond to calls from her own aircraft, and *Zuikaku* began sending homing signals and recovering them. These efforts were witnessed by the intercept operators, who, throughout the afternoon and evening, reported many aircraft lost at sea or landed on isolated beaches.

After the *Yorktown*'s air group completed their attacks, intercept confirmed for Fletcher the damage reports he was receiving from his aviators. At 1237 local time, Fletcher notified Nimitz and MacArthur that he had damaged an enemy carrier with two 1,000-pound bombs and two torpedo hits. He also reported that his own force had sustained some damage. This message was probably welcome in Hawaii, where, a few minutes earlier, a Tokyo report that an American carrier was sunk had been received from the COMINT center in Melbourne. A message from *Zuikaku*, intercepted by

Hypo at about the same time, contained even more ominous news. It said that one carrier had been sunk and another sustained three sure direct hits. This was a truly remarkable situation.

Both centers combined to advise CINCPAC of the extent of damage to his own force based on enemy sources before he received damage reports from his own commanders. Fletcher and Inouye were apparently unable to assimilate and evaluate the completely unique and voluminous reports both received about plane losses and carrier damage sustained by their enemy counterparts.

Accordingly, each chose similar courses of action late in the afternoon of May 8. Each broke contact with the enemy and retired from the scene. Fletcher advised Nimitz of his plans to retire overnight. Similarly, Admiral Inouye, aware of his own losses, particularly in aircraft of all types, postponed the attack on Port Moresby and ordered the strike force to break contact. The postponement order was intercepted and reported by Hawaii. The order to break contact was abruptly rescinded by Admiral Yamamoto at midnight on the eighth, and Admiral Takagi was peremptorily ordered to find and destroy the American task force. In a short time, however, the tight Japanese schedule for Port Moresby took over and the search was dropped.

Meanwhile, at combined fleet headquarters, Admiral Yamamoto was keenly aware that the attack on Pearl Harbor had not damaged a single American carrier. Though he knew that a Saratoga class carrier had been torpedoed in January, he was uncertain as to the exact number of American carriers in the Pacific. In his mind, however, the remaining carriers and their escorting cruisers and destroyers represented a significant threat to the Japanese homeland and to the gains the fleet had realized since Pearl Harbor. In addition, Yamamoto and his staff in the combined fleet were aware that the United States shipbuilding program, initiated in 1940, would make the United States Fleet superior to the Japanese Fleet in carriers by 1943.

Another factor weighed heavily in Admiral Yamamoto's considerations. Vulnerable from the east and northeast, a fundamental tenet of Japanese naval policy was to guard these approaches at whatever cost. Here we have the major ingredients of the challenge confronting Admiral Yamamoto in early 1942. Protect the Japanese homeland and create a defensive perimeter to protect the enormous and unexpected gains realized during the opening months of the war. To do so effectively, Yamamoto believed that the combined fleet must engage the United States Pacific Fleet in a victorious showdown battle as early in 1942 as possible. His immediate challenge was to convince the Imperial General Staff that he was right in his choice of locations.

In Hatori's history, the name of Midway as a desirable objective came up early in 1942 because its airfield and anchorage represented a possible solution to eastern vulnerability. It was also an objective which, unlike Wake, when threatened would undoubtedly bring out the United States Fleet in its defense. On April 16 the Imperial General Staff reluctantly approved the combined fleet's Midway proposal. The operation was to occur after Fiji and Samoa were secured.

On April 10 and 14, however, Japanese communications intelligence warned the home defense forces of an impending carrier attack by an American carrier task force. This force was led by Capt. Mark Mitcher and Lt. Col. James Doolittle. The shocking reality of April 18 convinced the Imperial General Staff to move Midway ahead of Fiji, New Caledonia, and Samoa. By the end of April, a Midway-Aleutian timetable was hurriedly approved under great pressure from the combined fleet staff. A new schedule placed the operation in early June. Then the carriers of Carrier Division 5 would return to the 1st Air Fleet from the seizure of Moresby, ready to become part of a six-carrier Midway strike force.

Reports by communications analysts in the Pacific centers also contained many early indicators of Japanese intentions in the central and northern Pacific. The first Japanese K campaign, for example, was an abortive attempt to bomb Pearl Harbor, or AK in the Japanese designator system, using long-range seaplanes based in the Marshalls. The so-called attack occurred as predicted on the night of March 4–5. After dropping their bombs harmlessly at sea, the attacking aircraft fled to the northwest. They landed and were refueled by submarines in a protected lagoon at French Frigate Shoals, a small island near Midway in the Hawaiian group.

Reactions in Washington to the attack and to the details reported by the Pacific center were so disproportionate to the threat that the analysts were especially alert and quick to recognize its reprise as a second K campaign which was planned for early May, when the Japanese hoped to divert our attention from Midway. The first overt indication of Midway as a possible Japanese military target also occurred on March 4, when the geographic designator AF initially appeared in Japanese communications. After March 13, when it began to appear regularly, it was firmly identified by the Pacific analysts as a likely objective.

Analysts in OP-20G in Washington and in Admiral Turner's War Plans Staff did not agree with the correlation of AF and Midway until late May. In late April, Vice Adm. Nobutake Kondo, the commander in chief of the Second Fleet, the largest of Japan's six fleets, revealed to COMINT analysts the Japanese interest in Alaska. On April 27, one of his messages was intercepted which requested navigational charts for the area from the gulf of Alaska to Vancouver. On the same day, a message containing the geographic designators AOE and KCN appeared. They were identified as Dutch Harbor and Kodiak Island, respectively. These two developments prompted Layton to warn that a Japanese offensive in the Aleutian chain was possible in late May.

On May 7, a translation was published by Melbourne which revealed the details of a 1st Air Fleet aviation conference to be held in Kagashima on May 16. According to the translation, this was to be a conference on the tactics to be employed by naval air in an amphibious assault. It included such items as the battle for air superiority, dive bombing, torpedo attacks, bombing and strafing, all in the battle for wiping out local resistance.

On May 8, a translation was published by Hypo analysts containing an order of battle for what they described as the Midway strike force. This strike force comprised the four carriers of Carrier Divisions 1 and 2, Cruiser Division 8, two battleships from Battleship Division 3, and other Second Fleet elements. This message was particularly interesting because it revealed that Admiral Yamamoto and Admiral Nagumo had already accepted the loss of Carrier Division 5's two carriers, *Shokaku* and *Zuikaku*, in the Coral Sea.

Melbourne published a translation of First Air Fleet Striking Force Order Number 6 on May 9. This important translation revealed that a major movement was to occur on May 21, when battleships and carriers were to depart Sasebo. Thus, within a week's time, the Japanese Fleet's intentions to launch an amphibious assault against Midway, the make-up of the strike force, and the time the collective assault and invasion forces would leave their anchorages were provided by communications intelligence.

The sum of all this evidence convinced the officer in charge at

Hypo, Lt. Cmdr. Joe Rochefort, and Cmdr. Layton that a major Japanese navy operation would occur soon. On May 9, they advised Admiral Nimitz that he could expect a combined Second Fleet/First Air Fleet operation at the end of May. Nimitz's response was immediate and to the point. Based on what was learned of Japanese capabilities during the first K campaign, and aware by now that a second K campaign was being planned, Admiral Nimitz on May 13 ordered a constant patrol of French Frigate Shoals.

One major question remained unresolved, however. When would the attack come? Between May 17 and 27, the answer to that question changed almost every day. The most significant clue into the date of the expected attack was discovered on the eighteenth. Buried in a message requesting weather information, Melbourne and Hawaii each discovered something far more important. Their translations revealed that Admiral Nagumo planned to launch his planes fifty miles northwest of AF and attack on N-minus-2. N-day was unknown, but after weeks of uncertainty and concern that right decisions were being made, this information was treated as a godsend.

The effects in headquarters CINCPAC were instantaneous. Nimitz superseded his casual orders of May 15 to Halsey and Fletcher and ordered them both to return to Pearl Harbor immediately, stressing that radio silence be observed, particularly when approaching port. In addition, wary of doing anything which might arouse Japanese suspicions, Admiral Nimitz directed submarines rather than airplanes to begin patrolling fifty miles northwest of Midway. CINCPAC Operations Plan 29-42 for Midway was published initially on May 20.

In the first version of this plan, Admiral Nimitz estimated that the Japanese attack on the Aleutians should begin about June 1. This was an educated guess based on earlier COMINT reports that a Japanese naval deployment would begin on May 21. On May 23, he changed his date to June 2, when COMINT reported cruiser deployments from Ominato for the Alaska campaign would begin on May 26 or 27. On May 25, Hypo solved the date cipher in the general purpose code. Two days later, Rochefort predicted that the Japanese attack on the Aleutians would begin on June 3 and Midway on the fourth.

Despite objections from his staff, Nimitz decided to base his final timetable on these dates. Nimitz published the final revisions to CINCPAC Op. Plan 29-42 on May 27. Throughout this process,

Admiral King raised no major objections to Admiral Nimitz's actions. At one point, after the loss of *Lexington*, King became apprehensive over the safety of the three remaining carriers, but his ideas quickly adjusted to the onrushing events. In addition to agreeing with Nimitz's strategy, vis-à-vis Midway, King, in his May 17 message to Nimitz, warned that Yamamoto's primary objective was "to trap and destroy the United States Pacific Fleet." This warning weighed heavily in Nimitz's advice to Fletcher and Spruance. King also warned, apparently based only on his own intuition, that the Japanese First Fleet might "take up a supporting position west of Midway." This last item turned out to be the only accurate illusion to the Japanese main body to appear until the air battle was over.

This was a powerful force, commanded by Admiral Yamamoto himself. It consisted of battleships, cruisers, destroyers, and a light carrier. From his flagship, the *Yamato*, Yamamoto controlled the combined fleet. In the Midway campaign, the 1st Fleet was to swoop down on and destroy an unsuspecting American fleet, belatedly coming to the rescue of either Midway or the Aleutians. No provision to deal with this fleet was made in Op. Plan 29-42.

May 27 was a momentous day in Hawaii. *Yorktown* finally limped into Pearl Harbor twenty-four hours after *Hornet* and *Enterprise*. Admiral Nimitz published the final versions of Op. Plan 29-42, a new cipher was introduced into the Japanese navy's general purpose code, and an American submarine on patrol 600 miles west of Midway reported sighting a searchlight, which everyone in headquarters CINCPAC agreed could only have originated on a Japanese vessel. By changing the cipher of their general purpose code, Japanese cryptographers rendered the text unreadable of almost all JN-25 messages intercepted after May 27. This development was accompanied by radio silence which began among the carriers of the strike forces.

Intercept did not cease, however. Organizational relationships were quickly recovered with the aid of radio-direction finding, and many older messages were found which had a current value. Thus, between what he learned before May 27 and what he learned after JN-25 became unreadable, the commander of each American task force entered the month of June with a tremendous advantage over his Japanese counterparts.

Adm. Robert Theobald, commander of Task Force 8, departed Hawaii on May 22, charged with the defense of Alaska. When he left

Hawaii, he knew the order of battle of the Japanese northern force, and the approximate date to expect an attack. He arrived in Kodiak in time to receive Admiral Nimitz's final revisions to Op. Plan 29-42, which contained the actual date of when the Japanese planned to launch their attack. In the same message, Nimitz also brought him up to date on what else had been learned from COMINT while he had been on his five-day journey. Specifically, Admiral Theobald was warned that the Japanese Aleutian force included one group for Kiska and one for Attu. He was also alerted that the Japanese were placing heavy bombers at their airbase on the Kurile island of Paramushiro, a move which represented a potential threat to both his own task force and the American bases in the Aleutians. Daily thereafter, Admiral Theobald received CINCPAC bulletins containing the latest from COMINT and air reconnaissance reports concerning the Japanese force he faced. This included a message outlining the probable Japanese plan of attack, another warning that Carrier Division 3, with its two carriers, was in the northern force, and another warning message containing the latest order of battle for the northern force.

Admiral Theobald did not believe any of these reports, thinking that they represented a Japanese plan to deceive him. Accordingly, he deployed his main force 400 miles south of Kodiak, ostensibly to prevent the Japanese in the Aleutians from getting between him and the eastern Aleutians and Alaska.

Admiral Spruance's Task Force 16 left Pearl Harbor on May 28. Task Force 17, under Admiral Fletcher, sailed late in the day on May 30. When each departed, he knew the very latest radio intelligence available to CINCPAC headquarters. Due to radio silence, the precise location of the Japanese Midway strike force was unknown, but based on COMINT provided before May 27, CINCPAC estimated that the Japanese rendezvous point was at 32 north, 173 west — a point about 400 miles west-northwest of Midway and almost astride the strike force's course.

Once at sea, the commanders of Task Forces 16 and 17 also began to receive daily intelligence bulletins based on communications intelligence from Admiral Nimitz and his intelligence staff. On May 30, they learned that the Japanese were also deploying heavy bombers to the Marshalls and to Wake. These planes would be in a position to attack United States forces on Midway by June 3, 1942, and to harass American shipping whenever it ventured within their range. They were also advised of submarine concentrations in the central Pacific, now being controlled from the Marshals, where the Japanese apparently planned to relocate their central Pacific headquarters.

On May 31, they received Admiral Nimitz's final appreciation for the Japanese navy's support, occupation, and strike force's Order of Battle for Midway. Between the end of May and the eve of the expected attack, they continued to receive a bulletin each day, each one containing intelligence concerning the impending confrontation. The attack on Alaska began as predicted when Japanese carrier aircraft attacked Dutch Harbor early in the morning of June 3. During a second Japanese attack on Dutch Harbor, Nimitz received word from a patrol plane that the Japanese Main Body was sighted 700 miles southwest of Midway. A few minutes later, a second, smaller group of warships and cargo vessels was reported 470 miles west of Midway. In his report to Admiral King and to the task force commanders, which he sent immediately after the second sighting report, Nimitz referred to these forces as the attack and occupation forces. He also reminded them that he expected the strike force to be separated.

On June 4, Hypo reported that radio silence was being maintained by the Japanese despite their repeated attacks by planes from Midway. Of the mobile detachments on the *Hornet*, *Yorktown*, and *Enterprise*, we know only by inference what type of contribution they probably made to the commander's tactical decisions. Thanks to the reports from naval aircraft of all types, however, Admiral Nimitz was in an excellent position to keep track of events and control the movements of his own forces.

As the record now stands, therefore, it was from visual observation and not communications intelligence that Admiral Nimitz and his task force commanders, Spruance and Fletcher, were able to follow the battle's progress and appreciate the magnitude of victory. But it was communications intelligence provided before the battle which shaped the victory.

Thus ended the battles of Coral Sea and Midway. Based on Japanese navy radio communications, American radio intelligence during the battles themselves and their preliminary preparations provided accurate and timely warnings of Japanese intentions to task force commanders and to three major shore-based headquarters, Washington, Pearl Harbor, and Melbourne. The warnings began as early as January 1942, and covered both strategic and tactical developments until the battles were over.

According to Admiral Nimitz's biographer, Professor E. M. Potter, communications intelligence gave the United States a priceless advantage over the Japanese. The Battle of the Coral Sea was unique to military history and to communications intelligence for another reason. The idea for special intercept/linguist detachments to monitor Japanese tactical communications can be traced to the Philippines and the Imperial naval exercises of the mid-1930s, when an intercept station assigned to the 16th Naval District in the Philippines attempted to monitor Japanese navy tactical communications from aboard ships belonging to the Asiatic Fleet. During the Battle of the Coral Sea, the latest versions of these intercept detachments more than proved the wisdom of these early efforts. They provided invaluable services to the American commanders of both task forces by following the communications between Japanese carriers and their aircraft. When not occupied with periods of actual fighting, they may have helped to explain COMINT reports sent by Hawaii and Melbourne. According to the limited number of accounts available, however, this linkage cannot be said to have functioned smoothly at this stage of the war.

I would like now to add a brief footnote to this chapter of American COMINT history. Because of the confusion which in early 1942 surrounded the United States government's policies concerning secrecy and the need to know, a United States naval officer mistakenly revealed to Stanley Johnston, a British correspondent working for the Hearst newspapers, Admiral Nimitz's final assessment of the Japanese Midway Support, Occupation, and Strike Force Orders of Battle, which was issued as a message to the commanders of Task Forces 16 and 17 on May 31. As a direct result of this act, the Battle of Midway continued in the newspapers and courthouses of three major United States cities — New York, Chicago, and Washington — for several weeks after the combatants retired from the scene of their efforts.[4]

The controversy began on June 7, when the story broke in the Hearst-controlled newspapers in these cities. At the center were several critical issues, including how the navy knew of the Japanese plans, how that knowledge came into the possession of a newspaper reporter, and how the government should handle a serious violation of the public trust. In the end, no one was ever formally punished for revealing to the public the role communications intelligence played in the Japanese defeat. Whether or not the Japanese ever discovered the fact that United States cryptologists had successfully penetrated their most secret operational code or even suspected the magnitude of the warning provided by communications intelligence remains a matter of conjecture even today. At the time, however, officials within OP-20G were certain that subsequent, almost draconian corrections in Japanese communications procedures and cryptography were traceable directly to these revelations.

By June 11, all the principals had been interviewed. Those aboard the ships returning *Lexington* survivors were interviewed more than once. Out of this work emerged the very unpleasant picture of official neglect and confusion concerning the safeguarding of communications intelligence, both within the navy and within the Hearst organization.

Because newsmen accompanying our forces were sworn to secrecy, indictments of the principal employees of the Hearst newspapers were sought on June 9, even before inquiries were completed. They were returned on July 7 by a Chicago grand jury. A week later, on July 14, the special prosecutor, William D. Mitchell, recommended to the attorney general, Francis Biddle, and the secretary of the navy, Frank Knox, that the case be dropped, saying that "the game may not be worth the candle." In his summary of the case, he concluded by saying that "some officer left a copy of that dispatch lying around and that it may fairly be said that there was as much carelessness on the ship as the *Tribune* was guilty of and the jury may think so."

No further action was taken until August 15, when the British Admiralty Delegation in Washington sent a letter to Admiral King expressing concern that the Hearst revelations posed a danger to special intelligence methods, that a trial would further compromise this source, and that preservation of this invaluable weapon outweighed almost any other consideration. King's response reassured the British that the United States would not do anything which would increase the harm already inflicted by the original news stories. Five days later, the *Chicago Daily Tribune* carried the front-page story: "U.S. Clears Tribune."

Questions concerning the appropriate applications of communications intelligence to wartime emergencies of all types continued to arise. One problem, which was addressed in December 1942, affected how newspapermen and radio broadcasters treated information which they knew originated from within enemy communications. A new paragraph was prepared for insertion in the Code of Wartime Practices for the American Press by the secretaries of war and navy, and sent to the director of censorship for implementation: "To the end that the enemy may not have information concerning any success we may attain in deciphering his encoded or enciphered communications, no mention should be made of available or captured enemy codes or enemy ciphers, or about the intelligence gain from intercepting and studying enemy radio messages." A prestigious trade journal gave immediate approval to the addition, while at the same time registering editorially the idea that after the war, censorship should not continue.

After citing a post-Pearl Harbor report which "monstrously exaggerated" our losses as an example of irresponsible behavior, the editorial concluded with some ideas which are still very relevant: "As between an ethical professional requirement that a journalist hold nothing back and a patriotic duty not to shoot one's own soldiers in the back, we have found no difficulty in making a choice. Freedom of the press does not carry with it a general license to reveal our secret strengths and weaknesses to the enemy."

John Costello is an expert on code-breaking operations in the early days of World War II. His perceptions and data suggest a slightly different version of the code-breaking events surrounding the Battle of Midway than Fred Parker's.

John Costello

You have just had one version of the contributions code-breaking made to the Pacific War. Now I am going to present the controversy. It is given to very few people to actually have the opportunity to rewrite history. My association with the late Adm. Edwin T. Layton was entirely accidental. He had no particular favor for Brits in that he was rather like Admiral King. After writing about the Pacific War, he was interested in the fact that I had started to read and detail the Japanese signals that the NSA, Fred Parker's organization, started to make available. They were depositied in the National Archives with no indication as to their significance. Even the code designators had been removed and the intercepts were not in chronological order.

Over a period of five years, Layton and I helped to reconstruct with Capt. Roger Pineau (a wartime Japanese linguist and postwar assistant to Samuel Eliot Morison) what had really gone on in the run up to the Battle of Midway. The real story proved to be very different from the official version. And the reason I can say that with some authority is because Layton spent a great deal of time at the Naval Language School in Monterey, California, going through all the CINCPAC intercepts, and annotating the wartime intelligence histories that had been classified until the late 1970s. Parker's paper was based on their "official" accounts prepared in 1942 by Naval Intelligence in Washington. What I am going to give you is the revision to those histories that Layton added. His account lays bare the secret Battle of Midway, fought between Station Hypo and Station Negat in Washington. If Washington had been allowed to call the shots, instead of Nimitz, who trusted his own staff at Pearl Harbor above the code-breakers, the Battle of Midway would have been lost. The Japanese would have occupied Hawaii, and the war in the Pacific might have ended in the summer of 1942.

"To know your enemy's intentions is fine, but such knowledge does not always stop him," Samuel Morrison wrote in his magisterial history of United States naval relations in World War II. But as this distinguished Harvard professor acknowledged, Adm. Chester W. Nimitz had to have advanced knowledge of Japan's movements in May 1942, or it would not have been possible for him to have turned the tide of the war in the Pacific. Just how Nimitz and his staff learned of Japan's intentions, Morrison was not permitted to know when he wrote his volumes on the Battles of the Coral Sea and Midway and the other volumes up to the last two. Even in the 1950s, the official appointed historian of the navy, with the rank of rear admiral, could not be let into the secret that the United States Navy cryptanalysts had broken the principal Japanese naval cipher. The NSA is unable to find some of the essential signals of this codebreaking operation.

Captain Pineau, with whom I was privileged to work alongside Adm. Edwin T. Layton on his book *And I Was There*, the memoir of his service as the Pacific Fleet's wartime intelligence officer, was not permitted to discuss the vital role played by communications intelligence with Morrison when he wrote up Battles of the Coral Sea and Midway. It was not until the mid-1960s, when historians learned of the Midway water signal, that the role of code-breaking became apparent. In fact, Pineau recalled how frequently he had to bite his tongue, because he was not allowed to indoctrinate Morrison into the secrets that explained why Nimitz had accepted such long odds at Midway. As we now know, radio intelligence and code-breaking had enabled him to know, in advance, precisely where and when to deploy the Pacific Fleet for the maximum carrier strength to ambush a vastly superior Japanese force.

While the general outline of this remarkable achievement has been celebrated in books since Walter Lord's in the 1960s, it was Admiral Layton's inside story of the Midway code-breaking operation that made public for the first time the secret Battle of Midway that had preceded the actual naval engagement. This had not been a fight with the enemy, but a long and bitter internecine struggle waged by Nimitz, his CINCPAC intelligence staff, and the code-breakers at Hypo combat intelligence unit at Pearl Harbor against Adm. Ernest J. King, the COMINCH Intelligence Staff, and the Negat code-breakers of OP-20G in the Navy Department in Washington. Had the repeatedly wrong estimate of Japanese intentions made by King and his intelligence staff prevailed over the correct interpretations of Nimitz's intelligence staff, then the combined fleet would have won the smashing victory at Midway that Adm. Isoroku Yamamoto had planned it to be.

Radio intelligence, as Layton repeatedly emphasized to me and in his book, was not an exact science. Determining the order of battle from traffic analysis based on interception and directional bearings of transmissions is at best an interpretive art. But whenever it could be combined with the breaking of intercepted orders, as in the case of Coral Sea and Midway, it did provide a war-winning weapon.

Nimitz had given Layton the task of providing him with the intelligence picture from the Japanese point of view. He was, in Nimitz's own words, "to be CINCPAC's Yamamoto." The information from which he had to make his assessments during the critical months of 1942 was often fragmentary. Making sense of these partially intercepted transmissions was like trying to divine the picture on a jigsaw of the Mona Lisa, when only half the pieces were available. You didn't know where the eyes were, you didn't know where the lips went, or the hands, or the dress. When it came to both cryptanalysis and interpretation, Nimitz and his fleet intelligence officer had a great advantage over King and his staff in Washington when it came to indefinable things such as determining the direction of the eyes and the enigmatic expression on the Mona Lisa's face.

They had at station Hypo, as it was code-named, under Lt. Cmdr. Joseph J. Rochefort, a Japanese-speaking intelligence officer whose team had the edge in both talent and track record over the code-breakers at station Negat in the Navy Department in Washington and station Cast (Cavite) and later Belconnen station in Australia. Hypo's dedicated band of "crippies," led by Capt. Thomas Dyer and Captain Hamwright, were the finest in the United States Navy. They had been sent out to Pearl Harbor in the summer of 1941 specifically to concentrate on breaking the Japanese admiral's code, which they never succeeded in doing. Had they spent more of that effort trying to penetrate JN-25, which they were not allowed to begin until a week after Pearl Harbor, the whole outcome of the Pacific war might have started off on a different foot.

But with the assistance of the *Maryland*'s displaced bandsmen manning the batteries of IBM punch-card tabulating machines,[5] this team proved their abilities by accurately tracking, as Fred has explained, Japan's southward advance toward New Guinea that led to the strategic United States victory in the carrier actions of May 6 and 7 in Coral Sea.

But the feud between Hypo and Negat over the interpretation of these signals and the analysis to be put upon them had begun in January 1942, when the acerbic Admiral King became commander in chief of the United States Fleet. He had not only changed the traditional acronym CINCUS to COMINCH, because he disliked its negative alliteration, but set about establishing direct control of the navy, and this included the evaluation and distribution of intelligence from Washington. He found willing allies in this in the deputy director of naval communications, Capt. Joseph R. Redman, whose brother, Cmdr. John R. Redman, was one of the deputies of Cmdr. Lawrence F. Safford, whose sixty-man OP-20G unit was responsible for communications security in the navy and its code-breaking effort in Washington.

Safford, the father of radio intelligence in the United States Navy (and Rochefort's close friend), preferred to run a loose ship, understanding that code-breaking was a more creative than technical science. He protested the potential disruption of this delicate relationship between Negat and its division of labor with the outlying stations at Pearl Harbor and Corregidor. For his pains, he was replaced in February 1942 at OP-20G by John Redman, who took over as head of the Communications Combat Intelligence unit in Washington.

The determination of Washington to dictate and control the radio intelligence function soon brought about a clash of jurisdiction and personalities, and it had nearly proved disastrous in the run up to the Coral Sea Battle because of Negat's predisposition to magnify the threat to Australia. Part of this was in response to Admiral King's ongoing efforts to affect a redirection of the strategic priorities of the United States Joint Chiefs of Staff away from the Atlantic theater to the Pacific. Therefore, different perspectives and priorities colored the intelligence estimates made by Negat, tending to overestimate the threat to Australia. This was one of the things that led to a running feud with Hypo, who saw the Japanese movement contained in the south but moving toward the central Pacific.

Stung by the American carrier raids in the Marshalls and Rabaul, Yamamoto called for the addition of a Midway and Aleutians invasion to the second operational phase of the Japanese strategic plan. His intention was to lure out and smash the Pacific Fleet once and for all. Any lingering Japanese army doubts about backing Yamamoto's plans for completing the unfinished work begun by Pearl Harbor vanished when Colonel Doolittle and his B-25 bombers roared in from Halsey's carrier to make their token bombing raid on Tokyo on April 18.

To avenge this national insult, the Midway operation was now made the cornerstone of the combined fleet strategy, so setting the stage for the Pacific Fleet to cause the surprise upset of the second operational phase. Doolittle had indeed done it in a way that not even the American headline writers in the Hearst newspapers could have guessed at the time.

The delay in getting out the new fleet codebooks caused by the building complexity of Yamamoto's back-to-back offensives in Port Moresby and toward Midway permitted Rochefort's cryptanalysts to continue peeling away successive layers of Japan's plans. In the ongoing battle over the true readings of the fragmentary JN-25 intercepts, it proved critical for Nimitz and the Pacific Fleet that the Japanese postpone until May 27 their scheduled change-over from the B to the C version of the main fleet cipher because through radio intelligence they were able to discover the when and where of the Japanese operations.

Before the Coral Sea, as we've read, Rochefort had already discovered one of the "wheres" — the request for the maps of the Aleutians that appeared in the May 27 enemy signal intercept. But the first specific indication of "when" came from a May 4 decrypt of a battleship commander radioing the combined fleet headquarters that his vessel's refit would not be completed until May 21, therefore making it "impossible to accompany you in the campaign." The next day, Yamamoto's flagship ordered delivery of a large quantity of fueling hose, "for scheduled operations." The large quantity of refueling hose suggested an operation to take place far deeper into the Pacific than the already-uncovered Japanese plans to land on Ocean and Narrow Island in the Phosphate group.

But they still did not know whether the main attack was heading for the Aleutians or, as Rochefort had a hunch, the central Pacific. A pointer came in the May 6 signal from the submarine flotilla commander at Kwajalein requesting the delivery, by May 17, of radio transmitter crystals, "for use in aircraft in the second K campaign." Remembering how he had been caught out by the first K operation, in which the Japanese flying boat had dropped two bombs on Honolulu on March 6, Rochefort advised Layton to tell Nimitz that this was probably a second sea reconnaissance of AK, the known alphabetic designator for Pearl Harbor.

Nimitz immediately ordered a minelayer out to patrol French Frigate Shoals, where the enemy flying boats had previously been refueled by submarine. This action was critical because it disrupted the reconnaissance operation that Yamamoto himself had added on to his plan after the surprise appearance of a second United States Navy carrier task force in the Coral Sea. The centerpiece of this whole operation consisted of five carriers of Admiral Nagumo's Kido Butai. Their mission was to support amphibious landings on Midway while a northern force escorted by two carriers created a diversion by landing troops of Kiska and Attu in the Aleutians. An advance force of submarines off the Hawaiian Islands was to attack the Pacific Fleet as it sortied out to relieve Midway.

Once it had been lured out, Yamamoto intended to pounce on it with the battleships of the main force as the jaws of a gigantic floating trap which would snap shut when the Aleutian force steamed south to cut off the American retreat to Pearl Harbor. The combined fleet's total force of more than 700 planes, 200 ships, including 11 battleships, eight carriers, 23 cruisers, 65 destroyers, and 20 submarines, monumentally outnumbered the Pacific Fleet's capital ship strength by more than three to one. But as the tabletop rehearsals aboard the *Yamato* showed, Yamamoto's elaborately choreographed operation was dependent on the United States carriers not appearing on the scene of battle until after Midway Island had been captured. The disruption that could result from an unscripted and premature arrival of the Pacific Fleet was in fact exposed in one of the run-throughs, when the combined fleet lost two carriers and the Midway task force had to retreat during one of those exercises.

Such was Yamamoto's confidence that providence would continue to favor Nippon, that the two sunk carriers were promptly refloated by his umpires to continue in the operation. According to the official history, the commander in chief of the combined fleet was affected by *Shorebo,* or "victory disease." The Japanese have always been adept at turning a portentous phrase to blame fate for the inherent shortcomings of human nature. We can now see that it was nothing more than a bad dose of hubris that caused Yamamoto to launch his cumbersome offensive without the key reconnaissance flight over Pearl Harbor after the second K operation had been thwarted by the American navy patrols. This, as we can now see, was the blunder that tripped up the whole of his carefully choreographed Midway battle plan.

Rochefort himself could not have foreseen, and never pretended to have seen, the importance of spiking the K operation when it was uncovered in that May 6 signal. But Hypo's ability to beat Negat to the draw in breaking out this type of vital intelligence clues from the fragmentary JN-25 traffic was galling to Washington. The Redman brothers had already let their boss down badly over the Coral Sea intelligence estimates, and by May 11 they were out to impress Admiral King by demonstrating their renewed prowess at finding evidence to confirm King's belief that Yamamoto's next objective was indeed toward cutting off Australia by driving down the Solomon Islands chain through the southwest Pacific. CINCPAC's forecast of a major Japanese operation building in the central Pacific was sour music indeed to the ears of the Redmans. The essence of the strategic appreciations King was receiving from Negat was that the enemy would attack in the south or the southwest Pacific, not in the central Pacific. And this can be tracked in those reports that have actually survived from the time, even though the Naval Intelligence staff afterwards sought to prove (as Fred Parker has asserted) that Negat and CINCPAC were thinking alike. They were most definitely not, as Layton's reconstruction from the actual records proves.

King was misdirected by those in Washington who gave the wrong spin to the intelligence in an effort to try to prove that they were right, and the CINCPAC's estimate was wrong. The principal culprits were the Redman brothers, who nearly derailed the entire strategic direction of the war in the Pacific. As one of the staff at Pearl Harbor said at the time, "If we listen to Washington, we will all end up prisoners of war of the Japanese."

This continuing feud with Hypo made it more difficult to educate Negat to the errors of their misinterpretation because the Redmans were not prepared to lose face again. Rochefort and Layton were equally determined not to let Nimitz be misled as his predecessor Admiral Kimmel had been before the Pearl Harbor attack. In this case, Washington's erroneous deductions arose from slanted misreadings of partial operational orders and intercepts of the advance preparations for the subsequent third operational phase of Yamamoto's plans, which did indeed call for a combined fleet to strike southward to Fiji, Samoa, and New Caledonia in preparation for the invasion of Hawaii.

Layton pointed out that one of the fundamental errors that Negat had made was to interpret a May 2 signal that carrier *Kaga*, on completion of repairs, "will depart Sasebo and anchor [date indecipherable] in Truk." The missing date, because it was in a superencipher group, allowed Negat to read this signal in conjunction with another message to the Truk fleet base allocating berths for the Third Battleship Division and assigning the 1st Air Fleet commander to the *Kaga*. From this mistaken amalgamation of intelligence to do with the third operational phase after Midway, Washington concluded that the combined fleets of the Kido Butai would shortly be heading for Truk and down for a southward campaign.

Rochefort assembled the pieces differently and discovered how Negat, through an additive group confusion, had mistakenly read Truk for what was actually Kagoshima in Japan. His correct reading was that Yamamoto's fleet commander had called for May 17 conference of Kido Butai commanders aboard *Kaga*, then at anchor in Kagoshima, the southern port of the home islands. Furthermore, traffic analysis supported Rochefort's contention that operational exercises were taking place in southern Japan. Ten days later, the recovery of further additives enabled Hypo to produce a more accurate, though still incomplete, breakout of the second decrypt to read, "Kido Butai may be in Truk for a period of about two weeks after 94539 [the indecipherable group of the time and date] please arrange for [indecipherable] and designate anchorages." But what Rochefort and Layton spotted in this signal was that it related to the Kido Butai's move to Truk for the southern offensive after the Midway operation. The crucial date was actually June 20, which proved them right, but was at the time locked in the superenciphered code group represented by the numbers. But at this critical moment in Hypo's battle with Negat, Rochefort could offer no more conclusive proof that he was right than that virtually every destroyer in the combined fleet was then at that point moving west to Saipan, corroborating but not proving a major impending offensive in the central Pacific.

Rochefort, however, soon unlocked another critical clue. On May 14 a partially decrypted message contained the Japanese expression "Koyaku Butai," a proven value for "invasion force," which was ordered to effect a landing on the AF geographic designator. This was obviously the same operation referred to, according to Rochefort, in a Second Fleet command instruction to an AF occupation force which was ordered to the Saipan-Guam area to await the forthcoming campaign. Rochefort was convinced these two messages were also linked to a third, ordering another unit to load its ground-based equipment and crews and advance to AFG: "Everything in the way of base equipment and military supplies that will be needed for the K campaign will be included."

From these, Rochefort argued that the signals tied the second K operation for a flying boat reconnaissance at Pearl Harbor to the AF target for the Japanese forces gathering at Saipan. This was the invasion of Midway, he reasoned, because AF was listed as such in the April 30 decryption intelligence bulletin put out by OpNav in Washington. AF had to be within flying range of Pearl Harbor, and since Midway was 150 miles closer to the Japanese advance base in Wake than the alternative, Johnston Island to the south, Nimitz deduced correctly that Midway must be the operational focus of the enemy's plan.

When Layton reported Rochefort's analysis to Nimitz on May

14, he knew he would have the admiral's attention, because two weeks earlier Nimitz had in fact made a flying visit to Midway. This trip was undertaken, not as many historians have argued, because Nimitz already knew at that point that Midway was a target, but in response to King's urging that he take personal steps to "make the atoll more secure." It had convinced Nimitz of the strategic importance of the island, and Layton found it relatively easy to persuade him to accept Rochefort's reasoning. Henceforth, Layton stated that "Nimitz never once wavered in his conviction that AF was Midway."

That was not, of course, the case in Washington. The Washington Navy Intelligence analysts, in spite of what you've read from Fred Parker (who based his account on the official 1942 internal history), had changed their minds since their April bulletin about the correct reading of the AF designator in the Japanese messages. OP-20G now believed it was not Midway but Johnston Island, and this is what Layton called a classic case of cooking the data so the facts fit a predisposed conclusion. "There is no doubt that Washington was totally in error," Capt. Thomas Dyer told me. He had been Rochefort's chief cryptanalyst. "There was never any question in our minds about AF being Midway," he said. The records show that Washington continued to insist that the Hypo additives were erroneous, and in fact their AF should be read as AG, the Japanese designator for Johnston Island. "It was a mess," Capt. Wesley Hamwright described the blazing row that erupted and spilled over into the padding. Those sections of the messages before and after the main contents were put in there as a security to cover the possibility that anyone might be eavesdropping and make it more difficult to break them out of the messages that were exchanged on the secure Copek circuits.

Wright said, "Washington wanted to take complete charge and tell us what to do in detail, but Rochefort would have no part of it. You see, Negat was determined to impose their own incorrect values on the JN-25 code recoveries, even though Hypo had proven their superior record before the Coral Sea battle. It all boiled down to who was going to do the work and who was going to get the credit. Negat cryptanalysts," he said, "did not want to trust our additives and would not use them." In fact he told us he was in Washington one time and found a bunch of them in the wastepaper basket. Nor did Hypo trust Negat's values, with better reason. When Rochefort challenged OP-20G over the additives relating to the AF group, Commander Redman began openly accusing him of being insubordinate.

Any doubt about AF's identity ought to have been dispelled on May 14, after Hypo had decrypted a signal listing a series of American charts to be sent to Saipan. Of the seventy-six reference numbers given in the signal by the Japanese, all but one were found to be map sections of the Hawaiian Islands. Yet far from persuading Redman that he was wrong, the intercept only caused him to dig in his heels deeper in supporting Negat's claim that the intending Japanese capture of Johnston Island heralded the invasion of New Caledonia and Fiji as a probable prelude to a raid on the Panama Canal.

Neither Rochefort nor Layton could fathom where on earth Negat was finding the evidence to back up this claim in the Japanese signals. Simple arithmetic would have shown that the logistical support for such a far-flung operation as an attack on the Panama Canal over ranges that were now way beyond the combined fleet's ability to sustain. "Evidently COMINCH believes we will strike a poppy in roses," was how Nimitz cryptically noted King's latest blast on May 25, demanding that Halsey's Carrier Task Force 16 immediately be sent to the bases in Noumea, New Caledonia, Suva, and Fiji.

If Nimitz had been forced to keep these two carriers in the southwest Pacific, as COMINCH had directed him to, it would have crippled CINCPAC's ability to meet the main threat in the central Pacific. Moreover, the enormous distances involved in their redeployment meant that time was running out for Nimitz to concentrate his forces off Midway. King's previous order forbidding Halsey to take his task force within range of enemy land-based air cover had effectively scotched CINCPAC's operation to thwart the already uncovered Japanese attempt to invade Ocean and Narrow islands.

It was Layton who told me that he suggested a ruse by which Nimitz could short-circuit having to wait for COMINCH's approval before recalling Halsey. It was a totally illegal operation. It involved relaying King's cautionary caveat to Task Force 16 and then following it up with a personal eyes-only message instructing Halsey to steam north toward the Phosphate Islands, within range of the Japanese reconnaissance planes in the Solomons, and to report as soon as his force had been spotted. Since Halsey was effectively being told to ignore a direct COMINCH order, Layton explained that no record was kept of the second signal and no copies of it filed in the log. But it worked.

On the morning of May 17, Halsey duly arranged for his carriers to be sighted some 450 miles east of the Solomons by a Japanese long-range flying boat. He then held to the northerly course until dusk and only turned to withdraw to the east after his "mobile radio intelligence unit" aboard had received confirmation that the Japanese command at Rabaul had dispatched a powerful force to intercept his carriers off the Phosphate Islands. Halsey's stratagem not only received the desired effect of canceling the Japanese invasion plan for the islands, but Nimitz was not intending that his deployment would last for any longer than was necessary to fool the Japanese.

"Desire you proceed to Hawaiian area on 16th of May," Nimitz signaled Halsey the very next morning. Simultaneously, he drafted a long message of explanation to King justifying his decision to recall Task Force 16, since it was his estimate "that attack Midway and raid Oahu is due for the first part of June." The confidential tenor of this May 16 CINCPAC signal shows Nimitz's absolute confidence in his own intelligence staff, because at that point he had put himself right out on a limb as far as COMINCH was concerned, with Layton and Rochefort clinging on behind him. The next day, after receiving reassuring news from Numea that the preliminary damage estimates that the *Yorktown* could be repaired at Pearl Harbor, Nimitz returned to the attack by telling King, "Considerable differences in estimates probably on the same data." This does not suggest, as Mr. Parker has told us, that King and Nimitz were thinking alike at that time. The latest CINCPAC intelligence Nimitz reported on May 17, "does not confirm future enemy concentration at Truk," which Washington at the time was telling them it did.

Much to the relief of everyone at CINCPAC's staff, COMINCH finally capitulated in a dispatch of May 17. Effectively, it had taken them more than twenty-four hours to adjust to the new situation. "Difference in estimate due to earlier receipt by you of decryption intelligence," was the face-saving formula that King had adopted. Never a commander to be made a fall-guy by his own staff, COMINCH had been obliged to eat his own words for the second time in a month. He conceded now that Hypo had been right all along, and that Negat was incorrect in its assessed estimate that the Midway and Aleutian operations would precede the enemy's South Pacific campaign. This operation, he now said, was to be slated for the middle or end of June. "I have now revised my estimate and now generally agree with you," King assured Nimitz. He changed his

mind, giving approval for the Pacific Fleet to deploy a strong concentration in the Hawaiian area. They were to use a strong attrition
tactic and not ("repeat *not*") allow our forces to accept such decisive
action as would be unlikely to incur heavy losses.

Nimitz put King's guidelines before the CINCPAC staff on
May 18 in a conference which set May 25 as the deadline for reinforcing Midway and dispatching the cruiser force to intercept the
Japanese invasion of the Aleutians. With Halsey's force now due
back on May 26, and Fletcher's the following day, there was good
reason to hope that *Yorktown* might be patched up in time for the
Pacific Fleet to get three carriers off Midway in time to ambush the
five or possibly six Japanese carriers that might be expected there by
the end of the following week.

Now that the internal battle over intelligence had finally been
won, Nimitz's staff set about trying to shorten the odds that were
stacked against the numerical inferior force by trying to discover the
precise details and timing of Yamamoto's tactical choreography that
he had put into the operational plan. But what neither Nimitz nor
King appreciated at the time was that the whole rationale on which
the ambush by the Pacific Fleet enabled it to accept battle against
superior odds had been thrown into jeopardy by an astonishing
lapse of security by their British Allies.

A week earlier, the unescorted British steamer *Nankin*, two
days out of the western Australian port of Fremantle, en route from
Wellington, New Zealand to Ceylon, had been intercepted on May
10 by the German surface raider *Thor*. Aboard, in the captain's safe,
were secret Royal Navy mailbags which contained the latest weekly
summaries of the so-called combined operations intelligence center
of the New Zealand armed forces. Amongst them were the most
secret assessments and summaries circulated on an officer-only basis to some twenty-two senior members in the chain of Allied command, including Admiral Layton. Some of these estimates were
based on Layton's daily CINCPAC intelligence bulletins.

Any Japanese intelligence officer worth his salt would have at
once been able to have deduced the nature of their contents, which
included such precise details as the transfer of their flag officers and
the location of new seaplane bases in the Mandates. This sort of information could only have come from enemy code-breaking. If the
Germans had communicated the contents of the Royal Navy code
bags promptly to the Japanese, instead of waiting two months, when

the supply ship *Regansburg*, docked in Yokahama, the Japanese would have been alerted that the Americans were reading their naval codes. The Battle of Midway, if it had been fought at all, might well have ended in the decisive victory that Yamamoto wanted.

It is significant, and I find it particularly significant working with Layton, to find that the British never told their Allies about the loss of the *Thor*, which put the whole of their Japanese code-breaking operation in hazard. Forty years on, Layton was shocked but he recalled the wisdom of Nimitz's instruction at the time to not put anything in intelligence bulletins about the possibility of an attack on Midway. Once again, it was Rochefort's detective work on May 19 which pieced together a May 16 Japanese signal referring to the softening up of Midway by the Kido Butai prior to N-day.

By calculating the time taken for an occupation force to reach the island from Saipan, N-day could be the second or third of June, a week earlier than had previously been estimated. When Washington refused to buy that date, a fresh dispute erupted over the interpretation of the intercepts, for the same reasons. By again confusing orders from the current offensive with the third operational phase of the Japanese plan, the Redmans argued in OP-20G analysis, which revealed that the logistics of the Midway operation had forced a delay in the enemy plans, and that the invasion would not now take place until "about the middle of June."

When Rochefort tried to point the error out to OP-20G, Redman hit back, accusing Hypo of being suckered in by a clever Japanese radio deception operation. He reasserted that in his view the enemy was not, after all, intending to attack Johnston Island as a prelude to raiding the west coast. It was in response to this eleventh hour *fax paus* from Washington that Rochefort and his assistant, Lt. Cmdr. Jasper Holmes, came up with the famous water message. Nimitz authorized the ruse on May 19, when instructions were sent to the garrison commander by submarine cable (to prevent interception) to transmit an emergency radio message, in clear, reporting an explosion in the water distillation plant. Within hours, the United States Navy listening posts had picked up the Japanese intercept at Kwajalein, the Japanese listening post rebroadcasting from Kwajalein atoll, the news that the AF water emergency was considered important enough to go to the Owada Naval Communications Center.

"This will confirm AF Midway," Rochefort triumphantly reminded Negat on May 22. It did nothing for his stock with the

Redmans, but it did in fact provide the foundation for the Pacific Fleet's victory at Midway. Until the publication of Layton's memoirs, it was not publicly even known that the famous AF water message was transmitted not to persuade Nimitz that Hypo was right about the Midway designator, but to prove that Washington was wrong, that the Japanese were heading south for Johnston Island. Now that the AF designator had been established as Midway, Negat responded with an analysis that the Japanese had postponed their offensive until June 15.

The sense of exasperation to Pearl Harbor can be sensed in the communications traffic that emanated from there. Nimitz now had to disabuse Washington of its latest intention, which was again seized upon by King because it fit in with his strategic notions. If he was to deploy his forces in time to ambush the Kido Butai, with Midway three hard days' steaming from Oahu, and Halsey due on May 26, there was no time for Hypo to lose and no margin for error. Rochefort and his team began reviewing thousands of signals to find corroboration for their estimate for N-day, that it was indeed in the first week of June. There were plenty of sailing orders from which the date could be bracketed by calculation, but the vital day remained stubbornly locked in the superenciphered code, whose key still eluded Hypo. And when the conflicting assessments of Negat and Hypo over the date were discussed at the CINCPAC staff meeting on May 26, Layton admitted he still could not pinpoint the date on which the deployment of the Pacific Fleet depended. His best estimate was within "a day or so," and it was based on extrapolations from the sailing dates of the Aleutians and Midway forces. This required, he said, that the Pacific Fleet unit should have to be off Alaska by the first of June and Midway by the third of June.

But without precise foreknowledge of when the Kido Butai would show up off Midway, the argument with Washington hadn't been settled. A day or so late would cost the United States Navy the chance to ambush the Japanese, and that was essential to make up for the more than two-to-one numerical odds against it. Spurred on by the determination to vindicate their reputation once and for all, Rochefort's team worked around the clock in an exhaustive review of all previous recovers to try to break out the superencipherment in which the dates were locked.

It was Lt. Joseph Finnegan who finally hit upon the correct formula late in the afternoon of May 26. The solution of the date superencipherment code was simple, but neat. It proved to be a table with a built-in garble check built on a grid matrix, constructed along twelve rows for the months at the top by thirty-one columns for the day. It was a transposition cipher which, when tested against a number of dates in the intercepts, revealed that N-day had to be June 5.

This was heartening news to Nimitz, who only the previous afternoon had been shaken to find that Halsey's carriers had docked and that his fighting admiral on whom he was going to depend to run the battle had to be hospitalized with a severe case of shingles. It was therefore Task Force 16's cruiser commander, Rear Adm. Raymond A. Spruance, Halsey's choice to take over the flag bridge on the *Enterprise*, who attended the crucial task force staff briefing next day, at which Layton gave a final rundown on what he knew of the Japanese operational plan. He estimated that the carriers of the Kido Butai would be within striking range of air of Midway by the third or possibly the fourth of June to carry out the softening raids which had been set for N-2.

Nimitz, according to Layton, ordered him to be more specific, with the injunction, "This is the order I have given you: To be the admiral commanding the Japanese forces. Tell me precisely what is going on."

"I told Nimitz that the carriers would probably attack on the morning of the 4th of June," Layton wrote, "from the northwest, on a bearing of 325 degrees. They will be sighted about 175 miles from Midway at around 0700 local time." On the basis of this estimate, Nimitz crossed his Rubicon that morning, setting the seal on CINCPAC Operational Plan 29-42. This ten-page document was the blueprint for the forthcoming operation. And since not all officers who would read it had been cleared for receiving radio intelligence data, it noted only that the intelligence of Japanese movements had come from a "very reliable source."

"That man of ours in Tokyo is worth every cent we pay him," was the jocular comment of the *Enterprise*'s navigating officer.

Yet only those who had been inducted into the restrictive circuit of radio intelligence knew how close that call had been, and in fact, on the night of May 27, that very reliable source went dead, as the long bespoken changeover from the B to the C version of the JN-25 navy's code went into effect. But that three-week delay had been enough of a window of opportunity for Hypo to unravel the main elements of Yamamoto's Midway strategy and to prove that

Washington had been wrong about theirs. In the words of this secret United States Navy wartime assessment that Layton had corrected, there is one statement that is pertinent and accurate, which neither he nor I would challenge, and it was the statement that from the date of May 27, it was "all over but the shooting."

The next day, *Enterprise* and *Hornet* sailed for the designated poised position off of Midway, followed on May 28 by *Yorktown*, her hull damage patched with welded steel plates. Task Forces 16 and 17 set course for Midway, observing strict radio silence while the seaplane tender *Tangier*, off New Hebrides, and the heavy cruiser *Salt Lake City*, in the Coral Sea, executed elaborate radio transmissions to fool the Japanese into believing that both American carrier groups were still in southwest Pacific headquarters. After a week of intense waiting, the CINCPAC operations room learned on the morning of June 3 that their stratagem had worked to perfection. A report came in from a Midway-based PBY, "Main body bearing 262, distance 700 miles. 11 ships, course 090, speed 19 knots." This was the invasion force.

Layton, who happened to be in Nimitz's office when the electrifying message came in, recalled how "Nimitz's blue eyes lit up like searchlights."

"Have you seen this?" he said, handing the signal to Layton. "The Japanese forces are exactly where we have put them on our plot. This will clear up the doubters now. They have just to see this to know what I have told them is correct." This, I would submit, does not suggest that he and Admiral King had been agreeing on where they were going to appear since May 17.

Early the next morning, when the main force of the Japanese carriers were sighted shortly after 0600, some 180 miles northwest of Midway, Nimitz joshed Layton that his May 27 estimate had been "only 5 minutes, 5 degrees, and 5 miles out." But a large measure of the credit for the Midway ambush Nimitz accorded to Rochefort and his Hypo team. It was they who triumphed over Japanese naval ciphers and won the second secret battle with Washington that had allowed Nimitz to set the stage for the pilots of the Pacific Fleet's three carriers to surprise and sink four Japanese carriers and a heavy cruiser. Their air strikes succeeded in downing 220 enemy planes and taking 2,500 lives, for the loss of one American carrier, taking 147 aircraft and 347 lives. In contrast to the Coral Sea, Midway was a smashing tactical and strategic victory for the United States. It was a climactic triumph that at a stroke restored the balance of naval power in the Pacific and dammed the floodtide of Japanese expansion, turning it onto its head.

While the heroism of the navy fliers was immediately made public, and justifiably enshrined in the hallowed annals of the finest moments of United States military history, the vital contribution that intelligence and code-breaking made to the Midway victory had necessarily to be kept secret during the war. Forty years were to pass before the true dimension of that struggle and that victory emerged. Nimitz had put Rochefort up to receive the Distinguished Service Medal immediately after the battle. But his strong personal recommendation was doomed by Admiral King's curt disapproval of June 22, 1942. The specious reason King gave for blocking Rochefort's decoration was that "equal credit is due to the COMINCH planning section for the correct evaluation of enemy intelligence."

We can see that this does not jibe with the actual records. Rochefort had lost out in the final round of his feud with the Redman brothers. They had King's ear on a daily basis and wasted no opportunity to acquaint him with what they portrayed as Rochefort's insubordination. Cmdr. Joseph Redman was, shortly after Midway, promoted to captain and later received the Distinguished Service Medal. He, at the same time, questioned Rochefort's fitness to lead Hypo. In a memorandum he described the unit as suffering from being "in the hands of an ex-Japanese language student," who was "not technically trained in naval communications." Talk about damning with faint praise. The Redmans bandied about that it was Rochefort who had endangered the entire Allied radio intelligence effort by leaking the code-breaking signals to the Hearst newspapers, whose sensational story made headlines that went around the United States.

Within six months, Rochefort had been recalled to Washington, and despite Nimitz's protests was not permitted to return. He was assigned to sea duties, commanding a floating dock for the rest of the war, when his real talents were sorely needed during the Guadalcanal campaign, as a new version of the Japanese code had to be reconstructed.

Layton was saved from the Redmans' vindictiveness by Nimitz's personal intervention. He got a letter from Admiral King saying, "Now I have dealt with Rochefort. You will deal with Layton." Layton remained incensed throughout his life at the way his friend

Rochefort had been "speared like a frog and hung out to dry for the rest of the war." He knew the degree to which the Redmans had adjusted the record to camouflage that they had been right and, incredibly, that Rochefort had been wrong about Midway. In 1943 the older brother brazenly asserted that "Pearl Harbor had missed the boat at the Battle of Midway, but the Navy Department had saved the day." This lie, coming from the lips of Joseph Redman, "took the breath away of Commander Jack S. Holtwick, a former member of Rochefort's team at the time, who protested to the man who was now a Rear Admiral, that this was most certainly not the case. Redman dissuasively and dismissively told him he 'must be misinformed.'"

Nimitz tried again in 1958 to get Rochefort the credit, hoping that the wartime personal feuds would have died down. Even from his distinguished retirement he was rebuffed for a second time. Twenty-five more years were to pass until November 1985, on the eve of the publication of Layton's posthumous memoirs, that the long campaign, which had laterally been led by Rear Adm. Donald M. Showers, a former high post staffer at the time of the Midway operation, had finally persuaded the Navy Department to relent and agree to award Rochefort the decoration for which Nimitz had recommended him in 1942.

"Rarely has a book righted an old wrong, even before it is published," observed the *Baltimore Sun* in a headline story that noted how the memoirs of Adm. Edwin T. Layton had accomplished this remarkable feat. Rarely is it given to a historian to have the satisfaction of helping rewrite the history of a great country, but it is a special satisfaction to me for the role I played as a foreigner in helping write this long wrong. And when Rochefort's achievement was publicly acknowledged, I felt a special pride on May 30, 1986. At a special ceremony in the White House, President Ronald Reagan presented Rochefort's son and daughter with their father's Distinguished Service Medal on the eve of the 44th anniversary of the Battle of Midway.

Sometimes I'm asked why I spend so much time writing history. And I give the remark, "Well, those who can't make history are condemned to rewrite it." But nothing has given me more pride and more confidence in the profession I have chosen than in working with Admiral Layton and Adm. Roger Pineau in order to set this particular part of the record right. There you have the controversy. The controversy justified itself, and that is the real story of the secret Battle of Midway.

Midway

The Battle of Midway occurred June 4–6, 1942, and was a combination of luck and skill. One of the fascinating stories of Midway, and one which Walter Lord later discusses and can be seen in the other selections in this chapter, is the large role luck played in deciding the outcome. Almost all of this luck befell the American forces. Beginning before the battle, Cmdr. Joseph Rochefort and the Hypo codebreakers at Pearl Harbor intercepted and decoded enough Japanese communications transmissions to make an educated guess concerning the destination of Yamamoto's forces. Rochefort had Midway send, in the clear, a message indicating the water purifiers were broken and that the need for fresh water was crucial.[6] Shortly thereafter, Japanese communications relayed a message to the fleet that island "AF" faced a critical shortage of water.

A scout plane from the *Tone* was unable to launch due to a faulty catapult, and the Japanese did not discover the American carriers. A later Japanese scout plane did discover the American carriers, but the plane's radio malfunctioned. Admiral Nagumo, Strike Force commander, and Air Group Officer Genda aboard the *Akagi* made a crucial error in judgment at the incorrect time, allowing American aviators virtually free skies to sink the Japanese carriers *Akagi*, *Kaga*, *Soryu*, and the destroyer *Isokaze*. The one carrier the Japanese did strike, *Yorktown*, had experienced battle damage at Coral Sea. Because of this experience, the captain of the *Yorktown* had ordered the fuel lines filled with carbon dioxide and the magazines flooded, thus keeping the carrier from sinking. Any other American carrier would have been sunk. After the strike against the *Yorktown*, Captain Yamaguchi ordered the pilots of the *Hiryu* fed and rested before allowing them to resume their search for the other American carriers. While the pilots were dining, Dauntless dive bombers from the *Enterprise* attacked and sank the *Hiryu*. On the night of June 4, Admiral Yamamoto recalled Admiral Kakuta's strike force from Dutch Harbor in the North Pacific and was planning to draw the American forces into a night battle. Admiral Spruance, however, had received radio intelligence concerning Japanese intentions and withdrew, not wanting to risk a night engagement against a superior force. On June 5, during the Japanese withdrawal, the heavy cruisers *Mikuma* and *Mogami* collided, damaging both. *Enterprise* SBD dive bombers found the hapless ships and sank the *Mikuma*.

Midway, however, was more than luck. It was the skill, ability, and daring of the United States in engaging a battle-experienced enemy. The information gained from the Hypo code-breakers was the result of hard work and dedication on the part of these men isolated to an underground building at Pearl Harbor. Using Hypo information wisely, Admiral Nimitz dispatched four task forces to surprise the Japanese. Rear Admiral Spruance was given Task Force 16 and the carriers *Enterprise* and *Hornet*, Rear Admiral Fletcher commanded Task Force 17 with the *Yorktown*, Rear Adm. Aubrey W. Fitch commanded Task Force 11 and the *Saratoga* (although Task Force 11 did not arrive at Midway until the battle had ended), and Rear Adm. Robert H. English commanded Submarine Task Force 7.

The Battle of Midway cost the United States one aircraft carrier, one destroyer, and over eighty airplanes. It cost the Japanese the backbone of its Pacific Fleet: four aircraft carriers, one heavy cruiser, 234 airplanes, and 2,200 men.

The Japanese had more firepower, more men, and more combat experience. The United States knew enemy intentions. A bookmaker would consider the odds "even-up." Sometimes the oddsmakers are wrong, not because they are bad at setting odds but because the intangibles take control. Very seldom does chance conspire to control and change the course of history. Midway was that exception.

Situational Overview

Walter Lord is an outstanding writer, historian, and speaker. He has written on Pearl Harbor, Midway, the evacuation of Dunkirk, the Coastwatchers of the Solomon Islands during World War II, the good years (the period between the turn of the century and World War I), the Alamo, and the sinking of the *Titanic.* He will discuss the role of Lady Luck in the Battle of Midway.

Walter Lord

Adm. Isoroku Yamamoto was a born gambler. He was betting that his great victory at Pearl Harbor would give him about a year to consolidate his conquests in Southeast Asia. Then just possibly, Washington might settle for a negotiated peace favorable to Japan rather than face the agony of the long road back. At least it seemed worth the gamble.

America refused to go along with this scenario. Far from folding under pressure, Admiral Nimitz, the new CINCPAC, showed daring and resourcefulness. The battleships might be gone, but three carriers staged bold hit-and-run raids on outlying islands in Japanese possession. In a gesture of almost contempt, Col. Jimmy Doolittle staged a surprise bombing raid on Tokyo itself. When the Japanese tried to push south for Port Moresby, a large American task force stopped them cold in the Battle of the Coral Sea.

But the Japanese fleet was still immeasurably stronger, and Admiral Yamamoto decided to act accordingly. He would lure the Pacific Fleet into the open sea, where the Imperial Fleet could crush it. The bait would be Midway, a tiny but invaluable island outpost about a thousand miles northwest of Hawaii. The Japanese would seize it, and when the American fleet came rushing to the rescue, Yamamoto would ambush the Americans with one shattering blow.

On May 29, 1942, Yamamoto was on his way, commanding a huge force, some 190 ships altogether. He outgunned the Americans in every class of ship. He had 11 battleships, the Americans only two. He had 23 cruisers, the Americans eight. He had 66 destroyers, the Americans 14. Above all, he had seven carriers, the Americans only two or three — perhaps none, if Japanese plane sightings in the Solomons were accurate. These sightings suggested no carrier could get back in time to take him on.

Instead of concentrating his ships, Yamamoto broke his force down into nine separate groups, each with its own role to play. For instance, one group including a small carrier peeled off and attacked the Aleutians in a sort of sideshow. Yamamoto himself would be toward the rear with the main body in his flagship *Yamato*, the biggest battleship in the world. Some 300 miles ahead steamed Admiral Nagumo's First Carrier Striking Force, built around four splendid carriers, the *Akagi*, *Kaga*, *Soryu*, and *Hiryu*, all veterans of Pearl Harbor. They would spearhead the advance.

It would be misleading to say that Admiral Nimitz had no idea of what was up. A more defense-minded man might have prepared to pull back, but starting early in May, Nimitz poured men, munitions, and planes into Midway. He called Admiral Halsey and Task Force 16, built around the carriers *Enterprise* and *Hornet*, back from the Solomons. He summoned Admiral Fletcher's Task Force 17 home from Tonga, where the carrier *Yorktown* was nursing wounds received at Coral Sea.

By May 28, all three carriers lay in Pearl Harbor, taking on new ammunition and provisions. A bulging dispatch case was brought aboard the *Enterprise*, containing a thick document labeled CINCPAC Operation Plan Number 29-42. It was classified Top Secret, and for those who had the necessary security clearance, the contents were mind-boggling. It stated that the Japanese were expected to attempt to capture, in the near future, Midway, and went on to tick off the Japanese strength: two to four fast battleships, four to five carriers, eight to nine heavy cruisers, 16 to 24 destroyers, and eight to 14 submarines. Op. Plan 29-42 then went on to list the countermeasures the United States fleet must take. Cmdr. Richard Ruble, the *Enterprise*'s navigator, reacted with the comment that is my personal favorite of all the quotes that came out of Midway. Ruble took one look at it and said, "That man of ours in Tokyo is worth every cent we pay him." Actually, "that man in Tokyo" worked just a few yards away in a cellar office designated "Combat Intelligence Unit." The name was deliberately ambiguous in deference to the unit's line of work — code-breaking.

In charge was Cmdr. Joseph J. Rochefort, Jr. He was humorous, caustic, and slightly eccentric. He padded about the office, usually wearing carpet slippers and an old red smoking jacket. Joe Rochefort had been breaking codes forever. In the boredom of the uneventful 1920s, he even amused himself by breaking the State Department's "Gray Code." "They were mad as hell," he told me. Now his target was JN-25, the Japanese naval code, and by the fall of 1941 he was getting results there too. For security reasons, Tokyo changed the key to the code just before December 7, but by the end of the month Rochefort and his unit had mastered the new key and were back in business.

I asked Joe, when I saw him, what made a good code-breaker. He said, "You have to be a sailor, you have to have knowledge of Japanese, and you have to love puzzles." He went on to add that bridge players make the best code-breakers.

All through the spring, the intercepts pointed to increasing Japanese activity in the central Pacific, with a major operation scheduled for the end of May or early June. But where? The Japanese never mentioned the word Midway, and in a sort of code within the code, they referred to the target only as AF. From past traffic,

Rochefort felt sure that AF was Midway, but others in the code-breaking fraternity felt AF might stand for Alaska, Panama, Hawaii, or even San Francisco. This led to the famous ruse: Rochefort staged a fake message in the clear, stating that Midway's fresh water was low. Japanese eavesdroppers obligingly reported, "AF low in fresh water."

That settled, Nimitz's next problem was the command of Task Force 16. Normally it would, of course, go to Bull Halsey, everybody's favorite admiral. But he had come down with acute dermatitis and been packed off to the naval hospital at Pearl Harbor.

For a replacement, Nimitz looked at his list of flag officers and picked, at Halsey's recommendation, Rear Adm. Raymond Spruance. It was an odd choice. Halsey had practically cut his teeth on carriers. Spruance had never set foot on one. Halsey was warm, emotional, and volatile. Spruance was cool, logical, and utterly methodical. I remember the day I interviewed him. He showed me the tool shed in his garden. There every tool had its exact place, with its outline neatly painted on the wall.

Task Force 17 presented an entirely different problem. Admiral Fletcher's flagship, the *Yorktown*, had been seriously damaged at Coral Sea. Summoned back to Pearl Harbor, she lay utterly helpless in dry dock, where the experts estimated she would take several weeks to repair. Not good enough, said Nimitz. He must have her back in three days.

No one knows what red tape was slashed, what corners were cut, and what procedures were abandoned. The fact remains that three days later, the *Yorktown* was refloated and pronounced ready to fight again. Covered by her screen of destroyers and cruisers, she led Task Force 17 out of Pearl Harbor on May 30, and headed for a spot some 200 miles northeast of Midway. There she met Spruance and Task Force 16, and the two American forces began waiting at a position euphemistically called Point Luck. If all went as planned, early on June 4, Admiral Nagumo and his great carrier fleet would come steaming into range on his way to bomb Midway. His four carriers would make a prime target for the outnumbered Americans. In this way the ambusher might suddenly find himself the ambushed.

Early on the morning of June 4, there was still no sign of Nagumo's force, but that was the way Joe Rochefort said it would be. Then, at about 0630 hours, a patrol plane finally sighted the Japanese carriers and radioed their position. In a wild scramble the Mid-way-based planes took off, while at sea the three United States carriers prepared to launch. At 0700, the *Enterprise* and *Hornet*'s planes began taking off. The *Yorktown* planes followed nearly two hours later.

Admiral Nagumo, still unaware of the American carriers, launched his own planes on an all-out attack on Midway. They caused great damage, but less than expected, and recommended a second strike.

Meanwhile, the Midway-based American planes found the Japanese carriers, but had little success. The motley collection of United States army, navy, and marine aircraft was simply no match for Nagumo's Zeros and their brilliant pilots. The Americans scored no hits. As the last of the survivors headed back to Midway, the torpedo planes from the *Hornet, Enterprise,* and *Yorktown* began boring in. Unlike the inexperienced Midway airmen, the American carrier force torpedo pilots were excellently trained, though their equipment was deplorable. Their planes could make only 100 miles an hour, and the torpedoes were often duds. The Zeros had a field day. All 15 torpedo planes from the *Hornet* were lost, as were 10 of 14 from the *Enterprise,* and 11 of 13 from the *Yorktown.* They registered no hits.

But they did accomplish one thing. They flew so low that they forced the Zeros protecting the carriers to come down, too, leaving the skies almost completely empty of fighter protection.

And so we come to 1022 hours, June 4, 1942. Admiral Nagumo has just heard that an American fleet was in the area after all. Plans are canceled for a second strike on Midway. Orders go out to shift the bombs back to torpedoes, and the box formation of carriers turns to meet the new challenge. Suddenly, without any warning whatsoever, three squadrons of American dive bombers come hurtling down from the sky, each aiming at a carrier. The *Akagi,* the *Kaga,* and the *Soryu* explode in flames. It is still only 1028. It all happened in six minutes. The Battle of Midway dragged on for another two and one-half days. The Americans got the fourth Japanese carrier, the *Hiryu,* the afternoon of the fourth. But not until the *Hiryu*'s pilots got a moment of revenge by fatally wounding the *Yorktown* around the same time their own ship was under attack.

The next day, June 5, the American dive bombers plastered two more Japanese ships, the cruisers *Mogami* and *Mikuma,* which had

Crews ready bombs for carrier bomber airstrikes at the Battle of Midway while crews (middle left) receive preflight briefings. *Photo source unknown*

sailed ahead of the invasion force, presumably to soften up the defenses of Midway. The *Mikuma* sank; the shattered *Mogami* managed to limp back to Japan.

Everything else was really anti-climactical. Nothing came close to those six historic minutes when Nagumo's crack carriers were almost simultaneously knocked out. Never again would the Japanese navy's air arm be so overwhelmingly affected in such a short time.

"I can't think of any other occasion where luck played such an important part in such a decisive battle," Admiral Spruance told me when I interviewed him twenty-four years later. In a way he was right. Luck did indeed play a fantastic part in the victory. Because fitting out took longer than planned, the Japanese cordon of submarines failed to get into proper position in time to intercept the American fleet on its way to Point Luck. The failure of a catapult on the cruiser *Tone* meant a thirty-minute delay in launching the search plane that ultimately found the American carriers. Those thirty minutes meant the difference between clear flight decks and decks cluttered with planes, loose torpedoes, and high-octane gasoline.

Above all, there was the simultaneous attack of the dive bombers from the *Enterprise* and the *Yorktown* on the three Japanese carriers. It looked like a product of years of meticulous planning and training and months of careful, well-rehearsed practice. Actually, it was a matter of total coincidence. The *Yorktown* planes were launched two hours after the *Enterprise* Air Group, but the *Enterprise* planes took so long to get going and then so long to find the Japanese Fleet that they all ended up attacking together. Still another piece of fantastic luck was that each of the three squadrons of dive bombers picked a different carrier to attack.

But there were other factors besides good luck. There was the calm, clear judgment of Admiral Spruance himself. He was bold enough to launch a full load of planes an hour before it was safe to do so, yet he was cautious enough to end his pursuit of the fleeing Nagumo, just when Admiral Yamamoto was planning one last trap, this time built around the mighty *Yamato*. There was the clever mind

Adm. Chester W. Nimitz gives awards on Midway Island following the June 1942 battle. *U.S. Navy photo, Naval History Division, print courtesy Admiral Nimitz Museum*

of Joe Rochefort and his crustiness in sticking to his guns that the Japanese target was really Midway. There was also the cool, clear head of Cmdr. Wade McClusky, skipper of the *Enterprise* Air Group, who didn't give up when he found no one at the supposed position of the Japanese carriers, but searched instead until he found them. Finally, there was the downright courage and determination of the fliers themselves, many of whom gave their lives for our country.

The Participants Speak

The eyes of the navy were airplanes. Before World War II, the primary function of the airplane was to find the enemy and then direct the fleet to a favorable position by which to engage the enemy. In World War II, the airplane became not only the eyes of the fleet, but also the "long-range guns" of the fleet. Richard Best flew one of those "long-range guns."

Richard Best graduated from the Naval Academy at Annapolis in 1932 and earned his wings in 1935. He was attached to Bombing Squadron Six aboard the USS *Enterprise* when the Japanese attacked Pearl Harbor. Best flew in support of the Doolittle raid and then in a Dauntless during the Battle of Midway.

Richard Best

I'm going to try to convey what it felt like to be a dive bomber in the Pacific during the Battle of Midway. I will try to avoid technical jargon and organization and go into them only to the degree necessary to describe who was there.

A dive-bombing ride is something like a roller-coaster. The proper approach during combat is to come in at a good altitude, preferably around 20,000 feet. You head directly toward the carrier. The two wing divisions split out to either side. They'll follow you through right up tight, and as you get to what you know to be the proper pushover point, you push the stick straight forward, go right over the top, and come into a vertical dive that is known as "standing on your rudder pedals." At 3,500 feet, you pull your plane up to put your bombsight on the target, advance it 50 feet for bomb trail, and at 2,500 feet drop the bomb, start a high-G pullout so that you don't go any lower than a thousand feet, and thus avoid the bomb blast of the plane ahead. The leader, obviously, has no such worry about a plane ahead, so he goes in as low as he thinks he can possibly get out of. The ride itself, I would say, would be something like a ride on a roller-coaster. As you go over the top, when you push the stick forward, it's just as you feel when you go over the top of a bump in the road, the top of the hill in the roller-coaster, before you take that long death-dive down to the bottom and wonder which way it's going to go, whether it will stay together or not. But like a roller-coaster, if you ride it a number of times, it gets to be very much of an old-hat sort of thing, and the only excitement is what you can do at the bottom of the dive.

On April 12, 1942, we joined the *Enterprise* at sea. It was trailed by the *Hornet*. We went aboard south of Kauai, the island west of Oahu. After we were out of sight of land, the *Enterprise* turned northwest, followed by the *Hornet*. That evening, we wondered where we were going, because we had an oil tanker accompanying us. It was a fleet oiler, which means it is a fast-speed oiler and can keep up with the fleet and company. I went up to the bridge and looked at the compass up there and found that the course was something like 335 degrees, which is well northwest. I asked the junior officer of the deck if he could let me see the night orders that the captain leaves. I saw those and saw the change of course we would make during the night, and it was quite obvious that we were on a great circle course that would take us right into the mouth of Tokyo Bay. And then I had my worries. I knew I could get out, but I didn't see any way I could get my other seventeen planes out with me. For two days I worried about this.

On the third morning, on the predawn launch, we were told that we would be joined by the *Hornet* that morning. We were told to be on the lookout for her and not take her for an enemy vessel, but be careful to ascertain it was she. We were launched just at the beginning of morning twilight — twilight being that time where it's light enough to see the horizon and dark enough to also see the stars. It is a navigation period for celestial navigation. As it turned out, about twenty-five minutes out on my sector, I spotted this long, dark object to port. After taking a hard look, I discovered it was clearly the *Hornet*, our sister ship, along with *Yorktown*. What I couldn't make out in the dark is what she had on her decks. There was a very strange jumble there that looked as if they had taken some of the engines up and strewn them out on deck. They were much too large for planes and much too irregular shaped.

When I came home three hours later it was daylight. I could see they were the army B-25s and the jumbled machinery were the deck tractors they used to move them around freely. We were along because the Doolittle raiders being on deck immobilized the *Yorktown* Air Group. The B-25s were too big to run down the elevators. I understand the plans were that if we were attacked at that time they would be pushed over the side so that the bombers, scouts, torpedoes, and fighters could be brought up from below.

During the time when the *Hornet* planes were below, the *Enterprise* was flying the combat patrols all throughout the day. They flew the morning search. They went out 200 miles on either bow and flew in the evening, 80 miles astern to be sure somebody didn't overrun you during the night and surprise you. When I got back on deck, the word was just being spread that Lieutenant Colonel Doolittle was leading sixteen B-25s in to bomb Tokyo. My exultation of being released from the doubts was immediately replaced by envy that they should be the first ones to get to Japan. I thought of all the glory we could have had when we got all eighteen out ourselves. We returned to port.

We made a fruitless trip down to the Coral Sea to strengthen the forces down there. It was fruitless because we got there thirty-six hours too late. The planning was not bad, we just couldn't move that fast. We came back to Pearl Harbor, and on May 28 we departed Pearl and joined the *Enterprise* at sea. The *Hornet* again was in company. Admiral Spruance by this time had replaced Admiral Halsey.

The first day there was no news. The fleet all went along as usual. On the following day, May 29, Admiral Spruance had a conference in his cabin with his staff attending. Present was our group commander, who was to coordinate the attack, and the four squadron commanders of the scouts, bombers, torpedoes, and fighters. He laid out the whole plan of the Japanese attack, including the fact that they would hit the Aleutians on June 3 as a diversionary tactic to attempt to start the fleet moving in defense toward the Aleutians and giving them extra time to reduce Midway and gain control of it. He not only gave us the names, *Akagi, Kaga, Soryu, Hiryu*, as the carriers that would be there, but also told us about the battleship force coming up from the southwest and the transport force coming up with troops that would be landed on Midway. He told us the carriers would be coming in from the northwest while the others came from the southwest, at daybreak on May 4. The details of the

intelligence were unbelievable. A submarine could not possibly observe all that he told us because he gave us the battleship divisions by
number, the cruiser divisions by number, the names of the battleships, and the destroyers that were along.

When the briefing had been completed and he asked if there
were any questions, I spoke up boldly and said, "Admiral, suppose
they don't hit Midway but keep going east and hit Honolulu or hit
Pearl again?" I had a wife and a four-year-old daughter there. I was
greatly concerned about back home, not about us. He regarded me
silently for almost a minute, and then he finally said, "Well, we just
hope they won't." I thought that was pretty cold comfort, but after
all, he was the admiral. My doubts were redoubled by the long silence. Clearly, what he had been thinking of was, "Do I raise their
morale? Do I give them a big boost by telling them we're reading the
Japanese mail? We've broken the codes. We know what they are going to do because we've read all of their operations orders." And
then he decided, "No, somebody may be forced down, they may be
captured, and forced to reveal how we happened to be out there,
how we know they are there, and we will spoil the greatest surprise
we have ever had for them and we'll ruin possibilities for later on in
the war," which would have happened. Two pilots, in fact, were
forced to land, one in a scout bomber and one in a fighter. They were
interrogated. They were executed by the Japanese that evening. The
two destroyer captains that did this died during the war, and there
was obviously nothing that came of that one.

The afternoon before, we had received a report that the Japanese transport force had been sighted. On the third we had heard of
the attack in the Aleutians. So all of a sudden this becomes fairly
real. It was almost unbelievable, almost too good to be true. Everything before then we had been fighting in Japanese areas. If you
went down, you were dead or you were a Japanese prisoner of war.
Now they were in our backyard and we were lying behind the
Golden Gate with a bat in our hand. We were going to show them
what a surprise was this time.

There was a PBY group called the Black Cat Squadron that
made an attack on the transports that night. The picture was beginning to clear. The next morning we started getting reports of the
carrier force that was seen near Midway. We had been at flight quarters since 0200 in the morning, so it was no problem getting us
ready. Planes warmed up on deck from time to time so they would

be ready to go instantly. Admiral Spruance made the decision that he would start then.

Admiral Fletcher, who had given a junior admiral command of the *Enterprise* and *Hornet* while he commanded the *Yorktown*, was running his own operation north of us. He sent a scouting squadron out, Bombing Squadron 5. It was forced to take the number of Scouting 5. He returned Bombing Squadron 3 on board ship. Incidentally, the scouts and bombers flew the same planes, they flew the same searches, they did the same kind of dive-bombing. It was an antiquated nomenclature from the days when the navy thought the aircraft were the eyes of the fleet rather than the long-distance punch.

We started launching by local time, a little after 0700 in the morning. The scouts went off first because they were carrying a 500-pound bomb underneath. The dive bombers had a 1,000-pound full load of gas, which makes them fairly heavy. To start us off they put us in the landing wires back on the stern so that I saw the island structure well ahead of me when I started off. By the time I passed the bridge I was lifting. We got the bombers into the air and joined up with the scouts. The torpedo planes went separately because they climbed so slowly. They would have held us up so much that we would have unnecessarily used a great deal of gas to stay with them.

The attack was to be coordinated. They were to arrive at the same time we did, which would divert the fighter protection by having dive bombers to contend with in addition to torpedo planes. That went astray, because when we got to where we thought they were, led by the group commander, there was nobody there. So we had to cast around and then recover from our casting around, which took us about an additional hour. The torpedo squadrons did excellent navigation. They went right to the target, so they arrived almost an hour before we did. They were decimated. Only one in ten made it through. Torpedo 8 was one of the worst hit. We lost ten out of the fourteen in our squadron, and two out of twelve survived in the other squadron.

As we finally picked up the Japanese Fleet, we first saw only two carriers, the southern and westernmost carriers. I started in for the nearest carrier, since I was the trailing squadron. I should get the nearest target, but as I got almost there and split my divisions out to the side the group commander of the scouts came pouring in from above me, so I had to pick another target. I tried to join my squadron up but only my two wingmen stayed with me. They were already in a column getting ready for the dive. We tore across as fast as we could, putting the nose down, giving up altitude for speed until we got over there, and then we had to pull way up in the air in order to open our dive flaps. We rode up on a vertical climb, turned over at 14,000 feet, and started down again. The Japanese carrier was the most beautiful sight I had ever seen. As I recall, it had a yellow-orangish deck with a great rising sun up near the forward elevator. I had a perfect point of aim. I went so low in my dive that my number-two,[7] when we got back to ship, told me he had thought I'd gone in because when he released his bomb I was in his bombsights between him and the carrier.

I pulled up. The best way to do it is to pull up sharply, turn over and look back over your right shoulder as you do in practice bombing, and see where your bomb hits. If you don't do it you never know where the bomb is and what your accuracy is. My bomb hit right near the forward elevator. There was a tremendous burst of flame and smoke, and the deck peeled back. Things scattered off. While I was hanging up there in the air, there was not a gun turned on me all the way in the attack, all the way in the dive. As I watched, the second bomb hit on the lead fighter plane that was getting ready to take off on the stern (why they were launched from the stern I never learned), and the third bomb hit among the fighter planes that were warming up. There was no near miss.

One of the feelings that I remember best was as I pulled up at 3,500 feet and put my sights on deck, a Zero ran through my sights, trying to take off. I hadn't even observed that up to that time because they were insignificant. I thought to myself, "Best, if you were a real hero, after you released you would aileron on around and you would shoot him down." But I realized that if I missed on the first pass I was a dead duck. I was a dive bomber. I had seen a fourth carrier up to the north on attack, and it was clearly in everybody's interest on our side that I get back home and get some more bombs.

I went back and went right up to the admiral's bridge. I was intercepted by Miles Browning, chief of staff. I said, "There's another carrier out there. We should gather all the planes we have got and shoot them out right away." Captain Browning was of a different opinion. He didn't approve of me and I returned the compliment. So we waited for about four hours before we went out again, with the remnants of three squadrons that had done all the damage in the morning. In the interim they bombed the *Yorktown*.

We got out there in the afternoon and the *Hiryu* saw us coming. They had their fighters aloft. They had finished launching and had turned back. They were heading for Japan when we saw them. They reversed 180 degrees, steaming into the wind and toward us, which gave us a beautiful dive because you steepen your dive when you come in from the bow. She was lying with fire all down the decks. Every ship in the force was firing. I didn't pull up and observe the fall of shot because I would have been a dead duck if I had been there. I jinked out. My rear seat man said I had been hit, but I don't believe anything unless I see it myself.

The next morning I started coughing up blood. The doctors finally decided after months in the hospital I had amiliary tuberculosis, known in those days as "galloping consumption." I spent two years in the hospital and thirty-two months with pneumo-thorax treatment. I retired as 100 percent physically disabled. I spent another year in with a tubercular spine and fusion and a plastic jacket from my left knee cap up to my shoulder pits. And that was the rest of my naval career, most unfortunately.

Luck works two ways. Depending upon one's perspective and point of view, luck can work for you or against you. Sometimes luck works both ways at once. Such was the case with George "Tex" Gay on June 4, 1942. Flying as a member of Torpedo Squadron 8, Gay witnessed his entire squadron shot down and killed by attacking Zeros. He was also shot down and wounded, but luck intervened on his behalf. He not only survived, but, as he will relate, he was the first American to return to Pearl Harbor following the Battle of Midway.

George "Tex" Gay was an ensign at the Battle of Midway. He later wrote a book about the fate of Torpedo Squadron 8, *Sole Survivor.*

George Gay

The biggest problem that I have in trying to explain this whole thing to most people is to get them to understand that what actually happened at Midway, as far as the torpedo people are concerned, was a logistics problem. They keep saying, "Where were all the fighters?

Why don't you have fighter cover?" Well, hell, we only had a few fighters. When they ask me what the complement of an airplane squadron was in those days, the answer is, "Every damn thing you could find."

When Torpedo Squadron 8 was first formed, two months before I got there, they didn't even have torpedo planes. We had a brand new aircraft carrier and a brand new torpedo squadron. They went all over the United States to get airplanes for them, and all they could find were eleven.

The dive bombers and the fighters at Midway were going to altitude so that the dive bombers could do their thing. Since we had never done any of this before, but had talked to the people who came back from the Coral Sea Battle, the fighters didn't want us halfway up and down between the 18,000 feet that the dive bombers were going to. We also knew that we had to be down on the water to drop those torpedoes. The old TBD Devastator that we were flying — you couldn't get that old kite up to 18,000 feet with a hydraulic jack, so we couldn't go up there. We had to be down on the water to drop that old Mark 13 World War I submarine torpedo, the best we had. We knew that we were going to be low, so the whole operation was predicated on the Japanese having gone in and hit Midway Island, and coming back to their fleet out of gas and ammunition. That's when we were going to try to hit them. They had us outnumbered so greatly that the only odds we had were to try to catch them at whatever kind of a weak moment that might be. So that's what predicated our takeoff time that morning.

The dive bombers and the fighters took off. Some of the torpedo planes (even as few as we had) had to be down on the hangar deck. By the time the torpedo planes got into the air, the dive bombers and the fighters had departed by about eighteen minutes.

I was the navigation officer. Commander Waldron (Torpedo 8) told me to follow him, and we didn't go where everybody else did. I have been told here that I don't know where I went. Some historians here are trying to talk me into saying that somebody else can tell me more about where I was than I know where I was, but that seems to be the way history is written. I've been trying for fifty years to straighten this thing out, and everybody I talk to about it argues with me. The point is that we did not go in the same direction as the dive bombers and the fighters. Cmdr. John Waldron took us just as straight to that Japanese navy as we could fly. Now they tell me we went and made all kinds of turns and did all kinds of things. How can you follow somebody all over the damned ocean and get there ahead of them? I don't understand that. The point is that on the way over, we didn't need any fighter protection between our navy and their navy. The fight was going to be around their navy, hopefully, at least as far as we could arrange it.

We took off and started following Commander Waldron, and during the flight from our navy over to where I first saw the Japanese, nothing happened too much. We did see one scout plane. I think that was one of the first inklings that the Japanese knew that we were in that area. They had a scout plane that was supposed to cover our section from their fleet. He had a catapult problem and was about fifteen to twenty minutes late. They sent out a replacement, and I think the aircraft we saw was that replacement. And would you believe it, out of all the radios in that whole damned fracas, that radio wouldn't work and he couldn't tell them that we were there or where our navy was.

We got over to where we spotted the Japanese navy and I thought that we were late. There was a lot of activity over there. The B-17s were throwing bombs all over the ocean, there was a lot of smoke, and one cruiser was putting out a smokescreen. The one thing that they were doing that we could not tolerate was that they were landing aircraft. We had anticipated that they would send everything they had on that first raid. They very wisely kept half of their air force back, but the big mistake that they made was to send out half of the aircraft off of each of four carriers. Had they sent out everything off of two carriers and kept two back completely ready, it would have been a different ballgame. So, what we were trying to do was catch them at the right time, and it works out to within five minutes. At one point the Japanese had this battle won. Five minutes later, *zap.* They were out of it.

We started in. You will hear that Commander Waldron radioed in for permission to retire and refuel, and that's a bunch of baloney.[8] First of all, it goes completely against his nature, and second, we knew that we had to do something about them landing those airplanes. He gave the order to attack, and I would have been surprised if he hadn't. We were immediately jumped by the Japanese CAP, their combat air patrol. We had by this time fifteen airplanes. We did not carry the bombardier, so there were two men in each airplane. I was tail-end Charlie and in a position where I could see the whole thing. It was all in front of me. I thought we were jumped by about 30 Zeros. The Japanese told us after the war there were 75 Zeros in that CAP and they all came down to get us. So it didn't take them long to wipe out Torpedo 8.

I saw, I'm almost positive, every one of my friends killed except those in one airplane. I remember when my gunner said he was hit. I looked back, and when I looked forward again there was one plane over on my left that was missing. The Zeros shot down all of our aircraft. I don't think, unless it was fluke, their anti-aircraft fire got any of our planes. When I got into the flak, it was so heavy that the Zeros left. One of the first things that happened, my gunner said that he was hit. I said, "How bad have you been hit?" I never heard from him again.

Somewhere in this fracas, I got a bullet in my left arm, knocked my arm around and I reached over and worked that thing out through the sleeve and looked at it. I remember thinking, "What do you know? A souvenir." Well, I had safety harness over a parachute harness over an inflatable life jacket. I had pockets down on my knees and stuff, but I'm kind of busy. I stuck this thing in my mouth. Talking about this at a news conference sometime later, the reporter said, "Wasn't that thing all bloody?" I said, "What the hell? It's my blood. I just wanted to keep it."

I was the only one who got in close enough to drop a torpedo. Now I've got a problem. I've never carried a torpedo before and I have never seen it done. I have to think back to the blackboard and Commander Waldron. The drill was, you get in to about a thousand yards, you get down to about 80 feet, and you slow down to 80 knots. Why? That's a Mark 13, World War I submarine torpedo, and it isn't worth a damn. The submariners had told us, "You're dropping them out of airplanes? You're crazy." They said, "We've been squirting them out of torpedo tubes and we don't know where they are going to go. The gyros will tumble over and we're afraid they will come back and hit our submarine. That isn't too big a problem, because the detonators are no good and they haven't been exploding." Isn't that a pretty poor way for big old muscle-bound Uncle Sam to have to go into a war? And believe it or not, we were better off then than we are now, and we've got people trying to work up a situation today to disarm the United States and put us under the United Nations and have foreign troops in here supervising this country. What do you think of that?

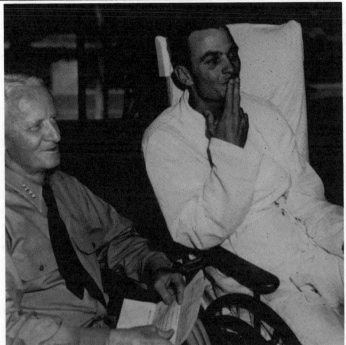

Adm. Chester W. Nimitz and Ens. George "Tex" Gay at the naval hospital at Pearl Harbor. *Photo courtesy of Admiral Nimitz Museum*

The point is, I got in there. I got a bullet in my left hand trying to slow that torpedo plane down. I got about where I thought I ought to be and I think I dropped that torpedo. I don't know whether I did or not — my electrical system was all shot out. I had to pull the emergency release handle and get rid of it. I remember looking up at the target, the *Kaga*. Regardless of what anybody else says, I know it was one of the two biggest ones there and the island was on the starboard side. It was the *Kaga*. I remember looking at it and thinking, "My God, that's a big mother. Why don't the *Hornet* look that big when I'm trying to land on it?" I went through there, went through the whole Japanese navy, got out on the far side, and got shot down. I tried to help my gunner. My liferaft came out of my airplane. The Japanese almost ran over me, but looking up at a cruiser going right by me, I saw our dive bombers and our fighters coming. They hit those three carriers right by me, as they were going by me, and then they went off and came back and stopped right where I was. So I sat in the middle of what many historians consider to be the most decisive naval battle in history. I not only witnessed it for thirty hours, but I was picked up the next day, flown in to Midway Island and debriefed, flown down to Pearl Harbor, and was the first guy from our navy to get back to our admiral to tell him what was going on.

Some people ask occasionally about the TBFs based on Midway that were part of Torpedo 8.⁹ Six left from Midway and attacked the Japanese Fleet before we arrived. Of those, only one survived. Bert Earnest was the guy who came back from that. He has three Navy Crosses and he is "Mister Torpedo," as far as I am concerned. Bert had one dead gunner and one very badly wounded gunner. The gun turrets on the TBFs were inadequate. That .50-caliber turret had 300 rounds of ammunition. You can't get one of them hot with that kind of stuff. It only had one little .30-caliber forward. We never did have a fighting chance as torpedo people with that airplane. I tried to get the Navy Department to put .50-caliber guns in the wings of a TBF, and they said it is not an offensive airplane. I can't tell you my comment about that.

One of the things I have never been able to understand is why some of those earlier contacts did not make contact reports, so that we would have been more advised as to where to go looking for the Japanese.

VII. The Fight for New Guinea: A Military Nightmare

Overview of New Guinea

New Guinea contains some of the harshest and most inhospitable climate on earth. The jungle, mountains, monsoon rains, and wildlife all conspired together to become the enemy of the soldier, friend and foe alike. The terrain played no favorites; it fought all armies equally. In addition, the soldier had to contend with the tribal headhunters. The headhunters were masters of the jungle and could kill silently and swiftly. Any soldier who got separated from his unit or any airman who got shot down had to fear the headhunters as much as, if not more than, the enemy.

On July 2, 1942, Gen. George C. Marshall, army chief of staff, ordered Gen. Douglas MacArthur to conduct a three-prong United States offensive against Japanese forces. First, Admiral Nimitz's Pacific Fleet was to capture the Santa Cruz Islands by August 1, 1942, as a prelude to the Allied invasion of Tulagi. Second, and at the same time, MacArthur's forces were to capture New Guinea. Third, after the taking of the Santa Cruz Islands and New Guinea, the Allies were going to capture New Britain and Rabaul.

The battle plan for New Guinea was code-named "Operation Providence" and was simplicity itself. Approximately 3,000 Australian ground forces were to advance over the Kokoda Trail in the Owen Stanley Mountains and open an airstrip on the Papuan Peninsula by August 10, 1942. In late July, however, Maj. Gen. Tomitaro Horii and the South Seas Detachment landed at Buna and Gona and marched across the spine of Papua in the Owen Stanley Mountains. On July 29, 1942, the Japanese took Kokoda airfield and immediately based fighters and bombers there. Because of the importance of the Kokoda airfield, the Allies made its recapture their number-one priority. Recalled from North Africa, the 7th Australian Division was taken to Port Moresby with orders to recapture Kokoda.

At the same time, General Hyakutake at Rabaul commanded a Japanese assault on Milne Bay. Maj. Gen. Cyril A. Clones, Allied commander at Milne Bay, requested immediate reinforcements. He was given the 18th Australian Infantry Brigade, 1,300 United States troops, the Fifth Air Force, and 2 RAAF (Royal Australian Air Force) fighter squadrons. On September 5, after a fierce, three-day battle, General Hyakutake ordered the retreat and evacuation of all Japanese forces from Milne Bay. For the first time in World War II, a Japanese amphibious assault had been defeated.

On September 5, General Horii's army captured the Gap. The difficulty Horii had was in keeping his troops resupplied. His resupply line areas stretched for over sixty-five miles through the Owen Stanley Mountains. Using his air forces wisely, General MacArthur concentrated on strategically bombing Horii's resupply lines rather than concentrate his bombing on the main body of enemy forces. In a serious blow to resupply efforts, Allied fighters destroyed the Wairopi Bridge. Horii was still able to capture Ioribaiwa and advance on Imita Ridge less than thirty miles from Port Moresby. Because of no resupply, on September 18 Horii was forced to retreat to Buna. The Imperial Japanese Army had been stopped short of their goal of Papua.

Horii's surviving troops were attacked by the 16th Australian Infantry, led by General Blamey, at Eora Creek on October 21. Horii took up a defensive position at the Kumusi River and was able to hold off the Australians until November 10, 1942. General Blamey had been replaced by Major General Vassey just two days prior, and with morale high, the Australians forced the Japanese to retreat across the Kumusi River. The retreat across the Kumusi cost Japan several hundred men, as the bridge had been destroyed by bombing attacks and the Japanese were forced to cross the raging river in collapsible rafts, on logs, or by swimming. General Horii, in fact, drowned while attempting to cross the Kumusi.

On November 17, 1942, the Allies began a counteroffensive on the Papuan coast (across from Milne Bay) and pushed forward to retake Buna and Gona. This counteroffensive was led by Gen. Edwin F. Harding, who was able to drive to the outskirts of Buna before the Japanese halted the Allies. On December 1, General Harding was fired by General MacArthur and replaced by Lt. Gen.

Australian soldiers struggle through the dense New Guinea jungle in the Owen Stanley Mountains. *(Photo #13947) Australian War Memorial, Canberra, Australia*

Robert L. Eichelberger. Eichelberger's orders were quite specific: "Go out there, Bob, and take Buna — or don't come back alive," MacArthur told him. On December 5, Eichelberger received a company of Australian Bren gun carriers. Supported by the Fifth Air Force, the Australians tried their mightiest to recapture Buna, but to no avail. The Japanese, heavily fortified in log bunkers, repelled every Australian attack. By December 7, the 25th Brigade, 7th Australian Division, had lost two-thirds of its manpower and most of the Bren gun carriers. Finally, on December 9, after setting delayed-action fuses on the mortar shells (so they would penetrate the Japanese bunkers before detonating) and a fierce night of hand-to-hand combat, Gona fell. Almost a week later, on December 13, Buna was captured by the Allies, and by mid-January 1943 the Sanananda region of New Guinea had been cleared of Japanese. The battle for Buna and Gona had cost the Allies 1,600 men.

On February 1, 1943, a Japanese convoy attempted to cross the

The Battle for Buna. Australian soldiers advance on Japanese bunkers. *Australian War Memorial, print courtesy Admiral Nimitz Museum*

Bismarck Sea from Rabaul to Lae and Salamaua. This convoy contained eight transports, eight destroyers, and a 6,000-man invasion force. They were attacked by 200 B-25s using the newly developed technique of skip bombing. Using this new technique, the B-25s sank eight transports and four destroyers. The surviving convoy was attacked by American PT boats based in Milne Bay. The Japanese called off the reinforcement and resupply effort and returned to Rabaul. Less than 2,000 Japanese soldiers survived. This was the final attempt made by Japan to resupply New Guinea.

The battle had turned, and the strategic areas of New Guinea belonged to the Allies. It wasn't until July 1944, however, that the Allies had recaptured the whole of New Guinea. On August 17, 1942, the Japanese were surprised at Wewak Air Field. The Fifth Air Force bombing attack destroyed approximately 200 enemy planes, leaving only six in flyable condition. On September 25, 1943, the 41st United States Army Division and the 9th Australian Division took Lae. About 9,000 Japanese soldiers fled into the mountains on

New Guinea's northern coast. In December 1943, the 7th Australian Division moved from Lae into the Finisterre Range north to the Huon Peninsula, cutting off and trapping the fleeing Japanese. The 22nd Infantry Battalion, 9th Australian Division, held Finscha Fen at the end of the Huon Peninsula, and on January 2, 1944, the 32nd Division landed at Saidor, preventing the Japanese from retreating to Madang. Piece by piece, the cornered Japanese were beaten.

In April 1944, the Allies landed at Hollandia (41st Division), Tanahmerah Bay (24th Division), and Aitape (41st Division). In May, the 163rd Regimental Combat Team captured the Japanese airfields at Maffin Bay and Wake Island. Later that same month, the Allies captured Biak Island. In July, the Allies wiped out the last organized enemy resistance at the Driniumer River, Mar, and Sansapor. By the end of August, the Allies had regained control of the whole of New Guinea.

During the New Guinea campaign, which was worse, the enemy or the jungle? Many who were there and many historians (such as Dr. Goldstein) would argue the elements and the jungle did more damage to the soldiers of both sides than did the opposing forces. In their attack on the Australian forces at Kokoda, the Japanese had to cut holes in their trenching tools so the mud would not stick to them. One Japanese soldier wrote in his diary, "The sun is fierce here. We make our way through a jungle where there are no roads. The jungle is beyond description. Thirst for water, stomach empty." (Costello, 1981; page 317) When the survivors of Horii's South Seas Detachment finally surrendered after spending less than four months in the Owen Stanley jungles, their clothes had rotted completely off their bodies. To survive, many had eaten Kunai grass, bushes, dirt, leaves, tree limbs, etc. These items had torn their stomachs so badly that they could not digest food and died in the Allied hospitals, vomiting up clots of blood. At the siege at Buna, many resorted to cannibalism to survive.

But the jungle was no kinder to the Allies. During a tour of duty, a pilot could expect to lose thirty pounds. The pilot's staple, canned meat and vegetables, quickly spoiled, contributing to the spread of malaria and endemic dysentery. The troops rapidly learned the "New Guinea salute," the constant brushing away of flies and mosquitoes. Ground crews joked that at night they would not refuel the mosquitoes because they did not have landing lights. The monsoons, which the Australians called "the wet," could easily dump an inch of rain within five minutes. Boots and clothes rotted within days. Open sores rapidly developed and festered, each infection compounded by the hordes of insects which attacked. Wrote George H. Johnson, Australian journalist, "The insect life, from scorpions to butterflies, is impressive. Only for a time though. You eventually reach a stage when flora and fauna, and even the Japs, gradually lose interest. Your mental processes allow you to be conscious of only one thing: 'The Track,' or more usually, 'The Bloody Track.' You listen to your legs creaking and stare at the ground and think of the next stretch of mud, and you wonder if the hills will ever end . . . Each step is two feet high. You slip on one in three . . . Life changes as you push up the track. Standards of living deteriorate, sometimes below normally accepted standards even of primitive existence. Thoughts become somber, humor takes on a grim, almost macabre quality. When men reach the nadir of mental and physical agony there are times when sickness or injury or even death seem like things to be welcomed." (Costello, 1981; page 375)

New Guinea was not so much the struggle of soldier against soldier, but rather soldier against jungle. The elements of nature were a more harsh, severe, and uncompromising foe than all mortal enemies combined. At the individual battles on New Guinea, the soldier would defeat his human foe only to lose to the relentlessness of the jungle.

Analysis and Ingenuity

Americans are known for their creativity, ingenuity, and adaptability, even in the worst of situations. Nowhere during World War II was this more evident than on New Guinea. Nowhere were human capabilities stretched to such a limit, nor resourcefulness ever more needed, as Dr. Donald Goldstein will explain. On New Guinea, the worst brought out the best. Dr. Goldstein also offers some valuable lessons for today.

Dr. Donald Goldstein is on the faculty at the University of Pittsburgh. He spent many years working with Gordon Prange and was co-author of *At Dawn We Slept*. He has authored several books on the Pearl Harbor attack and is presently working on a book covering the Aleutian Campaign. Dr. Goldstein has edited the diaries of Admiral Ugaki, who was Admiral Yamamoto's chief of staff, a superb book titled *Fading Victory*.

Dr. Donald Goldstein

The Situation in Early 1942

Early in 1942, the situation in the Pacific became extremely bleak for Allied forces. The triumphant Japanese swept down through China and across Thailand. They marched through Malaya and Burma and captured what had once been called the impregnable port of Singapore. They took the Philippines and lost no time in adding Sumatra, Java, Borneo, and the Celebes Islands to the imperial realm of Hirohito. They grabbed New Britain, New Ireland, and the Dutch East Indies, and when they took the Solomons only New Guinea stood between them and the projected conquest of Australia. Here, for various reasons, they hesitated. Douglas MacArthur believed the Japanese paused because they had overexpanded and had to wait for their supply lines to be established. He also thought that the enemy stopped because they were tied up in the Solomon Islands[1] and did not have the forces available to capture Port Moresby and continue to support their forces in the Solomons.[2]

In any event, whatever the reasons were for halting, most of the men this writer has interviewed believed that had the Japanese Command struck Port Moresby in New Guinea with the same force that they had used in other areas of the Pacific, Port Moresby would have fallen and northern Australia would have been open to the Golden Horde of the Rising Sun.[3]

How the Japanese accomplished so much in such a short time is another story,[4] but their tactics were relatively simple. As they pushed south against token opposition they built airfields so that the bomb line[5] could be extended and targets in the next projected area of attack could be saturated by their air arm.[6] In the early days, when the Japanese were not making mistakes, no land or sea force moved anywhere until it was assured of effective air cover. Relatively maximum harmony existed between their army, navy, and air force. Thus using their airpower to the maximum extent possible against token Allied resistance,[7] the Japanese took their objectives with a high degree of precision and little expenditure of human life. There were no massive attacks with men marching shoulder to shoulder. There was no front line of the World War I, 1914–1918 pattern. Instead, the Japanese fought as an invisible enemy. They appeared behind retiring Allied columns; blocked roads; staged ambushes; and when the battle got too hot they disappeared into the jungle. It was the simplicity of their tactics, more than anything else, that made them such a formidable foe.[8]

The Allies were unprepared for war, as was witnessed by the devastating attack on Pearl Harbor and the subsequent Allied defeats through Asia, and as other chapters in this volume have so ably depicted. Against the Japanese type of tactics they were doubly unprepared. They had never fought against an adversary that used such unorthodox methods of warfare. Despite their unreadiness, they fought well and may have done better except for two major errors in judgment. These errors were to initially underestimate the capabilities of the Japanese Armed Forces, and then, following the early Japanese victories, to overestimate them.[9] Thus the myth of the invincible Japanese superman was born and played a very important role in their early victories.[10] This myth was nurtured by Japanese propaganda and fifth column whispers and propagated by the many war correspondents who wrote about their invincibility.[11]

As the supposedly invincible Japanese tide drew closer and closer to Australia, there was a shake-up in the Allied high command.[12] On April 18, 1942, Gen. Douglas MacArthur formally became supreme allied commander of the Southwest Pacific area (SWPA).[13] This area included Australia, the Philippines, and New Guinea. Admiral Nimitz was given responsibility for the rest of the Pacific.[14] He was dubbed commander in chief of the Pacific area (POA). The headquarters was at Pearl Harbor. To create simplicity in span of control, Admiral Nimitz broke his vast command into three sectors — the North, the Central, and the South Pacific areas.[15]

By agreement between MacArthur and Nimitz, the operational dividing line between the SWPA and the South Pacific air units was set east at the 159th meridian and south from the equator.[16]

After a quick survey of the situation, MacArthur and his new staff decided that the Allies in SWPA would retreat no more. They would make their stand in New Guinea. The battle for Australia would be fought and won, or lost, there.[17]

Japanese Strategy

As the Japanese pushed further south, MacArthur in Australia began to consolidate what little forces he had. The Japanese, after securing their flank with a victory in Tulagi, in the South Solomons, paused in northern New Guinea to regroup. They had several options. Among them: to attack Hawaii, the Aleutians, or to consolidate their defenses and wait for the Allies to move against them. But after some deliberation they realized that their flank was exposed to the Allied forces in Australia and New Zealand. They reasoned that in order to protect what they had won, both Australia and New Zealand would have to be captured.[18] With this in mind, early in May 1942, a Japanese fleet set sail for New Guinea with a force of two aircraft carriers, seven cruisers, 17 destroyers, two submarines, one submarine tender, and 21 troop transport ships. Their objective appeared to be Port Moresby, the gateway to Australia.[19] American naval and air forces engaged the huge Japanese convoy from the seventh through the ninth of May 1942, in the famous Battle of the Coral Sea. In this battle, the Japanese lost one carrier (*Shoho*), four cruisers, two destroyers, four gunboats, four transports, and a hundred planes, and two carriers (*Zuikaku* and *Shokaku*) were badly damaged. American losses were: the carrier *Lexington*, one destroyer, one tanker, and 17 aircraft.[20] When the battle concluded, although the Japanese had achieved a tactical victory, strategically they had soundly been defeated.[21]

The Coral Sea debacle did not cause the Japanese command to relinquish its plans for procuring more territory in the Pacific. They next sought to extend their bases further eastward by trying to seize the American base at Midway Island. A feint at the Aleutian Island chain, near the coast of Alaska, did not deceive the U.S. naval command, and its naval forces and carrier planes were in a position to deal the Japanese the most lethal blow they had received in the Pacific up to that date.[22] Japanese losses included four carriers, two cruisers, three destroyers, and one transport. The U.S. lost one cruiser, one destroyer, and the carrier *Yorktown*. While it is not in the purview of this paper to talk about these famous battles, they must be mentioned to put the battle for New Guinea in the proper perspective.

The Coral Sea and Midway battles in May and June of 1942 were significant for four reasons. First, they were the first major defeats for the Japanese in World War II and descredited the thesis of Japanese invincibility. Second, they proved the value and effect of air power, even though it was naval air power, against floating navies.[23] Third, the two victories slowed the Japanese offense, which had been unstoppable for almost six months, to a temporary standstill. And finally, the immediate threat to Australia was effectively stymied.[24] But the long-range threat was still there.

The United States Strategy

When first established, the two commands in the Pacific, SWPA under General MacArthur, and the Pacific Command (POA) under Admiral Nimitz, had no set missions. However, MacArthur continued to consolidate his forces for the Japanese attack on Australia, which he believed was inevitable. On July 2, 1942, the Joint Chiefs of Staff issued a directorate outlining the plans for an operation by American forces in the Pacific. This was called the "Elkton Plan."[25] Under this plan of operation there were three tasks for Allied forces in the Pacific to perform. Task one was the reoccupation of Santa Cruz and Tulagi in the lower Solomons.[26] This was to be accomplished by Admiral Ghormley's South Pacific force with help from the SWPA Command.[27] Task two was to be the reoccupation by Allied forces from both the SWPA and the South Pacific areas, of the northeast coast of New Guinea together with the capture of the upper Solomon Islands. Task three, the reconquest of New Britain, became the responsibility of General MacArthur's forces. The target date set by the Joint Chiefs of Staff for the implementation of the "Elkton Plan" was August 1, 1942.[28]

In support of the "Elkton Plan," the Fifth Air Force was given the mission to harass, and obstruct if possible, the supply lines of the attacking Japanese who were slowly edging toward Port Moresby.[29] With the limited number of aircraft available they were employed around the clock against the Japanese force that was advancing through the almost completely covered jungle. Despite valiant efforts, the Australians, outmanned and continually outflanked, fell back steadily under the attacks delivered by the jungle-wise Japanese.[30] Allied problems were further complicated by available air strength in SWPA. In the New Guinea area and Port Moresby there presently were not enough airstrips to accommodate an increase in Allied aircraft over Australia. This was necessary because flights over the almost three-mile-high Owen Stanley Mountain ranges were often limited by adverse weather.[31] In addition, pilots had to fly missions which took them from thirty-six to forty-eight hours away from their home base.[32] The crews had to fly as much as eighteen hours to drop a load of bombs. Adding to their discomfort, the

Japanese usually met them over the target with swarms of fighters. Under the above adverse conditions, the efficiency of both planes and crews suffered.[33] Such circumstances pointed to the necessity of obtaining airbases, not merely staging areas on the northern coast of Papua. Ironically, many of these same unfavorable conditions impelled the Japanese to seek an airbase on the northeastern coast of Papua for this purpose. Thus, when the Japanese landed at Buna on July 21, 1942, they proceeded immediately to build airstrips there.[34]

Much of MacArthur's time during his first months in New Guinea was devoted to obtaining a substantial increase in engineer troops and equipment for construction of the additional airdromes, operating facilities, and housing.[35] Construction began immediately to enable the basing of all combat elements of the Fifth Air Force in New Guinea and to eliminate hazardous flying from Australia to the operational areas in New Guinea.

For the conquest of Papua and New Guinea, the air strength of Allied forces in New Guinea and Australia was very meager.[36] American operational forces consisted of three bombardment groups, three fighter groups, and two partially equipped troop carrier squadrons.[37]

The typical bomber squadron was supposed to contain forty-eight aircraft. However, in reality most fighter squadrons were lucky to have eight operational aircraft and most bomber squadrons six operational aircraft during the lean years of 1942 through 1944. Thus, SWPA air forces were constantly under strength. The Royal Australian Air Force[38] had thirty squadrons of assorted aircraft, but twenty-seven of them were outmoded. The Australians had to turn primarily to the United States for new aircraft.[39] The Dutch Air Forces consisted of one B-25 squadron.[40] Two American medium bombardment squadrons had been detached to help the South Pacific forces invasion of Guadalcanal and the rest of the Solomon Islands operation. Also supporting the Guadalcanal and Solomon Islands campaigns, which was top priority in the Pacific under the "Elkton Plan," was one bombardment group which belonged to SWPA.[41] In short, the Allies had less than 100 aircraft to work with.

On the other hand, the Japanese had close to 1,000 planes in the area. They could also call on aircraft from nearby bases in Singapore, Malaya, and the Dutch East Indies.[42] Allied intelligence in the early days never did know how many aircraft the enemy had.

Fitting the Weapon to the Mission

In order to accomplish the overall strategy of driving the Japanese from New Guinea, the Allies had to resort to ingenuity and unorthodox methods to overcome the shortage of personnel and aircraft which existed. One such example of the ingenuity was the introduction of skip bombing. In skip bombing, the plane dived close to the water and released the bomb so that it would bounce off the water and into the side of the enemy ship, creating damage with as great an effect as a torpedo. Thus, skip bombing worked on the same principle as a small boy skipping a stone across the surface of a small lake or pond. Maj. Bill Benn, former aide to Gen. George Kenney, introduced the tactic of skip bombing in the SWPA. And by the middle of 1943, most B-17s and B-25s specialized in the skip-bombing method and torpedo training was discontinued in the Fifth Air Force.[43] Skip bombing was used in the sinking of many Japanese vessels and played a most important part in the Battle of the Bismarck Sea.[44]

Another example of ingenuity was the parafrag bomb. A parafrag bomb was a twenty-pound bomb with a parachute attachment. The pilot dropped it from low altitudes, and in the few seconds that it took for the bomb to reach the target, the aircraft was flown out of the range of the bomb fragments.[45] Because the bomb was usually released at low altitudes, it was very accurate. Among all the various types of bombs used by the Allies, the Japanese feared the parafrag the most because they had no defense against it. They could not shoot up at the parachute because that would bring the bomb down faster on their heads, and if they exposed themselves by running away, skilled Allied snipers who were using aircraft deploying parafrag bombs for close air support would pick them off.[46]

A third innovation was the placing of additional firepower on each bomber aircraft. This became necessary because the Japanese in New Guinea concentrated their air defense weapons in constricted zones.[47] The heavy firepower of these defenses made them tough to penetrate. If Allied bombers were ever going to be successful in cracking the Japanese defenses, they would need some additional firepower. In order to rectify this deficiency, Lt. Col. P. I. Gunn experimented with the installation of additional forward firing guns in each bomber's nose. Since only local Australian materials were available, it was necessary to fabricate each installation by hand.[48]

After several experiments and extensive combat tests, eight fixed forward firing .50-caliber machine guns were established as standard equipment. This weapon proved so efficient and effective that by the first part of 1943, two groups of B-25s had been fully equipped and were operating against Japanese targets at minimum-altitude missions instead of medium-altitude missions. By the middle of 1943, production models with this equipment were arriving directly from the United States, made in accordance with the specifications developed in the SWPA.[49]

A fourth major innovation was an increase in the range of all aircraft. Although the increase of firepower on strafer-type airplanes had given the Allies a strong weapon against Japanese airstrips, ground installations, and shipping, the range of these aircraft was still limited. Beginning with their retreat in New Guinea, the Japanese, as the Allied strikes became more effective, pulled their forward bases back beyond what they considered the range of Allied aircraft. This countermeasure in turn required the Allies either to establish new forward bases or extend the range of its weapons. The former solution obviously was not easy to achieve; the second solution, with a little resourcefulness, was.

Additional gasoline tanks were installed on all aircraft. This installation on the B-25s eventually gave them a combat radius of 720 to 750 nautical miles. Fighter ranges from points of takeoff were increased to over 700 nautical miles; heavy bomber formations flew missions from 860 to 1,020 nautical miles. Thus, with the added fuel capacity, it became possible to provide fighter-escorted strikes to places that the enemy had felt secure.[50]

Other new methods employed included the use of heavy bombers on low-level attacks and on pinpoint targets; the placing of high air-burst phosphorus bombs over airfields to burn enemy aircraft and aerial support personnel on the airstrip; and finally, the addition of 80mm cannons on heavy bomber aircraft, making them almost like deadly flying buzz saws.[51] As previously pointed out, their first attempt to take Port Moresby by an amphibious operation was frustrated at the Battle of Coral Sea. Their second attempt, which will now be related, was made both by land and by sea — a march over the mountains from Buna and a swing around the island via Milne Bay.[52]

The Japanese Advance

In late July 1942, they began to advance from Buna, on the northeastern coast of New Guinea[53] toward the crest of the Owen Stanley Mountains. With their new air base they hoped their land-based aircraft would be able to provide adequate cover for their naval invasion force, which would then steer around the southeastern corner of New Guinea to assail Port Moresby.[54] The Allies, not knowing that the Japanese were so well entrenched in Buna, had the same idea. They wanted an air base in Buna to protect their flank. They sent a reconnaissance party to survey sites for the future air base. This party ran into the Japanese force at Buna. After a brief skirmish, the Allied forces beat a hasty retreat and reported on the Japanese activities.[55]

The occupation of Buna by this large Japanese force put a damper on Allied plans to occupy the Buna-Dobadura area and establish a complex of airdromes in that vicinity so that air superiority could be obtained and the range of aircraft increased.[56]

As soon as the strong Japanese force was reported to MacArthur, the main mission of Allied forces in New Guinea became the envelopment of this Japanese force's left flank located over the eastern mountain trail called Kokoda.[57] This trail, although rugged, was the main route from Buna to Port Moresby.

The course adopted was a compromise between total airlift, as advocated by the air force, and ground travel, as advocated by the army's General Eichelberger, who was in command. One regiment of the 32nd Division proceeded on foot to Genou[58] and then into the Dobodura area; the other two regiments were flown to hastily cleared airdromes on the Japanese eastern flank. From there they attacked the enemy positions in Buna.[59] Although the flanking movement was unsuccessful and the operation did not stop the Japanese advance, the troop carrier phase was a huge success. There were no major complications and the paratroops were in place on time and caused the Japanese much trouble. According to at least three sources, this was the first use of cargo planes to carry troops into battle in U.S. aviation history.[60]

After the capture of Buna, the Japanese plans called for the capture of Milne Bay. They hoped to use this bay as a staging point for a land movement along the southern Papua Coast toward Port Moresby. The plan called for Port Moresby to be assaulted from the flank and the eastern tip of Papua to be neutralized to prevent the Allies from reinforcing their command by convoy.[61] They thus proceeded to send a convoy to Milne Bay, where they were successful in landing 12,000 fresh troops.[62] Because of this, the Allied command in New Guinea was faced with two strong forces, one at Buna and the other at Milne Bay, both advancing toward Port Moresby.

The situation was very grave, and despite the constant harassment from the air the Japanese continued to push southward on the Kokoda Trail. By the middle of September 1942, they were through the gap of the Owen Stanley range and only thirty miles from Port Moresby.[63] Beginning an all-out drive and fighting for every mile, the Japanese edged closer and closer to Port Moresby, but finally the heavy bombing of their supply lines and the stiff ground resistance by Allied forces began to pay off and they were halted approximately eighteen miles from Port Moresby.[64] They had overextended themselves. The Allies had control of the air on their side, the southern part of the mountain range, and the A-20s and B-25s now began to take a heavy toll.

The Allied planes attacked not only the Japanese and the Buna area but also enemy airdromes in eastern New Guinea as well as key supply points and airfields in New Britain.[65] Attacks on their left flank against Lae and Salamaua,[66] two major enemy bases in New Guinea, and periodic attacks against Rabaul, the major Japanese base in New Britain, kept the bomber and dive bomber strength of the Japanese down to proportions much lower than they were when the drive was at its zenith.[67] This made it possible for the air defenses of the 5th Fighter Command, under Brig. Gen. "Squeeze" Wurtsmith, to handle Japanese air raids with assurance and competence.[68]

Through surveillance the Allies observed the Japanese construction of large bases at Wewak and Hollandia in Dutch New Guinea and kept them under close scrutiny.[69] Unable to reconnoiter Truk because of the distance involved and the vulnerability of a single reconnaissance airplane of the bomber type, they were restricted in their surveillance to the north, in the area of Rabaul and Kavieng,[70] until the bomb line could be advanced.

In the hectic days of the Papuan campaign, thirty troop carrier airplanes worked around the clock. Their main objective was to transport supplies to the Allied ground forces.[71] In early September 1942, all thirty troop carriers moved an entire Australian infantry division to Port Moresby. On October 6, 1942, the troop carriers transported an Australian infantry battalion to Collingwood Bay, sixty-five miles southeast of Buna, where the engineers hacked out of the jungle and the swamps an airfield at Wageo.[72] Between October 14 and November 10, a company of Australian troops and two regiments of an American division were flown into the Collingwood Bay area.[73] Because of the initial success of the troop carrier aircraft, the Army Air Force headquarters authorized more troop carrier squadrons and a troop carrier group was organized in the Fifth Air Force.[74]

The importance of the use of troop carrier aircraft can hardly be exaggerated. Other theaters in World War II subsequently used such tactics on a larger scale. The use of air transportation[75] gave the ground troops in SWPA new legs and made the infantry a long-range strategic striking force.

By November 2, 1942, aided by a vigorous air arm which had gained air superiority, isolated the battlefield, and interdicted Japanese air bases within range of Port Moresby, Allied forces had pushed the Japanese back across the Owen Stanley Mountains and the myth of Japanese invincibility was broken forever. Late in November, Japanese forces were enveloped by the Allies at Buna, so they decided to risk the resupply of Lae and Salamaua, their main bases in New Guinea. For they realized that if they were to retain a foothold in eastern New Guinea and Papua, it was imperative that they strengthen their bases. Therefore, on January 6 and 7, 1943, they sent several small convoys to reinforce Lae. Although they lost a few transports, troops and supplies were landed and their mission was a success.[76] This success encouraged them to attempt a larger convoy in the near future.

The Battle of the Bismarck Sea

It is now widely known that American crytographers had broken the Japanese top secret codes prior to Pearl Harbor.[77] However, during the war in the SWPA, this fact was a closely guarded secret and the payoff was tremendous. On April 8, 1943, it resulted in the destruction of the aircraft carrying the leading Japanese naval leader, Admiral Yamamoto, and his staff and it was a potent factor in the outcome of the Battle of the Bismarck Sea.[78]

In February 1943, an intercepted Japanese message called for the reinforcement of Lae and Salamaua by a full division.[79] The convoy carrying these reinforcements was to assemble near Kavieng, in the New Ireland Island group, later that month. The Allied forces were directed in this message to prevent this attempt with all the forces at their disposal.[80]

Prior to the receipt of the intercepted Japanese message, army and air force attacks against Japanese convoys had a rather dismal record.[81] This, along with the minor success earlier that year, undoubtedly encouraged the Japanese to believe that they could now successfully operate in the face of the growing Allied air power. However, they underestimated the Allies.

On March 1, a reconnaissance report was flashed: "Convoy heading south through the Vitiaz Straits — weather over target clear and unlimited."[82] The entire Fifth Air Force took off accompanied by a squadron of Australian Beaufighters.[83] The B-17s and B-24s struck the convoy just preceding a low-level attack by B-25s. While Beaufighters and A-20s strafed the convoy, the fighter escort took care of a swarm of Zeros attempting to protect the convoy.[84] The attack went off "without a hitch" and when it was over, there was no convoy left; not one man in the Japanese division being transported in the convoy reached Lae or Salamaua. The number of Japanese aircraft shot down and the number of ships in the convoy varied.[85] First reports indicated that twenty-two ships were sunk.[86] This was the number which the press and news media used, but after the war interrogation reports, diaries, and confiscated Japanese documents indicated there were only sixteen ships in the convoy that were sunk. The Joint Army-Navy Assessment Committee, appointed by the War Department, concluded that there was a total of sixteen vessels in the convoy and that only twelve were sunk.[87]

The number of ships actually destroyed will probably never be known. The Japanese kept their records on 4x5 sheets of tissue paper.[88] Many of these records, not being very durable, were destroyed or ruined. Regardless of which figures are accepted, it was a great triumph for the Allied forces.

After the war, Japanese military leaders, when interrogated, confirmed that the Battle of the Bismarck Sea was a great victory for the Allies. They also claimed that it was the turning point of the war for New Guinea, New Britain, and subsequently Australia.

The Papuan Campaign had been a costly one for the Allies. In addition to normal casualties, which included 8,546 Australians and Americans killed, some 7,000 Americans and Australians were disabled by disease, in testing the strength and will of the Japanese defense system and in providing Allied commanders with the proving ground for tactics which would be of great value in the subsequent defeat of the Japanese Empire.[89]

A Final Word

When Helen McDonald asked me to speak at the symposium about New Guinea, and then asked me for a title, the first title that came to mind was "New Guinea: A Military Nightmare." New Guinea was a military nightmare. Perhaps one veteran, in a vulgar sense, put it best. He said, "You know if the world at that time had to take an enema, it would have probably taken it there."

In the parlance of World War II folklore, one never sees the rich and famous going to or talking about New Guinea. There is no movie, *The Sands of Buna*. One never sees William Holden, John Wayne, or other Hollywood stars playing in movies about the Southwest Pacific area. Not many people in World War II knew much about New Guinea. It really was an enigma. Geography, weather, equipment, logistics, and living conditions were terrible. Yet, in a way, this is what war is all about.

In war many fight, but few get credit. New Guinea is an excellent example of a place where the second-echelon commanders never really got credit. MacArthur and his leading airman, George Kenney, got most of the credit, but it was the Eichelburgers, Krugers, Whiteheads, Crabbs, and Smiths who really did the planning and the fighting.

In New Guinea, the Allies won because of good old-fashioned ingenuity and because of blood and sweat. They did not have much help, they had to improvise. Maybe there is a lesson to be learned there. Yes, they moaned and groaned, but in the final analysis what they did was they won because they would not be defeated. Maybe today we should be thinking about this instead of complaining about the economy and other problems. Maybe with a little old ingenuity and a little grit, this country could learn something from the men of the army and navy who fought and died in New Guinea, a place that was truly a military nightmare.

The Worst of All Possible Worlds

For the first time in the Pacific theater, Australians and Americans fought a land battle side-by-side. It is a wonder the two countries are still Allies. Evan H. M. Barnet was one of those Australians unfortunate enough to be sent to New Guinea. Even though the climate played a significant role in his misery on New Guinea, the Japanese proved worse than nature. As he will describe, his stay on New Guinea was indeed short.

Evan H. M Barnet joined an artillery survey unit in Australia at the outbreak of the war with Germany. After a year, he transferred to a horse cavalry unit, then to the 6th Armored Regiment. He fought with this unit in Buna, New Guinea, where he was severely wounded.

Evan H. M. Barnet

The last shall be first, and the first shall be last. What I have to tell you is my part in the early stages of the Buna Campaign, beginning the conquest of the Japanese in the Pacific on land. You have heard about air forces and navies and all sorts of things up to date, but the land did take a large part in it eventually.

I joined the army in June 1941, with the understanding that after some initial training in Australia we would go to the Middle East to fight the Germans. However, at this stage, the First Armored Division was being formed. And instead of going to the Middle East, I volunteered to join the 6th Armored Regiment, which was the first tank regiment to be formed in the new armored division. We were trained as a specialist force and it is doubtful that there had ever been an Australian division or regiment fitter than this one, prouder, or keener. The division was one in which the discipline and the *esprit de corps* had never been higher, nor one where the bearing of the officers and the men was better. The crews were men who had been specially selected for their intelligence and their capabilities.

All of our training was for desert warfare, being eventually issued American M-3 light tanks, General Stuarts, or Honeys, as they were called. They weighed 14 tons, armed with a .37mm cannon, as well as a .30-caliber Browning co-axially mounted with the cannon in the turret and another one in the hull. We had a crew of five: a crew commander, a gunner, a driver, a wireless operator, and a hull gunner. We were fast, lightly armored reconnaissance vehicles, ideal for desert warfare. We had our final leave, our camp was established in the Middle East, Japan attacked Pearl Harbor, and we were at war with Japan. We were moved to Townsville as part of the line of defense of Australia. We were not there long before the regiment was moved to New Guinea, Port Moresby, and Moon Bay. My squadron went to Moon Bay, on the southeastern tip of New Guinea. The Australian troops were pushing the Japanese over the Owen Stanley range, and it became our job to go up the east coast and attack Buna in support of the Americans, who were already there and who were having a pretty tough time.

We loaded our tanks in the Dutch ship called the *Karsick* after much hassle with the Dutch skipper, who was not at all keen on the idea. However, once loaded with eight tanks, we went around to Oro Bay, where after a lot of fuss and bother again with our skipper, we off-loaded our tanks onto flat-topped barges. These barges had been used previously in Sydney Harbor to cut timber. War in the Pacific was relatively new. There were no tanks and no tank landing craft. These were the first Australian tanks to be used in the Pacific.

Our two tanks plus crews were then taken by MTBs (motor torpedo boats) and towed up the coast. When daylight came they cast us off, and we had to pole ourselves like coolies into the shore, where we tied up to what we thought was a large, camouflaged barge, the ideal spot. And a bronze Danzac (New Guinea native) came out and said, "Where do you think you are?" And we said, "Well, we're on the coast of New Guinea somewhere." And he said, "Well, you're tied up to the ammunition dump for the east coast." Unperturbed, we stayed there until the next morning, when we were picked up again and towed up and landed south of Buna. We dropped our tanks off the barges and into the sea and onto an ingoing tide, so that our tank tracks were concealed. We also had air cover at that stage, to conceal from the Japanese that there were tanks about. As we started up, the planes flew over until we got into the jungle and under cover.

The next day we were getting ready to go into action against the Japanese, who were well entrenched in concealed bunkers. We made contact with the American and Australian soldiers, whom we were going to support. That evening, a Lieutenant Macintosh, an Australian, and myself crawled forward into the front of the first line of the troops to investigate the enemy positions. We found strongly logged posts (dugouts) manned by five Japanese with two machine guns. There were a lot of these bunkers, and each of them was a small fortress cunningly concealed and camouflaged. Some were protected by interlaced logs covered by six feet of earth; some had metal roofs and some had concrete.

Precisely at 0700 hours on December 18 we commenced our advance. My tank was on the right flank and on the edge of another overgrown plantation going up the beach. As we went forward we found that the Japanese trenches and dugouts were at right angles to the beach, so we were able to fire down their lines and create great confusion. The Japanese put up very strong resistance, and we supported our infantry by firing through the slits into the bunkers, and periodically chopping down the coconut palms which had snipers hidden up in them. Eventually, we made our objective to Cape Endiadea and then turned inland to help Sergeant Lattimore and rescue his tank. I told my gunner, who was an excellent gunner, probably the best in the squadron, to take the point of Lattimore's tank to hunt the Japanese away as they were sneaking up and trying to plant sticky-bombs (magnetic mines that could be attached to vehicles and delay-detonated) under the side of his tank. Eventually we rescued Lattimore. I left my vehicle, actually, to supervise the rescue of Lattimore and his crew, and we got them away safely.

We continued to assist American and Australian infantry in their push. The Japanese had considered a creek and a swamp in their rear impassable. However, the brave and tireless 2nd Lt. James E. Dowty, an American engineer, prepared and constructed a bridge to enable us to go around them, creating great confusion with the Japanese. On December 24, we were to take the old air strip with the four remaining tanks. Due to incorrect intelligence, there was concealed a 6-inch anti-aircraft gun at the end of the strip. With the last three shells this 6-inch gun had, it put out of action three of the four tanks. Lattimore's tank was hit, the shell going straight through the middle, killing the gunner and severely wounding Lattimore. The second tank's tracks were knocked off. On my tank the turret was opened like a tin opener. My driver was killed and I was severely wounded. We had given instructions to our drivers that if anything like this happened to go for hell and clear out and go back. So the fourth tank saw this was happening, turned around, and tipped over into a shell hole.

Sergeant Lattimore's Stuart tank on New Guinea. The Japanese shell entered through the gunner's hatch below the gun. It killed the gunner and took the legs of Sergeant Lattimore. This tank is now on display at the Admiral Nimitz Museum. *Photo courtesy of Admiral Nimitz Museum*

I had an amputation the next day in a field hospital under a tree with a tent tarpaulin. I was carried by seven fuzzy-wuzzy angels, fuzzy-wuzzy men — New Guinea men who acted as porters and were christened "fuzzy-wuzzy angels" by the Australians because of the wonderful work they did carrying the wounded and generally doing porter work. I had seven men in my carrier group. There was a boss man and six carriers (four carrying me and two supporting the others). Periodically along the fourteen-mile trek, the boss boy used to send a boy up into the trees to pick a coconut and bring it down to give me a drink. I was badly damaged and I couldn't do much, so these drinks of coconut, I can assure you, were wonderful all the way along the trek.

On arrival at the airstrip, I was met by an American medical orderly who asked me if I would like a drink. I said, "Yes I would." I was on the ground and he had one look at me and went away. He came back with a bowl. He put the bowl on the ground beside me and a plastic tube in my mouth, and I had my first drink of real American coffee. And I can tell you, it's not nearly as good these days.

I was then flown over the Owen Stanley range to Port Moresby and to the hospital. That was the end of my war effort. Reinforcements from my unit continued to assist in the push, and with the Allies, we eventually moved the Japanese out of New Guinea.

★　★　★

The recollections of James Kincaid combine the elements of fighting two enemies at one time: the Japanese and nature. Being part of an infantry unit, Kincaid experienced firsthand the worst New Guinea had to offer.

James Kincaid served as an enlisted man in the United States Army during World War II. He participated in the Battle of Buna, New Guinea, in the first offensive action of the war in which Americans and Australians fought side-by-side.

James Kincaid

My military instruction began when I joined the Junior ROTC program in the fall of my sophomore year at Beloit Memorial High School, Beloit, Wisconsin, in the fall of 1938. In the spring of 1939, I joined Company L of 128th Infantry, 32nd Division, Wisconsin National Guard in Beloit, Wisconsin. In October of 1940, we were activated into federal service and transported to Camp Beauregard, Louisiana, for training. We were shipped to Australia in the early part of 1942 for more training and preparation for what was to come.

Because the Japanese were closing in on Port Moresby, New Guinea, we were taken to Townsville, Queensland, Australia, and airlifted to Port Moresby to give support to the Australian army, who were trying to stop the advancing Japanese attacking over the Owen Stanley range on the Kokoda Trail.

From there, the 3rd Battalion, 128th Infantry, was airlifted over the Owen Stanley range to a small kunai-grass covered field near Wanigela, New Guinea. In order for the planes to land, the local natives had cut the kunai-grass at ground level by hand under the supervision of Australian Overseers.

From there, we hiked overland across Cape Nelson carrying all of our weapons, ammunition, food, and other gear on our backs. For two weeks we slogged through the dense jungle, existing on one-third ration a day (I was only about twenty years old at the time so I could take this). We only saw glimpses of sunshine through the overhanging canopy of trees, and only saw bright sunshine when we came to occasional fields of shoulder-high kunai-grass, which was sharp enough to slice through skin if dragged across it.

Our one-third ration consisted of one-day's C-ration supplemented by a little rice divided by three men. The C-ration was air dropped to us by C-47s flying over a marked field at about fifty feet high and kicking the cases out of the open door of the plane. Needless to say, when the cases hit the ground, they burst open and scattered cans for hundreds of feet. Some were damaged beyond use.

On our trek, we came to Totore, on the Musa River, which was in flood stage due to the incessant rain, which never seemed to cease, and made the trail very hard to traverse. We could not ford the river, so we were forced to camp at Guri Guri for a couple of days. Our Colonel Miller said that it was the most filthy, swampy, mosquito-infested area that he had seen in New Guinea.

We were then sent north through the swamp to Gobe, which was on the coast. As soon as the Luggers arrived, which were small fishing boats of about 100-ton capacity, we were taken out to them by native outrigger canoe, taken aboard, and transported to Pongani overnight. Well, coming in to Pongani, the Lugger I was on was hung up on the reef, and we threw a lot of stuff overboard to lighten it up enough to raise it up at high tide to go in to shore. After unloading at Pongani, we proceeded to Embi and went into bivouac until further orders.

The middle of November, we started for Dobodura and then along the Simemi Trail toward Buna, between the airstrips. The trail was only about ten feet wide, with deep swamp on both sides. Our company was the point and had the baptism of fire along the way. We attacked along the trail, and the point crossed the bridge over the Simemi Creek into the kunai-grass-covered field into the airstrips. The Japanese had a regular strip and a new strip that was a dummy strip, built so that it would be bombed instead of the other strip.

The Japanese let the lead men come within a few feet of their camouflaged pillboxes and then opened fire on them, pinning them down. After they were pinned down, they started dropping mortar shells and grenades from grenade launchers onto them. There was so much crossfire and lead flying that they had to crawl back when they were told to withdraw. The camouflage was so well done that you couldn't see the fortifications just a few feet from them. They also had snipers and observers in the coconut trees, which we didn't know about until later.

Company L pulled back on the other side of the bridge and set up a defense. The light machine-gun section, of which I was in charge, and the rest of the weapons platoon hadn't crossed the bridge yet when the rest of the company had to pull back. So we backed down the trail to let the rest of the company withdraw. The company commander came along the trail and asked for volunteers to return to the field to bring back some wounded who couldn't get out.

Several others and I volunteered. We took .45-caliber automatic pistols and headed for the field. We couldn't cross the bridge, so we waded across the creek in water up to our necks to find the wounded. A short ways into the kunai-grass we found several wounded. Every time we moved the kunai-grass, it brought a burst of machine-gun fire in our direction. One of the wounded was a fellow I had gone to school with. He had been shot through the ankle, just above the foot. The bullet had entered the back of the leg, exiting through the front, taking about an inch of bone with it. The foot was dangling by a little flesh and skin. He begged me to shoot him because he didn't want to go home with just one leg. I talked him out of that idea and we proceeded to get him out of there.

We didn't take time for any first aid, as the bleeding had stopped by then, probably from shock. I slipped into the water and took him onto my shoulders in the sitting position, with his leg dangling in the slimy water, and me up to my neck. I crossed the stream and took him to the first aid station, or the aid station, where they set his foot and leg in a cast and sent him back to a hospital. They then took him back to the States and put him in the hospital and let his leg heal, break it, stretch it, let it heal again, break it, stretch it. Today he walks today with hardly a limp. For this, I received the Silver Star award.

We spent that night along the trail just before the bridge. I lay in a shallow ditch alongside the trail, trying to get a little sleep. During the early part of the night, it started to rain and the ditch started to fill with water, so I took my helmet liner and used it as a pillow to hold my head up out of the water so I wouldn't drown. I was lying on my side and the water was half way up my body, but I slept until 0200 hours when it was my turn to do guard duty.

The next day we didn't attack as we were out of rations and

almost out of ammunition. Being resupplied that day, we were to attack the next morning after the air force bombed the enemy positions. Due to faulty communications, the order never came through to the battalion commander to start the attack. The air force was supposed to drop some flares to let us know when the bombing was through. The flares were never dropped, so we didn't get the orders. Worse still, one of the planes, instead of bombing across our front, bombed directly down the trail onto Company L, which was the point company, killing four of our own men and wounding two others. It was quite a frightening experience, lying on the ground and looking up at the underside of our own planes with the bomb bay doors open, and watching a 500-pound bomb exit a plane and get larger and larger as it falls, and wondering if it will land where you happen to be. The only thing that saved more people from being hurt or killed was that it landed on one side of the trail in the swamp and buried itself before it exploded. The force of the explosion went upward instead of out.

We made another attack that afternoon late, but that also failed. At 2015 that night, we were ordered to march to the coast to resume our attack on the right flank against Cape Endiadea. In that series of encounters, Company L lost thirty to forty percent of its people.

We set up a line of defense in case the Japanese counter-attacked. In the process of setting up this defense, I lost my mess kit spoon on which I had scratched my name to better identify it. I had discarded my knife and fork to make the load lighter, because everything we had we carried on our backs. In the process of checking on the light machine guns a couple of days later, while going through the brush, right behind the line, I looked down and saw a mess kit spoon on the ground. As I bent over to pick up the spoon, a Japanese bullet cracked right where I had been standing. Needless to say, I didn't stand back up in that spot but scooted out of the area. It was my spoon with my name on it.

An attack was planned for Thanksgiving Day, which was November 26 of that year. But it also failed. For Thursday dinner, I had a can of Australian hardtack and a can of Australian corned beef, which we called bully-beef.

A short time later, five or six of us were standing and talking under a large spreading tree about forty yards in from the coast when we heard a thump in the tree overhead. We looked up to see a Japanese grenade from a grenade-launcher falling through the branches to land right in the center of our circle. Needless to say, there was a mass exodus from that spot as everyone dove for cover. The grenade turned out to be a dud, which we later threw into the ocean.

Later they brought in Australian troops with Bren gun carriers, who proceeded to attack the enemy positions in the Duropa Coconut Plantation. These were repulsed by the Japanese, who took all of the Bren gun carriers out of action. The carriers hung up on the uneven ground and the stumps. Snipers picked off the men in the vehicles while the men on the ground threw grenades into them, wounding or killing a great number. Company L, who was supporting the attack, was also hit very hard.

While we were on the coast, a flight of eighteen Japanese BETTY Bombers circled our position. We wondered where our fighters were. There were none to be seen. All of a sudden, out of a cloud, four P-39 fighters appeared, diving on the rear planes of the formation. As they passed down under the formation, four BETTY Bombers fell off. They nosed up under the formation toward the lead planes and four more fell off. We were told later that they downed the whole formation before they could return to Rabaul.

Next, they brought in fresh Australian troops with Stuart tanks and overran the Japanese fortifications in the Duropa Plantation. The 3rd Battalion, 128th Infantry, followed the attack to mop up.

We were then moved to a defensive position along the northern edge of the Simemi Creek. While there, a Japanese plane, in broad daylight, flew at about forty feet high the whole length of the airstrip. We waved as he went by, and not a shot was fired at him. While in this area, we witnessed an aerial dogfight between the air forces and the Japanese of about one hundred aircraft, bombers and fighters. I watched one Japanese Zero on the tail of a P-38. The pilot of the P-38 realized a Zero was on his tail, so he pushed full throttle and stood the P-38 on its tail, leaving the Zero behind like it was standing still. We then moved over to the south side of this old strip in a defensive position. That was around Christmas time.

For Christmas dinner there, I had a real treat. I had a tin of Australian hardtack and a can of salmon. It came out in all the American papers that every serviceman had turkey for Christmas dinner that year.

Right after that, Buna was captured. We were moved back to Dobodura, put aboard planes, flown to Port Moresby, put aboard ship, and taken back to Australia for rest and relaxation.

VIII. The Hardest Fight of All: Guadalcanal

Guadalcanal

Sitting in the blue Pacific was a small island chain that seemed to be one of the most insignificant places on earth in mid-1942, the Solomon Islands. The Solomons were a small chain of islands. The largest was only nine miles long by twenty-five miles wide. It had mountains, forests, and swamps, as did most of the South Pacific islands. Islands in the Solomons had strange-sounding names like Tulagi, Florida, Malaita, Ndai, Santa Isabel, San Gorge, New Georgia, Kolombangara, Vella Lavella, Faisi, Shortland, Choiseul, Bougainville, Buka, and Guadalcanal. The only thing that made these islands significant in the world around them was that the Japanese had a small airfield on the island of Guadalcanal. From this airfield, they could control the Allied shipping lanes to Australia and New Zealand. Because of this isolated airfield, the Solomon Islands would earn an eternal place in military and American history.

The fight for the Solomons was important in another respect for the United States military. For the first time in the Pacific, all United States military branches and forces would unite and combine *en masse* to fight the Japanese. From August 7, 1942, to February 8, 1943, the American army, navy, and marine corps fought together to present a unified front against a superior foe. As with any combined unit action, there were flaws. Coordination between American forces was lacking, supplies and equipment were not delivered where needed, and communications mistakes plagued the Americans. The military forces of the United States were able, however, to put aside their egos and inter-service rivalries and work out the differences. This cooperation not only paid dividends at Guadalcanal, but would also pay even bigger dividends later in the war.

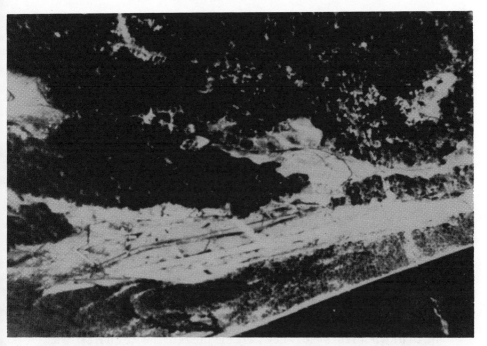

This piece of real estate on Guadalcanal became the most important land in the entire Pacific theater in 1942 and led to one of the most protracted battles of WWII in the Pacific. The Japanese had built this airstrip, and the United States desperately needed it to conduct the war. The United States named it Henderson Field after a pilot at Midway. *Photo source unknown, print courtesy Admiral Nimitz Museum*

For six months, navies, armies, and air forces clashed, and the tide of battle turned almost daily. But in the end the United States held. The sea and air lanes to Australia and New Zealand were open for good, and the tide of war had definitely turned. No longer did the Japanese have the trained, experienced pilots to challenge the American airmen. In fact, the Japanese would become so desperate for qualified airmen that they would begin using teenagers to pilot their aircraft.

Overview and Analysis

Walter Lord speaks of the battles, suffering, and valiant effort put forth by Allied forces on Guadalcanal.

Walter Lord

Midway permanently blunted any further Japanese thrust into the central Pacific, forcing Tokyo to direct its future efforts to the south instead. Having established a major new naval base at Rabaul, Yamamoto turned his attention to the Solomon Islands, some 200 miles to the southeast. The Solomons lay like a spear, pointing directly at the supply line between Australia and America.

Unlike Midway, the Solomons were no flat coral atoll. Volcanic in origin, they towered upward from the sea in a spectacular display of tumbling green mountains. Little of this terrain was suitable for land-based planes, with one big exception. About two-thirds of the way down the chain lay the Guadalcanal. On its north side was a flat grassy plain which could easily be converted into a landing field. At the end of June and the beginning of July, Japanese construction crews began building and burning away the grass in order to build a runway.

They did not come unobserved. Most of the 650 Europeans who lived in the Solomons had fled before the Japanese advance, but here and there a few remained. They were members of the Royal Australian Navy's Island Coastwatching Service. Recruited by Cmdr. Eric Feldt of the Australian Navy, and equipped with portable teleradios, they lived in jungle hideaways, watching and reporting Japanese movements. Friendly natives served as scouts and carriers.

There were three of these Coastwatchers on Guadalcanal. Snowy Rhoadès, a planter, was stationed on the western end of the island. Don MacFarland, formerly a department store buyer, hid in the middle, high up on a mountain called Gold Ridge. Finally, Martin Clemens, the Colonial Offices district officer in better times, served all the way to the east.

News of the Japanese movement into the Solomons struck a raw nerve in Washington. Adm. Ernest J. King, COMINCH, had always been skeptical of the Allies' Europe First strategy. Now he urged at least some sort of holding action in the South Pacific. The Japanese, he argued, must not be allowed to take over the Solomons. King was a rough man in a Washington power struggle. It was said he shaved with a blow-torch and he got his way. Parts of two marine divisions were slapped together under Maj. Gen. Archibald Vandegrift, and on August 7 they launched a two-pronged invasion.[1] One group landed on Tulagi, the traditional seat of the British government. The other stormed ashore on Guadalcanal, where they quickly captured the airfield. Resistance was barely more than token.

By the evening of August 8, 19,000 men were ashore. The main problem seemed to be the orderly unloading and storage of the supplies. Half a dozen American and Australian cruisers stood guard, covering the unloading of the transports.

At 0138 hours early on the morning of August 9, a Japanese task force under Vice Adm. Gunichi Mikawa slipped in by the American picket destroyers and caught the cruisers, which were protecting the landing, completely by surprise. In less than twenty-five minutes, Mikawa sank four Allied cruisers and badly damaged a fifth.[2] With the transports stripped of their protection, they steamed off on the ninth without unloading more than a fraction of the marine supplies. To make matters worse, Admiral Fletcher, covering the landings with three carriers, felt he was running low on fuel and ordered them to retire, leaving the marines without any air cover.[3]

They were isolated deep within Japanese territory, but managed to hang on with the help of two more Coastwatchers, stationed on the island of Bougainville, the northernmost of the Solomons. Japanese planes flying from Rabaul to Guadalcanal usually passed directly over the hideouts of these two Coastwatchers. They were Jack Reed and Paul Mason, who would observe the planes and then flash a warning to Guadalcanal that the Japanese were coming. Guadalcanal had two hours to get ready for the blow. Those two advanced hours were priceless in holding Guadalcanal. Coastwatchers made it possible with their brief messages.

Meanwhile, the marines managed to turn back seven successive attempts to retake the landing field, living off captured Japanese supplies. All the time they worked on the airfield, now christened Henderson Field after one of the marine heroes of Midway. The fighting took on an odd pattern. The Americans seemed to control the sky in the day, but come dark, the Japanese fleet took over and controlled the night. It went on this way day after day until the night of November 14-15, when a great naval battle permanently swung the balance to America. What can we learn from these two great victories at Midway and Guadalcanal, so different in detail yet so much alike in other ways? Well, we learned a lot about the nuts and bolts of war, such as the need for better torpedoes, the need for better procedures in loading and unloading vessels. But the lesson I really want to leave with you is nothing so practical. It is this:

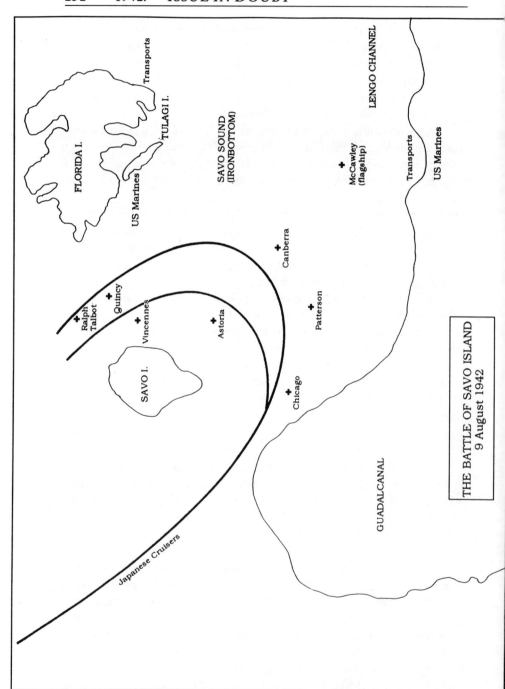

THE BATTLE OF SAVO ISLAND
9 August 1942

There's a special blend of skill, faith, and valor, plus a little bit of luck, that can turn almost any certain defeat into incredible victory. This rare mixture was present at both Midway and Guadalcanal, and every American can take pride in what was accomplished.

★   ★   ★

One of the most complex battles of World War II was fought at Guadalcanal. The interplay of air, sea, and land forces, the drastic shifts in fortune experienced by both sides, the nip-and-tuck between navies, the intelligence information obtained from Coastwatchers, and the interrelationships between intentions and battles, all made Guadalcanal an enigma to military planners and strategists. Even today, most historians have difficulty in comprehending and explaining the complex correlations of battle actions which transpired at Guadalcanal. Not so with Richard Frank. He presents a synthesis of the battle which can easily be grasped by novice and expert alike.

Richard S. Frank obtained his degree at the University of Missouri and was then commissioned in the United States Army. He served in Vietnam before his discharge. He is the author of *Guadalcanal: The Definitive Account of the Landmark Battle*, which received the General Wallace M. Greene, Jr. Award for outstanding nonfiction work relevant to marine history.

Richard S. Frank

On August 7, 1942, in Tokyo, Japan, there was an important briefing at Imperial General Headquarters. Senior staff officers of the Imperial Army assembled to listen to a lecture by Lieutenant Colonel Sugita, who was billed as an expert on the United States and American forces. Colonel Sugita conducted a tour of the strategic horizons and delivered his opinions. The United States would not strike anywhere along the Pacific front in the foreseeable future. The most likely course of action that the United States would take would be to establish bases in Soviet maritime provinces, which are to the north and northwest of Japan, and from those bases to conduct air and submarine attacks upon Japan.

That same day, across the International Date Line, U.S. marines splashed ashore on the then very obscure South Pacific island of Guadalcanal, approximately 4,270 miles away from where Colonel Sugita had projected the Americans would next move. Now, the documentary sources don't tell us everything, but they do suggest that this briefing was a turning point in Colonel Sugita's career. When we next encounter Colonel Sugita, he is not leading the cushy life of a staff officer in Tokyo, but he is not wearing the dirty, sweat-stained uniform of a field officer, as he peers through the brambles on the island of Guadalcanal, as the intelligence officer for the Imperial Army's Second Infantry Division.

What makes Guadalcanal one of the most evocative names from World War II for Americans? I think the answers to this are several. First of all, it was ferociously fought, on land, on sea, and in the air, by forces that were closely balanced. Second, the campaign witnessed such marked oscillations of fortune that so vastly exceed what anyone would dare to propose in fiction, that it had a riveting narrative drive entirely its own. And third, and I think most important, it is what I would call a fundamental rite of passage for a generation. To understand this, I think we have to put ourselves back into that high summer of 1942 and try to appraise the world as it appeared then. It was a world whose borders were very severely darkened by the economic downfall of the 1930s — the depression and the serious depravation that human beings suffered here and abroad. It was also a period of political dissary. It looked like the center could not hold, that market economy and democracy was on the way out. The world was dividing up left and right, and the tired American experiment was simply not going to deliver for the future.

It was marked militarily by almost a decade of what seemed like unending and unrelenting triumphs by forces, principally the Axis, against everyone that we enjoyed common values with and that we wished well. It was not merely defeat; it was humiliation. One after another, ancient and famous peoples fell, and not in a fashion of a heroic battle, but seemingly collapsing. The fall of France was a tremendous shock to the United States and throughout the world. It seemed to indicate that there was simply a rot that was present within the western nations, and those who shared their values and attempted to uphold the principles that we stand for today.

There had been some successes. There had been the Battle of Britain. There had been the repulse of the Germans before Moscow in December of 1941. But all of these victories were essentially defensive successes that merely denied to the Axis powers an extension of their conquests, deprived them of none of the spoils of their victories since the 1930s, and left us a long, long, long way from any decisive achievement. I think the best barometer of just how grim and dim the prospects seemed in the summer of 1942 is provided by Sir Winston Churchill. He is rightly regarded as the very epitomy of bulldog determination, of resolution in the face of defeat. Yet we know from the diary of his physician, Lord Moran, that in June 1942, Churchill himself, in tears, questioned whether the youth of democracy would be capable of standing up and prevailing against the Axis. Therefore, I think, you can really appreciate the fact there was this visceral sense that was abroad: were we tough enough to bear it out and carry through?

Why, then, was there a campaign on Guadalcanal? On the Allied side, I think the answer is clearly political. In a strategic appreciation prepared in early 1942 by Dwight Eisenhower, the United States Army was quite prepared to simply write off Australia as expendable. This was not to the taste of either Prime Minister Churchill or President Roosevelt. They insisted that Australia must be held, and to hold Australia meant that the lines of communication, the sea lanes to Australia and New Zealand, had to be secured. Now, the Allies of course were not writing on a blank sheet of paper in terms of strategy. The Japanese were also active.

At Midway, in June 1942, certainly the Japanese were checked in their thrust in the central Pacific, and a tremendous defeat was inflicted upon the Imperial Navy. But it is quite wrong to think that after Midway, Japan simply sat back and awaited an offensive from the Allies. Quite the contrary. The Imperial Army was quite determined to continue with its offensive operations and was indeed continuing a thrust on New Guinea, and preparing further thrusts down to the Solomons to cut the supply lines to Australia and New Zealand.

This combination of the political decision at the highest levels in the United States and Great Britain and the Japanese efforts in the South Pacific clearly created a demand for a defensive disposition. Translating those circumstances into an offensive, I think, must be entirely attributed simply to the unrelenting will of Ernest Joseph King, the commander in chief of the United States Navy. He was tough but was also very, very intelligent. As to his toughness, if I had to sum him up, I would simply say he basically was an SOB's SOB, and as to his unrelenting dedication to his career, I think you can get some flavor of this from a comment he once made: "You ought to be very suspicious of anyone who won't take a drink or who doesn't like women." Admiral King was no slouch in either category. In fact, his biographer tells us that in the midst of this global war, every afternoon about 1600, he used to steal away for a couple of hours and no one knew where he was. But we can be pretty sure that he wasn't curled up with a copy of *Jane's Fighting Ships*.

Admiral King's intentions were quite clear. He wished to exploit the victory at Midway, he was determined to start an offensive in the Pacific before accounts were settled with Germany, and most of all, he was determined that the offensive, when it started, would be under naval command and not under command of Gen. Douglas MacArthur.

What was the role of radio intelligence during the Guadalcanal campaign? It was sort of paradoxical. I would say on the one hand it was limited, but on the other hand it was profound in some areas. The Japanese changed their main cipher system in May 1942, and that basically caused an eclipse in code-breaking that extended through most of the campaign with a few very important exceptions. One of the minor exceptions was that the harbor master at the main Japanese base of Truk continued to use a cipher system that we were very happily able to read, and therefore his reports to Tokyo of the comings and goings of major Japanese warships were shared also in Washington and Pearl Harbor.

At the time of the landing on Guadalcanal, there was a Japanese code book that was captured and from the information I saw, it appeared as though it was captured ashore. This prompted the Japanese to switch to what the code-breakers labeled the "D" version of the code around August 18. The Command War Diary of Admiral Nimitz has a very interesting reference to the next change in the Japanese cipher system, which states that about September 30 or October 1, the Japanese did not merely change their cipher system, but changed the entire methodology of their communications system. One can speculate that the time frame would be just about right for the Japanese to react to the fact the *Chicago Tribune* and other newspapers had compromised communications intelligence with articles that were printed after the Battle of Midway. Overall, however, the Guadalcanal campaign highlights the terrific work done by Hypo traffic analysts having only limited dashes of radio intelligence.

I think code-breaking, of course, is just an incredibly fascinating activity that seems to stir up a lot of interest within the normal gene pool, and it produces papers that have titles, one of which I'll share with you here that I like very much: "The Principles of Indirect Symmetry of Position in Secondary Alphabets and Their Application to the Solution of Poly-alphabetic Substitution Ciphers." I can commend that to you if you are having insomnia. Probably, radio intelligence's most single important contribution was to provide the catalyst for the campaign. Determinations made by radio intelligence analysts that the Japanese were moving construction troops to the island of Guadalcanal to erect an airfield provided the immediate catalyst for the decision to launch the campaign.

This was reached in agreement on July 2, 1942, between Admiral King and General Marshall. Interestingly enough, the campaign plan specified that the initial effort would be made to land at "Tulagi and adjacent positions." The island of Guadalcanal was not even mentioned. Fortunately, and I think in the first instance of what was to be the hallmark of a truly illustrious page in Marine Corps history, the commander and staff of the 1st Marine Division, quite on their own and without direction from anyone else, immediately determined that they would have to land on the island of Guadalcanal and seize the airfield.

They, of course, were not the first Allied forces in the Solomons. That title was held, of course, by the Coastwatchers. They were a wonderfully diverse group. My favorite among the group, I think, was Paul Mason, who was described by Eric Feldt as follows, "He looked less like the sort of hard-bitten character properly imagined for a Coastwatcher, than any other Caucasian in the area, missionaries not excepted."

On August 7, 1942, the marines did indeed seize Tulagi and adjacent positions. They seized Guadalcanal, achieving complete strategic and tactical surprise. That success, however, marked the high point of a roller-coaster ride that then began. Immediately following that was the humiliating defeat of the United States Navy at Savo Island, which prompted a withdrawal of the transports and their covering forces, and a decision by Admiral Fletcher to withdraw his carriers. The marines were left stranded and, in effect, under seige. They were enormously aided initially by the fact that the Japanese grossly underestimated both the numbers of Americans on Guadalcanal and their morale.

The first Japanese effort to recapture the island was mounted by merely a reinforced battalion under Col. Kiyano Ichiki. Ichiki, as a mere company commander in 1937, originally had gone a long way toward starting hostilities in China. Repeating his rash tactics, this time against the marines, he came to a place called the Tenaru River. Actually, it was Alligator Creek. Ichiki was killed and most of his command was annihilated.[4] Immediately following upon this action, there was the third carrier battle of the war, at Eastern Solomons, which clearly was a tactical American victory.[5]

The Japanese, however, were not dissuaded and indeed renewed their effort in September, this time with a brigade under Gen. Kiyotaki Kawaguchi. Kawaguchi's brigade launched a series of night attacks in September 1942, at a place called Edson's Ridge, or Bloody Ridge, and was repulsed.[6] Immediately thereafter, the marines received their first significant reinforcements, but that was at the cost of the carrier *Wasp*, which was torpedoed and sunk by a Japanese submarine.

During these days of late August and into September, the air

The USS *Wasp* is torpedoed at Guadalcanal on September 15, 1942.
U.S. Navy photo, print courtesy Admiral Nimitz Museum

campaign began at Guadalcanal, which in the long run was perhaps its most significant element. What I would emphasize about the air campaign is that while the fighters of course correctly achieved great fame and glory in their defense of the island, the efforts of the dive bomber and the attack crews effectively throttled the Japanese and forced them into using destroyer reinforcement, which made the Japanese logistical arrangements for Guadalcanal quite as bad as ours.

There is a saying in the military that amateurs study tactics and professionals study logistics. The Guadalcanal campaign was, for both sides, very much of an amateur hour. Both sides suffered great depravations. Ultimately, of course, the Japanese did more so. One of the captured diaries that was found on Guadalcanal contained an entry from a Japanese soldier that read like this: "Our bodies are so tired they are like raw cotton."

The Japanese, having been turned back in August and September, renewed the effort in October. By this time, Admiral Nimitz in Pearl Harbor had become disillusioned with his theater commander, Adm. Robert L. Ghormley. Nimitz decided that he would have to be replaced, and after some soul searching appointed Adm. William "Bull" Halsey as the commander. There are many things you can say about Admiral Halsey, but I want to share with you one simple thing I think epitomizes his leadership. When he reached the South Pacific, he issued, in staccato fashion, a series of intelligent and well-thought-out orders, but he also issued one other. He said, "Henceforth, Naval officers in the South Pacific will remove their ties from their tropical uniforms." And there was something visceral about this order that he issued, the sense of a brawler stripping down for action, I think, that illustrated the keen grasp of psychology that Halsey had. He came just in time, because the campaign then moved into a furious climax in a period of a little over three weeks.

A Japanese offensive, this time by divisional size units, at the battle of Henderson Field was once again repulsed by the marines.[7] This was followed immediately thereafter by the Battles of Cape Esperance[8] and Santa Cruz islands, in which the carrier *Hornet* was sunk.[9] Although the Japanese suffered very grievously in losses of aircraft (97) and particularly of aircrew (148), they were prepared to renew an effort in one final supreme campaign to recapture Guadalcanal in November.

This decision, I would indicate to you, was based upon two things. First, it was their appreciation of the situation that they

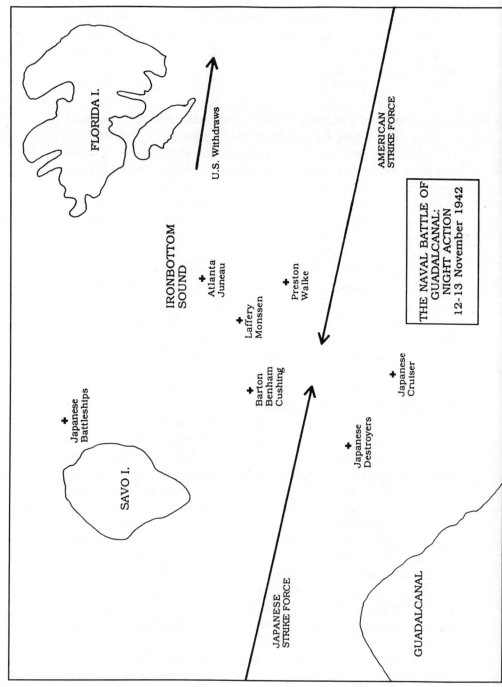

FLORIDA I.

U.S. Withdraws

AMERICAN
STRIKE FORCE

IRONBOTTOM
SOUND

Atlanta
Juneau

Preston
Walke

Laffery
Monssen

THE NAVAL BATTLE OF
GUADALCANAL:
NIGHT ACTION
12-13 November 1942

Barton
Benham
Cushing

Japanese
Cruiser

Japanese
Battleships

Japanese
Destroyers

SAVO I.

JAPANESE
STRIKE FORCE

GUADALCANAL

thought they were close to achieving victory, and that if they rebuffed the first Allied offensive of the war, they would achieve both a victory and gain an important psychological effect they were basing their entire strategic plan on. The second reason why they renewed their effort, however, is that basically the morale in Washington had been cracked. There was a decision in October 1942 to start releasing a great deal more candid information about what was happening in the Solomons. Now, this was not done merely for the purposes of providing more information to the public. It was done expressly, I think, for the purpose of preparing the public for the notion that Guadalcanal was about to become an enormous disaster and a defeat.

Having been spurred on by this, the Japanese cobbled together a plan that led to the naval Battle of Guadalcanal (November 14–15, 1942). In one of the very few moments in which radio intelligence played a critical role in the campaign, a break of the most important message that Admiral Yamamoto sent out was achieved that provided invaluable information upon which actions could be based. The first of these was a furious night action on November 13.[10]

The day after, several damaged cruisers were withdrawing, and during that withdrawal the cruiser *Juneau* was torpedoed and sunk. There were 697 men who were on the *Juneau* on November 13, 1942. When the ship sank, approximately 100 to 120 got off the ship. They were in the water for up to ten days. The circumstances of the sinking, and subsequently exposure and the sun, one by one killed them off. But they also attracted and were attacked by a large flotilla of sharks. One of the individuals who was on one of the rafts was attempting to move from the raft to the net. And as he did so, a shark attacked him and literally gouged out a large portion of one of his shoulders. What happens next I'll tell to you in the words of Lester Zook, one of the survivors: "He looked at his shipmates there and realized that he was making them nauseated, that he was driving them crazy by just being there. And the sharks were getting around close in the water because of his blood being around there, and knowingly, he pushed himself off the lifenets and swam out about five or six feet and let the sharks have him rather than lie there and die like a coward and jeopardize the lives of his shipmates."

On November 14, a Japanese convoy was savaged by American aircraft from both Henderson Field and the *Enterprise*. On the night of November 14 and 15, a battleship action was won by Admiral

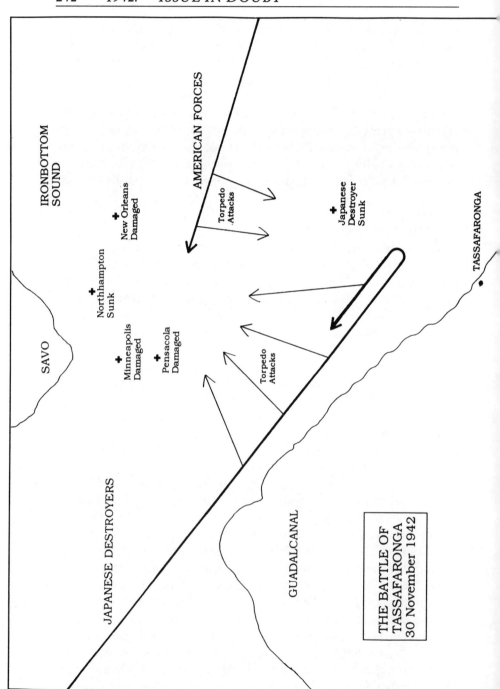

IRONBOTTOM
SOUND

AMERICAN FORCES

New Orleans
Damaged

Japanese
Destroyer
Sunk

Torpedo
Attacks

Northampton
Sunk

TASSAFARONGA

SAVO

Minneapolis
Damaged

Pensacola
Damaged

Torpedo
Attacks

JAPANESE DESTROYERS

GUADALCANAL

THE BATTLE OF
TASSAFARONGA
30 November 1942

Lee, and this was the turning point of the campaign, although it took another month before the Imperial Army could be convinced that Guadalcanal would have to be abandoned.[11] During this period, Japanese supplies were almost entirely severed and the Imperial Army's forces began dying from starvation at a very rapid rate.

In January 1943, a final offensive began that thrust Japanese back on the island. Meanwhile, a decision to evacuate the island was made and brilliantly executed by the Japanese. Indeed, one could say that nothing so became them as their departure from the island. By February 9, 1943, almost exactly six months after the campaign began, it was over. The statistics were 7,100 Americans and Allied soldiers, sailors, and airmen died. Of those, nearly 4,900 were sailors and marines in shipboard complements. At least 30,343 Japanese perished on and around Guadalcanal. Twenty-five American and twenty-four Japanese warships were sunk, in addition to 615 Allied and 683 Japanese aircraft shot down or destroyed as a result of the campaign.

I want to close with some comments that I have borrowed from James Michener. These are words he uses in his book *South Pacific:* "They will live a long time, these men of the south Pacific. They had an American quality. They, like their victories will be remembered as long as our generation lives. After that, like the men of the confederacy, they will become strangers. Longer and longer shadows will obscure them until their Guadalcanal sounds distant on the air, like Shiloh and Valley Forge." To which I would add, Guadalcanal may already sound distant on the air to many, but while distance is inevitable, immortality is not.

The Tossing Sea: Naval Horror

The complexity of the Battle of Guadalcanal was lost on the individual sailor, airman, and soldier who fought for survival at Guadalcanal. Of all military forces at Guadalcanal, the sailors suffered the most. Unlike the airman and infantryman, the sailor has no control over his fate. His life (or death) is completely controlled by the decisions and actions of others. Ted Waller and Teiji Nakamura both allude to the fear in battle which comes from having no control over one's own fate.

Ted Waller served aboard the cruiser USS *Portland* during the Battles of the Coral Sea and Midway. He was also aboard the USS

Portland when the ship provided critical support for the marine landings on Guadalcanal and Tulagi.

Ted Waller

I want to share with you the experiences and thoughts of what was then an eighteen-year-old kid who was just out of high school. I was proud and honored enough to be assigned to the USS *Portland* in February of 1942. I proudly served on there until August of 1946. It was briefly mentioned that we served in the Battle of the Coral Sea and Midway. After that we did go on and participate in the screening of the *Enterprise* in the first battle of landing of the marines on Guadalcanal. The *Enterprise* had been damaged at that time. We escorted her back to Pearl Harbor, and then for a very brief time (for some reason and I never want to find out) the navy decided we should be a lone raider and they sent us to Tarawa to reconnoiter that area and fire on a couple of ships. Fortunately, we only spent about fifteen minutes there and high-tailed back and joined up with the cruiser fleet that was then going back in to Guadalcanal. That was with the *Atlanta*, the *San Francisco*, and the *Juneau*.

On October 24, in the Battle of Santa Cruz, once again we were screening the *Enterprise* and being attacked by torpedo planes and dive bombers. And during that time we lost, temporarily, our steering control. Sometime during that same action the battleship *South Dakota* and the cruiser *San Juan* also lost temporary steering control, and I tell you, if you've ever seen some ships supposedly in formation firing at the enemy and one or two of them get out of control, the nearest thing to describe it is a couple of Aggies in a fire drill.

The *Portland* was mighty lucky that particular day because as the action drew to a close, we spotted three torpedoes coming directly at our starboard side. You could almost hold your breath waiting for them to hit. All three of them hit within seconds of each other. All three of them were duds. So, as a result, we were able to continue on some of the other battles for the next couple of years.

Later on we joined up with the task force of the *San Francisco*, the *Helena*, the *Juneau*, the *Atlanta*, and several other destroyers. My battle station at that particular time was as a sight spotter on one of the anti-aircraft batteries, and my location was up near the bridge area. So during the night battle of November 13, all I got to do was watch. I do remember that particular night that it was pitch black. We couldn't see anything. I was on the sight with a lieutenant that was standing next to me, and we knew that we were about to go into action. All of a sudden, a searchlight came on and firing commenced immediately.

At that time I thought that the lieutenant had kicked me in the leg because I fell to the deck and I was probably thinking about kicking him back, but then I would be a seaman second for the rest of my life. I decided not to. But then I found out that I had been hit by shrapnel. Our starboard hangar was hit and there was a twelve-inch hole put in there. At that time several of our crew members were wounded.

I really didn't know much about what went on at the time because I was carried in to the bridge area, but I could hear the captain and the officers giving instructions on what to do. And about that time, I do remember the loud explosion where the torpedo hit our stern and we immediately lost control of the ship and could only go in circles. When the torpedo hit our stern, the hull plates blew out and formed I guess what could be called a temporary rudder, so that no matter what we wanted to do, all we could do was steam around in a circle. The torpedo hit just aft of our number-three turret, jamming the turret in an elevated position.

The next morning, still steaming in circles, the captain announced and the crew could all see a burning Japanese destroyer. I don't know how many yards away it was, but he announced that as we went around in a circle, we were going to fire on it and sink it. We did not know that the destroyer had been abandoned. But anyway, after the sixth salvo, we did hit it. We probably hit a magazine and the ship blew up and sunk immediately. Historians who have studied the battle and the ship formations of both sides seem to indicate that the *Yudachi* probably fired the torpedo that struck the *Portland*, and Mr. Nakamura was the torpedo officer that night. The ship that we sunk the next morning was the *Yudachi*, so I guess it was kind of even-even on that. In fact, when I met him the other day, I laughed at him and said, "I'm still mad at you because I've got a piece of shrapnel in my right leg," and I pointed to it. And he laughed and he pointed at his leg, and he said, "Me too." So once again we're even. Isn't that something?

We were still steaming in circles when the navy sent out the navy tug *Bobolink* and a little yard patrol boat that attempted to tow us in to Tulagi Harbor. It took just about fifteen hours for them to maneuver us by pushing on our bow and some marine Higgins boats pushing on the stern and the action of our own screws to get us in to Tulagi. It was late that night when we did finally round the area, and just as we rounded the area to tie up alongside the shore, a Japanese battleship rounded the area and shone a spotlight, but failed to see us. So once again, I'd say the *Portland* was a very lucky and fortunate ship.

That next morning we tied up along shore in Tulagi. The next day we went ashore and cut down trees, shrubs, bushes, whatever we could and covered the entire ship with camouflage so we couldn't be seen from the air. Repairs were commenced by our divers to try to cut off the area of the hull that was acting as a rudder,[12] and a couple of days later the fleet tug *Navahoe* came along and we tied up to that. They towed us out to sea, where we proceeded on down to Sydney, Australia, for repairs and a couple of months of wonderful liberty.

Teiji Nakamura also served at Guadalcanal. He was assigned as a torpedo officer aboard the *Yudachi*. The *Yudachi* and *Portland* faced each other off the coast of Guadalcanal.

Teiji Nakamura

Let me just briefly preface this by commenting the Imperial Navy was of the practice of naming destroyers, of giving them poetic names for weather phenomenon. The *Yudachi* means "evening rain." *Yudachi* arrived at Rabaul on August 22, 1942, escorting a seaplane tender after being parted from consorts of the 2nd Destroyer Division. Thereafter, she conducted reinforcement operations to Guadalcanal as on November 13, mainly based from the Shortland Islands. During these three months, we conducted more than sixteen sorties toward Guadalcanal to reinforce and supply soldiers fighting there or to destroy enemy ships at night. As the enemy commanded the skies over and near there, we had to make numerous anti-aircraft actions beside some anti-submarine actions and two surface actions.

In retrospect, I cannot help but wonder how the ship and crew withstood these trials. Cmdr. Kiyoshi Kikkawa was the commander of the *Yudachi*. He was later promoted to rear admiral, following his death in action at the Battle of Cape Saint George. Commander Kikkawa was a very brave but cool man in battle, who always considered best how to contribute to the overall situation. Blessed with an open-hearted and warm personality, he was loved and respected by the entire crew. Notwithstanding of the terrible hot air and high humidity aboard the ship, the endless air raids, the fatigue and want of sleep, no gloomy atmosphere existed among the crew. Morale was quite high, and the fighting-will to take back Guadalcanal was like fire.

The transport operation was not considered a proper task of destroyers, but as there was no other useful means to reinforce and supply in the face of the enemy command of the sky, every destroyer designated to this task did its utmost, utilizing her trained night operations capability. As the operational radius of enemy small planes based at Guadalcanal was 150 miles, it was essential to enter in this circle after sunset and to get out before dawn next day. But because of the time required for landing and other operations, it was the reality that the ships could not avoid several air attacks in almost every reinforcement operation. Many ships could not escape from being damaged by the close support from friendly fighters, especially the utmost efforts by our float planes.

In addition to destroyers, seaplane tenders and cruisers were also used to transport heavy equipment until, at last, it was decided to make a bold attempt with a convoy of six merchant ships in the middle of October, combining this effort with the bombardment of the enemy airfield by our battleships. It was the most severe trial for the crew of the *Yudachi*, as she escorted this convoy, breaking through repeated air attacks and supported landings just off the airfield in full daylight. When we came back safely, all the crew thought that this was just a miracle.

Anti-air warfare was a field in which the Imperial Japanese Navy considerably lacked in research and development. However, *Yudachi* could evade severe damage throughout numerous air raids. It seemed to me that this was due to two facts: one was the enthusiastic lookout maintained by the entire crew, even including the supply officer. Another was the excellent command of the ship by the captain. He tried to make the maximum effect of the weapons and took the most suitable evasive action at the very last moment.

Our first surface action off Guadalcanal occurred on September 4, when the captain of the *Yudachi* commanded two other destroyers as the senior officer present. After landing soldiers at Cape Tevu, three destroyers began firing on the airfield to help the land forces on the commander's own initiative. Two ships were then sighted which were identified as the foe. The commander ordered us to suspend bombardment, and after closing he reopened fire on the enemy ships. He made three runs to make sure of their destruction at the range of between 4,000 and 10,000 meters. After the war, we learned that they were the United States destroyer transports *Little* and *Gregory*.

Our second surface firing was the Battle of Guadalcanal on November 13. The *Yudachi* was proceeding for Lunga Point, and was about eight miles southeast of Savo Island, as one of the warning pickets for the battleships, *Hiei* and *Kirishima*, when we sighted more than seven enemy cruisers and destroyers. *Hiei* and *Kirishima* were to fire on the Guadalcanal airfield with their 14-inch guns. The *Yudachi*, while immediately reporting as the enemy sighted, went across ahead of the enemy course to the east and then dashed alone to the enemy cruisers, which had just commenced firing on the *Hiei*. We launched eight torpedoes at the best position, about 15 meters from the target, and soon thereafter recognized two or three explosions on the leading anti-aircraft cruiser and one of the heavy cruisers.

After launching torpedoes, the *Yudachi* went across the rear of the enemy column to take the position from which she could attack the enemy ships on the opposite side of the firing to assist our main body. We fiercely fired at enemy bridge and fire-control systems from the short distance of 3,000 to 1,000 meters. The targets were changed one after another, from a heavy cruiser to a light cruiser, an anti-aircraft cruiser, and then two destroyers. The *Yudachi* was also fired upon and received some damage, but it was not severe. After fighting twenty minutes, the *Yudachi* left the enemy to rejoin friendly forces. When she approached them, she was hit heavily by a cruiser which had been sighted and identified as friendly as beforehand by the *Yudachi*.

She became immobile due to the damage to the main engine and the boiler. A big fire also started in the forward compartment around the magazine. Most of the crew tried desperately to resume mobility and to fight the fire, while some of them even spread out canvas and hammocks, with the desire that they be used as a sail to head for the northern coast of Guadalcanal with the assistance of tide and thereby beach the ship and become a land battery. About 0200 on November 13, a consort, *Samidare,* arrived to help us and it became clear that the recovery of mobility was impossible and that towing was not practical. The captain decided to abandon ship, and all survivors moved to the *Samidare.* The *Samidare* launched one torpedo to sink the *Yudachi,* and it was recognized as a hit. But as there was no evidence of her sure sinking, the captain of the *Yudachi* asked one more torpedo be fired. At that moment an enemy heavy cruiser was sighted and planes started to take off. So the *Samidare* decided to retire at 0300 after firing on the *Yudachi.*

In such a melee, the identification of friends and foe was quite difficult by eyesight, although Japanese forces hoisted a marking streamer. So it was recommended that there be developed some means of identification of friend and foe, such as infrared rays. As for the radar, we were told that the United States Navy was using it and it had showed its effect in the Battle of Cape Esperance on October 11. But on the *Yudachi,* and other destroyers, we still had the self-confidence in our capability and lookout at night and did not feel that radar was a great threat at this stage.

The Most Unusual Job of All: The Coastwatchers

Imagine yourself to be at war with a merciless enemy. You are placed in an unfamiliar, hostile environment (both from enemy forces and nature) all alone. Furthermore, you are given no food, no bulky packs of life-sustaining equipment, no supplies, and no provisions. Additionally, you are not even given any weapons to defend yourself with. You are instructed to watch, monitor, and report on enemy movements so you cannot stay hidden all of the time. And if all that were not bad enough, assume you volunteered to do this. That is the basic scenario for the story of Martin Clemens.

Martin Clemens was assigned to the Solomon Islands in 1938 as a colonial officer cadet. When the war began, he was pressed into service as a Coastwatcher on Guadalcanal. He provided the Allies with valuable information concerning Japanese aircraft, ship, and troop movements. The Coastwatchers proved to be invaluable during the early stages of the American invasion of Guadalcanal.

Martin Clemens

In November 1941, I had done just over three years in the government in the Solomons, two as a cadet on Malaita and one as the district officer on San Cristobal. My home leave had been canceled, but I was allowed to go to Australia for a month. I got on board the *Malaita* about November 30, leaving Tulagi its usual self apart from the occasional Japanese float planes that came in for a sticky-beak. At the same time, everyone was worried about what was going to happen.

We tied up in Sydney on December 7 and I was handed a newspaper. "Pearl Harbor Devastated," it said on the front. Right down at the bottom in small print it said, "Tulagi Bombed." I and Jack Keenan, a New Guinea district officer, leaned over the stern rail, tore a pound note in half and dropped them in the water. We said, "We won't need these much longer." We were both fed up as we had offered our services to the armed forces, and had been told we were in a reserved occupation. None of the Sydney recruiting offices would have us.

About February 3, I left Sydney on the old *Morinda*, a coal-burner making its presence felt with a plume of black smoke trailing behind. When I got on board, I found I was one of two passengers, and that made me think. We were met outside the harbor in Tulagi by MacFarlan, the naval liaison officer, in a launch looking terribly grim. He shouted at us, "The morning raid is on in twenty minutes time, so I'll let direct you up Port Purvis." Right on the dot, the Kawanishi flying boat hove in sight and made a few circles. The engines had stopped on the *Morinda*, and we all laid down on the deck. There was an awful period of waiting, during which I looked up and counted eight bombs and wondered which one was for me. He let the first two go early, I thought, and then two more followed them down till they fell off the starboard quarter and the port bow. The old ship heaved up but collapsed again in one piece. Then a few more circles and down came the other four. They seemed to drop vertically over us, but he had not allowed for his own speed and they all ended up about a hundred yards ahead.

After that ordeal, we tied up at Lever's Wharf at Gavutu. It was crowded with people and piles of luggage. There were crying women, screaming, woebegone children, and men arguing. I realized my worst fears. I had guessed the place was going to be evacuated, as

I had been one of only two passengers on board. I heard that most of the managers of plantations, particularly on Guadalcanal, had just shot off and left their laborers, most of whom came from Malaita or other islands. The resident commissioner was at his office, but all the other government offices and private homes had been evacuated. They couldn't get all of the Europeans on board, so the Solomon Islanders were to be left to their fate. I couldn't stand this.

I talked to the district officer of Gizo, one of the western districts. He had evacuated under orders and was intending to go out on the ship. Then the government secretary saw me and said, "What the hell did you come back for?" I didn't like that. I got to the resident commissioner and he offered me Gizo. I was furious. I had never served in Gizo and I couldn't go back there once it was evacuated. "No sir," I said firmly. He said, "Well, you'll have to come with me or go to Guadalcanal." Naturally, I chose Guadalcanal, though I had never been there before either. There were two others there. One was Horton, who was tidying up court cases, and Joselyn, who was busy collecting laborers and getting them back to Malaita with six cutters and a schooner. It had to be done quickly, as they were all smashing and looting the plantation houses. An alarm system had to be set up, and we had to get the mission-folk to get off the coast or evacuate. Mostly they would not budge, but expected me to be responsible for them.

The alarm system that was first set up was a platform high up in a banyan tree with a rope ladder and a length of rope and a bucket to ferry up the sentry's lunch, or his pipe, or whatever. We had a conch shell to sound one blast for a ship or two for a plane. When enemy planes came, we all had to take cover so that the place would look deserted.

I had to go around all the coastal villages, but first only the ones on the northern coast, and tell them about reporting strange ships or planes as quickly as they could. Sometime later, I persuaded each village to build a temporary village at least a mile from the coast so that the women and children could avoid contact with the enemy. Medical supplies had to be divided up into several caches throughout the island to be available to the people. Josselyn finished the labor transport and was whipped off to take records to the New Hebrides. After another few weeks, Horton shot off on another special task and so I had the whole shooting match to myself. Tulagi, with its harbor, was a likely place for the enemy to occupy, and although we could see ships coming in and out, it was only twenty miles away. So I had to plan where I would go in the bush if I had to. There was no doubt but that I would have to.

By this time, we were regularly overflown daily by these Kawanishi flying boats. But they kept all of their bombs for the RAAF stationed on Tanambogo Island, near Gavutu. They serviced PBY reconnaissance planes and the long distance Sunderlands and had a big radio and listened in on our frequency for warnings. We could warn them of approaching aircraft. By the way, I got fed up coding Kawanishi, and substituted the word "usual." It was much shorter.

Having decided where to go, the job fell to my Solomon Island clerk, Daniel Pule, to list all the government movables, pack them all up, and get ready for evacuation. I was still the district officer and had to maintain law and order. However, this took some time and he gradually got everything ready for evacuation. But it was further delayed by the departure of the RAAF and the arrival of the Japs in Tulagi, at the beginning of May. We started digging up all the station roads and lawns and planting them with yams and sweet potatoes. We would get no more supplies from outside. I could see that training and accurate observation were badly needed. I checked over what I had. I had fourteen policemen with rifles. I had a doctor and three or four dressers. I had an agricultural officer, four public works chaps, one or two boats crew, and the warder and nine prisoners. They were all lifers (life in prison with no parole), by the way. They had all committed murder. We had some Japanese plane identification sheets, and once they had seen one of the types the Solomon Islander could tell what type of plane it was by its sound at about fifteen miles, which was very useful.

In the beginning, no watchers recruited had any arms. We didn't have any more. After much agitation, I was allowed to recruit a few former police to strengthen us up a bit. I had to promise them rifles, until we got some left behind by the RAAF. Later on, when the enemy had arrived, I gave recruits four days' leave to get a rifle and fifty rounds of ammunition. If they could do that, I could trust them.

MacFarlan, the naval officer (naval liaison officer), had come with me when he should have been with the resident commissioner. He was ignorant of the way things were done in the Solomons and so had to be led by the hand. At least he could keep schedules on the radio. In peacetime, we had used government code for ordinary messages and navy code for secret messages. They both had large, clumsy books, no good for the bush. Eric Feldt had wisely hit upon a simple code called Play Fair, where you drew a square on a sheet of paper and divided it up into I've forgotten how many squares. You wrote the code word down and followed it with all the remaining letters of the alphabet and then you coded it in pairs. And you could always tear it up so there would be no trace of it. We had a new word every month.

At the end of April, I was still too busy to contemplate going into the bush, but Kennedy at Segi, at the south end of New Georgia, reported that a fleet was approaching down the slot. The bombing of the RAAF was stepped up. Traffic on the radio had stepped up, both ours and the enemies. On April 31 the RAAF launch arrived towing a damaged PBY. We had put out warnings that morning but the PBYs were getting their orders from Port Moresby. The other PBY was damaged, but it taxied off over the water and was never seen again. They towed it in as close to the beach as they could, and I gave the crew various jobs. The bombing continued.

MacFarlan went up the coast in a hurry to Berande Plantation, where Ken Hay, the manager, had everything on board his truck including his refrigerator and his famous butter dish to take the path to Gold Ridge. They would have a fine view of the proceedings from there, because it was about 2,000 feet up. The RAAF base became untenable, and two days later we got the RAAF evacuation signal "Steak and eggs, steak and eggs." They arrived the next morning. The AIF platoon that they had with them remained to demolish everything.

The RAAF were a tired and sorry lot. I fed them, the whole exhausted party of forty, rested them, and cursed them for leaving the PBY on my doorstep and for not staying to give me a hand. They left for the south on a requisitioned recruiting vessel that night. I also got rid of a small squadron of Tulagi Chinese, who went over to Malaita to meet a ship, but it did not come and they sailed on to San Cristobal.

It was time to move, but coding and sending was quite hectic. I blew the conch one morning at 0700 and 500 carriers picked up their loads and they were all away in twenty minutes. I followed two hours later, and after four hours of walking over a few rivers and hills, got to a village called Paripao, which was on a ridge about 1,800 feet up with a splendid view of Tulagi and along the Guadalcanal coast. My clerk Daniel showed me to a native hut with a beetlenut palm floor and a table, all laid out with a clean blotter and all the current files laid out. In my dairy I said, "How kind it was, but was it really necessary." On May 4, Tulagi received a good plastering by dive bombers and torpedo bombers. We counted about a dozen ships coming out of the harbor, most of them smoking profusely, and some of them sank later.

My agricultural officer, Anthony Bingiti, belonged to Ngela and so volunteered to go over in a canoe. He set up his own coast watch over there, and from then on we got a daily report of what was going on in Tulagi. We were able to report Japanese casualties and the damage done. It seemed that the bodies were just heaped together and burnt.

I went back to Aola to finish getting rid of the PBY. We dug a channel in the beach, tied ropes to her, and then 300 of us got her up about a foot with the tide. This was not good, so we took to it with axes and burnt what we could. We were left with the engines and the main plane, so we felled some of the front row of coconut trees and covered it all with palm fronds. The Japs never noticed it. I had sent the PBY captain, Ken Ekins, off to collect a couple of my policemen from Milaita and he got stuck on a reef coming back. They sat there all day, hiding in the cabin, while a couple of Kawanishis came and circled them a couple of times but didn't shoot. They got home in the dingy, so I sent them all off south as quickly as I could.

Then Vouza appeared from Milaita with his family, where he had been police sergeant major. He had served twenty-five years in the police and he was fifty-five years old. Bengough, the district officer, sent me a brief note with him, to say that he'd retired, perhaps I could use him. I couldn't understand what had happened, because I wouldn't have got rid of Vouza at all, and I was very glad to have him. Anyway, he volunteered to help and so I sent him off to Tasimboko, his own area near Koli Point, which included the plantations where the marines landed, and asked him to keep them quiet and to get a coast watch set up properly, which he did.

On May 8 a report came in of two United States Navy fighter pilots who had managed to beach their planes at Cape Henshaw on the southern coast. The pilots, Plott and McCaskey, I think their names were, had been picked up by a destroyer. Their parachutes, navigation boards, rubber dinghies, and batteries were all brought over. They were off the *Yorktown*, which I presumed was a carrier.

Then on May 13, Brother James, a missionary, arrived from Marau with another pilot and his number-two (gunner). I had come down the night before and was having breakfast when I heard the tramp of European feet. I grabbed for my gun but was relieved to see Brother James. He introduced Spike Ewoldt, who said, "Could you please get us back to Pearl Harbor?" I said, "Sit down and have a cup of tea and I'll see what can be done." I said, "I suppose you're from the *Yorktown?*" So he gripped his chair and he stiffened and said, "How did you know?" So I told him about the other two and I sent he and his number-two chap off to KiraKira on a schooner to catch up with a Chinese family sailing down to the New Hebrides. They got back to Pearl Harbor three weeks after their ship. So I would like to claim the honor of returning the first pilot to duty.

That was the first of very many pilots that the Coastwatchers did return. The funny thing was, I gave him a blue ensign with an anchor device in the quarter to fly if a friendly plane doubted their intentions. I thought it was a Trinity House Flag, but thirty years later, when he kindly returned it with his thank-you letter when he found out where I was, I found out that it was the quarantine flag. Just as well he didn't have to fly it.

I just have a few anecdotes to tell you about before I joined the marines. Life got tougher and tougher and I got very depressed. I read Shakespeare, *Henry the V,* a number of times. It was one of the few books I had with me and I read one day, "We are in God's hand, brother." And there was not an Australian around to say, "Too bloody right."

We went on to starvation rations. The rains came and the rivers flooded and we couldn't get food up and I went further into the bush. We had no food at all for three days, which is really rather hungry-making. We had tea but no sugar. I sent someone down to make some from a coconut spath. I won't tell you how that's done, but that's what you have to do when you haven't got something in the bush. He came back with a bottle full of a brown syrupy substance, which came in very handy.

Then the teleradio set started rusting and the switch wouldn't work, the switch for the different frequencies. I knew nothing about the mechanics of a radio set, but I opened it up and I found that there were two spring plates with holes in them and ball-bearings in them and they had all rusted up. Today you go to the hardware store and buy some emery paper or something like that. We didn't have a hardware store within 500 miles. So I sent a chap down to come back with a small bottle and a cork and some lemons, and we put the lemon juice into the bottle and followed it with the ball-bearings, and two or three people were told to shake the bottle. After about two hours they were bright and shiny. We just greased them with a little coconut oil and put them back and they worked. However, the thing to do is to keep the set dry, so we found a tiny hurricane lantern and we put some kerosene in it and burnt a very low flame underneath the set and that did the trick for the rest of the time.

However, the next thing that happened, the charging engine (for the teleradio) conked out. I couldn't get it to work, but there was another I knew about in a hut in Kukum, at the back of the plantation, which by this time was occupied by the Japanese building the airfield. I sent a scout down to get a job. He actually got a job as cook to some of the officers, and when Sunday came, he said he had to go to church in his village. And so he nipped the charging engine and brought it up. We took the two engines to pieces completely and cleaned the whole lot and put the best bits together and after I had pulled the rope 120 times it actually worked. Those were some of the problems we had as Coastwatchers.

The coding and the collection of messages was much simpler. I was getting requests then for details of the Japanese airfield. Scouts went down there after dark and paced out the distances between the ack-ack guns and measured their caliber. We had to put two lines on the chart with a magnetic bearing as a sort of grid reference as to where all these things were. We actually pointed out the radio station, but I'm afraid our dive bombers were not able to hit the radio shack, which was just as well because General Vandegrift found that he hadn't got a decent-sized radio set and we were able to use the Japanese one for quite a long time.

The Solomon Islanders came to me about halfway through this and said, "What will happen to us?" They were very sad and very tearful. There were about 200 of them outside the office. I said, "Be quite sure that I'm staying with you and I can't say when, but one day someone will come and all will be all right."

"What do we do, for instance, if a Jap says, where is the district officer?"

I said, "You just say he is gone." And that seemed to work quite well at the time. But I heard many years later from one of my old scouts that he'd said this to a Japanese officer and all the officer said was, "Bullshit."

Then one glorious morning, we were awakened by a frightful racket, a bombardment I thought. One scout rushed in and said,

"The Jap fleet has arrived, master." "Rubbish," I said, for I had turned on the teleradio and I could hear all the targets that I had given being allotted, and then see them hit. What a sight. What a wonderful sight. I counted over eighty ships. And I drew a little sketch which Walter Lord very kindly published some years later. On the ninth, I got a field message telling me to come down and what route to take. We packed up and off we went. I was barefoot by then. My shoes had all fallen apart and all I had was a pair of MacFarlan's "winkle-pickers." They are of the sort store managers wear with the sharp points and they were too small for me. So I didn't put them on until we got down to the beach. But as we crossed the grass plains, we saw some two-engine bombers going over and we waved at them, rather stupidly, until we saw the red blobs on the side. We then rushed off to the trees and during that rush, two wicker-wick baskets were dropped by parachute, which we collected like collecting the football, and that was food for the Japanese. So I thought there must be some of them about there, so we moved very fast.

We reached the beach and we could see troops unloading gear. I put on my black shiny shoes. I got my dozen scouts into two lines with sloped arms and waving the Union Jack, and accompanied by my dog, I joined the marines. The general manager of Lever Brothers came up as a scout with the 1st Marine Regiment and that's where I spent my first night. And as bit of an anti-climax, lying on a poncho on a blanket in the middle of a plantation, Charles Widdy, the general manager, said to me, "God, if somebody had told me a month ago that I would have been sleeping in the middle of one of my plantations, I would have eaten my bloomin' hat." And so we joined the 1st Marine Division, and I and my scouts became their eyes and ears.

Skies of Blood: In the Air Over Guadalcanal

Two air combatants, heros both, tell of the air battle over and around Guadalcanal. Brig. Gen. (Ret.) Robert D. Galer and Keiichi Arima both fought in the skies above and around Guadalcanal for the duration of the battle. That feat, in itself, is a claim not many others can make.

Brig. Gen. (Ret.) Robert D. Galer was stationed at Ewa Marine Corps Air Station during the attack on Pearl Harbor. He flew a land-based Wildcat during the Battle of Midway. He was one of the first pilots assigned to Guadalcanal. He is credited with thirteen and a half victories and was shot down three times during his tour on Guadalcanal. For his actions on Guadalcanal, he was awarded the Congressional Medal of Honor.

Brig. Gen. Robert Galer, USMC (Ret.)

I make one claim. I'm the marine's luckiest pilot. Many of our pilots are better pilots, but I'm the luckiest. I was shot down four times and had to ditch one time at sea because of engine failure. This is why I have so much admiration for Australian Martin Clemens and his Coastwatchers. They treat you nice when they pick you up and bring you back so you can "do it again."

There are a lot of lessons to learn when they have a worldwide war like World War II. As mentioned, the marines went to Ewa in January of 1941, before the war started. The marines stayed there through the end of the war. It originally was built as a mooring mast for the dirigible's around-the-world flight. The dirigible, as some of you know, caught fire going around the world and never made it to Ewa. Ewa was out in the middle of a sugar plantation about five miles from Pearl Harbor. It initially had a 2,000-foot runway. Technically, the historians say that for the Pearl Harbor attack, the Japanese strafed Ewa two minutes before they hit the *Arizona*. Being there and seeing what happened to the *Arizona* and all the people on it, from that point on, everybody that I was associated with were gung-ho and wanted to get on with this war and fight the Japanese.

After frantically reorganizing after Pearl Harbor, I was designated a squadron commander in March of 1942 with two airplanes, two other pilots, and about six enlisted men. Four months later, with twenty-three pilots and nineteen aircraft, we were on our way to war. So you can understand, we were not a well-trained squadron. We were getting new pilots from the States and qualifying them and training them and doing the best we could. When ordered, we went to Guadalcanal. In Marine Air Group 23 at that time, there were two fighter squadrons and two dive bomber squadrons. One fighter squadron and one dive bomber squadron went to war on a carrier. That wasn't mine. I was the lucky one. We went to war about three or four days later on the USS *Kitty Hawk*. The USS *Kitty Hawk* used to be the automobile ferry that ran between Key West and Havana with a top speed of eight knots. We taxied aboard and were off on a 2,000–3,000 mile trip.

When we got to Espiritu Santo, which is south of Guadalcanal, the little jeep carrier which had brought out the other two squadrons was anchored there. They tied us up alongside, lifted us off with a derrick, put us on a catapult, launched us off the catapult, and we landed at Espiritu Santo to refuel to go to Guadalcanal. It only took our ship two weeks longer for us to get there.

When we arrived at Guadalcanal, we landed at about 1600 in the afternoon. The Japanese started shelling and bombarding us about 1700. They must have known we had arrived because from then on, every night we were either shelled, bombed, or what have you. Admiral Fletcher took the carrier task group back out of Guadalcanal after D-Day, on D-plus-1, which did not provide sufficient time to get all the marine equipment and supplies ashore. So we lived in the mud, ate some Japanese food that we had captured, and things were pretty miserable and pretty tough. After living in tents at Ewa we

Left to right are Maj. John Smith, Maj. Robert D. Galer, and Capt. Marion E. Carl. These three pilots accounted for forty-six kills in the skies over Guadalcanal. *USMC Defense Department Photo #A50012*

got into some miserable conditions. I and most of my men had dysentery and a few other things such as malaria.

Our normal operation could not have taken place if it had not been for Martin Clemens and his Coastwatchers. I'll explain that. We were short of fuel, short of ammunition, short of airplanes, and operating off of a field that initially had been under construction by the Japanese. Our Sea Bees, marine engineers, and everybody available pitched in and enlarged the airfield. We called this Henderson Field, named after a marine pilot killed at Midway a couple of months earlier. It was a gung-ho outfit, whether you were army air corps, navy, or marines. We called it the Cactus Air Force!

One advantage of Clemens' Coastwatcher operation was that it was our early warning net. They acted as our early warning radar. They would have somebody who was physically counting airplanes taking off on the Japanese fields. They would radio down the information, such as, "twenty-four bombers, twenty fighters just departing." We would know what time they were going to get there. We would save all that gas. We would save a lot of time. Then we would climb to altitude.

Our primary mission was, if possible, to hit the lead bomber. We had discovered that if you got the lead bomber, particularly if you could get him before he got to the field, he would drop his bombs and everybody in the formation would drop on his signal. So if you were successful, he would bomb the area of the jungle where some of his own people might be. But those were the odds. Because of a shortage of fuel, shortage of airplanes, and shortage of ammunition, we took every advantage we could get. Sometimes the force that went up to meet the enemy might only be four airplanes, sometimes it might be eight airplanes. You were always fighting a tough battle.

The second advantage we had was that we were fighting over our own field — the field the Japanese had started building. On one occasion that comes to mind, just to prove the point, eight planes took off, and three of us got shot down. We made successful deadstick landings on the field, saving airplanes and spare parts if the aircraft was too badly shot up to fly again. The first time I was shot down I was about to come out of the clouds and the word was out, "Don't parachute. You might be strafed in the parachute." So the normal operation was to land in the water, even though you had a land plane. That will get you a very sudden stop. I made a landing about a hundred yards offshore with my equipment on. I swam ashore and, looking up the beach, I could see three people coming, carrying rifles. So I scrambled across the beach, got behind a log, dried out my weapon, and they came along, and I said, "Drop your guns." The response was, "Me friendly." I said, "Drop your guns." "Me friendly, me Christian," came the reply. So I captured those three and decided that I would go with them. They took me back to Tulagi and the navy came and picked me up.[13]

When our people got shot down, Clemens' people brought them back. One example was that of Marion Carl. Just to give you a feel of the gung-ho attitude of the pilots, Marion Carl was executive officer to John Smith, VMF-223. Both very proficient, excellent aviators. When Marion got back, he asked, "How many did John Smith shoot down?" John had shot down three while Marion was gone and Marion asked the general, "Please ground him for a couple of days so I can catch up to him in the number of airplanes shot down." But still, the conditions were miserable. Dysentery was very open and around, and as I say, the Japanese visited us every night.

Our navy pretty much took over the waters during the day, but the Japanese would come back at night. They came down a couple of times with battleships, and other interesting things. When they shoot a sixteen-inch shell at you at night you can see it come out of the gun. You almost know where it's going to hit. Another unique thing that occurred is one night we were bombed, a 500-pound bomb took out the tent that we normally were in. We were in an adjacent foxhole because the air raid was going on. It eliminated the tent but didn't break the mosquito netting that was over the cot. Obviously, there is a place real close to a bomb crater caused by a bomb explosion where you can survive if you are below the surface (i.e., in a "fox hole").

For two to three months, Tokyo Rose was on the radio and would tell us we were going to be captured the next day. Washington was saying there was doubt about who was going to win the Battle for Guadalcanal. But it was very interesting three months there under miserable conditions but getting beautiful cooperation from the army air corps. They had miserable airplanes, so-called fighters that could not go above 12,000 feet. They did an outstanding job. They learned how to do dive bombing and they supported the troops, and nothing could be said that could take any credit away from them. They did a great job. Most people don't understand that in roughly three to four months we thoroughly dominated the island. To give you an idea of how bad we were hurting the Japanese, I'll quote Adm. Raizo Tanaka. He said, "On the ninth of December, 1942, there is no question that Japan's doom was sealed with the closing of the struggle for Guadalcanal." Maj. Gen. Kiyota-ki Kawaguchi said, "Guadalcanal is no longer merely the name of an island in Japan's military history. It is a name of the graveyard of the Japanese army." They threw a whole army at a small number of people. They made the terrible mistake of doing it piecemeal, trying to walk through the jungle. Our raiders, our ground troops, navy, army and marines fought them every inch of the way. Obviously, I think they did a very outstanding job.

★   ★   ★

Keiichi Arima served in the Imperial Japanese Navy. He graduated from the Japanese Naval Academy at Ita Jima in 1937 and was a dive bomb pilot in central China in 1938 and 1939. In 1942 he fought against American forces in the Guadalcanal campaign. He was assigned aboard the aircraft carrier *Shokaku*.

Keiichi Arima

At the outbreak of the war, I was a training officer at the Suzu-ka Air Base after coming back from central China, where I was a combat air officer and engaged in bombing surface targets for more than one year.

Until May 1942, we were quite optimistic about the future of the war due to the unexpected grand success of the battles at the beginning of the war. However, the terrible result of the Midway Sea Battle brought about great shock to the higher echelon of the military command. Although the return flight crews were isolated at a remote air base located in Kyushu to prevent leakage of the severe defeat, including the loss of four aircraft carriers, the fact was known to navy officers.

To deliver an aerial attack on the United States carrier fleet sighted west of the Solomon Islands, a new task force was organized as the Third Fleet, composed of the three aircraft carriers, two battleships, several cruisers, and many other warships. I had been assigned as the *buntaicho*, the leader of nine bombers with their crew members, as well as their maintenance personnel, on the aircraft carrier *Shokaku*. Practical training was carried out and the fleet set sail on August 15, headed for the South Pacific.

Until the night of August 23, we had no information about the United States carriers, partly because bad weather hampered reconnaissance by land-based planes stationed in the Solomon Islands. Our carriers dispatched planes to reconnoiter, but obtained no results. The fleet took a southerly course, then reversed to the north several times. We called it the piston maneuver. We feared of being discovered by United States planes and submarines, which might make us the second mover, as in chess.

Early on the morning of August 24, both cruiser seaplanes and carrier-based Kanko (torpedo plane) made a fan-shaped 250-300 nautical mile reconnaissance. Again they obtained no information as to the location of the United States carriers. Around noon, a seaplane dispatched from the cruiser *Chikuma* discovered the United States carrier fleet.

The attack mission, which comprised twenty-seven dive bombers and ten supporting Zero fighters, left the carriers at 1255 under the command of Lt. Cmdr. Momoro Seki. I led the second squadron of nine dive bombers. Our altitude was about 8,000 meters (or 24,000 feet) and visibility was clear. At 1400 we sighted ships in a ring formation. Instantly, Lieutenant Commander Seki ordered the attack. When our planes were encountered by enemy fighters, several of our planes burst into flames. The Kanbaku, as we called our dive bombers, took the bombing formation of a straight line to the target carrier. Anti-aircraft fire directed at us from the surface ships was much more severe than I had experienced many times in China during the previous year. I was rather surprised to note the oncoming shells and bullets were recognizable in the daylight. Several bullets hit my plane, which made considerable noise but no fatal blow, fortunately.

After bombing the United States carrier, my plane pulled out low, less than ten meters above the sea. I passed near the bow of the cruiser until reaching the area out of range of the ship's guns. It was planned to circle there and rendezvous with our fighters because they did not have the ability to find their way back to the carrier without turning on their radio homing devices. With only two dive bombers following me, we cruised within sight of the smoking United States carrier for about fifteen minutes, looking for our fighters. I sighted four small planes in the distance. I ordered a change of course to rendezvous with them and approached them. Surprisingly, they were not Zero fighters, but four F4F Grumman fighters. At that instance they seemed to recognize us and headed for us. We turned in haste and increased speed. They pursued us, firing with their machine guns, but the bullets could not reach us and made many splashes on the sea. Our height was only several meters above the sea, and the distance was narrowing little by little. Then I noticed the sun was setting a little to the left. We changed course toward the sun. The speed superiority of the F4F was not enough to overcome the distance, and probably the glare of the setting sun made them unable to pinpoint us. They departed. I ordered a new course to return to our carrier. Our three planes were heading for the calculated position of our fleet but we did not worry about having to land on the carrier deck.

The dusk changed to night and we could see only stars twinkling above us, under which we proceeded more than thirty minutes. We should have found our carriers by that time, but did not. I started my search maneuver. At last we found our carrier, on which we landed, but my engine stopped running at that second. One of my subordinate planes made a forced landing on the sea due to a shortage of fuel. The crew was rescued by a destroyer. Later we noted that our carriers had changed their originally scheduled course after receiving an attack by United States bombers, but failed to inform us of the change.

Our attack planes and crews were severely damaged by the battle, but surface ships were safe other than the damaged carrier *Ryujo*, which sank. The fleet returned to Truk for reorganization. The crews and planes were filled up, replacements were allotted, and then we underwent air fighting training for the coming battle.

The South Pacific sea battle occurred in relation to an attack and defense at Guadalcanal island. Our task force departed Truk on October 11, looking for the United States carrier fleet. Until midnight on the 25th, we had no information about the correct location of United States carriers despite reconnaissance made by both land-based planes and ship-board planes. Our fleet was contacted by a United States plane and was bombed.

Early in the morning of the 26th, one of our reconnaissance planes radioed a finding of the United States carrier fleet. The first air attack wave left our carriers and attacked a United States carrier around 0700. The second attack wave, to which I belonged, was composed of nineteen dive bombers and five fighters and left our fleet around 0600 under the command Lieutenant Commander Seki. I myself led nine dive bombers. We reached the battle area around 0820 and dived against the United States carrier. This time I did not sight many United States fighters, but the anti-aircraft fire was more severe on the battle of August 24. I recognized several planes, including Lieutenant Commander Seki's, take hits and become enveloped in flames. After dropping my bomb, I noted a hit on the carrier deck.

This time we were not intercepted by United States fighters and returned to my carrier, *Shokaku*. I found she was bombed by United States planes and the flight deck had a large hole from which heavy smoke was coming up. Inevitably, I gave up landing on my own ship and flew to the *Zuikaku*, on which we landed. When I was back aboard the *Shokaku* later, I was notified of my death in battle, a mistake presumably made in the confusion.

Jungle of Death: The Ground Forces

Hopelessness and helplessness are two words that often describe the plight of the infantry and ground soldier. The enemy, the elements, and the weariness hinder the physical, mental, and emotional condition of the ground soldier. There is a unique psychological state of mind developed by the ground soldier which allows the soldier to survive from day-to-day under the worst of conditions. This mindset enables the infantryman to survive the total environment. Victor Branch and Shiro Hashimoto both experienced that peculiar psyche and re-create it in their accounts of life on the ground at Guadalcanal.

Victor Branch was a sergeant in the Signal Battalion of the 1st Marine Division and participated in the initial invasion of Guadalcanal on August 7, 1942.

Victor Branch

I landed on the canal on August 7, D-Day, H-hour plus one. D-Day was a very significant day. I was proud to be a part of this great division, the 1st Marine Division. I was privileged to be with them in this campaign.

We had looked forward to this, the 1st Signal Company, Headquarters Battalion, all of the special weapons companies that were in headquarters, and the 1st Tank Company. All of us were on the same ship, on the *McCawley*, when we left New Zealand, and it was about two weeks later when we hit the canal.

When we left New Zealand, they told us we were going on maneuvers. Well, if they tell you to pack two sets of skivvies, two pair of socks, a set of fatigues, and your helmet, and the rest of it is weapons and your radio gear, you know you are not just going on maneuvers and you are not coming back to New Zealand. When you packed your sea bag and sent it off to San Francisco with all of your gear, except the bare necessities of apparel and combat equipment, you knew something was going to happen.

I was a field radio operator and we had radio operator teams. There were four men to a team: one carried a receiver, one carried a transmitter, one carried a generator, and the team chief carried spare receiver batteries. All those field units combined weighed somewhere in the neighborhood of seventy-five pounds. When we talk about setting up a command post with the radios, we are not talking about some radio station studio; we are talking about field radio setups.

We thought it was very glorious to be involved in D-Day, H-hour plus one. We went down the cargo nets and got into Higgins boats. I landed with Col. Gerald Thomas and Lt. Sanford B. Hunt. Sanford Hunt was the cryptographer. I'll tell how we got to go on H-hour plus one. Our section chief had Sgt. Willie Wagner and I draw cards. Whoever got the highest card stayed on board the *McCawley*, and whoever got the lowest card went in right behind the 1st Marines and the 5th Marines. I drew the lowest card and was kind of happy about it.

We were looking forward to getting on the beach. We were a little bit apprehensive, but nonetheless, we were going to be the first ones to set up a command post on Beach Red. That's another thing I thought about later. Why don't they call it Blue Beach? Red Beach connotes blood, doesn't it?

Red Beach was the main point of the landing, with Colonel Thomas, who was the operations officer for the 1st Marine Division. We landed around 1000 hours without any opposition. H-hour was around 0630 to 0700 hours, when all the shelling took place from our cruisers and destroyers.

By the time we got to the beach, it was around 1000 or 1030

Red Beach, Guadalcanal, late 1942. *Jason E. Everts collection*

hours. It didn't take us long to get on the beach. The 1st and 3rd Battalions, 5th Marines, went to the right of the beach and went inland. The 1st Marines went straight toward Mount Austin, which was supposed to be about half a mile to a mile away. It turned out they couldn't get there; it was about ten miles away.

We set up our command about fifty yards off the beach right under a coconut grove. We set up the radio and secured the generator. This was done by securing the generator with a chain around the tree trunk while someone hand cranked the generator for power to the transmitter.

We made contact with the men that landed on Tulagi and found out that they were catching holy hell. According to the word we received, there were about 1,500 to 1,700 Japanese on the island. It took three days of fighting, but in three days' time, the marines on Tulagi wiped out the Japanese. I believe there were about seven Japanese out of that 1,500 who were captured or surrendered.

We stayed on Red Beach until the following day. At around 1200 hours, or shortly after, we had set up, and all hell broke loose.

About fifteen dive and torpedo bombers came along. We could look out at them from where our radio set was located. The USS *Eliot* took a direct hit, and it had to be beached close to Red Beach. We found out later that all of those dive and torpedo bombers were knocked out. We felt they were knocked out mostly by the cruisers USS *San Juan* and the USS *Chicago*. All of the cruisers were firing 6-inch, 8-inch, and 40mm guns at the Japanese. That night we found the best thing to do was to sleep in a bomb crater. At least I felt that way, so I laid in a bomb crater right off the beach. You slept in a bomb crater because you believed lightning was not going to strike twice in the same place.

The next day we went up the beach to the Tenaru River, where in approximately two weeks a famous battle would take place. We got there on August 8 and set up our command post. All I can tell you about that night is that we had advanced warning of the Japanese attack force. We were optimistic. We knew a task force was coming down. We said, "Boy, this is great. We're going to lay back off Savo Island and when they come down the Slot we're going to nail them."

Well, that night at about 2300 hours, all hell broke loose. We felt like our cruisers and destroyers were doing a good job on the Japanese task force, but they were dropping flares all over the beach. During the night I received a message from the *McCawley* (we were in touch with them by radio). The message was, "Enemy troops landing on Red Beach." Colonel Thomas said to the effect, "Send another message back and ask them to confirm." I radioed the USS *McCawley*, "Please confirm." It turned out that it was a false alarm. We were relieved when they radioed back, "Disregard last message . . . troops friendly." We left that command post the next morning.

Some navy survivors of the night naval battle came ashore. They came to the division command post and told us the bad news: the USS *Quincy*, the USS *Astoria*, and the USS *Vincennes* had gone down in about five to ten minutes with almost everybody aboard. We were told there were very few survivors. The Australian cruiser *Canberra* also went down. We were still on the beach up by the Tenaru spit and you could see a great, gaping hole in the *Chicago*, another cruiser. I didn't know at the time how many destroyers we had lost, but it was a bitter pill to swallow.

We were disillusioned but not depressed. On August 9, we moved up to the other command post, on the northwestern edge of the airstrip. As we were moving to the command post, we encountered strafing by Japanese Zeros.

On August 16 at about 1200 hours, twenty-five Japanese BETTYs came over and this lasted for days. From August 9 until December 9, some four months later, when I left along with all of the rest of the survivors to go to Australia for R and R, we were shelled from the sea and bombed from the air on an almost daily basis.

We suffered from malaria, dengue fever, and malnutrition. I weighed 155 pounds when I landed on the canal and I was 118 when I left. I was barely able to climb a cargo net to get on board the USS *Barnett*, a troop ship.

I would be remiss if I didn't tell you something about Shiro Hashimoto, better known as "Pistol Pete." We suffered the pangs of his trying to shell us. I can't tell you how much profanity he provoked on that island. I guarantee there was more cussing, more beating of gums, and more chipping at him than at anyone else I have ever known. You never knew where the shells were going to hit. You never knew which ones were duds. He would do it at the most inappropriate times, such as at one or two in the morning or at 1200, when you might be trying to eat some of that fish and meal that we captured. So many times he thought it was chow time and there wasn't much chow, anyway. Pistol Pete would send a salvo and he usually would be in and around the airport.

One day, Command decided to move the command post. They decided to move it to the south side of the airstrip. We thought that was a good deal. We're going to get away from the shelling, get away from the bombing, and would be protected. But it was apparently unknown to the top brass that this is where the Japs would make their charge. The Japanese were concentrating all their forces on both sides of the island. We knew the Japanese had control of the seaways and were landing troops on either side of the island. So what did they do? They amassed enough troops to come through — guess where? There was the 1st Raider Battalion that was resting after their fight on Tulagi. There was the Parachute Battalion that was used in the fighting on Tanambogo and Gavutu islands — what was left of them were resting. The Japanese came through what became known as "Bloody Ridge." That was where the command post had been moved and that was where the Japanese came through. But fortunately, we had Edson's Raiders and the 11th Marines there and the 1st Parachute Battalion. The artillery officers did a good job.

On September 12 and 13, I believe, the Raiders and the 11th Marines held the Japanese back.

But I want to tell you, the artillery officer went to great lengths to locate Pistol Pete because he didn't stay in one place. He would move around. Pistol Pete would shell here, then shell there, and then he would go someplace else. So what the artillery officer did was measure the angle the dud shells went into the ground to determine where Pistol Pete's position might be located. Of course, that didn't work because Pistol Pete would move, and we were never able to find him. In any event, that artillery officer went to great lengths to locate Pistol Pete.

There was also "Washing Machine Charley." We had some 90mm anti-aircraft right around the airstrip that came in with the 3rd Defense Battalion, and they finally put their lights on trying to locate this Washing Machine Charley. I guess it was a scout plane that came off a cruiser. That's what it appeared to be. He caused a lot of harassment, but did very little damage to our men or equipment. He was like Pistol Pete, an irritant more than anything.

Shiro Hashimoto was Pistol Pete. He served in the Imperial Japanese Army and was a sergeant major assigned to an artillery battalion on Guadalcanal from October 1942 to January 1943. At war's end, he was a warrant officer on Bougainville Island.

Shiro Hashimoto

Time is like a flying arrow. Truly fifty years of time has flown by like an arrow. However, the blue feelings of the stormy Pacific have not been extinguished in everyone's heart.

I will address three themes concerning my experiences on Guadalcanal. One is the process of movement of my artillery unit to Guadalcanal. Two is the process of withdrawal from Guadalcanal. Three is the ration situation and troop morale. I shall attempt to simplify and put into order these things.

In the late summer and autumn of 1942 my unit, the 4th Field Heavy Artillery, was in northeastern China. We were occupying Mutan Kiang near the Soviet border in Manchuria. In the middle of

September, we received, unexpectedly, orders to depart. We even changed from winter clothing to summer wear. We boarded the ship *Miike Maru* in Puson, Korea.

At that time, crowded on the *Miike Maru,* was also an infantry unit and my unit, which was the 1st Battalion of the 4th Field Heavy Artillery, with twelve new 150mm howitzers. My good friend, Akio Tani, was a lieutenant in the 2nd Battalion of the 7th Regiment Field Heavy Artillery, which had four 100mm cannons. Also aboard was the 2nd Battery of the 21st Battalion of Field Heavy Artillery. This was a horse-drawn artillery unit with four 150mm howitzers.

Our troop transport, the *Miike Maru,* approached Shetland Island of the Solomon Island Group. In addition, we were joined by a naval escort ship. On the way, we saw the Rabaul port and on October 7, we arrived at Erebenta on Bougainville Island.

My assigned regimental headquarters was placed on board a destroyer, the *Natsu Kumo,* which we also boarded. It was here that Lieutenant Tani and I became separated. The morning of October 7, at about 0100, the seaplane tender *Chitose* landed our guns at Guadalcanal Island. At last we had arrived at Tassafaronga, on Guadalcanal's north coast.

At that time, the Japanese army on Guadalcanal was engaged in a pitched battle. Since August, the infantry had attacked the American airfield. The Ichiki unit and the Kawaguchi unit and others had attacked violently, but were counterattacked by the American defenders. We received heavy losses. Again and again, effective attacks came against us. As we listened, headquarters was discussing the effectiveness of the Japanese army's forces on Guadalcanal. It was here that the power of artillery was judged and heavy artillery was brought in to support a frontal attack on the Guadalcanal airfield. An all-out attack was ordered in the middle of October. The chief of the Army General Staff, General Sugiyama, received this order from the Emperor.

Then, on October 14, at Tassafaronga, much equipment was lost from the transport vessels. On the next day, air attacks caused heavy casualties. We lost twelve 150mm howitzers. There were about 200 to 300 bombs dropped on those positions. We prepared our food on the high ground at Tassafaronga. Why? Of what did we speak? We probably thought the worst. As for us, the time had come for our final regular meal.

Finally, Guadalcanal's routine had begun. In order to simplify the events of Guadalcanal, we say that these were but the initials. Then the sound of hunger became apparent. Before long we had the actual feeling that Guadalcanal Island became known as Starvation Island.

After that, our unit advanced to Hill 903, where we took up a position in one location. Again, the 1st Battery advanced to Cape Kurutsu and the bombardment of Henderson Field began. The enemy fire was being neutralized. Supporting fire was provided to the high ground by a friendly unit. At this time, First Lieutenant Tani's company also reached the high ground and this was how we got to the island's high ground.

After that, my unit's main force advanced toward the Matinikau River in order to attack the coastline. There was insufficient ammunition. Here, please permit me to use a nickname given to us by the Americans, Pistol Pete. From near the shore we, Pistol Pete, bombarded the airport and with the cooperation of the Sumiyoshi unit, also shelled American marine positions.

As for our 17th Army's offensive operation, we planned to take the airfield on October 7, but to assure the success of this attack supplies were needed. Such resupply from the sea was very difficult. Finally, ammunition, rations, and such were exhausted.

On October 22, our troops crossed the Lunga River and attacked the airport in full force. Every day we attacked, but inside the jungle, movement was so truly difficult that it proved impossible. In front of the superior American forces' positions, again like jungle phantoms, we stood naked and suffered. With these burdens and the American defense, the Japanese forces suffered great losses. The 29th Infantry Regiment of the Second Division took part in the battle from the evening of October 24 until the morning of October 26. Of the 2,554 soldiers, 552 lost their lives, 479 were wounded, and one was missing, a total of 43 percent casualties. Whatever happened to the regimental commander is not known. He allegedly disappeared in the jungle with the regimental colors. His unit sent out search parties but they could discover nothing. However, afterwards, according to the Americans, his remains had been found and identified.

The attack of October 26 ended. This military operation was criticized by many military critics. This was truly a foolish military operation, such that rations, ammunition, materials, sufficient preparation, and fatigue and troop morale were completely ignored. However, such operations as this were still being examined.

In the middle of November, the 38th Division's main body was sent from the eastern part of New Guinea to reinforce the troops on Guadalcanal. They traveled in a convoy of eleven troop ships, and as they raced for Guadalcanal, on the way they were attacked by American aircraft. Some were sunk, others set afire. Barely reaching Guadalcanal were four ships. Such were the events of those times. In the waters around Guadalcanal rest a number of ships.

Thus the Guadalcanal battlefront came under miserable circumstances. Counterattack was out of the question, or so thought Tokyo headquarters. At last we should cease operations. It was decided to call back the troops from Guadalcanal. That was on December 31, 1942. About that time, the American forces on all fronts gradually increased their attacks. From the island's interior, troop casualties grew. Our miserable feelings left us speechless. It was the beginning of 1943. I faced a mysterious morning. In truth, it was a quiet morning. The American attack had stopped. Naturally, we couldn't stand the silence. It was a very special January event. Every person got two small *kanpars* (sweetbread) and there was one cigarette for every ten men. For these goods, we all were very grateful. We faced our homeland and bowed. We then prayed to the Emperor and for the safety of our families.

Then the time for our withdrawal had come. Our 17th Army split into three groups on February 1, 4, and 7 and began our withdrawal. While there was no direct combat, the withdrawal was a very dangerous and difficult exercise. Until it could be completed, how many units might be completely annihilated? We, the Pistol Pete artillery, lined up in advance on the beach to retreat. While friendly forces gave us covering fire, we destroyed our big guns. Then we were just barely able to embark on the ship. The destroyed cannons even now remain on the beach. Finally, my unit had brought some 1,300 men onto the island the previous October. Now 504 were fortunate to depart on the destroyer *Arashio*.

The next issue I would like to address is ration and supply conditions and troop morale. In those days, the Japanese soldiers' orders were from the higher authority of the Emperor's orders. Absolute obedience was expected, regardless of the difficulties encountered. The Guadalcanal battle site was, as far as human living conditions were concerned, horrible. As food and ammunition shortages became more serious, the strength to do battle became abated. At the time that the ration conditions were calculated, the army believed resupply would not present a problem, so we were given rations to last only a few days. The Americans, of course, stopped all resupply movements and soon our rations had been used. One hundred percent hunger was the norm. There were many cases of starvation. Even then, around the beaches, the circumstances were better. There were coconuts, tuber leaves, and weeds. Anything edible was eaten. Since taking fish was dangerous, none were taken.[14]

The infantry unit that desperately defended the Gifu Highlands, the 228th Regiment and the 124th Regiment, ate ants and lice. There was no rice. Some even ate earthworms. Ultimately, these units were completely destroyed.

As for abnormal battle conditions, abnormal psychological problems occurred. Abnormal phenomena grew to be an increased problem. It was something no one could specifically explain and presented a serious problem. I am not an expert in this, so all I can offer is an abbreviated summary.

In closing, I am thinking of Hunger Island. To me, Guadalcanal was not an island of despair. Recalling it again today, I believe this with all my heart. I will read from my grandfather's favorite book: "To everything there is a season and a time to every purpose under heaven. A time to love and a time to hate. A time of war and a time of peace." May a time of love and a time of peace continue to eternity.

IX. 1942 Draws to a Close

Finally, 1942 was over. The new year looked much brighter than had 1942. America had been challenged and had more than met the challenge. The darkest was over, and a new dawn was on the horizon.

The war was far from over, however. Much remained in the Pacific to reclaim. The Philippines were still under Japanese control, and MacArthur had made their recapture his number-one priority (more for vanity than military necessity). Places like Tarawa, Eniwetok, Kwajalein, Saipan, Tinian, and Iwo Jima were still waiting to earn their place in the collective American memory.

At the University of Chicago, a small group of physicists had begun development of the weapon which would bring the war in the Pacific to a close and change the way the world perceived warfare.

Was there any good to be found in the shattered remains of 1942? For all the misery and suffering, war did bring about some positives for the American people. The economy was fully recovered, and the Great Depression was now an unpleasant memory. The economy dictated by war made money flow freely. Jobs and opportunities were plentiful for everyone who wished to prosper.

American business had been revitalized and was surging ahead with new technologies and business practices. Manufacturing techniques were improved and streamlined. The assembly-line first used by Henry Ford became widespread and efficient. Because workers performed only one task, training time was minimized and replacement workers could easily fill in line openings. Women were accepted as part of the labor force. Growth far outpaced manpower, and industry was forced to hire women, who proved they were every bit as capable as men. Shift work helped increase the number of leisure hours Americans had each week, and this leisure time further stimulated the economy.

There was an explosion in science and technology. The war required the think tanks and laboratories to maintain the pace. Physics, chemistry, biology, and the social sciences all participated in an exponential growth of discovery and knowledge. Nuclear physics, plastics and polymers, synthetics, herbicides, faster and bigger crops, metallurgy, and geophysics all saw quantum advances. Even more miraculous, the discoveries in laboratories quickly made their way to useful technology. The application of scientific discovery was a matter of weeks or months, not years or decades (as is the case today).

Medicine benefited from the war. Penicillin and other antibiotics replaced the crude and damaging sulfa drugs. New medicines were developed at a breakneck pace to combat the new diseases and infections our fighting men were exposed to in the Pacific jungles. Surgical techniques were refined and surgeons became healers. Gone were the days of sawing off damaged limbs and leaving the ambulatory alone to see if they lived or died. Surgeons learned to repair mangled tissues and to fight against loss and death.

Education benefited from the war. Prior to World War II, the colleges and universities of America were filled only with the upperclass and the offspring of the wealthy. World War II brought about the advent of the G.I. Bill, which enabled men and women from all walks of life to enter institutions of higher education. This may have been the greatest benefit to come out of World War II.

The transportation industry improved and flourished. The war placed two major demands on the industry. One, to move military personnel and equipment efficiently, and two, to provide for nonmilitary personnel. The automobile had become a staple of life for Americans. The war caused shortages in automobiles, parts needed for repair, and gasoline. America had to depend less on the automobile. The airlines, railroads, bus lines, and trolleys all worked harmoniously to move America from point-to-point in a timely, efficient manner.

The fields of engineering, aviation, communications, chemistry, geology, zoology, and economics benefited from the war. The list could go on *ad infinitum* (or *ad nauseum*). Every segment of American society ultimately prospered and improved because of a small band of pilots who flew over a small Pacific island on December 7, 1941. To me, one of the great tragedies of life is that suffering, agony, and death in war are required to produce the greatest triumphs of a nation. Neil Armstrong's historic walk on the moon, the greatest achievement in the history of mankind, began in 1942 with a group of scientists in an obscure military laboratory who were attempting to push an airborne warhead faster, farther, and higher.

I hope you have enjoyed reaching in and touching the lives and souls of the veterans who were brave enough to bare their hearts and souls. Andy Warhol once said that everybody would be famous for fifteen minutes. I hope the veterans within these pages are famous for eternity, for the lessons they teach within these pages are ones we dare not forget or repeat. If we, our children, and the children of our children read, memorize, and remember the lessons taught here, then World War II can truly be the "war to end all wars."

List of Contributors

Keiichi Arima

Mr. Arima served in the Imperial Japanese Navy. He graduated from the Japanese Naval Academy at Etajima in 1937 and was a dive bomb pilot in central China in 1938 and 1939. In 1942 he fought against American forces in the Guadalcanal campaign aboard the aircraft carrier *Shokaku.*

Evan H. M. Barnet

Mr. Barnet joined an artillery survey unit in Australia at the outbreak of war with Germany. After a year, he transferred to a horse cavalry unit, then to the 6th Armored Regiment. He fought with this unit in Buna, New Guinea, where he was severely wounded.

Richard Best

Mr. Best was attached to Bombing Squadron 6 aboard the USS *Enterprise* when the Japanese attacked Pearl Harbor. Following Pearl Harbor, he supported the Doolittle raid on Tokyo and later flew a Dauntless during the Battle of Midway.

Victor Branch

Mr. Branch was a sergeant in the Signal Battalion of the 1st Marine Division and participated in the initial invasion of Guadalcanal on August 7, 1942.

279

Hattie Brantley

Ms. Brantley graduated from the Baylor School of Nursing and became an army nurse in 1939. She was a member of the first medical group assigned to Bataan, on Christmas Eve 1941. She became a prisoner of war when Corregidor fell and continued to provide care for Americans until her release in 1945.

Martin Clemens

Mr. Clemens was assigned to the Solomon Islands in 1938 as a colonial officer cadet. When the war began, he was pressed into service as a Coastwatcher on Guadalcanal. He provided the Allies with valuable information concerning Japanese aircraft, ship, and troop movements, and proved invaluable during the early stages of the American invasion of Guadalcanal.

John Costello

Mr. Costello was educated at Cambridge as a historian. He is the author of a number of books on World War II, including *The Pacific War, Virtue Under Fire,* and *And I Was There.* His new book on Pearl Harbor is the result of the 1991 symposium sponsored by the Admiral Nimitz Museum.

Frank W. Ficklin

Mr. Ficklin joined the 131st Field Artillery in 1939 and traveled with his battalion to Java in January 1942. His unit surrendered to the Japanese in March 1943. Mr. Ficklin was a prisoner of war for more than three years in Java, Singapore, and Thailand.

Lt. Col. Wallace Fields, USA (Ret.)

Lieutenant Colonel Fields joined the Army Air Corps in 1940 and flew in the first heavy bombardment of the Japanese stronghold of Rabaul in February 1942. He flew fifty-one combat missions in B-17s, most with the 435th Reconnaissance Squadron, 19th Bombardment Group.

Richard S. Frank

Mr. Frank obtained his degree at the University of Missouri and was then commissioned in the United States Army. He served in Vietnam before his discharge. Mr. Frank wrote *Guadalcanal: The Definitive Account of the Landmark Battle*. This book received the General Wallace M. Greene, Jr. Award for outstanding nonfiction work relevant to marine history.

Brig. Gen. Robert Galer, USMC (Ret.)

Brigadier General Galer was stationed at Eva MCAS during the attack on Pearl Harbor. He flew a land-based Wildcat during the Battle of Midway. He was one of the first pilots assigned to Guadalcanal. He is credited with thirteen and a half victories and was shot down three times during this tour. For his actions on Guadalcanal, he was awarded the Congressional Medal of Honor.

George Gay

In 1942 Mr. Gay was an ensign and served with Patrol Wing 8 during the Battle of Midway. He was the only survivor of his squadron at Midway. He later wrote a book about the fate of Torpedo 8, *Sole Survivor*.

Margaret Gillooly

Ms. Gillooly was sixteen when the Japanese invaded the Philippines and took her parents prisoner. After hiding in the mountains for six months, Ms. Gillooly turned herself in to the Japanese and was eventually reunited with her parents at the Santo Tomas Internment Camp, where she graduated from the Internment School.

Donald Goldstein, Ph.D.

Dr. Goldstein is on the faculty at the University of Pittsburgh. He spent many years working with Gordon Prange and was co-author of *At Dawn We Slept.* He has authored several books on the Pearl Harbor attack and is presently working on a book covering the Aleutian campaign.

Shiro Hashimoto

Mr. Hashimoto served in the Imperial Japanese Army. He was a sergeant major assigned to an artillery battalion of Guadalcanal from October 1942 to January 1943. At war's end, he was a warrant officer on Bougainville Island.

James Kincaid

Mr. Kincaid served as an enlisted man in the United States Army during World War II. He participated in the Battle of Buna, New Guinea, in the first offensive action of the war in which Americans and Australians fought side by side.

CWO Cecil King, Jr., USN (Ret.)

CWO Cecil King, Jr., was assigned to the Flag of the Asiatic Fleet under Adm. Thomas Hart. He left the Philippines for Java and then to Australia. Three of the ships he had been on were subsequently sunk: USS *Houston,* USS *Perry,* and USS *Langley.*

Brig. Gen. Richard A. Knobloch, USAF (Ret.)

Brigadier General Knobloch became a pilot in the Army Air Corps in 1940 and volunteered for the Doolittle raid on Tokyo in 1942. He then flew fifty additional missions against the Japanese and was awarded the Distinguished Service Medal, the Distinguished Flying Cross with clusters, and many other medals.

Rear Adm. William N. Leonard, USN (Ret.)

Rear Admiral Leonard graduated from the Naval Academy in 1938 and served as a fighter pilot for the first part of the Pacific War. He participated in the Battles of Coral Sea and Midway. He ended the war an ace.

Walter Lord

Mr. Lord is a distinguished historian of the war in the Pacific. He is the author of many best-selling books, including *Day of Infamy, A Night to Remember,* and *The Freemantle Diary.* He has written on the Battle of Midway *(Incredible Victory)* and on the Australian Coastwatchers *(Lonely Vigil).*

John Lundstrom

Mr. Lundstrom is associate curator of the Milwaukee Public Museum. His expertise is in the early phases of World War II in the Pacific. Mr. Lundstrom has published several books on World War II, including *The First Team.*

Dwight Messimer

Mr. Messimer is a former tank commander, United States Army, and currently teaches history at San Jose State University. He has authored several books on American and German naval history, including *Pawns of War, The Loss of the USS Langley and the USS Pecos,* and *In the Hands of Fate: The Story of Patrol Wing Ten, 8 December 1941–11 May 1942.*

Lt. Gen. Joseph H. Moore, USAF (Ret.)

Lieutenant General Moore flew with the Army Air Corps in the early days of World War II in the Pacific, then took part in the Normandy and other invasions in Europe. He served at the Pentagon, in the fighter-bomber command in the United States and France, and as air operations commander in Vietnam, vice commander in chief of Pacific Air Forces, and tactical Air Force commander for NATO in Turkey.

Adm. Thomas H. Moorer, USN (Ret.)

Admiral Moorer graduated from the Naval Academy in 1933 and was at Pearl Harbor in a PBY squadron on December 7, 1941. He later served throughout the Pacific and was named as chief of naval operations by Presidents Johnson and Nixon.

Teiji Nakamura

Mr. Nakamura served in the Imperial Japanese Navy during World War II. He graduated from Etajima Naval Academy and became a torpedo officer on the *Yudachi* in October 1941. He participated in the invasion of the Philippines, Dutch East Indies, Midway, and Guadalcanal. When the *Yudachi* was sunk, he was assigned to the battleship *Nagato.* He completed his career as an instructor at the academy.

Fred Parker

Mr. Parker is senior historian in the Center for Cryptological History at the National Security Agency. His field of concentration is communications intelligence in the navy's decision-making process during the Pacific War.

Col. Arthur Poindexter, USMC (Ret.)

Colonel Poindexter was a Marine Corps officer for the heroic defense of Wake Island in December 1941. He spent the remainder of the war as a prisoner of war in Japan.

Walt Whitman Rostow, Ph.D.

Dr. Rostow was special assistant for National Security Affairs for both Presidents Kennedy and Johnson. During World War II, he served as a major in the OSS. In 1969, Dr. Rostow returned to teaching at the University of Texas. His specialty is U.S. foreign policy, economic theory, and world history.

Paul Stillwell

Mr. Stillwell is editor-in-chief of *Naval History* magazine and director of oral history for the U.S. Naval Institute in Annapolis, Maryland. He is the editor of *Air Raid Pearl Harbor!* and the author of *Battleship Arizona: An Illustrated History*.

Ted Waller

Mr. Waller served aboard the cruiser USS *Portland* during the Battles of Coral Sea and Midway. The USS *Portland* provided critical support for the marine landings on Guadalcanal and Tulagi.

Col. Donald Wills, USA (Ret.)

Colonel Wills is a 1940 graduate of VMI. He then joined the 14th Horse Cavalry and was transferred to the 26th Cavalry in the Philippines. After surrender on Bataan, Colonel Wills spent two years as a prisoner of war, when he managed to escape. After his escape, he served with the guerrilla forces on Mindanao. He received the Silver Star, Bronze Star, and Purple Heart.

Notes

I. 1942: The Pacific at War

1. The *Prince of Wales* and *Repulse* had no air cover off the east coast of Malaya. One question which has arisen concerns why the *Prince of Wales* and *Repulse* left Singapore and went out into the Malaya area, where they knew the Japanese had air patrols. Part of the answer lies in a mix-up of signals between the military of different nations. In Singapore Harbor, the destroyer *John D. Edwards* was refueling, and, as was standard American naval practice, had raised the flag "Baker" at the foretop. When other American ships saw the *John D. Edwards* with "Baker" raised, they did likewise, as was required. The air marshal of Singapore, who was British, kept all air cover in the area because he thought the signal signified an air attack by the enemy.

Second, and probably a more important factor, was that Commander Phillips of the *Prince of Wales* was a headstrong individual and he did not really believe airplanes were a threat to a battleship. He had decided to sail to Manila Bay and the protection offered by air cover provided by MacArthur. He took the risk and paid for it with his life and the lives of 2,000 of his men.

2. The 26th Cavalry was the last horse-mounted cavalry unit in the United States Army.

3. War Plan Orange was the war plan developed by the Joint Chiefs of Staff in the event Japan attacked the Philippine Islands. Basically, War Plan Orange called for the United States and Filipino militaries to resist Japanese attacks until reinforcements could be sent from the United States. Military planners had estimated that reinforcements would arrive within six months at the most.

II. A Different Kind of War: Goliath on the Seas

1. The six aircraft carriers were the *Akagi, Hiryu, Shokaku, Soryu,* and *Zuikaku.* They were protected by the battleships *Hiei* and *Kirishima,* the heavy cruisers *Chikuma* and *Tone,* the light cruiser *Abukuma,* the destroyers *Akigumo, Arare, Hamakaze, Isokaze, Kagero, Kasumi, Sazanami, Shiranuhi, Tanikaze, Urakaze,* and *Ushio,* and three I-class submarines.

2. The Japanese failure to provide their aircraft pilots armor and self-sealing fuel tanks concerned their great emphasis on offense (attack), not defense. They did not want to waste excess weight on defensive attributes. Attack meant everything. Unlike other cultures, Samurai warriors never used shields, but put their faith in their two-handed swords.

3.   The Japanese were quite interested in radar, but had to develop the technology. They were aided by capturing British radar sets at Singapore. They installed radar sets on two old battleships, *Ise* and *Hyuga*, in May 1942, and on the carriers *Shokaku* and *Kirishima* in July 1942. United States Marines discovered two Japanese radar sets when they landed on Guadalcanal (not installed nor operational). The first Japanese radar contact with enemy planes took place on August 24, 1942, at the Battle of the Eastern Solomons. At the Battle of Santa Cruz (October 26), the *Shokaku*'s radar picked up American planes at ranges which considerably exceeded that of radars on the *Enterprise* and *Hornet*.

4.   The light carriers were the *Hoshu*, *Ryujo*, and *Shoho*.

III.   The Demise of the Asiatic Fleet

1.   The lessons learned from ABDA regarding communications were lessons remembered later in the war. Much of the success of the Normandy invasion, for example, was due to communications lessons learned from the ABDA experience.

2.   Gen. Sir Archibald Wavell.

3.   This was the project immortalized in the 1954 film *Bridge Over the River Kwai*. The wooden bridge was replaced by a concrete and steel bridge in 1943. Even today, the wooden pillars are visible when the river is at low stage.

IV.   Situation Grim

1.   Escape attempts on POW camps were discouraged by POWs because of retaliation by the Japanese. At some camps, for every POW who attempted or successfully escaped, up to ten of the remaining POWs would be executed.

2.   Under American leadership (and with the assistance of hundreds of American soldiers), a para-military guerrilla resistance was organized throughout the Philippines. The guerrilla resistance was organized and operated under a military structure and defined chain-of-command. Operations against the Japanese had to be reviewed and approved. "Free-lance" operations were not permitted.

3.   Admiral Kurusu's visit to Washington, D.C., was a final attempt by the Japanese to settle their differences with the United States. If he failed, he would notify Imperial Japanese Headquarters to proceed with their war plans.

4.   The United States military forces in the Pacific were under strict orders to do nothing to provoke a Japanese attack nor to initiate an attack unless war was declared or the Americans were fired upon first. This order was made very clear to the local commanders and troops.

5.   Mount Pinatubo recently erupted, forcing the closure of Clark Air Force Base.

6.   The Japanese attack was led by Rear Admiral Kajioka, and his armada consisted of the cruisers *Tatsuta*, *Tenryu*, and *Yubari* (flagship), the destroyers *Hayate*, *Kisaragi*, *Mochizuki*, *Mutsuki*, *Oite*, and *Yayoi*, the transports *Kongo Maru* and *Konryu Maru*, two APD patrol boats, and a 450-man Special Naval Landing Force.

7.   On December 14, the Imperial Japanese Navy reformed the Wake ar-

mada, again giving Admiral Kajioka command. The second armada consisted of the cruisers *Tatsuta*, *Tenryu*, and *Yubari*, the destroyers *Asanagi*, *Oboro*, *Tusagaru*, and *Yunagi*, one mine-layer, one seaplane tender, two transports, several submarines, and 1,500 men of the Maizuru 2nd Special Landing Force. In addition, the Imperial Japanese Navy aircraft carriers *Hiryu* and *Soryu* and Cruiser Division 6 were dispatched to support the second assault.

On December 21, Maj. Walter Bayler departed Wake on a PBY, the last American to leave the island. On December 22, VMF-211 lost their last two airplanes. In addition to the Japanese ships hit in the first attack, VMF-211 claimed twenty-one enemy planes shot down and fifty damaged. In fact, the Japanese later reported that during the air attacks against Wake, over fifty-five airplanes were damaged and several crew members killed by anti-aircraft fire.

8. Capt. Herbert C. Freuler was so badly wounded and his plane so heavily damaged that he was obliged to make a crash landing. He was dragged from the cockpit of a plane that was irreparably damaged. 2nd Lt. Carl R. Davidson never returned to base from this last mission.

9. Some of the aviators and ground crewmen of the squadron were killed or mortally wounded, including the gallant Maj. Henry T. Elrod.

10. An account of the combat operations of one element of the defense force which was holding its own and even counterattacking after the island had been surrendered is contained in an article by A. A.Poindexter, "Last Hurrah on Wake Island," *American History Illustrated* 26, no. 6 (1992).

11. All Presidential Unit Citations issued thereafter were issued by direction of and signed by the secretaries of war and navy.

V. A Ray of Hope in a Stormy Sea

1. The Japanese had placed submarines off the West Coast of the United States in December 1941. Nine I-class submarines patrolled the waters from Vancouver, Canada, to San Diego, California. Their job was twofold. One, they were to stop military ships and merchant shipping designed to reinforce the Pacific Fleet. Two, they were to gather pre-invasion intelligence for a possible Japanese invasion of the American West Coast.

2. Moe Berg, a major league baseball player for the Washington Senators and Boston Red Sox, was a highly intelligent man. He did not fit the "dumb jock" image of baseball players. He was accomplished in many fields, including art, music, and foreign languages. In 1934, when an American all-star baseball team went to play the Japanese all-star team, the United States government recruited Moe Berg to gather intelligence. He smuggled a small movie camera under his clothes and went to the hospital in Tokyo, the tallest building there, ostensibly to visit an American patient. He instead went to the top floor of the hospital and took movies of the Tokyo skyline. These movies were the intelligence pictures for the Doolittle raid.

3. To airplane pilots in World War II, a sun shot was equivalent to a ship navigator using celestial navigation to find the position of a ship. Short-distance flights used dead reckoning, landmarks on the ground, or compass readings to determine relative position. Long-distance flights had to rely on the sextant and the position of celestial bodies to determine location.

4.   The surviving sailors from the *Sims* were not rescued for ten days. Only sixty-eight crew members ultimately survived the attack and exposure in the sea.

VI.   The Tide Turns: Midway

1.   Code-breakers of Hypo and Negat.

2.   It seems somewhat inconceivable, even to a nonhistorian, that plans to invade the United States did not indicate a desire for "total victory" over the United States.

3.   Part of this message is now unintelligible.

4.   This naval officer turned out to be the executive officer aboard the *Enterprise.* Because of security considerations, this officer was never formally charged with any crime, for to do so would have meant publicity concerning United States intelligence activities. But, according to Paul Stillwell, this officer was assigned a shore billet and basically his naval career was over.

5.   The *Maryland* band members were assigned to shore duty while their ship was being repaired following the attack of December 7, 1941. They were just assigned to Hypo by chance.

6.   The ruse was the brain-child of Jasper Holmes, one of Rochefort's code-breakers at Hypo. The purpose of the message was not to convince Admiral Nimitz that AF was Midway, but to convince Negat in Washington, D.C.

7.   Number-two is the trailing bomber in a tow-plane attack.

8.   Some historians have indicated that Commander Waldron did not want to strike the Japanese because the planes of Torpedo 8 were low on fuel. They argue that Commander Waldron requested to return to the carrier, refuel, and then return to attack the Japanese.

9.   It was common practice in the 1930s and 1940s for the United States Navy to split its carrier squadrons into land-based and ship-based complements. About half of a squadron's planes would be assigned to land, the other half to a carrier. This was done because the navy had many more airplanes than carrier spaces could accommodate.

VII.   The Fight for New Guinea: A Military Nightmare

1.   For details on the Solomon Islands campaign, see Samuel E. Morrison, *History of United States Naval Operations in World War II* (Boston: 1949), v; and W. F. Craven and J. L. Cate, *The Army Air Forces in World War II* (Chicago: 1948), Vol. 4.

2.   Letters, E. C. Whitehead to Gen. D. Wilson, October 15, 1942; D. Wilson to E. C. Whitehead, October 21, 1942. Interviews, F. H. Smith, June 10, 1969; J. Crabb, February 29, 1969.

3.   General MacArthur and Whitehead both said this. See Pat Robinson, *Fight for New Guinea* (New York: 1942), 5. Hugh Buggy, *Pacific Victory* (short history of Australia's part in World War II, Melbourne: 1943), 6. Letters, E. C. Whitehead to G. Kenney, August 10, 1942; E. C. Whitehead to Charles d'Olive, August 15, 1964.

4.   This story is amply covered in Craven and Cate, Vol. 4, and Morrison, *op. cit.*

5. To extend the bomb line is the process by which new bases are built in forward positions so that the radius in which troops can receive air support is increased.

6. Buggy, *Pacific Victory*, 1–15.

7. *Ibid.* See Craven and Cate, Introduction to Vol. 4; "Let the Bombs Talk," narrative of air war in Pacific by personnel of the Fifth Air Force (unpublished, undated), 1.

8. Robinson, *Fight for New Guinea*, 7; Buggy, *Pacific Victory*, 11; "Let the Bombs Talk," 3. In the command and the area of responsibility with Nimitz at the 159 Meridian, it was decided with much debate to stand at NG.

9. Buggy, *Pacific Victory*, 85–100. Buggy says many of the early Japanese victories in the Philippines were due to the underestimation of their forces by the Allies. Later, such places as Singapore fell because the Allies overestimated their adversaries' ability. While this thesis can be challenged and is certainly not valid in all aspects, it has merit, especially in New Guinea, where the Japanese myth of invincibility was prevalent. Robinson, *Fight for New Guinea*, 5–15, also alludes to this.

10. Buggy, *Pacific Victory*, 115.

11. Letters, E. C. Whitehead to Lee Van Atta (INS News correspondent), November 15, 1942; Lee Van Atta to E. C. Whitehead, December 1, 1942. Also Robinson, *Fight for New Guinea*, 125.

12. There had been a previous shake-up soon after Pearl Harbor when a unified command placed all the forces of the Dutch, British, New Zealanders, and Australians under one command. Gen. Sir A. Wavell was made commander of this unified command. However, because the Japanese conquest of Malaya was so fast and the bombing of Darwin was so intense, another change was thought to be in order, particularly with the availability of General MacArthur. For the composition of the new command, see Craven and Cate, 4:7.

13. South West Pacific Area hereafter SWPA.

14. Jealousy between the army and navy as to who was to get each command caused a division of the command in the Pacific. Letter, E. C. Whitehead to G. Kenney, August 15, 1942; Craven and Cate, 4:xiv.

15. Craven and Cate, 4:7; "Let the Bombs Talk," 13.

16. *Ibid.*

17. Buggy, *Pacific Victory*, 15. MacArthur is supposed to have said, "We shall win or we shall die in New Guinea." Robinson, *Fight for New Guinea*, 44.

18. "V Bomber Command Historical and Tactical," narrative (unpublished, undated), Data Volume 1:1. Also "Let the Bombs Talk," 20; Buggy, *Pacific Victory*, 19.

19. Craven and Cate, 4:6. "Let the Bombs Talk," 20; Vern Haugland, *The AAF in the War Against Japan* (New York: 1948), 79.

20. *St. Louis Dispatch*, June 10, 1942; *The United States Strategic Bombing Survey: The Campaigns of the Pacific War* (Washington: 1946), 53.

21. For comprehensive study, see Samuel F. Morrison's *The U.S. Naval Operations in World War II*; Craven and Cate, 4:3, 18–21, 46; Haugland, *The AAF*, 79–89; "Let the Bombs Talk," 25–27. Buggy, *Pacific Victory*, 145–160; Robinson, *Fight for New Guinea*, 19–54; *U.S. Bombing Survey: Campaigns*, 52–57.

22. *U.S. Bombing Survey: Campaigns,* 67; "Let the Bombs Talk," 11; *St. Louis Post Dispatch,* June 8, 1942, 1. The Battle of Midway is described in Samuel T. Morrison's *The U.S. Naval Operations in World War II;* Craven and Cate, 4:3, 19, 28, 58–59, 65; Haugland, *The AAF,* 79–89; M. Fuchida and M. Okumiya, *Midway: The Battle that Doomed Japan* (Anaprens: 1945).

23. "Let the Bombs Talk," 27; "V Bomber Command," 2. The Battle of the Coral Sea was the first naval engagement in which surface vessels did not exchange a single shot. It was a unique running battle between opposing forces which were hundreds of miles apart.

24. There was an axiom which was accepted by Allied intelligence: "He who holds Port Moresby holds the key to northern and northeast Australia." Quoted from Buggy, *Pacific Victory,* 9; Robinson, *Fight for New Guinea,* 17; Craven and Cate, 4:vi. These indirectly concur with the axiom.

25. "Let the Bombs Talk," 21; Craven and Cate, 4:ix.

26. MacArthur did not like this segment of the plan. He wanted to recapture New Guinea first. Interviews, F. H. Smith, June 10, 1969; J. V. Crabb, February 26, 1969.

27. MacArthur lent the South Pacific some army aircraft. This was of some help. He did not have anything else in the way of men and materials to give them. Letter, E. C. Whitehead to G. Kenney, August 18, 1942.

28. Craven and Cate, 4:ix, discuss the Elkton Plan in detail, as does Charles Willoughby, *MacArthur: 1941–1945* (New York: 1954), 107–125.

29. The threat to Port Moresby was real. The enemy planned to capture it by September 22, 1943. Buggy, *Pacific Victory,* 147; "Let the Bombs Talk," 30; "V Bomber Command," 2; Robinson, *Fight for New Guinea,* 194.

30. Buggy, *Pacific Victory,* 197.

31. "Let the Bombs Talk," 31; Buggy, *Pacific Victory,* 1–21. Vern Haugland, *Letter from New Guinea* (New York: 1943), is an excellent study on the geography and climate of New Guinea and its effect on the war in New Guinea

32. "V Bomber Command," 1:3; "Let the Bombs Talk," 32.

33. *Ibid.*

34. Craven and Cate, 4:21–25. "Let the Bombs Talk," 33; "V Bomber Command," 3.

35. Robinson, *Fight for New Guinea,* 149. For an excellent summary of the engineers in New Guinea see Volume 2 of *Army Engineers in South West Pacific* (New York: 1942).

36. It was a sad commentary on the prewar policy of the Allied nations that they had to begin preparing for war after the war had started.

37. Interviews, F. H. Smith, Commander V Fighter Command, June 10, 1969; J. V. Crabb, Commander V Bomber Command, February 28, 1969.

38. Royal Australian Air Force hereafter RAAF.

39. The U.S. was not much help. Priority was given to the Allied forces in Europe, and it was not until late 1942 that the Australians received any help. Buggy, *Pacific Victory,* 99; Robinson, *Fight for New Guinea,* 247; letter H. Arnold to G. Kenney, August 31, 1942.

40. Statistics for the Allied order of battle are in the Fifth Air Force History (1942), 5; "Let the Bombs Talk," 29–30.

41. For discussion of the Elkton Plan, see early pages of this essay. For the Guadalcanal campaign, see Morrison.

42. Interviews, F. H. Smith, June 10, 1969; J. V. Crabb, February 28, 1969. Also letter, E. C. Whitehead to G. Kenney, October 17, 1943; *U.S. Strategic Bombing Survey: Interrogations of Japanese Officials* (unsigned, 1946).

43. George Kenney, *General Kenney Reports* (New York: 1948) spends quite a lot of time and detail on skip bombing. Also, "V Bomber Command," 5; "Let the Bombs Talk," 32–34; and Robinson, *Fight for New Guinea*, 147–149.

44. The Bismarck Sea Battle is described in detail later in this chapter.

45. "Let the Bombs Talk," 33.

46. "Report on Use of Parafrag Bombs," September 17, 1943. In Whitehead collection, Maxwell AFB, Alabama. See also Robinson, *Fight for New Guinea*, 149.

47. The Japanese span of control extended so far in range and azimuth that they had to concentrate their defenses in certain sectors and at certain key points. Robinson, *Fight for New Guinea*, 164.

48. Kenney, *Kenney Reports*, 76, 144, 154, 155, 161–165; letters, E. C. Whitehead to G. Kenney, September 19 and October 21, 1942, March 17, 1943.

49. Letter, Gen. H. Arnold to G. Kenney, August 17, 1943. Arnold did not like the idea of SWPA doing the modification. He wanted factories in the U.S. to do it.

50. In 1944 Charles Lindbergh helped extend the range of P-38s by getting pilots to cut back on the richness of gas and the power needed to perform specific maneuvers. He doubled the range of the fighters but, of course, more engines were ruined and maintenance difficulties increased. Kenney, *Kenney Reports*, 411–415, 421. One attack on Wewak caught the Japanese unaware because they thought that the Allied aircraft could not reach them. (See Chapter 5 of this dissertation.)

51. "Let the Bombs Talk," 32. The cannon's recoil created such a back kick that the whole airplane shook and the idea had to be dropped. Letter, E. C. Whitehead to G. Kenney, March 13, 1942.

52. Craven and Cate, 4:92–93; "Let the Bombs Talk," 32.

53. This area was one of the narrowest on New Guinea.

54. Robinson, *Fight for New Guinea*, 149; Buggy, *Pacific Victory*, 187.

55. Unpublished report, July 27, 1942, 7; "Let the Bombs Talk," 32.

56. Letter, E. C. Whitehead to G. Kenney, no date.

57. Robinson, *Fight for New Guinea*, 297; Buggy, *Pacific Victory*, 185. The whole campaign is outlined in Craven and Cate, 4:92–128, and Raymond Pauil, *Retreat from Kokoda* (London: 1958).

58. Robinson, *Fight for New Guinea*, 148.

59. "Let the Bombs Talk," 37.

60. *Ibid.*

61. See "The Battle of the Bismarck Sea," later in this chapter.

62. "Let the Bombs Talk," 35.

63. Craven and Cate, 4:92–125.

64. Buggy, *Pacific Victory*, 101.

65. "Let the Bombs Talk," 33–37; "V Bomber Command," 3.

66. *Ibid.*

67. "Let the Bombs Talk," 37. Letter, E. C. Whitehead to G. Kenney, September 17, 1942.

68. *Ibid.*

69. Whitehead used his reconnaissance after every raid. The men flew two and three missions a day. It was an unglamorous but hairy job as enemy planes were always nearby. Interview, Lt. Col. John Jones, April 18, 1969; "Let the Bombs Talk," 37.

70. This is why it was so important to constantly extend the bomb line. "V Bomber Command," 3; "Let the Bombs Talk," 33–35.

71. Robinson, *Fight for New Guinea*, 245; "Let the Bombs Talk," 33–35.

72. This was important for the extension of the bomb line.

73. *Army Navy Journal*, Communiques October 14 to November 10. These are published on a daily basis and are in the Whitehead records of this writer at the USAF Academy, Colorado.

74. Letter, G. Kenney to E. C. Whitehead, October 29, 1942. A squadron consisted of from twelve to fifteen aircraft.

75. Later in Korea and Vietnam, commanders employed troop transport at a much greater rate than Whitehead. But Whitehead was truly the pioneer of the idea.

76. Craven and Cate, 4:129–136, discussed the prelude to the Bismarck Sea Battle. Also "Let the Bombs Talk," 41.

77. Ladislas Farago, *The Broken Seal* (1987); the *Bismarck Barrier* (1950); Elisson Zacharias, *Secret Mission* (1946).

78. Craven and Cate, 4:212–213; "Let the Bombs Talk," 19. These works and many others claim that Yamamoto was the driving genius behind Japanese naval strategy and was irreplaceable.

79. Message, G. Kenney to E. C. Whitehead, February 16, 1943; George Kenney, *Kenney Reports*, 197–198.

80. Letter, G. Kenney to E. C. Whitehead, February 20, 1943. See also Kenney, *Kenney Reports*, 198, for Kenney's account.

81. "Let the Bombs Talk," 43.

82. Letter, E. C. Whitehead to G. Kenney, March 9, 1943. Quoted from this letter.

83. *Ibid.* Interview F. H. Smith, June 10, 1969. Letter, E. C. Whitehead to Barry Goldwater, March 21, 1943.

84. *Ibid.*

85. *Ibid.* See also "V Bomber Command," 11; *New York Times*, March 6, 1943, 1. "Assembly by Janac," August 3, 1943.

86. All newspapers reported these statistics, as did Whitehead's report to General Kenney on March 9, 1943.

87. "Assessment by Janac," August 3, 1943. The argument over the exact number had never been resolved. As late as 1963 Whitehead still claimed twenty-two were sunk. Letter, E. C. Whitehead to J. V. Crabb, May 15, 1963. One author claims thirty were sunk. Haugland, *The AAF*, 79.

88. "Comments on the Bismarck Sea," 15.

89. Statistics from the Strategic Bombing Survey, *The War in the Pacific*, 13.

VIII.   The Hardest Fight of All: Guadalcanal

1.   Overall command of the Guadalcanal operation was given to Vice Adm. Robert L. Ghormley, commander, South Pacific.

2.   The Allies lost the heavy cruisers *Astoria, Canberra, Quincy,* and *Vincennes.* The heavy cruiser *Chicago,* and destroyers *Patterson* and *Ralph Talbot,* were damaged. The Japanese lost the heavy cruiser *Kako.* Damaged were the heavy cruisers *Aoba, Chokai,* and *Kinugasa,* and the light cruiser *Tenryo.*

3.   Other reasons have been given for Admiral Fletcher's decision, including that he was low on fuel. One historian has even accused him of "running scared." Neither of these explanations holds up under scrutiny. His carriers had been fueled shortly before arriving at Guadalcanal, and one does not become a fleet admiral by displaying cowardice during one's career.

4.   Colonel Ichiki actually committed suicide because of his failure to recapture Henderson Field.

5.   The naval battle of the Eastern Solomons took place on August 24–25. The American aircraft carrier *Enterprise* was damaged. The Japanese lost the aircraft carrier *Ryujo,* the destroyer *Mutsuki,* and the transport *Kinryu Maru.* Damaged was the seaplane carrier *Chitose,* the light cruiser *Jintsu,* and the destroyer *Mochizuki.* More importantly, the Americans lost only twenty-five planes to seventy-five for the Japanese.

6.   General Kawaguchi and over 3,000 soldiers of the IJA tried to storm the one-mile-long ridge protecting Henderson Field. The marines were commanded by Lt. Col. Merritt "Red Mike" Edson, who had 700 marines of the 1st Raider Battalion and 1st Parachute Battalion. The 1st Raiders were positioned at the Lunga River and the 1st Parachute Battalion was on the western and eastern sides of the slope leading to Henderson Field. In two days of bloody fighting, Colonel Edson and his troops had been pushed to the top of the ridge, only 1,000 yards from Henderson Field. On September 13, after a night of fierce artillery bombardment and hand-to-hand fighting, air support arrived at dawn to assist the marines. The air support turned the tide in favor of Edson, and the Japanese were repelled. Over 600 Japanese soldiers had been killed in the fight.

7.   By the first part of October, the Japanese had over 20,000 ground troops and a concentration of heavy artillery on Guadalcanal. The marines had been reinforced by the United States Army 164th Infantry, bringing total U.S. troop strength to 23,000. On October 24–25, Lt. Gen. Harukichi Hyakutake attacked Bloody Ridge again. The U.S. forces repelled the Japanese and held Henderson Field. For all practical purposes, the land battle for the Solomons was over.

8.   The Battle of Cape Esperance occurred on October 11–12. The Allies sank three Japanese destroyers (*Fubuki, Murakumo,* and *Natsugumo*) and one heavy cruiser (*Aoba*) at a cost to the Allies of one destroyer sunk (*Duncan*), two cruisers damaged (*Boise* and *Salt Lake City*), and two destroyers damaged (*Farenholt* and *McCalla*).

9.   In the Battle of Santa Cruz, the United States lost the acircraft carrier *Hornet* and the destroyer *Porter.* Japanese ships damaged included the heavy carrier *Shokaku,* the light carrier *Zuiho,* and the heavy cruiser *Chikuma.* More important than ship losses were the combat aircrew losses suffered by the Japa-

nese. The loss of experienced aircrews by the Japanese would prove to be devastating later in the war.

10.   The United States lost the destroyers *Barton, Benham, Cushing Laffery, Monssen, Preston,* and *Walke,* the light cruisers *Atlanta* and *Juneau,* and 1,732 sailors, marines, and airmen. The Japanese lost two battleships, one heavy cruiser, three destroyers, 40 airplanes, and 1,895 sailors, soldiers, and airmen. Of greater significance, the Japanese lost ten transports and all reinforcements, ammunition, and supplies intended for the ground troops on Guadalcanal. At the same time, the U.S. Navy was able to beach 6,000 men and tons of ammunition and supplies for the marines and soldiers defending Guadalcanal.

11.   The last major sea action in the Solomon Campaign occurred on November 20 at Tassafaronga. The Japanese had to resupply the 17th Army on Guadalcanal. The Japanese cleaned and half filled 55-gallon oil drums with food, rice, arms, or other supplies. These drums were tied to the decks of destroyers and were to be pushed overboard at designated points, where the ground soldiers would pull them ashore. On November 30, Adm. Raizo Tanaka led a Japanese fleet, including eight destroyers, into the straits between Guadalcanal and Savo Island to deliver these desperately needed supplies. The U.S. countered with four heavy cruisers, one light cruiser, and six destroyers. In a battle between American 5-, 6-, and 8-inch guns and Japanese Long Lance torpedoes, two ships were sunk: the *Takanami* (destroyer) and the *Northampton* (heavy cruiser). Several ships on both sides were heavily damaged, including the *New Orleans, Pensacola,* and *Minneapolis.* The significance of the Battle of Tassafaronga was in the fact that the U.S. prevented resupply and rearmament efforts to the 17th Army, thus ending Japanese plans to resume the ground and air wars in the Solomons. This was the last attempt made by the Japanese to resupply their ground-based troops.

12.   Each United States Navy ship carried a complement who were trained as scuba divers and could effect repairs on a damaged ship while under way or away from port facilities.

13.   General Galer was rescued by three Solomon Islanders who were members of the Coastwatcher cadre.

14.   Taking fish was dangerous because of the possibility of discovery by American planes or forces.

References and Additional Reading

Bowden, Tim. *Changi Photographer: George Aspinall's Record of Captivity*. Sydney, Australia: Australian Broadcasting Company Enterprises and William Collins, Pty. Ltd., 1984.

Cohen, Stan. *East Wind Rain: A Pictorial History of the Pearl Harbor Attack*. Missoula, MT: Pictorial Histories Publishing Company, 1981.

——. *Enemy on Island. Issue in Doubt: The Capture of Wake Island*: December 1941. Missoula, MT: Pictorial Histories Publishing Company, 1990.

Costello, John. *The Pacific War, 1941-1945*. New York: Quill, 1982.

Cressman, Robert J., Steve Ewing, Barrett Tillman, Mark Horan, Clark Reynolds, and Stan Cohen. *A Glorious Page in Our History: The Battle of Midway; 4-6 June 1942*. Missoula, MT: Pictorial Histories Publishing Co., 1990.

Dexter, David. *The New Guinea Offensives*. Canberra, Australia: Australian War Memorial, 1968.

Frank, Richard B. *Guadalcanal*. New York: Random House, 1990.

Layton, Edwin T., Roger Pineau, and John Costello. *And I Was There: Pearl Harbor and Midway – Breaking the Secrets*. New York: Quill, William Morrow, 1985.

Lord, Walter. *Day of Infamy*. Fredericksburg, TX: The Admiral Nimitz Foundation, 1957.

Lundstrom, John B. *The First Team: Pacific Naval Air Combat From Pearl Harbor To Midway*. Annapolis, MD: Naval Institute Press, 1984.

MacDonald, John. *Great Battles of World War II*. New York: Macmillan Publishing Company, 1986.

Mason, John T., Jr. *The Pacific War Remembered: An Oral History Collection*. Annapolis, MD: Naval Institute Press, 1986.

Messimer, Dwight R. *In the Hands of Fate: The Story of Patrol Wing Ten; 8 December 1941-11 May 1942*. Annapolis, MD: Naval Institute Press, 1985.

Payne, Alan. "The Battle of Sunda Strait." *Naval History* 6 (1992): 30-35.

Prange, Gordon W., Donald M. Goldstein, and Katherine V. Dillon. *December 7, 1941: The Day the Japanese Attacked Pearl Harbor*. New York: Warner Books, 1988.

——. *At Dawn We Slept: The Untold Story of Pearl Harbor*. New York: Penguin Books, 1981.

——. *Miracle at Midway*. New York: Penguin Books, 1983.

Rhoades, Lt. Cmdr. F. A. *Diary of a Coastwatcher in the Solomons*. Fredericksburg, TX: The Admiral Nimitz Foundation, 1982.

Ward, Geoffrey C., and Gary Wolinsky. "Douglas MacArthur: An American Soldier." *National Geographic* 181 (1982): 54–83.

Weintraub, Stanley. *Long Day's Journey Into War: December 7, 1941*. New York: Truman Talley Books, Dutton, 1991.

Index